EXPECTATIONS MATTER

Expectations Matter

THE NEW CAUSAL MACROECONOMICS OF SURVEYS AND EXPERIMENTS

OLIVIER COIBION &
YURIY GORODNICHENKO

PRINCETON UNIVERSITY PRESS
PRINCETON & OXFORD

Published by Princeton University Press
41 William Street, Princeton, New Jersey 08540
99 Banbury Road, Oxford OX2 6JX

press.princeton.edu

GPSR Authorized Representative: Easy Access System Europe - Mustamäe tee 50, 10621 Tallinn, Estonia, gpsr.requests@easproject.com

ISBN 978-0-691-26736-4
ISBN (e-book) 978-0-691-26738-8
Library of Congress Control Number: 2025947013

British Library Cataloging-in-Publication Data is available

Editorial: Joe Jackson and Rebecca Binnie
Production Editorial: Jenny Wolkowicki
Jacket design: Karl Spurzem
Production: Danielle Amatucci
Publicity: William Pagdatoon
Copyeditor: Bhisham Bherwani

This book has been composed in Arno

Printed in the United States of America

10 9 8 7 6 5 4 3 2 1

MIX
Paper | Supporting responsible forestry
FSC® C008955
FSC
www.fsc.org

CONTENTS

ILLUSTRATIONS

Figures

Tables

ACKNOWLEDGMENTS

THIS BOOK DESCRIBES research that we first started pursuing when we were in graduate school together, many years ago. Over that time, we have become increasingly indebted to many people for their support in allowing us to pursue this line of work.

First, and most importantly, we are grateful to our family and loved ones. To our parents, our partners, our siblings and children, all of whom have provided the love, support, and motivation for us to continue down this path and who have borne the cost of all of the time we have devoted to this endeavor: there are no words to express just how much we appreciate and cherish all of you.

Second, in developing this research agenda, we have received help and inspiration from many sources over the years. We owe a big debt of gratitude to those who encouraged us to pursue economics in the first place, including Barry Eichengreen, Susan Collins, Barry Bosworth, Iryna Lukianenko, and Charles Steele. We were then both fortunate enough to do our graduate studies at the University of Michigan, where surveys had long been an accepted tool in macroeconomics, under the supervision of our incredible advisers—Bob Barsky, Chris House, Susanto Basu, Serena Ng, and Matthew Shapiro—and alongside an extraordinary group of macro and international graduate students in our cohort, such as Edward Knotek, Eric Sims, Peter Morrow and Claudia Sahm, among others. It's from repeated conversations with this amazing group that our joint work eventually began to take shape.

Since then, we have been blessed with many exceptional coauthors who have allowed us to take this line of research far beyond anything we could have imagined or managed to do ourselves, and to all of them we are incredibly grateful. Also of great importance has been the support of our home institutions, the University of California at Berkeley and the University of Texas at Austin, which have consistently promoted our research endeavors and given us the freedom to explore new ideas, both good and bad, as they have arisen. The National Science Foundation has also played a critical role in funding our work (as that of many other young scientists). There are some research activities whose costs significantly exceed what typical or even generous academic budgets allow. By funding these types of projects, the Foundation plays a key role in advancing scientific progress, especially in the early stages when expected outcomes are most uncertain. We are where we are today because of the generous support of such state and federal institutions.

Finally, we would like to thank those who helped bring this book to fruition: our research assistants (Andres Larios, Michael Athanassiadis, and Lance Tong), our editorial team at Princeton University Press, and all our colleagues who provided extensive comments on early versions of the draft: Rudi Bachmann, Carola Binder, Lena Dräger, Jane Ryngaert, Saten Kumar, Johannes Wohlfart, and Francesco Zanetti, among others. Francesco also deserves special thanks for first suggesting to us that we write a book on expectations in macroeconomics. While we dismissed the idea at first, it slowly percolated in the back of our minds until we decided to follow his advice and take the plunge. This book also would not exist without the many other researchers working on expectations in macroeconomics. This incredibly active literature has grown tremendously in recent years, and we have learned so much from the work of others. We can only hope that our book will spur even more research in this exciting area.

Introduction

ON THE MORNING of December 21, 2015, we received an email from an editor of *The American Economic Review,* one of the top academic journals in the profession, giving us the opportunity to resubmit a revised version of a paper we had previously submitted to them, but only if we could implement the changes he and the anonymous reviewers requested. We were both thrilled and dismayed. Thrilled because publishing in top journals is what we academics live for and the opportunities to do so are few and far between. Dismayed because we had absolutely no idea how we could possibly do what they were asking us to do.

What was the problem? We had written, along with a wonderful new coauthor in New Zealand, Saten Kumar, a paper that described some properties of firms' inflation expectations using new surveys that we had run together in New Zealand. We were excited about the paper because there was essentially no evidence prior to this about how firms formed expectations about future inflation. And the results that came out were rather striking and unexpected (at least to us): the firms in the survey were remarkably uninformed about inflation and their beliefs about future inflation seemed out of line with what standard macroeconomic models would have predicted. The editor told us in his decision letter that while the results of the survey were intriguing, he didn't think inflation expectations were all that important by themselves. He asked us to provide ironclad evidence that the expectations actually mattered for firms' decisions. This seemed like a "mission impossible" request because we would have to tackle one of the major challenges that has long limited progress in macroeconomics.

When we write down models to describe how the economy functions, we start by characterizing the decisions of individual actors in the economy, such as how households choose how much to consume or save, how firms choose how much to invest or what prices to set, and so on. In most cases, those decisions are inherently forward-looking in nature: how much we choose to spend today, for example, depends on what we think our job prospects are and what we think will happen to prices in the future, amongst other expectations.

The resulting importance of what people believe about the future for macroeconomic outcomes has long been emphasized in the field. Keynes (1933), for example, described how "animal spirits," or investors' expectations about future returns on capital, could drive investment and economic activity. Economists in the 1970s speculated about how so-called "adaptive expectations" could generate persistent increases in inflation: if firms see that aggregate prices have gone up recently and infer that they will likely keep rising, they will choose to raise their own prices to keep them in line with their competitors', thus fueling more inflation. Wage-price spirals are another mechanism through which overall expectations, and inflation expectations in particular, can drive macroeconomic outcomes. If workers or labor unions expect that prices will rise more rapidly in the future, then they will try to bargain for larger wage increases, which will increase firms' costs and lead them to raise their prices, which would lead workers to want even larger wage increases, and so on.

But these expectations have historically gone unmeasured. The Bureau of Economic Analysis, for example, which provides exceptionally detailed measures of Gross Domestic Production, Consumption and Investment for the U.S. economy, does not publish a measure for investors' animal spirits or workers' inflation expectations. So one approach macroeconomists have long had to rely on is to simply *assume* an expectations formation process to plug into their models. In the 1960s and 1970s, this was typically backward looking: our belief for next year's inflation rate was assumed to be equal to this year's inflation rate. But if people are entirely backward-looking, policymakers will be able to systematically fool them, leading to outcomes that seemed implausible and counterfactual. In the 1980s and 1990s, macroeconomists instead started assuming that people formed beliefs about the future in a way that was consistent with the world in which they lived: the "rational expectations" revolution. But since the world in which these economic actors lived depended in part on how they formed their beliefs about the future, there was an inherent circularity that, when applied to formal models of the economy, sometimes implied multiple equilibria or indeterminacy. And even though macroeconomists could not seem to agree on how to describe the world in which we lived, the agents in our models were assumed to be much smarter and know precisely how that world functioned. Some macroeconomists thought such extreme rationality and informedness were not any more realistic than the assumption that people were completely backward-looking. But in the absence of evidence on how people actually formed beliefs about the future, macroeconomists were left with arguing about what assumptions to use with little reason to choose one over the other.

A natural solution to this would be to start measuring people's beliefs about the future to figure out exactly how they are formed. And this is exactly what some economists (including us) were actively doing in the 2000s and 2010s. This line of work used historical surveys of expectations and created new and larger surveys to help us better understand the nature of the expectations formation process. As we discuss in Chapters 3 and 4, this literature repeatedly and systematically rejected the benchmark assumption of full-information rational expectations (FIRE) that had become the dominant way of modeling expectations in macroeconomics. In doing so, it also provided support for models that allowed for a slow and/or imperfect adjustment of beliefs to changing economic conditions.

But surveys have many practical issues associated with them, making the measurement of beliefs a challenge. And when the results of the surveys turned out to look very different from what our standard models with FIRE were predicting, it wasn't obvious whether the issue was with the surveys or with the theoretical models. This was essentially the challenge posed to us by the editor: if you want me to believe that firms form expectations as your survey suggests, you need to convince me through direct empirical evidence that those survey expectations you are measuring are actually the relevant ones that affect the economic decisions of these firms.[1]

This required us to somehow address a fundamental identification issue to assign causality: how do beliefs affect decisions? Simply measuring expectations well and looking at how they correlate with firms' decisions is not enough. For example, suppose we observe a positive correlation between firms' inflation expectations and their actual price changes. This could be because if firms expect higher inflation, they anticipate that their prices will

1. To be fair, the editor gave us another option: develop a model of expectations that could explain all of the patterns that we observed and could then be used to consider the implications for policy. We didn't know how to deliver this option, and indeed it subsequently took years for smarter and younger economists (many of them our PhD students!) to write many papers that explained different parts of the results. See for example Afrouzi (2024), Yang (2022) and Kamdar and Ray (2024).

depreciate relative to their competitors' over time, and therefore they might choose to set higher prices in the first place. In this case, causality runs from expectations to prices. But causality could easily run in the opposite direction as well. Suppose a labor market shortage in Alabama caused wages there to rise; then firms in Alabama would tend to raise their prices more than in other states. If those firms in Alabama believe that the wage increase is occurring nationwide, then they would expect all other firms in the economy to progressively raise their prices as well. This would deliver a positive correlation between the prices and inflation expectations of firms across the country, but the expectations would not be *causing* the price changes at all. The editor was asking us to rule out the latter and prove that the former was actually at work, a tall order.

Assessing causality in economics is not new, of course. Applied microeconomists have been at the forefront of doing this using micro-level data for a long time. Joshua Angrist, David Card and Guido Imbens received a Nobel Prize in Economics in 2021 for devising different strategies for doing exactly that, by exploiting natural experiments, quasi-experimental variation, discontinuities, and other approaches. But in most settings, there is no such identifiable variation, or one has to be much more clever than we are to find it. We certainly did not see an easy way to apply these strategies to our surveys of firms in New Zealand. Our thought was then, can we *create* the exogenous variation in the data ourselves that would provide the identification necessary to address concerns about causality? In that respect, there is a gold standard out there that is well known to scientists: randomized control trials (RCTs).

In a typical RCT, participants are randomly assigned to one of two groups: a control group and a treatment group. The treatment group receives the "medicine" that is being tested, which can be a drug, a type of therapy, etc. The control group either does not receive any treatment or, at most, is given a placebo. Because of the randomization procedure used to allocate people to each group, the two groups will be essentially identical on average in terms of characteristics of individuals, but the treatment they receive will differ, which means any difference in outcomes across the two groups can be attributed exclusively to the treatment. In that sense, causality is clear and unambiguous; no fancy statistics are needed.

Applying this type of approach in macroeconomic contexts is not obvious. In a Bloomberg interview in October 2024, Donald Trump described running the Federal Reserve as "the greatest job in government. You show up at the office once a month and you say, 'Let's see, flip a coin,' and everybody treats you like you're a god." If his description of the Federal Reserve decision-making process as that of flipping a coin were correct, this would be an example of a repeated RCT applied to a macroeconomic context. Unfortunately for monetary economists interested in studying the effects of monetary policy on the economy, this description is far from correct, and most of the interest rate decisions by the Federal Reserve can instead be accounted for as an endogenous response to economic conditions (Romer and Romer 1989), and not as the result of a coin flip. The coin flip approach to monetary policy would obviously negatively affect millions of people, as would many applications of RCTs to macroeconomic environments. Only in development economics have RCTs become quite common, thanks in large part to the work of Esther Duflo and Abhijit Banerjee, for which they were awarded the Nobel Prize in Economics in 2019. RCTs were feasible in development and health economics because one could assign "treatments" (e.g., handing out malaria nets) to randomly selected villages and not others, allowing one to assess how these treatments affected outcomes across villages over time.

So how could we apply something similar in the case of firms' inflation expectations? Conceptually, the ideal experiment would be one in which, for each firm in our sample, we could flip a coin and if heads came up, we would raise their inflation expectations, but if tails came up, we would leave them alone. This would create new variation in inflation expectations that would be systematically unrelated to firms' characteristics. Our first draft of the paper included a simple experiment like this, in which some randomly selected firms had been provided with information about inflation or the central bank's inflation target. We used it to study how firms' expectations responded to the new information. Other papers had applied similar strategies to households (Armantier et al. 2016, Cavallo et al. 2017), but this by itself did not establish that those expectations were important for firms' actions in any way.

To address the editor's question, we had to take it one step further and determine whether changes in expectations actually had an effect on firms' actions. This would require an additional ingredient, namely, tracking the decisions of firms over time. If we could show that those firms whose inflation expectations were randomly changed subsequently set their prices or employment in a manner that differed from firms whose expectations were left untouched, this would provide clear causal evidence that those expectations mattered for their decisions. So we designed a two-stage experiment in which we would first run an RCT to change the inflation expectations of a randomly selected subset of firms. In the second stage, we would track their decisions over time. Through this combination, we would be able to estimate the degree to which changes in inflation expectations causally passed through into firms' decisions.

Excited at having this plan of attack, we went to our coauthor in New Zealand and proposed that we run two new survey waves: one to implement the RCT in which we would try to change some firms' inflation expectations and a subsequent one to enable us to assess whether their decisions had been altered relative to other firms whose expectations we did not affect. He agreed that this strategy might work but raised what turned out to be the first of many issues we've since learned can make this approach more challenging than how it first sounded: the cost! His funding had run out and implementing two more waves (and these needed to be large surveys to have enough power to detect effects on beliefs and decisions) would cost around $100,000, an amount that seemed insurmountably high. But after some time and the amazing support of our home universities (Go Bears! and Hook 'em Horns!) and the National Science Foundation, we were able to move forward and test out our new empirical strategy.

To be honest, we were not 100% confident that it would work. There were so many ways things could go wrong. The provision of information could fail to change the inflation expectations of firms in the treated group. The sample sizes could be too small to have a detectable effect on decisions even if there was one. Self-reported outcomes could be too imprecise. And, in our heart of hearts as trained macroeconomists, we shared some of the skepticism of our editor: if these expectations were important enough to actually matter for firms' decisions, wouldn't they have chosen to be well informed about inflation in the first place? Didn't the fact that they let themselves be uninformed about inflation imply that these beliefs did not matter? To cover our anxiety as we waited out the long months before the completion of the experiment, we would joke among ourselves about how this might turn out to be the most expensive failure to reject the null hypothesis of no effect ever, a little econ humor that provided us with little comfort.

Finally, the data came in and, to our great relief, the experiment had worked! We found that the information treatment was successful in changing the inflation expectations of firms that were initially uninformed, and that the change in their inflation expectations led them to alter their decisions over subsequent months. Firms that raised their inflation expectations due to the treatment (and relative to the control group) ended up hiring more workers and doing more investment than they had initially planned. And the implied pass-through of expectations into decisions was economically large along some margins: every 1 percentage point increase in inflation expectations raised employment growth by 2 percentage points and investment growth by 3 percentage points, for example. In contrast, the pass-through into prices was economically small and we could not reject the possibility that it was zero.

With this new causal evidence in hand showing the relevance of firms' inflation expectations for at least some of their decisions, we resubmitted the paper and it was ultimately accepted. Thanks to the skepticism of this editor, we ran our first RCT linking expectations and decisions, the first of what would turn out to be many. Since then, we have had the incredible good fortune to work with different research teams around the world who had access to surveys in which RCTs could be implemented. In addition to our initial surveys of firms in New Zealand with Saten Kumar, we have been able to work with surveys of firms in the U.S. with Brent Meyer, in Uruguay with Serafin Frache and Rodrigo Lluberas, in Italy with Tiziano Ropele and in France with Erwan Gautier and Frederique Savignac. We also began running similar experiments on surveys of households, initially in the U.S. with Michael Weber but then also in the Netherlands with Maarten van Rooij, and in the Euro area with Dimitris Georgarakos and Geoff Kenny. Through these research partnerships as well as through the work of our current and former graduate students and many other research teams working on similar topics and methods in parallel, we have learned much about the challenges and opportunities that come with using RCTs to study how beliefs affect economic decisions.

This book is the fruit of this research and is meant to provide guidance to current and future economists who may be interested in what this approach can bring to the table. Some of this guidance is simply a list of things not to do, lessons we have learned the hard way over time. Some of it is practical steps to raise the probability of success. Throughout, our goal is to help make this approach a more standard part of macroeconomists' toolkit, though the method is much broader and not restricted to macroeconomic questions. Since expectations affect decisions for households, firms, traders, and many other actors/participants in the economy, possible (and existing) applications include industrial organization, labor economics, public finance, and political economy among other fields.

We've divided the book into four parts. The first three focus on methodology, while the fourth describes different applications in the literature. The first part of the book discusses surveys of expectations, issues related to the design of questions to measure expectations, and some of the other challenges that arise in running surveys of expectations. The literature on expectations surveys has exploded in recent years and we provide an overview of some of the main empirical results to have come out of this literature, although due to space limitations we cannot do justice here to the breadth of this literature. Instead, we focus primarily on inflation expectations, both because of their particular relevance to macroeconomic policymaking and because they have been at the forefront of macroeconomic surveys and research. Finally, we discuss how these measures of expectations can be used to guide and discipline theoretical models of expectations formation.

The second part of the book turns to the RCT component of the strategy. This is the stage at which information is provided to randomly selected subsets of participants to assess whether and how it affects their economic expectations. We focus on how to implement these treatments and under what conditions we should expect them to be successful. Information treatments are not guaranteed to work, and indeed there are many cases where we should *not* expect them to work. Understanding ahead of time which treatments will likely work (and when) has been an important lesson from the very rapidly growing literature on information treatments in macroeconomics. Since the information treatments generate the exogenous variation in expectations that form the basis for identification, this is an essential component of the empirical strategy. We describe some of the main lessons from this line of research, for both policymaking and communication, as well as how results from information treatments can speak to theoretical models of learning and expectations formation.

The third part of the book describes how to estimate the passthrough of expectations into decisions. Ultimately, this is the question that we are interested in answering with our empirical strategy. In addition to the variation in beliefs created via the RCT, we need information on the decisions of economic agents to be able to relate changes in beliefs to decisions. We describe the different ways that one can try to measure outcomes, from the ideal scenario of matching the survey to external administrative datasets to the more common case where outcomes are measured using follow-up survey waves or even planned decisions from the same wave as that of the RCT. One chapter discusses different econometric approaches that can be used to estimate pass-through coefficients, as well as the many issues that can arise in both the implementation and the interpretation of estimated pass-through coefficients. We also discuss in a separate chapter how scenario-based questions (hypotheticals) can be used to identify the same theoretical object as the full-blown RCT strategy, but more quickly and at significantly lower cost. Finally, another chapter delves into how these estimates can be mapped into theoretical models, and the potential value of doing so.

Through all three of these initial parts of the book, we focus primarily on applications and examples involving inflation expectations to illustrate each of the components within a common framework. This reflects the fact that much of the literature on surveys, information treatments and estimated pass-throughs has been focused on inflation expectations. But the role of beliefs in affecting economic decisions is much broader than this specific application.

The final part of the book therefore covers other topics to which this approach has been applied. One such application is how uncertainty affects decision-making, an important line of research following the seminal work of Bloom (2009). We discuss how one can use RCTs to create exogenous variation in the economic uncertainty perceived by firms or households to study the different channels through which uncertainty affects their behavior, an essential ingredient for understanding the aggregate effects of uncertainty. In another application we consider how peer effects matter for individual decisions. "Keeping up with the Joneses" forces have long been emphasized for spending, but relative income standing could matter for other consumer decisions as well. We review recent papers, especially those relying on this type of RCT approach, that assess how perceived relative income standings affect spending decisions, labor supply decisions, investment decisions, political preferences and even the happiness of individuals in a causal framework. The final two applications are on how individuals' beliefs about future financial asset returns and future housing prices affect their decisions, respectively. In each case, recent research has utilized RCTs to generate variation in expectations of the future asset price changes and then related these changing beliefs to households' decisions, not only for their investment choices but also along other margins such as spending. Across the board, expectations are found to matter for economic decisions, although the quantitative magnitudes of the estimated effects in some cases are large whereas in other cases they are quite small. In all cases, the estimated pass-throughs can be used to discipline economic models in which these expectations channels are at work, and may also relate directly to policy communication objectives and tools.

Throughout, our primary objective is to present the main building blocks of this empirical strategy and identify potential pitfalls. As a result, much of the book concentrates on empirical topics and issues. But because another objective is to encourage macroeconomists in particular to adopt the strategy as part of their toolbox, we devote significant space to discussing how different steps of the approach can be mapped to theoretical models and the potential usefulness of doing so. There have been a few attempts to do so, and what we present should be thought of only as stepping stones to more systematically integrating the results from RCT studies into macroeconomic theory and modeling, an area we hope to see blossom in coming years. For non-macroeconomist readers, the theory chapters (Chapters 4, 8 and 12) may be of less relevance, and could be skipped without the reader losing understanding of the empirical methods.

Ultimately, this book is meant for students and future economists. Macroeconomics has changed dramatically in the twenty years since we were in graduate school ourselves. The field has become much more empirically driven than it has ever been and this trend is unlikely to reverse itself anytime soon. We view the methods in this book as an additional powerful set of tools that can be used to strengthen the empirical foundations of macroeconomics and guide the development of future models. We hope that students and practitioners of the field will embrace them and build upon them rapidly, hopefully making this book quickly outdated, as good science should do.

PART I

Measuring Expectations through Surveys

1

How Should We Measure Economic Expectations?

IN THE COURSE of making typical economic decisions, we rely on our views about the future. How much of your current income you choose to save today likely depends not just on your current salary but also how much you expect to earn in the future. If, for example, you expect a big raise next year, then the incentive to save today is reduced. If we want to assess how changes in beliefs about our future income might affect our current saving or spending decisions without imposing a lot of structure on beliefs (such as adaptive expectations or full-information rational expectations), we need to be able to measure what individuals believe their future income will be. Similarly, to the extent that real interest rates should also matter for spending decisions, we need to measure individuals' inflation expectations. The same logic applies to firms setting prices or making investment and employment decisions. These choices should all depend on expectations of the future.

It might seem like measuring these expectations would be straightforward. Just ask people what they expect about inflation, for example, and they will provide a precise and truthful answer. In practice, things are not simple. In fact, prominent economists like Nobel laureate Edward Prescott have claimed that expectations are not measurable at all. This is, in part, because a number of challenges arise very quickly in trying to measure expectations, and how these are tackled can matter quite a bit for the results. Indeed, existing surveys have used a variety of approaches to try to measure the very same expectations, some with greater success than others. In this chapter, we consider different ways of measuring expectations and the potential pitfalls associated with different approaches. We focus on inflation expectations both because they are of immediate interest to macroeconomists but also because the challenges associated with this particular variable speak to those arising from many other economic concepts as well.

There are four main choices to be made when framing questions to measure subjective beliefs. The first is about the specific language used to define what the expectation is over. The second involves whether to ask for qualitative or quantitative answers. The third choice concerns whether to ask for a single forecast or to elicit distributions over possible outcomes. The fourth key option involves the time horizon for the expectation. We discuss each of these choices in turn, focusing on the measurement of inflation expectations as an example. We then discuss potential challenges that can arise with the measurement of expectations through surveys, as well as alternative methods.

Question Wording

The long-running Michigan Survey of Consumers asks U.S. households what they expect will happen to prices in general over the next 12 months. The competing New York Fed's Survey of Consumer Expectations, in contrast, asks them about inflation in the U.S. economy. The Survey of Professional Forecasters instead asks for forecasts about the Consumer Price Index (CPI) and the Personal Consumption Expenditures Price Index (PCE) separately. Does this matter? Is one better than the other? The answers depend in part on the target audience of the question. In the case of professional forecasters who are often Ph.D.-trained macroeconomists, the CPI and PCE are not identical and professional economists will make separate forecasts for the two series. It makes sense to be precise when surveying this audience about their inflation expectations. But to paraphrase Greg Mankiw (1997), professional economists are not people and people are not professional economists. For a typical household, the difference between the CPI and PCE is of little relevance: providing this kind of precision in a question will likely add confusion rather than reduce it. The typical respondent in a firm survey will similarly not worry about the differences across price indices. For a nonexpert audience, asking for predictions of overly specific concepts can be counterproductive and lead to low response rates.

But being too general can raise its own set of issues. When the Michigan Survey, for example, asks a respondent, "During the next 12 months, do you think that prices in general will go up, or go down, or stay where they are now?" it's not immediately clear what the term "prices in general" is referring to. An economist would probably interpret it as a statement about inflation in the overall economy, but a survey respondent could just as easily interpret it as a question about the prices they typically pay for their own basket of goods (Bruine de Bruin et al. 2012). Both concepts are interesting to measure, but we should strive to avoid conflating different concepts by asking a question that is unnecessarily vague.

Two other surveys of U.S. households have each taken a different approach to separating these two concepts. The New York Fed's Survey of Consumer Expectations (SCE) asks explicitly about inflation: "Now we would like you to think about the different things that may happen to inflation over the next 12 months." While some individuals may not fully understand how inflation is measured by statistical agencies (how many of us really do?), at least the term "inflation" is commonly understood to be about the overall economy, not the specific prices paid by an individual. The Cleveland Fed's Indirect Consumer Inflation Expectations survey, on the other hand, targets the expected price changes that apply to each individual directly. They ask survey respondents, "Given your expectations about developments in prices of goods and services during the next 12 months, how would your income have to change to make you equally well-off relative to your current situation, such that you can buy the same amount of goods and services as today?" Since the question is formulated in terms of an individual being able to purchase the same set of goods and services as before, it deliberately captures the expected price changes for the specific bundle of goods used by that household, which is potentially quite different from what they might expect to happen to inflation in the overall economy. Both the New York Fed's and the Cleveland Fed's measures of inflation expectations are interesting, but they are distinct conceptually and there is no reason a priori for the two surveys to give very similar answers.

The Federal Reserve Bank of Cleveland is not the only organization to try to measure inflation expectations without directly asking about prices or inflation. The Atlanta Fed's Business Inflation Expectations (BIE) Survey, for example, asks firms to predict what will happen to their unit costs over the next twelve months. Because changes in unit costs should ultimately pass through into price changes, and averaging price changes across firms should approximate a measure of inflation, this survey is commonly referred to as measuring the inflation expectations of firms. But clearly it is measuring something different: firms' expectations about their own future cost changes. Again, this is a very interesting expectation to measure, but it is conceptually distinct from what firms expect aggregate inflation will be. For comparison, the Cleveland Fed's Survey of Firms' Inflation Expectations (SoFIE) asks firms directly about what they expect inflation will be over the same time horizon, and the answers from this survey tend to look quite different from what is found in the BIE (Candia, Coibion and Gorodnichenko 2024).

In short, what respondents are specifically asked about matters for the answers that are provided. Care must be taken in formulating questions that are on target in terms of the specific expectation we care about and that are appropriate to the respondents. This is especially the case for respondents who are less financially literate (Lusardi and Mitchell 2014).

Qualitative versus Quantitative Questions

Most of us have taken surveys at some point, be it for a company whose services we used or in response to an unsolicited email. The most common questions ask us to provide a qualitative answer, of the type, "On a scale of 1 to 5, how likely would you be to . . . (where 1 is very likely and 5 is not likely at all)." These questions are pervasive because they are very easy to answer for the respondent and generally sufficient for the needs of the surveyor. Most questions about economic expectations in surveys have also historically been of this type. And for some purposes, this is all we need. For example, for economic forecasting, the scale of answers does not matter much once a time series of answers is available. Consumer confidence measures are generally of this type and have long been used by economists and policymakers alike.

However, for many other purposes, these questions are insufficient. First, it is difficult to make interpersonal comparisons: one person's "somewhat likely" may be the same as someone else's "very likely." Second, in many cases, the numbers themselves are essential. For example, if a central bank wants to determine if inflation expectations are anchored, survey answers telling us that prices are expected to "go up" are not very informative without a metric of how fast they are expected to rise. Third, if we want to use survey answers to estimate elasticities or pass-through coefficients to relate to theory, quantitative answers are crucial. As a result, new surveys increasingly rely on questions that extract numerical answers, a feature that has allowed significant breakthroughs to take place in our understanding of economic behavior.

For those designing their own surveys, there is an important trade-off to keep in mind. Questions that are easy and quick to answer alleviate survey fatigue and help ensure higher response rates. They can also allow for more questions to be asked in the survey. More demanding questions, while often more useful, carry a higher opportunity cost in terms of the respondent's ability and willingness to continue with the survey. It is therefore up to the researcher to balance the need for more quantitative answers with the need to include enough questions in the survey. This is particularly important with surveys of firms. Getting chief executive officers to respond to surveys is a genuine challenge and they will typically only give you a few minutes of their time. The choice may therefore often come down to asking a small number of quantitative questions or a larger number of qualitative ones. The best choice will depend on the context and the objective of the survey. In many cases, researchers will use a mixed approach: asking a quantitative question for the key expectation they want to measure then asking qualitative follow-up questions that can speak to the mechanisms through which these expectations can affect decisions.

Point Forecasts versus Probability Distributions

A third important dimension to expectations questions is whether to ask for a point forecast or for a subjective probability distribution, which usually means assigning probabilities to a predetermined set of possible outcomes. Asking for a point forecast is conceptually straightforward. For example, the Michigan Survey of Consumers asks: "By about what percent do you expect prices to go (up/down) on average during the next 12 months?" While simple, one ambiguity about this type of question is that it is unclear if respondents are providing a mean, median, mode or other summary statistic from their distribution of expected outcomes. An alternative approach is to propose a range of possible outcomes to respondents and ask them to assign different probabilities to each. For example, the New York Fed's SCE asks respondents to assign probabilities to ten possible ranges of future inflation: "the rate of inflation will be 12% or higher," "the rate of inflation will be between 8% and 12%," . . . , "the rate of deflation (opposite of inflation) will be 12% or higher." The reported probability distributions can then be used to infer a central tendency (like the mean or mode).

This distributional question has two important advantages. First, it is much clearer which moment of the distribution is used, in contrast to the point forecast. Second, responses to these distributional forecasts allow the researcher to measure not just the first moment of the respondent's distribution but also their uncertainty as well as other higher moments of the distribution. Uncertainty can often be of interest in its own right, as in the extensive uncertainty literature following Bloom (2009), but also because it can matter in determining the extent to which respondents will adjust their beliefs to new information, as in Bayesian learning.

However, distributional questions have their own limitations. An important one is that the choice of what bins to present as options can shape the answers that respondents provide, for example, by making clear that some answers are extreme (e.g., "the rate of inflation will be 12% or higher") and by inducing answers to be close to the middle of the specified distribution. One illustrative example of this is the Bank of Canada's Business Outlook Survey (BOS) which offers only four bins for possible inflation outcomes: "less than 1%," "1% to 2%," "2% to 3%," "more than 3%." This survey tends to find inflation expectations that are close to 2% (coincidentally, the Bank of Canada's inflation target), but a skeptic could argue that this result is determined by the design of the survey. Another limitation of bins is having to assign a value to extreme bins. Again, the Bank of Canada's BOS survey is illustrative. When respondents assign high probabilities to the top or bottom bin, the choice over which value to assign to those bins (e.g., both 4% and 10% are above the 3% threshold to be in the top bin) can make a big difference for the resulting inflation expectations measures. A third important limitation of this type of question is that the appropriate bins may change over time as the level of inflation varies. For example, the specific bins used by the BOS make little sense when inflation is running close to 10%.[1] To address this limitation, we can either use a very large set of bins that cover many different outcomes over time or change the bins over time. Both are potentially a problem. Using a lot of bins increases the cognitive demand on respondents. Changing bins makes it difficult to have a consistent series of expectations over time. While appealing, these distribution questions therefore suffer from a number of drawbacks.

Broadly speaking, point forecasts and responses to distributional questions tend to be consistent with one another. For example, Figure 1.1 plots a binscatter of survey responses from U.S. households in the New York Fed's Survey of Consumer Expectations to questions asking them for a point forecast of inflation over the next 12 months, then asking them to assign probabilities to a wide range of different bins of possible inflation outcomes. On average, we see that the two line up fairly closely, with the slope of the relationship being close to 1. This is especially true for forecasts that are near the middle bins provided in the distributional question. Once beliefs approach the extreme bins, these

1. 78% of firms in BOS chose "above 3%" in the second quarter of 2022.

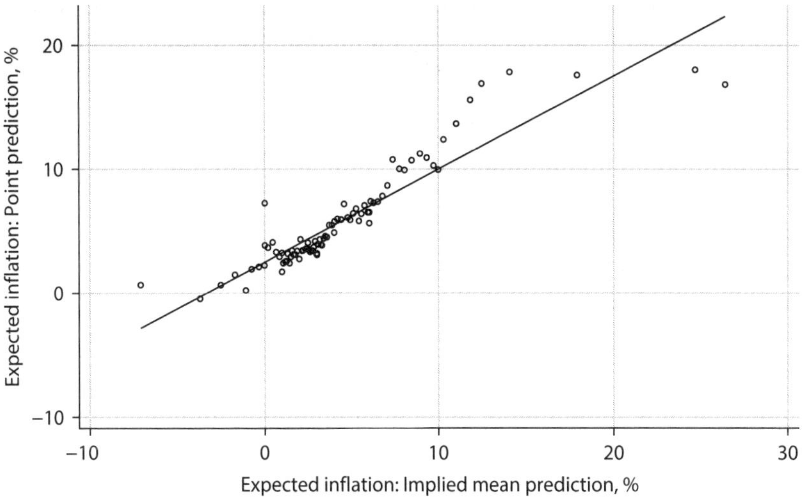

FIGURE 1.1. One-year-ahead inflation expectations.
Notes: The figure presents a binscatter plot and the fitted line for the joint distribution of point predictions vs. implied means for inflation expectations. The sample period covers 2013–2024. Own calculations. Data are from the New York Fed's Survey of Consumer Expectations.

questions do a worse job of characterizing expectations since there is so much ambiguity as to what values to assign to the top and bottom bins.

An alternative approach to pre-specified bins is to use a flexible scale such as the triangular questions from Manski (2004). In this formulation, we would first ask respondents to provide the minimum and maximum forecasts that they envision. If we assume a uniform distribution over these endpoints, this is sufficient to construct first (mean) and second (uncertainty) moments. To refine this measure, we can ask the follow-up question: "What is the probability that inflation is more than [(X+Y)/2]?" where X and Y correspond to the minimum and the maximum forecasts provided. Assuming a triangular probability distribution, then we can again readily compute first and second moments from this distribution. A very important advantage of this approach is it does not depend on pre-specified bins and therefore is immune to the concerns described above. However, it is now dependent on the assumption of uniform or triangular distributions to compute moments. Furthermore, the follow-up question is cognitively demanding to answer for many respondents, especially those who have low scores for numerical literacy.

In our opinion, the question formulation that best avoids all of these limitations is the one developed by Altig et al. (2022) in their attempts to measure the economic uncertainty perceived by firms. They proposed the following two-step question. First, ask respondents to provide numerical forecasts for five different possible outcomes ("very low," "low," "medium," "high," "very high"). Once respondents have provided these five possible outcomes, the second step is to ask them to assign probabilities to each outcome. The second step is therefore equivalent to what is done with typical distribution questions, but the first step of the question involved having the respondent define the bins themselves. The question can be simplified further, if need be, by reducing the number of outcomes from five to three, so that respondents are only asked to provide "low," "medium" and "high" outcomes. This approach has many advantages. First, there are no framing effects from having pre-specified bins presented to respondents.[2] Second, there are no end-bin issues, where one needs to assign a value to the extreme bins, since respondents have themselves specified the relevant values. Third, there is no issue over time with needing to change the bins to accommodate different economic conditions, since the respondents' bins will evolve as economic conditions change. While this question is not easy to answer per se, it does not appear to be more cognitively demanding than traditional bin questions. When asked what question formulation works best to measure uncertainty, this is the one we recommend.[3]

Conditional Expectations

A related approach to measuring beliefs focuses on *conditional* expectations, in which respondents are asked what they expect will happen under specific future scenarios. For example, a natural time to do this would be with presidential elections: asking respondents what they expect will happen if one candidate is elected. In Coibion, Gorodnichenko and Weber (2020a), we used this strategy to assess how economic expectations of U.S. households varied with their political beliefs and expected outcomes of the 2020 presidential election. Respondents were first asked to provide conditional expectations

2. The framing effect is a cognitive bias where respondents pick an option based on which and how options are presented.

3. The only time we ran into meaningful problems with this question was when trying to apply it to a survey of households in China, where respondents struggled to assign probabilities to the bins they had picked such that they summed to 100. The min-max question worked better in that setting.

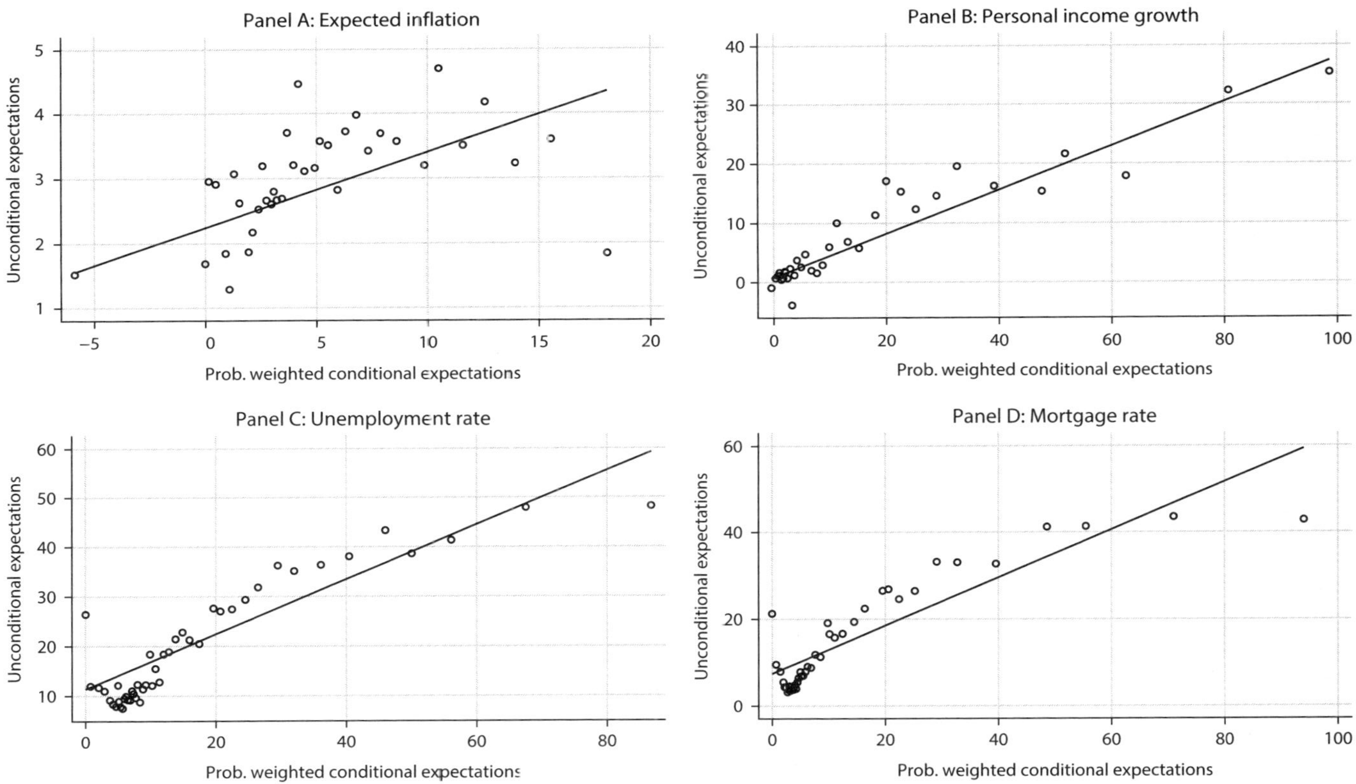

FIGURE 1.2. Distribution of unconditional and probability weighted conditional forecasts for macroeconomic variables.
Notes: Each panel presents a binscatter plot and the fitted line for expectations indicated in panel titles. Survey data are from the Nielsen Homescan Panel. The survey was conducted in October 2020
Source: Coibion, Gorodnichenko and Weber (2020a).

such as, "What do you think the inflation rate will be in 2021 if [Trump/Biden] is elected?" for both Trump and Biden. For both Republicans and Democrats, expectations of inflation were much higher if the other party was expected to win the election. An advantage of this type of question is that not only can it measure conditional expectations, but when combined with a question that measures the perceived probability of the relevant outcomes (e.g., "How likely do you think it is that [Trump/Biden] will be elected president?"), one can recover the *unconditional* expectation of a respondent as the probability-weighted sum of conditional expectations. Surprisingly, we found that using this indirect approach to measuring unconditional expectations yields, on average, similar answers as directly asking for unconditional expectations through point forecasts (e.g., "What do you expect inflation will be in 2021?"), as shown in Figure 1.2. Conditional variances and higher moments can also be recovered in the same fashion, and these can also be interesting on their own.

A potential disadvantage of this approach is that it is harder to implement when there are more than two or three possible outcomes, as we then need to

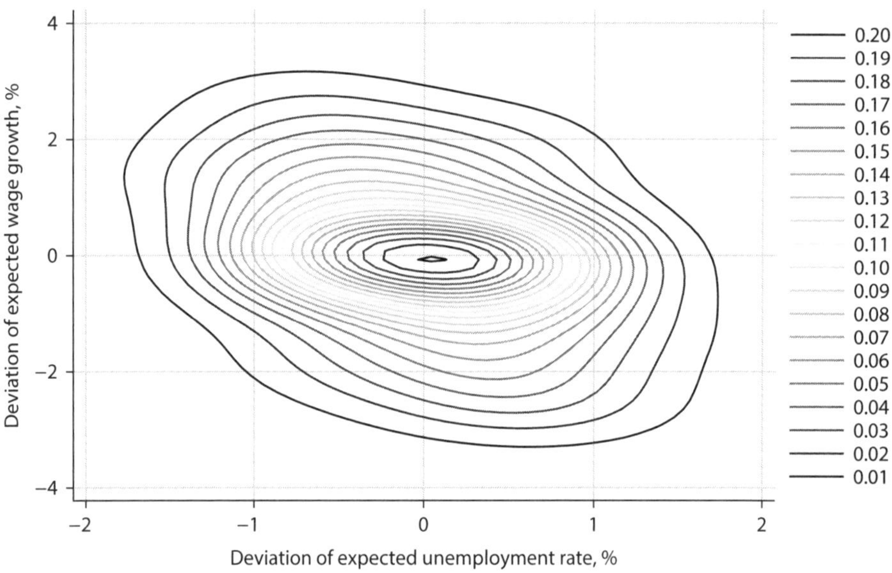

FIGURE 1.3. Joint distribution of managers' wage growth expectations and unemployment rate expectations in New Zealand.
Notes: The figure shows the contour map for the joint distribution of expectations for unemployment and wage growth. For each manager, the reported distribution is normalized to center at (0, 0) and then aggregated to the national level. See Candia, Coibion and Gorodnichenko (2020) for more details.

ask for conditional expectations and probabilities for each case. However, even this is feasible. For example, in a survey of firms in New Zealand, we first asked firms to assign probabilities to different possible unemployment rates. Then, for each unemployment rate with positive probability, we asked them to report probabilities for different wage growth rates, i.e., to report probability distributions for wage growth conditional on the level of unemployment. These questions yielded a *joint* distribution of forecasts of wage growth and unemployment for respondents, which we plot in Figure 1.3. The figure reveals a negative correlation between the two variables. Hence, on average, firms in New Zealand expect wage growth to be lower when unemployment is higher (a Phillips curve!).

Horizon of Expectations

In asking about people's expectations, the time horizon needs to be specified. A one-year horizon is often the default, but expectations can be defined over longer or shorter horizons as well, depending on what we are interested in. With inflation, it is not uncommon to be interested in longer run expectations, such as five or ten years ahead. One may similarly be interested in longer-run horizons for output growth, unemployment or personal income, for example. It is also often interesting to ask for backcasts or nowcasts, i.e., beliefs about past or current economic conditions, since these measures provide a direct metric of how informed individuals are about different economic outcomes.

There are two main issues that arise with different forecasting horizons. First, when deviating from the one-year horizon, we need to specify whether forecasts should be cumulative, at an annualized rate over the entire horizon, or at an annual rate at the forecasting horizon. Consider a five-year inflation forecast for example. We could ask a respondent: a) "How much higher or lower (in percent) do you think prices will be in five years?"; b) "What do you think will be the average annual inflation rate over the next five years?"; c) "What do you think will be the annual rate of inflation in five years?"; or d) "What inflation do you expect in year YYYY+5, where YYYY is the current year." These different formulations will likely lead to different responses, so researchers should take care in determining which horizon they are most interested in and using the language that is best tailored to that horizon (and least likely to confuse respondents). We find that option d) works best for measuring long-term inflation expectations because it gives a concrete period in the future.

A second issue that arises with the choice of horizon is the limited scope for asking for multiple horizons. It is often the case that researchers would like to know nowcasts and forecasts at multiple horizons, but this requires asking several related and nuanced questions of respondents, a tiring exercise for many people. One approach to dealing with this, which applies more generally as a strategy to expand the scope of a survey without increasing the overall number of questions, is to randomly assign different questions to respondents. For example, with inflation expectations, one might ask all respondents to provide their one-year ahead inflation expectations but then ask a randomly selected half of the sample to provide their nowcast while the other half is asked to provide a long-run inflation forecast. This would allow a researcher to connect nowcasts and forecasts, and separately map the term structure of inflation expectations, with only two questions, but it would prevent the joint analysis of nowcasts and long-run forecasts, at least in the cross-section.

Priming

When designing survey questions, extra care must be taken to avoid steering or "priming" respondents toward or away from particular answers. We have already discussed some ways in which priming can occur, such as through which bins are presented to respondents. To appreciate how much the wording of the questions can affect the responses, Figure 1.4 shows the average subjective probability distribution of inflation expectations of New Zealand firms when they are are presented with a narrow menu of possible inflation outcomes ("BIE grid") and a wide menu of possible outcomes ("NZ grid"). One can see that the narrow grid not only compresses the distribution but also moves the mean. Furthermore, presenting respondents with scenarios they are not thinking about (e.g., deflation) can prompt respondents to assign positive probabilities to these scenarios (Sergeyev and Gorodnichenko 2021).

There are other ways in which this can happen as well. One is by asking follow-up questions when respondents provide what may seem like extreme answers. For example, when households provide an inflation forecast that is greater than 5% in the Michigan Survey of Consumer Expectations, they are asked a follow-up question: "Let me make sure I have that correct. You said that you expect prices to go (up/down) during the next 12 months by (X) percent. Is that correct?" This type of follow-up question can make respondents question themselves (at least we would question ourselves) and provides an indication to them that their answer is not what was desired. As a result, they are likely to change them, in this case in a downward manner (Bruine de Bruin et al. 2017). Another form of priming can arise when a question provides a numerical

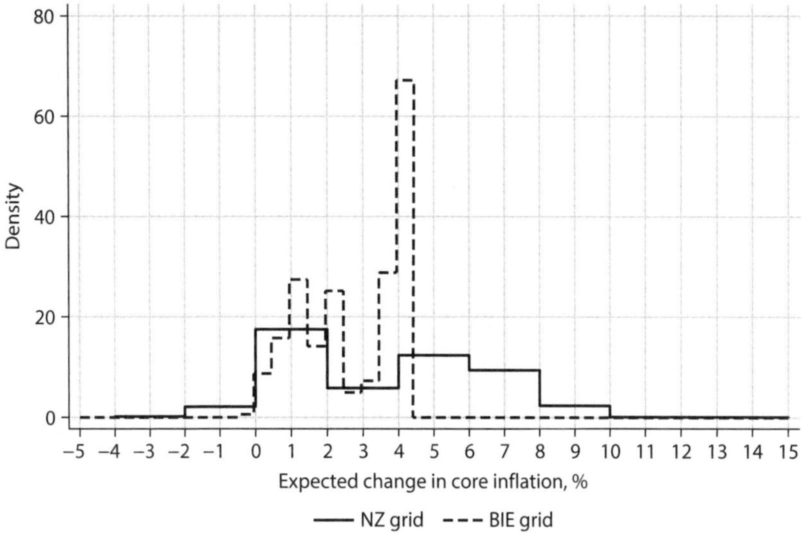

FIGURE 1.4. The effect of presented inflation outcomes (bins) on reported subjective distributions of inflation expectations of firms in New Zealand. *Notes:* The figure presents average probability distribution by the type of survey questions. The NZ grid has 16 bins ranging from "more than 25%" to "less than −25%." For the Business Inflation Expectations (BIE) of the Atlanta Fed, firms assign probabilities to 10 bins ranging from "4 percent or more" to "will decline." BIE bins have 0.5 percentage point increments. The NZ grid is centered at 0, while the BIE grid is centered at 2 percent. See Coibion, Gorodnichenko, Kumar and Pedemonte (2020) for more details.

example or explanation. As illustration, the Cleveland Fed's Indirect Consumer Inflation Expectations question is followed by, "For example, if you consider prices will fall by 2% over the next 12 months, you may still be able to buy the same goods and services if your income also decreases by 2%." Any provision of a numerical example can serve as an anchor that affects subsequent responses. Whenever possible, these should be avoided.

Rounding in Responses

A common outcome of survey responses is a disproportionate share of responses assigned to specific values, such as 0, 5, or 10, or to integer values when decimals are appropriate. Figure 1.5 plots the distribution of inflation point forecasts from the Michigan Survey of Consumers. While most answers are between 2 and 6%, we can see that there is disproportionate mass assigned to

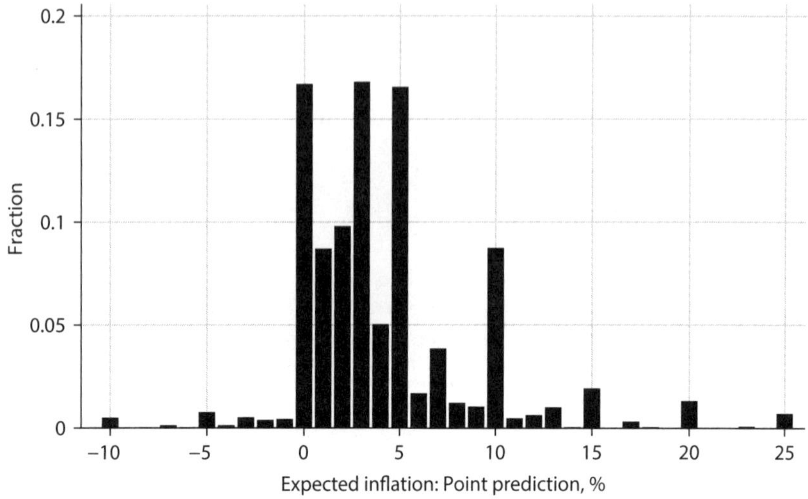

FIGURE 1.5. Inflation expectations (one-year-ahead) in the Michigan Survey of Consumers, 1978–2024.
Notes: Own calculations.

values like 5%, 10%, etc. Binder (2017) argued that the degree to which rounding occurs can be used as a measure of uncertainty about inflation among respondents. Using individual-level data for which distributional questions provide a direct measure of inflation uncertainty, she showed that respondents who are more uncertain about inflation are much more likely to provide point forecasts that are in multiples of 5. One implication of this phenomenon is that even when a survey asks respondents only for point forecasts, we can still create time series measures of uncertainty based on the extent to which they round their point forecasts. However, this approach can only measure uncertainty across all respondents and cannot provide an individual measure of uncertainty. Furthermore, when respondents use multiples of 5, the responses get coarser and thus affect the precision of aggregated measures. For example, the median may be stuck at 5 with rounding, while the truth may be 4 or 6.

Should Survey Responses Be Trusted?

Given that responses to surveys are sensitive to how questions are phrased, that respondents often report answers that are hard to believe, that respondents have little incentive to be truthful, and that measurement error seems to be pervasive, should we trust surveys to correctly measure the beliefs of respondents? Our answer is an emphatic "Yes, but. . . ."

There are many reasons to take seriously the responses that people provide to surveys. First, it has been found that surveys of economic expectations from households or firms commonly outperform asset prices or econometric models in predicting subsequent economic outcomes. A well-known paper by Ang, Bekaert and Wei (2007) showed this in the case of inflation. They compared the predictive power of inflation expectations from surveys of both U.S. households and professional forecasters to forecasts coming from asset prices (based on the term structure of interest rates) or from different econometric models. For different measures of inflation and different time periods, they found that survey forecasts—be they from households or professionals—systematically outperformed predictions from asset prices or time series models, with household forecasts being only slightly worse on average than those from professional forecasters. Researchers have documented similar evidence for other outcomes as well. For example, surveys that ask people whom they expect to win presidential elections outperform other electoral prediction methods such as vote intention polls, prediction markets, quantitative models and expert judgement (Rothschild and Wolfers 2012, Graefe 2014).

Second, there is extensive evidence that the forecasts provided by both households and firms in surveys about their own future actions strongly predict what they actually do in the future. If individuals were answering surveys at random or in the fastest way possible, their answers would be pure noise and would have no predictive content whatsoever. But this is far from what we observe in the data. For example, in a 2018 paper with Saten Kumar, we described a survey of firms in New Zealand in which we had asked managers, among other things, to tell us when they expected to change their prices next as well as by how much. Six months later, we reinterviewed managers and asked them, again among other things, what they had done with prices over the previous six months. The responses were striking: of those managers who reported initially that they expected to change their price within the first six months after our survey, 97% reported having done so six months later, and 98% of those who had initially said that they were not planning to change their price for at least six months later reported that they had indeed not changed their price over that six-month period. For those managers who did change their prices, the magnitudes of those price changes ended up being remarkably close to what they had predicted in the first wave of the survey.

Third, when survey responses are compared to external or administrative data on equivalent measures, the two generally line up quite well. For example, households' self-reported measures of spending are close, on average, to what can be inferred from administrative data (Kreiner, Lassen and Leth-Petersen 2015) or to measures of their spending from daily tracking of their purchases (Coibion, Gorodnichenko and Weber 2022a). Firms' survey responses about their employment and investment decisions also can be corroborated against administrative records and generally line up quite closely (Coibion, Gorodnichenko and Ropele 2020). When researchers use managers' discussions during earnings calls to create text-based measures of inflation expectations, these end up being highly correlated with survey measures of expectations (Albrizio, Dizioli and Simon 2023).

Fourth, as we will describe in more detail in later sections of the book, when survey participants are provided with new information that changes their beliefs, this often changes their economic decisions as well. For example, firms that are repeatedly provided with data on inflation not only change their expectations about inflation but also end up earning slightly higher profits than those who are not provided with this information. Households that are told about recent inflation numbers change both their inflation expectations and their spending. The fact that changes in reported expectations translate into economic decisions, especially when these can be measured through external sources, provides further validation that surveys can correctly capture the beliefs of individuals.

However, there are many potential caveats and pitfalls to avoid. We have already described some potential issues involving specific questions used to measure expectations, but there are many more. These include reaching the right respondents, getting them to participate, designing a survey that is representative and includes a sufficient but not excessively taxing set of questions, ensuring some repeated participation in the survey without contaminating the survey through panel conditioning effects, and so on. Without adequate solutions to these issues, even the best phrased expectations question is unlikely to provide results that can be used to address either policy or research topics.

2

What Makes a Good Survey of Expectations?

UNFORTUNATELY, IT TAKES much more than just well-designed expectations questions to be able to use surveys to study the determinants of individual beliefs and how these shape economic decisions. In this chapter, we describe the main characteristics of a successful survey of expectations. We emphasize seven key characteristics. No existing survey conforms to all of these desiderata (but we do not want the perfect to be the enemy of the good), and some otherwise excellent surveys depart from these along multiple dimensions. Indeed, surveys of expectations exist to serve different purposes, and certain characteristics are more important for certain purposes than others. Following our description of an ideal survey of expectations, we review the main existing surveys of household and firm expectations around the world, describing the strengths and weaknesses of each and the extent to which they are amenable to the type of research we are interested in. Finally, we consider the many potential benefits, but also the heavy costs, of developing and implementing new surveys.

Ideal Characteristics of a Survey

What would we ideally like to see in a survey of expectations? Given the discussion in chapter 1, clearly there is a need for *1) quantitative questions of expectations*. Without these, there is only limited scope for using the results for economic research. But observing a single quantitative expectation, however well measured, is generally insufficient for advancing our economic understanding. A good survey for research and policy purposes typically will *2) include space for many different questions*. Because respondents can have very different characteristics and their characteristics can shape their beliefs and decisions, a good survey should include 3) *a large representative sample drawn with high response rates*. To study expectations over time, or how different environments shape beliefs, we need a survey to be available 4) *at a high frequency over time*. Within those repetitions of the survey, it can be extremely useful to 5) *have some of the same respondents participating across different waves*. Because one ultimately wants to study expectations because they affect economic decisions, an important feature of a survey is 6) *the ability to link survey responses to external sources of information on decisions*. Finally, to create identifying variation in expectations, being able to 7) *run randomized information experiments* within the survey is essential. We discuss each of these in turn.

1. Quantitative questions

Chapter 1 has already covered, at length, the importance of measuring economic expectations in a quantitative way, as well as how best to do so. While traditional surveys of expectations often relied on purely qualitative questions, more modern surveys increasingly use quantitative expectations questions. These provide values that are easier to relate to economic models and that also speak more directly to the concerns of policymakers. They must be at the heart of any modern survey of economic expectations.

2. Space for many questions

In general, a survey that measures a single expectation or a very small set of expectations will be of limited use. Consider, for example, a survey that asked respondents only about inflation expectations. Repeated over time, this could be helpful to policymaking to track the evolution of those beliefs. It might also be useful to researchers in time series analysis, such as for estimating an expectations-augmented Phillips curve, for which a real-time measure of inflation expectations is necessary. One can also use a time series of a single expectation to study the nature of expectations formation, as we will discuss in Chapter 4. But being able to ask more questions in the survey opens the possibility of a much more systematic analysis of expectations and decisions.

There are several types of additional questions that can be of use. First, one may want to measure expectations of different variables to assess how jointly determined or correlated beliefs may be. For example, to understand how an individual interprets inflation, it is important to measure not only their inflation expectations but also how they think about unemployment or other variables measuring the real economy. Second, it is often helpful to ask for expectations of future decisions (e.g., future spending for households or future price changes for firms). These questions can provide an outlook for future macroeconomic dynamics (e.g., will consumer spending stay strong in the future?), but also give a benchmark for evaluating various policies and responses (e.g., do we see firms expecting to raise their prices more after an interest rate cut by the central bank?). Third, measuring some of the characteristics of the respondent (age, income, education, etc.) may be relevant to understanding their beliefs and decisions. Beliefs tend to be highly heterogeneous and it is important to understand the sources of this variation. Fourth, survey questions can help quantify past decisions (past spending, past price changes), which is essential when no external data on decisions is available. Fifth, qualitative questions can be added to help identify different possible mechanisms at work.

Another complement to quantitative questions of the type described in Chapter 1 is open-ended text-based questions. For example, sticking to the inflation expectation example, one could ask survey respondents a follow-up question, "You told us you expect inflation to be [X]% over the next year. Why do you think inflation will be this level?" Modern text-analysis methods can be used to characterize and summarize underlying narratives that people report in response to these open-ended questions, which can provide both a qualitative and quantitative complement to traditional survey questions. Andre et al. (2022b), for example, studied the narratives that households reported to explain the rise in inflation in 2021–2022 using such open-ended questions. They were able to show that the underlying narratives held by people shaped their quantitative expectations, thereby providing some of the first evidence on the potential importance of narratives in driving economic expectations. Haaland et al. (2024) provide an extensive discussion of how open-ended questions can be utilized to advance research.

There is, of course, always a trade-off between asking more questions and inducing survey fatigue. But it is better for the researcher to be the one to decide how to optimize questions subject to this trade-off rather than to face a hard constraint imposed by the survey provider on how many questions can be asked. The ability to ask many questions in a survey is therefore of paramount importance.

3. A large representative sample drawn with high response rates

Surveys are well known for the amount of disagreement in expectations responses they reveal and the noise associated with quantitative responses. This has several implications for designing a survey. First, large samples are crucial. It is very difficult to establish any result with small samples and noisy data. The presence of noise in surveys is unavoidable, so maximizing sample sizes is key to being able to identify underlying patterns through the noise. Large samples become even more important when information treatments are involved and samples have to be split into control and (potentially multiple) treatment groups. If ex post decisions are measured via the survey as well, there will be additional measurement error associated with these. Relating decisions to beliefs will therefore require even larger sample sizes.

The heterogeneity in beliefs and decisions at the individual level revealed in surveys also implies that it is important for a survey to be representative of the general population. Convenience samples or samples drawn with low response rates represent only a select subset of the population and in general should not be viewed as representative. Achieving high response rates is especially challenging for surveys of firms, but even with households, survey response rates have been falling over time and are becoming more of an issue (Brick and Williams 2013).

4. High-frequency observations

How frequently should a survey be repeated? For surveys that focus on the measurement of expectations, a high frequency of observations is a major attribute. Quarterly or even monthly observations allow users of the data to track how expectations change with economic conditions or policies and significantly increase the usefulness of a survey. A high frequency of observations is also useful for measuring outcomes. By tracking the days when respondents submit answers, surveys can even provide higher-frequency data than their official frequencies. For example, Lamla and Vinogradov (2019) and Binder, Campbell and Ryngaert (2024) used the specific days when households participating in the University of Michigan's Survey of Consumers and the New York Federal Reserve's Survey of Consumer Expectations respectively submitted their answers to study the high-frequency response of households to policy announcements. Lewis, Makridis and Mertens (2020) used daily data from the Gallup Poll to study the daily changes in household expectations around economic data releases.

5. A panel component

With repeated waves of a survey, one question that arises is whether new waves should consist of freshly drawn samples or whether the same participants should be surveyed again. For research purposes, it is generally helpful to observe the same respondents more than once. This is especially true when information treatments are applied, as described in Part 2 of the book. But even without information treatments, observing the same respondent repeatedly helps isolate differences in beliefs across individuals that reflect time-invariant characteristics of surveyed respondents. One caveat of relying on repeated panels is that the act of participating in the survey may change the beliefs of the respondents, thereby potentially making them unrepresentative thereafter. This possibility, commonly known as "panel conditioning," can occur if being presented with a question about a topic leads the respondent to learn about the topic or otherwise respond differently to the survey.[1] While generally thought to be of limited economic significance, there are occasions where panel conditioning can be meaningful. American households that are interviewed every month in the New York Fed's Survey of Consumer Expectations, for example, significantly change their beliefs about inflation after participating in their first survey wave or two, thereby making them less representative of the general population (Kim and Binder 2023). Similar results have been documented in the Euro area (Gautier and Montornes 2025). In contrast, repeat participants in the Michigan Survey of Consumers, because they are interviewed again only after six months, are much less affected by this learning mechanism. To minimize panel conditioning concerns while maintaining the advantages of having a panel dimension, repeated surveys should regularly introduce new respondents and potentially alternate waves in which respondents are asked to participate.

6. External information on decisions

Ultimately, the goal of this line of research is to relate how expectations translate into economic decisions. So, measuring those decisions is central to answering economic questions. Traditionally, aggregated survey expectations would be combined with aggregate data on outcomes (e.g., inflation, unemployment) to address this topic, but ideally one would like to be able to do this at the individual level as well. Hence, being able to match survey data on

1. One of the comments we received from somebody who completed our survey about monetary policy was revealing: "I just wanted to say that the study I just completed regarding inflation and the Fed really opened my eyes to how little I understand exactly what their purpose and methods are beyond 'economic growth/stable economy.' Thanks, I'll be reading up on that now." This of course would make this person more educated but likely less representative.

expectations to external data on decisions represents the ideal scenario. While this is often infeasible due to anonymity guarantees made to survey respondents, there are many settings where such mappings are possible, as we describe shortly. When there is no such possibility, questions about decisions can be asked in the survey itself, but these are generally subject to additional measurement error relative to external sources of information. This, combined with the fact that even more questions need to be asked in the survey to measure both decisions and expectations, generally makes this option the second best.

7. Ability to run experiments

Perhaps the most crucial element from an identification point of view, and at the heart of the methods that we emphasize in this book, is the ability to run experiments on survey participants. This requires being able to randomly assign participants to subgroups that will receive different information or questions. There are many existing surveys that do not allow for this possibility. The main reason is that if some respondents are provided with information during the survey, then they should no longer be viewed as representative of the general population if that information affects their expectations. When the survey's primary objective is the measurement of expectations in an economy, as is the case for many surveys run by government agencies and central banks, "treated" respondents (i.e., those who have been provided with additional information) are effectively contaminating the sample and should not be included in statistics that aim to measure the opinion of the general population. This can be addressed if the survey includes a large enough cross-section of respondents for the "control group" (i.e., the untreated respondents) to be representative. Despite its potential cost, the ability to run information experiments is crucial to creating the exogenous variation in beliefs that is needed to identify how expectations shape decisions and is therefore an imperative for this empirical strategy. Another possibility is to work with cohorts of survey participants who have left the survey ("retired") or are about to leave the survey ("outgoing").

Existing Surveys of Households' Economic Expectations

There now exist a large number of surveys of households' economic expectations around the world, far too many for us to cover in detail here (Dräger and Lamla (2024) as well as D'Acunto, Malmendier and Weber (2023) provide excellent descriptions of different household surveys). However, we will discuss some of the primary existing surveys that have been used for macroeconomic research. We focus on surveys in the U.S., which have received the most attention, but also cover some international surveys. Table 2.1 provides an overview of many household surveys that currently exist.

University of Michigan's Survey of Consumer (MSC): The MSC is one of the longest-running surveys of households in the world, with detailed micro-level data available since 1978. It consists of a monthly cross-section of 500 to 1,500 households, one-third of which are re-interviewed six months later. The survey is on the smaller end for a household survey and has a limited panel dimension. Many of the questions asked are qualitative in nature but the survey does include a point forecast for inflation, defined as "prices in general." The survey includes questions on a wide range of topics and can therefore be used to study different types of economic expectations. It also includes a broad set of demographic information about participants and is designed to be representative of the broader population. Because of anonymity requirements, it cannot be mapped to other sources of information about respondents, however, and information treatments are not allowed in the survey as of this time. Its rich dataset has been used to study a wide range of topics, for which Curtin (2019) provides an excellent overview.

Federal Reserve Bank of New York's Survey of Consumer Expectations (SCE): The SCE was designed with many of the perceived shortcomings of the MSC in mind. Started in 2013, this survey includes a larger cross-section of around 1,200 respondents per month, with households being asked to participate for 12 consecutive months. The survey includes distribution questions with fixed bins, in addition to asking for point forecasts. Like the MSC, it includes a broad set of demographic information about respondents and is designed to be nationally representative. Questions cover a wide range of topics, including aggregate expectations, housing, job search and individual decisions. It has been used to study the role of expectations in job search decisions (Faberman et al. 2022, Pilossoph and Ryngaert 2023, Mitra 2023), housing purchase decisions (Kuchler, Piazzesi and Stroebel 2022), and the effect of inflation expectations on consumption decisions (Crump et al. 2022), among many other topics. However, survey responses cannot be mapped to other data sources nor can information treatments be applied. Furthermore, to protect the confidentiality of responses, there is only limited geographic information made available in the public version of the data.

TABLE 2.1. Selected surveys of firms' and households' inflation expectations.

Country	Institution	Respondents	Price Definition	Sampling	Freq.	Start date	Bins	Horizon	Question
Canada	Conf. Board of Canada	Firms	Prices in general	Convenience	Quarterly	1997	9	6 months	Do you expect prices, in general, in Canada to increase over the next six months at an annual rate of . . . ?
Canada	Central Bank	Firms	Inflation (CPI)	Quota	Quarterly	1997	4	1 year	The firm's expectation for the average annual rate of inflation over the next two years as measured by the consumer price index (CPI) is: . . . .
Czech Republic	Central Bank	Firms	Inflation (CPI)	Representative	Quarterly	1999	open	1 and 3 years	What year-on-year consumer price change in percent do you expect in the next 12 months?
EU members	European Commission	Firms	Prices for consumers	Probabilistic sample	Monthly	1985	(up/down/same)	1 year	By what percentage would you say that prices will increase for the consumer in the next 12 months?
Euro area	Central Bank	Firms	Inflation	Probabilistic sample	Quarterly	2023	open	1, 3, and 5 years	What do you think the Euro area inflation rate will be at the following points in time?
Iran	Central Bank	Mnfg. Firms, ≥100 workers	Inflation	Probabilistic sample	Quarterly	2016	open	1 year	What do you think the [yearly] inflation will be during the next year?
Israel	Ungar and Zilberfarb (1993)	Firms	Inflation (CPI)	Representative	Quarterly	1980	open	1–4 quarters	The cumulative inflation rate (not monthly average), in %, which is expected for the following periods is as follows: The next 12 months: . . . .
Italy	Central Bank	Firms	Inflation	Probabilistic sample	Quarterly	1999	open	1 year	The last [month] consumer price inflation, measured by the 12-month change in the harmonized index of consumer prices, was equal to [IT] in Italy and to [EA] in the Euro area. What do you think it will be in Italy?
Japan	Central Bank	Firms	Prices in general (CPI)	Probabilistic sample	Quarterly	2014	10	1, 3, and 4 years	What are your institution's expectations of the annual % change in general prices (as measured by the CPI) for one year ahead, three years ahead, and five years ahead, respectively?

New Zealand	Central Bank	Firms and professionals	Inflation (CPI)	Convenience	Quarterly	1987	open	3 months and 1 year	What annual % change do you expect in the CPI for the: . . . ?
Poland	Central Bank	Firms	Prices	Sector representation	Quarterly	2008	5	1 year	In [month with the latest data available] of the current year, the CPI (inflation) was equal to x% in annual terms. In the enterprise's opinion, during the next 12 months, prices: . . . .
South Africa	Central Bank	Firms and consumers	Inflation (CPI)	Convenience	Quarterly	2000	open	1 year	What do you expect the average headline inflation rate (as measured by the % change in the CPI) to be during the year?
Sweden	Central Bank	Firms with ≥200 workers	Inflation (CPI)	Random	Quarterly	2000	open	1 year	n.a.
UK	Confed. of British Industry	Firms	Prices of competition	Convenience	Quarterly	2008	4	1 year	What has been the % change over the past 12 months in the general level of output prices in the UK markets that your firm competes in, and what is expected to occur over the next 12 months?
Ukraine	Central Bank	Firms	Inflation	Random	Quarterly	2006	8	1 year	How do you think the level of consumer prices will change in the next 12 months?
USA	Atlanta Fed	Firms	Individual unit costs	Nonrandom (regional)	Monthly	2011	5	1 year	Projecting ahead, to the best of your ability, please assign a percent likelihood to the following changes to unit costs over the next 12 months.
USA	Livingston, Philly Fed	Large firms	Inflation (CPI)	Convenience	Semi-annually	1946	open	1 year	n.a.
USA	Cleveland Fed	Firms	Inflation (CPI)	Representative	Quarterly	2018	open	1 and 5 years	What do you think will be the inflation rate (for the Consumer Price Index) over the next 12 months? **
Uruguay	Central Bank	Firms	Inflation (CPI)	Representative	Monthly	2009	open	1 year	What do you believe is going to be the change in the CPI?

(*continued on the next page*)

TABLE 2.1. (*continued*)

Country	Institution	Respondents	Price Definition	Sampling	Freq.	Start date	Bins	Horizon	Question
Turkey	Central Bank	Manufacturing firms	Inflation (PPI)	Sector representation	Monthly	1987	open	1 year	What is your expectation for inflation (producer prices) rate over the next 12 months (as an annual percentage)?
Argentina	UTDT	Households	Prices in general	-	Monthly	2006	open	1 year	Comparing prices now with those from a year ahead, around what percentage do you expect that, on average, prices will rise in the next 12 months?
Brazil	Instituto Brasileiro de Economia	Households	Rate of inflation	Convenience (7 cities surveyed)	Monthly	2005	open	1 year	In your opinion, how much will Brazilian Inflation be in the next 12 months?
Chile	University of Chile	Households	Inflation (CPI)	Convenience	Quarterly	2005	open	1 year	What do you think the inflation measure of the Consumer Price Index (CPI) will be in the next 12 months?
EU members	European Commission	Households	Prices in general	Probabilistic sample	Monthly	2020	open	1 year	How much higher (lower) do you think prices in general will be 12 months from now in the country you currently live in? Please give your best guess of the change in percentage terms. You can provide a number up to one decimal place.
Finland	Statistics Finland	Households	Prices in general	Representative	Monthly	1995	open	1 year	How much do you estimate prices will rise/fall in percentage in the next 12 months?
India	Central Bank	Households	Prices in general	Convenience	Bimonthly	2016	open	3 months and 1 year	NA
Japan	Central Bank	Households	Prices in general	Representative	Quarterly	1993	open	1 and 5 years	By what percent do you think prices will change one year from now?

Norway	Central Bank	Households	Inflation (CPI)	Representative	Quarterly	2002	3	1, 3, and 4 years	Do you think that over the next 12 months, prices for goods and services, as measured by the consumer price index, will be higher than or lower than they are currently or unchanged? About how much higher/lower, measured in percent?
Philippines	Central Bank	Households	Rate of inflation	Representative	Quarterly	2004	open	3 months and 1 year	What do you think the average inflation rate will be in the next 12 months?
Serbia	Central Bank	Households	Prices in general	Stratified	Monthly	2009	open	1 year	What is your expectation for consumer price growth in c+12, relative to c (c is current month)?
Sweden	NIER	Households	Prices in general	Representative	Monthly	1973	open	1 year	Compared with today, how much in percent do you think that prices will go up (i.e., what will be the rate of inflation 12 months from now)?
Ukraine	Central Bank/GfK	Households	Prices of consumer goods	Representative	Monthly	2014	8-12	1 year	In your opinion, how will prices for main consumer goods change over the next 12 months?
UK	Central Bank/IPSOS	Households	Prices in general	Representative	Monthly	1999	9	1 year	How much would you expect prices in the shops generally to change over the next 12 months?
USA	Federal Reserve Bank of New York	Households	Rate of inflation	Representative	Monthly	2013	6	1, 3, and 5 years	Now we would like you to think about the different things that may happen to inflation over the next 12 months. We realize that this question may take a little more effort. In your view, what would you say is the percent chance that, over the next 12 months. . . .?
USA	University of Michigan	Households	Prices in general	Representative	Monthly	1978	open	1 and 5 years	By about what percent do you expect prices to go up/down, on average, during the next 12 months?

Notes: Column "Representative sample" indicates whether respondents in a survey are representative of the group that is being surveyed. Column "Heterogeneous sample" indicates if a sample of firms covers various types (size, sector, etc.) of firms so that the resulting sample represents or resembles the population of firms in the economy. * last month annual inflation is given to 2/3 of the firms and firms are not allowed to report "extreme" values.

Federal Reserve Bank of Cleveland's Indirect Consumer Inflation Expectations (ICIE): The ICIE was started in 2021 by the Cleveland Fed with Morning Consult, an American business intelligence company. This survey asks respondents by how much their income would have to rise for them to be able to keep purchasing the same goods and services over time, thereby providing an "indirect" measure of inflation expectations. The survey includes around 20,000 representative households each week and is also applied across 14 countries each month. It is therefore significantly larger in size than the MSC or SCE but is much more narrow in scope, focusing primarily on inflation expectations. It includes demographic information on respondents and uses new cross-sections each week, so no panel component exists in the data. Like the MSC and the SCE, this survey cannot be mapped to external information on households, nor have information treatments been applied to it so far. The ICIE is described in detail in Hajdini et al. (2024).

Nielsen Surveys of Households (Nielsen): IHS Markit, commonly referred to as Nielsen, runs a panel of approximately 80,000 representative U.S. households that scan their individual grocery purchases each week (hence, it is often called the Nielsen Homescan Panel). Surveys of these households can be done by researchers and these survey responses can be mapped to the households' spending decisions, thereby providing a unique setting in which both expectations and spending decisions of households are jointly available. D'Acunto et al. (2021), for example, used this data combination to study how the shopping experiences of consumers shape their inflation expectations. Because survey response rates of Nielsen households are relatively high (generally around 25%), the resulting cross-sections are very large, usually 20,000–30,000 households. Importantly, Nielsen can accommodate information treatments in their surveys. In Coibion, Gorodnichenko and Weber (2022a), we used a combination of this unique household survey, an RCT and external data on spending to study in a causal framework how inflation expectations affect actual spending decisions, as described in more detail in Chapter 10. Surveys of Nielsen households can be run on a regular basis and, to the extent that some households choose to participate in multiple waves, include a panel component. The surveys can cover a wide range of quantitative questions and many different areas. To the best of our knowledge, this is the setting that comes closest to matching every one of the ideal survey features we describe. Researchers can apply to Nielsen to implement such a survey, with the main limitation being the large financial cost of doing so.

European Central Bank's Consumer Expectations Surveys (CES): The CES is a Euro area survey of households that has been running since 2020. It shares many features with the SCE, including the use of both point and distribution forecasts, a monthly frequency, a rotating representative panel in which respondents participate for up to a year, and a broad scope of questions that cover many areas. Unlike the SCE, it has grown to include 11 countries and has a monthly size of around 20,000 respondents. The implementation of the SCE is described in European Central Bank (2021) and Georgarakos and Kenny (2022). While the individual responses cannot be linked to external data, the CES differs from most official household surveys in that information experiments can be implemented. In Coibion et al. (2023), for example, we applied an experimental approach to the CES to assess how macroeconomic uncertainty affects household spending decisions; Ehrmann, Georgarakos and Kenny (2023) studied the response of Euro area households to information about the stabilizing role of monetary policy; and Christellis et al. (2022) estimated the causal effects of wealth shocks on the ownership of risky assets.

Other Household Surveys: In addition to these specific surveys of households, many countries typically host at least one official survey of household expectations. In general, these have structures that are close to the MSC or the SCE, depending upon when they were established, with newer surveys generally closely following the SCE structure and design. Like the MSC and the SCE, most of these household surveys cannot be mapped to external data sources and do not allow for information experiments. However, there are some exceptions worth highlighting.

The household surveys in the Netherlands and Germany are noteworthy in that, like the CES, they are open to information experiments. Chapter 15, for example, concentrates on an experiment done in the CentER Internet panel (sponsored by the Dutch National Bank and maintained by CentERdata at Tilburg University) that aimed to change people's perceptions of where they stood in the income distribution relative to their peers (van Rooij et al. 2024). The Bundesbank has been running a survey of households in Germany (Bundesbank Online Panel of Households) since 2019 that is actively engaged in research topics, including the use of information experiments. Unlike most other surveys, the Bundesbank actively solicits applications from outside researchers to implement new questions and apply the survey to specific research topics. This unique approach has led to a prolific use of the survey for research purposes. Two (of many) examples include Hoffmann et al. (2022), who studied whether households understand the difference between traditional inflation targeting and average inflation targeting, and Wehrhofer (2023), who assessed how energy prices shape household expectations. This is an excellent model for other surveys to follow.

Also worth noting is that the household surveys in the Netherlands and Denmark can be matched to administrative datasets on households. In the Netherlands, for example, Vellekoop and Wiederholt (2019) linked household survey responses with tax data on the wealth and income of the surveyed households to study how inflation expectations affect household savings decisions. In Denmark, Caplin et al. (2023) successfully matched the household survey to administrative data on earnings. This allowed them to compare the subjective earnings risk perceived by households to the actual earnings risk that they face. Another interesting case is Finland. D'Acunto et al. (2022) linked surveys of inflation expectations in Finland to military records that include IQ tests. Military records cover most men due to mandatory military service, and therefore allowed the authors to study how cognitive abilities affect beliefs and decisions. Over time, we anticipate that it will become increasingly feasible to match surveys of households to external sources of information on their actions and decisions, thereby significantly expanding the scope of research that can be implemented.

Existing Surveys of Firms' Economic Expectations

Surveying firms presents some special challenges. Top executives, especially at large firms, are difficult to reach and their time is protected by a legion of staff. Getting them to participate in surveys is therefore particularly challenging. As a result, most surveys of firms rely on the long-term development of a panel of willing participants who are asked a very narrow set of questions to minimize the time burden on respondents. Achieving all of the desired attributes of a survey in this context is therefore particularly challenging and most existing surveys focus on a subset of these desired qualities. Table 2.2 provides an overview of some of the most well-known existing surveys of firms, some of which we now describe in more detail.

Livingston Survey of Firms: This is the longest running survey of firms in the U.S. Participants provide forecasts for a wide range of macroeconomic variables on a semi-annual basis. The size of the survey is quite small, typically around 40–50, and consists of very large firms and banks as well as some academics and trade unions in the U.S. The survey results typically resemble those of professional forecasters. Responses are anonymized and cannot be matched with external data, nor can information experiments be run.

Ifo Business Survey (Ifo): The Ifo Institute in Germany has been running surveys of firms for more than 50 years and the resulting data constitute one of the richest firm survey datasets in the world. Firms are asked to provide forecasts about the aggregate economy and their own decisions, as well as information about their recent actions. The size of the survey is significant, typically 9,000 per month, and the survey is broadly representative of the industrial composition in Germany. Many of the questions are qualitative in nature rather than quantitative, a feature that is common to many other long-running surveys of firms. Responses are anonymized and cannot be matched to external data, nor can information treatments be applied to our knowledge, but additional questions are sometimes asked for research purposes (Demmelhuber, Sauer and Wohlrabe 2022). Bachmann et al. (2021), for example, used the survey to study how uncertainty affects firms' plans while Bachmann et al. (2020) showed how the Ifo survey could separate risk from uncertainty.

UK Decision Makers Panel (DMP): Like the Ifo survey, the UK Decision Maker Panel is a large representative survey of firms, but in the UK. The DMP covers approximately 10,000 firms per month and is representative of the UK economy. Started in August 2016, it is much more recent than the Ifo survey and also much more targeted. Its primary aim is to measure the economic uncertainty that firms perceive in terms of their *own* future sales, measured using the quantitative bin question designed by Altig et al. (2022). In addition, respondents are asked a small set of additional questions, but the survey is designed to be quick to answer to maximize participation by firms. It is discussed in detail in Bloom et al. (2017) and used to assess the effect of Brexit on the British economy in Bloom et al. (2019) and the effect of COVID-19 on productivity in Bloom et al. (2025).

Federal Reserve Bank of Cleveland's Survey of Firms' Inflation Expectations (SoFIE): Another recent and even more targeted survey of firms is SoFIE, run by the Federal Reserve Bank of Cleveland. This quarterly survey of 300–400 representative U.S. firms consists of just two questions added to a pre-existing privately run survey of firms. Firms in each survey are asked about their one-year-ahead inflation expectations, while the second question rotates

TABLE 2.2. Properties of selected surveys of firms' and households' inflation expectations.

Country	Institution	Respondents	Representative Sample	Heterogenous sample	Monthly or Quarterly Frequency	Large Sample Size (>350)	No Priming	Quantitative Question	Many/ wide bins	Distributional question	Agg. Inflation
Canada	Conference Board of Canada	Firms	✕	✓	✓	✓	✓	✕	✓	✕	✓
Canada	Central Bank	Firms	✕	✓	✓	✕	✕	✕	✕	✕	✓
Czech Republic	Central Bank	Firms	✓	✓	✓	✕	✓	✓	-	✕	✓
EU Members	European Commission	Firms	✓	✓	✓	✓	✓	✕	✕	✕	✓
Euro area	Central Bank	Firms	✓	✓	✓	✓	✓	✓	-	✕	✓
Iran	Central Bank	Firms	✓	✕	✓	✓	✓	✓	-	✕	✓
Israel	Ungar and Zilberfarb (1993)	Firms	✓	✕	✕	✕	✕	✓	-	✕	✓
Italy	Central Bank	Firms	✓	✕	✓	✓	✕	✓	-	✕	✓
Japan	Central Bank	Firms	✓	✓	✓	✓	✓	✕	✓	✕	✓
New Zealand	Central Bank	Firms	✕	✕	✓	✕	✓	✓	-	✕	✓
Poland	Central Bank	Firms	✕	✓	✓	✕	✕	✕	✕	✕	✓
South Africa	Central Bank	Firms	✕	✕	✓	✓	✓	✓	-	✕	✓
Sweden	Central Bank	Firms	✕	✕	✓	✕	✓	✓	-	✕	✓
UK	Confederation of British Industry	Firms	✕	✓	✓	✓	✓	✓	-	✕	✕
Ukraine	Central Bank	Firms	✓	✓	✓	✓	✓	✕	✓	✕	✓
USA	Atlanta Fed	Firms	✕	✕	✓	✕	✕	✕	✕	✕*	✕
USA	Livingston, Philadelphia Fed	Firms	✕	✕	✕	✕	✓	✓	-	✕	✓
USA	Cleveland Fed	Firms	✓	✓	✓	✓	✓	✕	✓	✓**	✓
Uruguay	Central Bank	Firms	✕	✕	✓	✕	✕	✕	✕	✕*	✕
Turkey	Central Bank	Firms	✓	✕	✓	✓	✓	✓	-	✕	✓

Argentina	UTDT	Households	-	-	✓	-	×	✓	×	×
Brazil	Instituto Brasileiro de Economia	Households	✓	×	✓	✓	×	✓	×	×
Chile	University of Chile	Households	✓	×	✓	✓	×	✓	✓	×
EU Members	European Commission	Households	✓	✓	✓	✓	✓	✓	×	×
Finland	Statistics Finland	Households	✓	×	✓	✓	✓	✓	×	×
India	Central Bank	Households	×	✓	✓	✓	-	✓	✓	×
Japan	Central bank	Households	✓	×	✓	✓	✓	✓	×	×
Norway	Central bank	Households	✓	✓	✓	✓	×	×	✓	×
Philippines	Central bank	Households	✓	✓	✓	✓	×	✓	×	×
Serbia	Central bank	Households	✓	✓	✓	✓	×	✓	×	×
Sweden	NIER	Households	✓	×	✓	✓	✓	✓	×	×
Ukraine	Central Bank/GfK	Households	✓	✓	✓	✓	✓	✓	✓	×
UK	Central Bank/IPSOS	Households	✓	✓	✓	✓	×	✓	✓	×
USA	Federal Reserve Bank of New York	Households	×	✓	✓	✓	✓	✓	✓	✓
USA	University of Michigan	Households	×	✓	✓	✓	✓	✓	×	×

Notes: Column "Representative sample" indicates whether respondents in a survey are representative of the group that is being surveyed. Column "Heterogeneous sample" indicates whether a sample of respondents covers various types so that the resulting sample represents or resembles the overall population in the economy. Column "Large sample size" indicates whether a survey has more than 350 respondents with non-missing responses. Column "No priming" indicates whether a survey does not provide information to participants before eliciting expectations, does not restrict the sample in any particular way (e.g., does not exclude respondents that do not understand the concept of inflation), and does not restrict possible responses (e.g., does not present respondents with a limited set of possible responses). Column "Quantitative question" indicates whether respondents are free to report an unrestricted inflation forecast (i.e., responses are not restricted to a binned/range/multiple-choice menu). Column "Many/wide bins" indicates whether a survey allows respondents to choose from a wide and detailed range of possible responses if quantitative response are not available. Column "Distributional question" indicates whether a survey elicits a probability distribution for future inflation. Column "Aggregate inflation" indicates whether a survey asks respondents to report an aggregate measure of inflation, changes in prices overall, etc. (rather than firm's unit costs or prices). * distributional questions are asked in ad hoc modules. ** distributional questions are asked occasionally at regular intervals.

each wave across four different formulations that measure long-run inflation expectations, perceptions of recent inflation, beliefs about the Fed's inflation target, and inflation uncertainty. This survey cannot be matched to external sources of information on firms, nor can information experiments be applied. The resulting inflation expectations were studied in detail in Candia, Coibion and Gorodnichenko (2024), and more information about the survey is in Garciga et al. (2023).

A similar approach is applied in the newly created survey of firms by the Bank of France, although that survey includes both inflation expectations and wage expectations, as described in Savignac et al. (2024). Furthermore, there is scope for matching survey responses of French firms to certain administrative databases.

Federal Reserve Bank of Atlanta's Business Inflation Expectations Survey (BIE): Another U.S. survey of firms is the BIE, run by the Federal Reserve Bank of Atlanta. This monthly survey of 300–400 firms in the district of the Federal Reserve Bank of Atlanta focuses on measuring firms' expectations about their future unit cost growth. Since theory predicts that firms' pricing decisions should be tied to their expected marginal costs, this survey provides significant predictive power for subsequent inflation developments (Meyer and Sheng 2024). The survey includes a number of other questions as well, although generally of a more qualitative nature, that speak to current economic developments. While this data cannot be matched to external data, information treatments can be applied on occasion, as described in Weber et al. (2025) and Meyer and Sheng (2024).

Other Surveys of Firms' Economic Expectations: There are now many surveys of firms around the world, some of which come even closer to meeting all of the desired characteristics than the ones described above. For example, the survey of firms run by the National Institute of Statistics (INE) on behalf of the Central Bank of Uruguay is a monthly representative survey of around 500 firms that includes questions on a number of quantitative expectations about inflation and other variables, as well as firm-specific forecasts (Frache and Lluberas 2019). The survey allows for information treatments, as explored in Weber et al. (2025). The Duke CFO Global Outlook Survey, run with the Atlanta and Richmond branches of the Federal Reserve, is a large quarterly survey of U.S. firms that measures a variety of macroeconomic expectations of participating firms that can be matched to external information on firms in Compustat, a database of financial, statistical, and market information on global companies (Gennaioli, Ma and Shleifer 2016). There is another excellent large representative survey of firms in Ukraine (see Coibion and Gorodnichenko (2015c) for more details on this survey) in which some external information on firms can be linked to the survey and there is scope for information treatments. However, it has not yet been fully utilized for research purposes since the barbaric Russian invasion of Ukraine. Columbia has a long-running large monthly survey of firms known as the Managerial Expectation Survey (or EOE for its name in Spanish), with approximately 500 firms per wave, that can be matched to trade data and in which information treatments can be applied, as done, for example, in Delgado et al. (2024). In the case of Turkey (Akarsu, Aktug and Torun 2024), a survey of firms can again include information treatments and be matched to external data. In Germany, the Bundesbank has been running a survey of firms since June 2020 that not only allows information treatments but can be used in conjunction with its household survey, as done, for example, in Wehrhofer (2023). The European Central Bank recently added an inflation expectations module to its Survey on the Access to Finance of Enterprises (Baumann et al. 2024).

The long-running Italian survey of firms (Survey on Inflation and Growth Expectations, SIGE) by the Bank of Italy has also been used to study firms' expectations and their decisions. The survey includes questions on some quantitative (e.g., for inflation, prices, and investment) and qualitative (for demand, economic growth, etc.) expectations. While information treatments cannot be added to the survey, it includes a repeated information experiment that has been ongoing since 2012, with one-third of the firms receiving no information and two-thirds of firms receiving information about recent inflation. The groups are reshuffled only infrequently, so that differences between control and treated firms accumulate over years. Furthermore, the survey can be linked to several administrative datasets, as shown in Coibion, Gorodnichenko and Ropele (2020) and Ropele, Gorodnichenko and Coibion (2022).

These surveys of firms are almost all run by central banks, statistical agencies, or other large organizations. This reflects the particular challenge of getting top executives of large firms to participate in surveys, a feat made easier when participation is mandated by law or requested by a major institution. Researchers can try to run their own surveys of firms, but this can be exceedingly costly and challenging. One solution that we proposed in McClure et al. (2025) is to use a large household survey to identify respondents with managerial responsibilities, then ask them the same set of questions that would have been asked in a survey of firms. This approach will likely miss top executives of large firms. However, when it comes to large firms, one may be interested in expectations at many different levels of the organization, since prices, wage and employment decisions are often made below the C-suite level. Identifying managers through surveys of households can therefore provide a complementary view to traditional firm surveys that target top managers.

Existing Surveys of Professional Forecasters and Financial Experts

The most commonly used forecasts in research are from neither households nor firms, but from professional forecasters. Surveys of professional economists exist for most countries, often for long time periods, different economic variables and different horizons. They are therefore a natural starting point for research on expectations and have formed the backbone of empirical work studying expectations formation for decades. To the extent that professional forecasters are some of the most informed agents in the economy, their use can help researchers identify a lower bound for how important deviations from full-information rational expectations may be. If professionals whose job it is to track the economy on a daily basis do not behave like *homo economicus*, then what hope is there for the rest of us? And as we discuss in the next couple of chapters, there is indeed quite a bit of evidence that even professional forecasters struggle to process information about the economy efficiently and in a timely manner. But because forecasts are so fundamental to their job and how they are evaluated, one should also worry that their incentives to provide truthful forecasts may be warped (e.g., Ehrbeck and Waldmann 1996, Lamont 2002, Ottaviani and Sorensen 2006), which calls into question how to interpret results based on these forecasts.

More fundamentally however, professional forecasters are simply less interesting for macroeconomists because their expectations do not directly map into economic choices. When households decide how much to save and consume, it is their own expectations that drive their behavior. When firms decide what price to set or how much to invest, it is their expectations that determine their decision. It is much less clear what economic outcomes are shaped by professional forecasters. It may be that the forecasts of professionals are reported in the media and gradually shape the expectations of firms and households, as modeled in Carroll (2003), but it is still the expectations of the latter that are the drivers of economic decisions. So while much of the literature on expectations formation has focused on professional forecasters (and we are as guilty of this as anyone else), this has been like the proverbial drunk looking for his keys under the light post, not because that's where he lost his keys but because that's where he can see. Fortunately, with the growing prevalence of expectations data on households and firms, our need to rely on surveys of professionals to proxy expectations of households and firms has declined over time.

Surveys of professional forecasters could also be important if they affect financial markets in a more direct manner. Indeed, many participants in surveys of forecasters are professional forecasters on staff at large financial institutions. But again, if our interest lies in identifying the expectations that directly affect decisions, one should be targeting the beliefs of traders, portfolio managers and others making decisions within those financial institutions, not the professional economists on staff who make their official forecasts. While the two may be linked, the former are likely to be much more important than the latter.

There are some surveys that explicitly target financial market professionals who are not economic forecasters. For example, MacroPolicy Perspectives runs the Shadow Survey of Market Participants (SSMP), a quarterly survey of various supply- and demand-side financial market professionals. This survey, with around 100 respondents per wave, is larger than typical surveys of professional forecasters (these usually include 20–40 forecasters) but is significantly smaller than surveys of households or firms given its targeted nature. This type of survey can include, on occasion, information treatments and can be potentially used for research purposes, although so far it has been underutilized.

Should You Run Your Own Survey?

Given all of the existing surveys of expectations, when should researchers run their own surveys? With the growing availability of online surveys, doing so has become increasingly feasible, especially to study households. These online surveys have a number of advantages. We can specify exactly the questions to use and the choice of respondents (e.g., representative sample or specific targeted subset), and information treatments are feasible. Online surveys also generally allow for the possibility of going back to the same respondents with a follow-up survey, albeit at a cost and subject to a limited response rate. They can also be used to pilot questions before they are implemented in larger-scale surveys. However, in general, these surveys cannot be matched with external information. Demographic information on respondents is very limited from survey providers, so some space in the survey has to be devoted to collecting the relevant information. And in our experience, online surveys yield much noisier responses than do official surveys, so researchers should plan to use larger sample sizes with online surveys.[2]

In some cases, it is possible to run surveys in new settings where external information on respondents is available. For example, D'Acunto et al. (2021) were the first macroeconomists to survey Nielsen Homescan participants, thereby linking expectations and detailed spending data. Giglio et al. (2021) surveyed retail investors from a large financial firm to whom they could match the underlying portfolios, thereby providing survey responses that were linked to detailed investment positions. This type of external information can prove invaluable in complementing survey responses. However, the representativeness of the resulting sample may be limited when respondents are drawn from clients or customers of a specific company.

With firms, it is much more difficult for researchers to run their own surveys. Because accessing top executives at large firms is so difficult, trying to start a new firm survey is likely to be very expensive and yield a very low response rate. In one attempt to create a survey of firms in the U.S., we achieved a spectacularly abysmal response rate of 0.1%. Two subsequent attempts fared no better. For those wishing to avoid such fiascos, one option to get around this is to try to use large surveys of households in which a subset of the respondents have managerial responsibilities, then target specific questions to those who indicate that they have sought-after professional characteristics, as discussed earlier. In general, though, the most realistic way to survey firms is to team up with an existing survey and add additional modules, questions or experiments to address the specific question at hand. Unfortunately, the ability to do so depends on whether the specific survey allows for such additions. With the notable exception of the Bundesbank, most surveys do not have a clear process for

2. A common problem in online surveys is "speeders," that is, respondents who click through the survey without giving much thought. One can occasionally force respondents to spend a minimum amount of time on a particular screen, but this cannot be a solution for all questions. To the extent speeders are computer bots, one can address this issue by using technologies like reCAPTCHA to identify and remove bots.

soliciting research project applications. Given the limited staffing and resources of most survey teams and the large pool of economists who lack access to the design of surveys, there is scope for much more collaboration to benefit both sides. Following the example of the Bundesbank and soliciting research proposals from outside academics would be one way for other surveys to expand their research contributions, even with fixed resources.

Summary

While conceptually straightforward, running surveys can be very challenging in practice, and there are countless ways in which a survey can go wrong, many of which we have experienced firsthand. Fortunately, in recent years, many new surveys of expectations have been developed around the world that provide a wealth of data on expectations of different kinds of economic agents. With online surveys, researchers also have the ability to run their own surveys independently of existing survey structures, which has allowed for a lot of experimenting in question design, topics and approaches by researchers. These surveys are at the heart of an increasing body of research shedding new light on how economic expectations are formed.

3

What Have We Learned from Existing Surveys of Expectations?

WITH ALL of these surveys out there now, what have we learned? The answer is, a lot! For now, we'll focus on five general stylized facts that emerge from the literature studying economic expectations. This is not meant to be an exhaustive list. As we'll see in subsequent chapters, there is much more that has been learned about expectations that we do not try to cover here. Instead, we focus on the "big picture," systematic patterns that consistently reveal themselves across surveys and time.

Fact 1: Disagreement about the future is pervasive and has many sources.

Ask five different people what country they think will win the next World Cup and you are likely to get five different answers. Economic forecasts are no different. One of the most immediately visible results from any survey of economic expectations is the extent to which respondents differ in their views about the future (Mankiw, Reis and Wolfers 2004). Consider, for example, a recent survey of households participating in the Nielsen Homescan panel run in December 2023. In Figure 3.1, we plot the distribution of responses for different economic expectations, specifically, inflation forecasts and unemployment forecasts one year out. In both cases, the amount of disagreement is striking. We can see some respondents predicting that inflation will be 0% while others are predicting that it will be over 10%. Unemployment forecasts are similar: some respondents expect unemployment of 3% while others expect an unemployment rate of over 10% in the next year. It might be tempting to dismiss this as reflecting the views of people who don't know anything about the economy and may not even understand percentages, but the truth

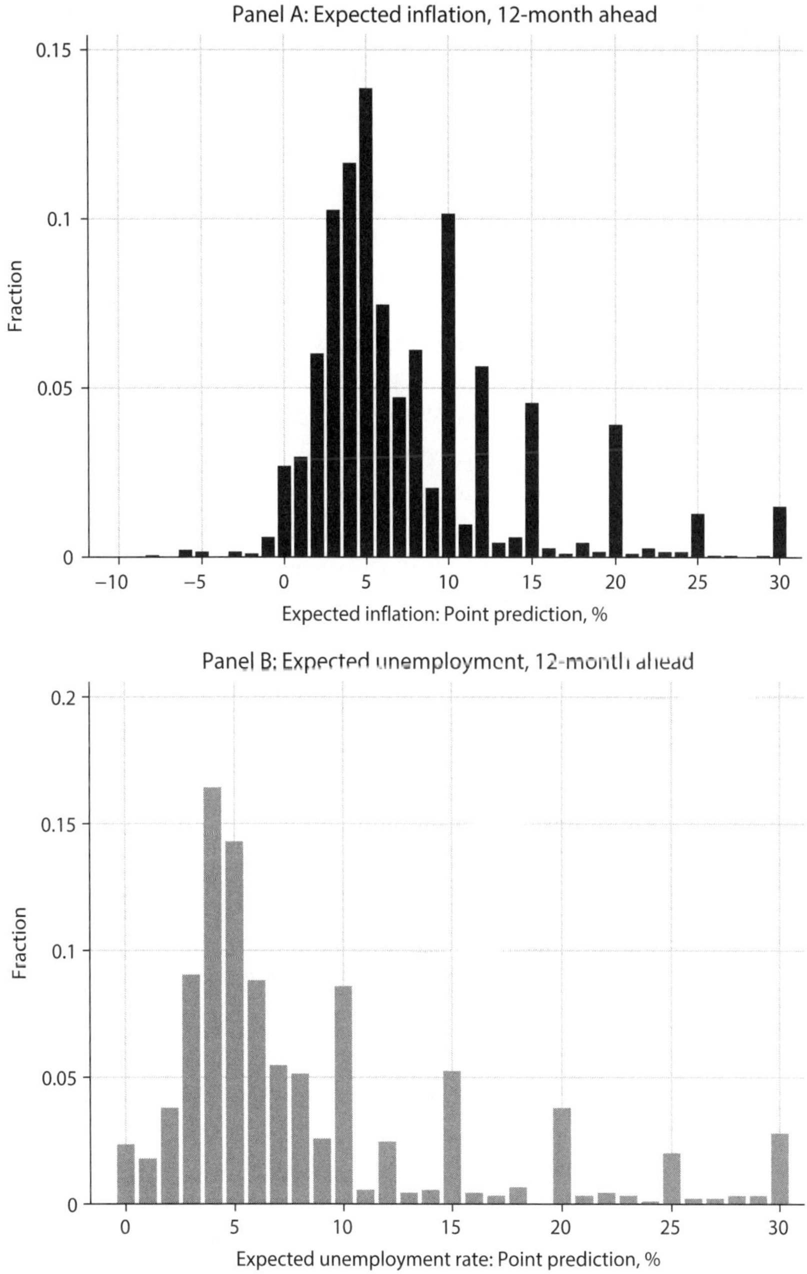

FIGURE 3.1. Distribution of one-year-ahead inflation and unemployment forecasts in the Nielsen Homescan Panel, 2023Q3.
Source: Own calculations.

is more complicated. Even amongst the highly educated and high-income respondents, disagreement is pervasive. This is not unique to households: firms' forecasts of economic conditions look broadly similar. For example, the Cleveland Fed's Survey of Firms' Inflation Expectations displayed a cross-sectional standard deviation of 1.8% in the second quarter of 2018, of the same order of magnitude as that for households. Finding similar amounts of disagreement about future economic conditions among firms and households is the norm rather than the exception: the same pattern holds for firms and households in New Zealand, for example (Coibion, Gorodnichenko and Kumar 2018).

Nor is this disagreement limited to forecasts of macroeconomic variables. When asked about future asset returns, such as for stocks and bonds, disagreement is also generally very high. In Weber et al. (2023), for example, we found that the cross-sectional standard deviation of expected returns for U.S. stocks among households was 8 to 9 percentage points, an enormous amount of disagreement. Those who owned stocks displayed only slightly less disagreement than individuals who did not own stocks. There was a similar amount of disagreement for other assets, such as bonds, gold, cryptocurrencies and even housing. Giglio et al. (2021), using a survey of investors from a large financial firm, documented the same kind of dispersion in expected returns on financial assets. Disagreement on electoral outcomes is just as pervasive as disagreement on financial returns (Coibion, Gorodnichenko and Weber 2020a). When U.S. households were asked immediately prior to the 2020 election to assign a probability of winning to a given candidate (Trump or Biden), cross-sectional standard deviations in reported probabilities were around 30 percentage points, with many respondents assigning 0% and 100% probabilities to either Trump or Biden winning, even though most polls were pointing toward a toss-up.

This disagreement is at odds with the benchmark assumption of full-information rational expectations (FIRE) commonly assumed in macroeconomic models. In a 2005 interview, Tom Sargent described FIRE as imposing a "communism" of models because "all agents inside the model, the econometrician and God share the same model." Allowing for disagreement requires relaxing the assumptions of FIRE. What can make individuals disagree so much about the future? One possibility is that people have different beliefs about the past, so they have different starting points from which to forecast. This notion is typically formalized by models of imperfect information (Mankiw and Reis 2002, Woodford 2001). A second possibility is that, even if they agree on recent outcomes, they may have different beliefs or interpretations about what is behind those outcomes, leading to different forecasts of the future. This interpretation is captured by models of learning (Evans and Honkapohja 2001). A third possibility is that they differ in where they think the economy will be in the long run, or they receive different news about possible future events, leading to different forecasts even if individuals agree about past and current conditions. As we will see, all three explanations contain an important element of truth when it comes to economic expectations, although the first explanation seems to be the most important quantitatively.

Sources of Disagreement about the Future: Beliefs about the Past

In 1981, Lars Jonung published a short paper in the *American Economic Review* titled "Perceived and Expected Rates of Inflation in Sweden." In it, he studied a survey of around 10,000 households in Sweden in 1977 that included questions not just about future inflation, as done in other surveys at the time, but also a question about perceived inflation—what households believed the inflation rate had been over the previous 12 months. He documented two striking facts. First, there was at least as much disagreement among households about recent inflation as there was about what inflation would be over the next 12 months, even though recent inflation rates were *publicly* available information. Second, he showed that the single strongest predictor of what someone expected inflation would be over the next year was what they thought inflation had been over the previous year. This paper therefore established a clear link between beliefs about the future (forecasts) and beliefs about the past (backcasts or nowcasts).

The predictive power of beliefs about the past in explaining beliefs about the future has since been extended to other countries, types of individuals, and types of forecasts. Similar evidence has been found for inflation forecasts of households in the U.S. (Axelrod, Lebow and Peneva 2018, Weber et al. 2022) and the Euro area (Andrade, Gautier and Mengus 2023, Huber, Minima and Schmidt 2023, Dräger 2015). Kuchler and Zafar (2019) documented a similar link for household beliefs about unemployment and housing prices. In a study of firms in New Zealand (Kumar et al. 2015), we found, as did Giglio et al. (2021) for individual beliefs about asset returns, that the result holds not just for firms' inflation forecasts, but also for their GDP, unemployment, and exchange rate forecasts.

Why would individuals hold different beliefs about the past? One potential explanation involves different experiences with inflation. For example, most individuals as well as top managers report that their primary source of information about aggregate inflation is their own shopping experience (D'Acunto et al. 2021, Kumar et al. 2015). Since we all purchase different goods and services from different stores on different days, the price changes we observe can vary significantly from one person to the next. Consistent with this, Kaplan and Schulhofer-Wohl (2017) used detailed data on prices paid by individual households to show that the rates of inflation experienced by different individuals vary widely. Building on this fact, D'Acunto et al. (2021) combined linked data on prices paid by consumers and their inflation expectations to show that those who faced more and larger price increases, especially on the goods they purchased frequently, tended to have higher inflation expectations than those who did not.

It is not just different experiences with very recent events that can matter: lifetime experiences can be important as well. Malmendier and Nagel (2011), for example, showed that living through the Great Depression profoundly shaped the beliefs and decisions of an entire generation. Lifetime experiences with inflation similarly affect beliefs about inflation (Malmendier and Nagel 2016). The German hyperinflation of the 1920s shaped not just one generation but subsequent ones as well, as parents transmitted knowledge to their children and local institutions were altered by the hyperinflation experience (Braggion et al. 2023). Despite this intergenerational transmission, because young people have a shorter life experience, they tend to adjust their expectations more to recent price changes than do older individuals. A related explanation involves selective recall or imperfect memory of lived experiences. Even for those of a similar age who have experienced the same events, their *recollections* of those events can differ significantly years later and what they do or do not remember can have profound effects on their expectations as well (Salle, Gorodnichenko and Coibion 2023).

Cognitive constraints and education play a role as well in affecting perceptions about inflation. The less educated may be less familiar with the concept of aggregate inflation and may deliberately report beliefs about the prices of their own consumption bundles, thinking the two are one and the same. Inflation perception errors are generally higher among those with lower education, those with lower incomes, or those who face financial constraints (Ehrmann, Pfajfar and Santoro 2017). D'Acunto et al. (2022) showed that individuals with lower IQs generally have larger errors with respect to recent inflation rates than do those with higher IQs.

Incentives are another factor that can matter for how informed people are about recent developments. For example, an individual is more likely to acquire information about inflation when they have to engage in a large financial transaction, such as buying a house. Homeowners spend more time researching financial markets and checking interest rates than do renters, and adjust their inflation expectations more rapidly to monetary policy changes (Ahn, Xie and Yang 2024). Firms that face more competitors or that expect to change their prices sooner tend to be more informed about recent inflation than do others (Coibion, Gorodnichenko and Kumar 2018, Afrouzi, Flynn and Yang 2024).

Sources of Disagreement about the Future: Narratives about the Present

Even if we all have the same information about recent conditions, we may still disagree about the underlying forces at work and what they mean for the future. For example, take the U.S. in 2024, with inflation falling after a sharp surge in 2021–23 and a strong job market. It would have been reasonable for an individual to believe that the U.S. economy had been hit with a bad supply shock that gradually dissipated, making the subsequent increases in interest rates by the Fed unnecessary and likely to lead to a downturn. Such an interpretation would likely lead to a pessimistic outlook for the economy. But one could alternatively believe that the surge in inflation was driven by high government spending and was only brought down *because* of the increase in interest rates, in which case this might call for a more optimistic outlook about the economy.

Different inferences about underlying dynamics are unavoidable in a world where, unlike in our typical models, we cannot observe the exact structure of the economy, nor observe shocks in real time, and we lack precision in our understanding of how policy responses affect outcomes. Andre et al. (2022b) tackled this topic by asking survey respondents to explain why they thought inflation surged in the post-COVID19 period. The authors then used text-processing methods to characterize the different types of narratives reported by households compared to those reported by experts. Both households and experts tended to report a wide range of different narratives, although experts were much more consistent in their explanations than were households. The researchers also found that these narratives systematically mattered for households' beliefs about the future path of inflation. Thus, different beliefs about the shocks driving current conditions can lead to very different predictions about the future.

A related explanation for differences in forecasts is heterogeneity in beliefs about the effects of different shocks: even if we agree on what shock has hit the economy, we may disagree about what *effect* this shock will have. Andre et al. (2022a) studied this possibility through survey questions that ask respondents what they think would happen under certain hypothetical scenarios. For example, they asked about the effects of an oil price shock on the economy to characterize how different individuals would view the same shock. They did this not just for oil prices but also for changes in monetary policy, taxes and government spending. Across vignettes, households displayed many differences in how they thought a shock would affect the economy, in terms of both inflation and unemployment, much more so than did experts. These differences were related in part to the experiences of the respondents, which shaped their views about which forces are important. Having worked for a military supplier in the past made someone more likely to think of mechanisms involving product demand and labor demand in the case of a government spending shock, for example.

Sources of Disagreement about the Future: News and Beliefs about the Long Run

Disagreement about future economic developments can also arise if we receive different news about future shocks or hold different views about long-run levels. What is news about future shocks? One possibility is forward guidance on the part of the central bank, which involves some communication about the future path of interest rates. If some individuals are more exposed to this news than others, then their inflation forecasts may differ (Andrade et al. 2019). Another possibility is news about future productivity, as studied in Barsky and Sims (2011, 2012). If announcements of a future technology are received by only some individuals, then their economic forecasts will likely differ from those who did not have access to this information. Alexopoulos (2011) provided evidence on the very gradual spread of knowledge about new technologies, consistent with this mechanism.

Alternatively, disagreement could be about long-run levels to which people expect variables to return after cycles or transitory forces dissipate. For inflation, this could be the inflation target for those who know there is one and trust the central bank. In advanced economies such as the U.S., knowledge about the inflation target is not widespread, with the majority of both households and firms being unable to correctly identify the 2% target. Similarly, individuals may naturally disagree about the natural rate of unemployment or the natural rate of interest, leading to disagreement about longer-run dynamics. Evidence of differences in beliefs about the long run among professional forecasters can be found in Patton and Timmermann (2010) and Andrade et al. (2016) and among firms in Candia, Coibion and Gorodnichenko (2022).

Fact 2: Forecast errors are predictable.

A basic tenet of FIRE—the standard assumption in macroeconomic models—is that all economic agents form beliefs using all of the available information in real time. As a result, it should not be possible to predict the forecasting errors that those individuals make ex post using information that was available to them when they made their forecast. If there is information that can help make better forecasts, it should have been used to make the forecasts in the first place.

One of the major results that has come out of existing surveys is that forecast errors are in fact predictable. This is true for the forecasts made by households, firms, professional forecasters and even central bankers. It is true for their forecasts of inflation and their forecasts of other variables as well.

Traditional tests of forecast error predictability consisted of regressing ex post forecast errors on a constant and variables that were available at the time that forecasts were made:

$$x_{t+j} - F_t x_{t+j} = \alpha + \beta \times z_t + error,$$

where x_{t+j} is the variable being forecasted, $F_t x_{t+j}$ is the forecast at time t of what x will be at $t+j$, and z_t is any variable that is available at the time the forecast is made. Under FIRE, one would expect that $\alpha = 0$, meaning that on average forecasts should not be systematically too high or too low, and also that $\beta = 0$ for any variable z, meaning that all available information was used to make the forecasts. Regressions of this type have yielded mixed results over time, often detecting some rejections of the FIRE hypothesis in shorter samples but less so over longer samples (Croushore 2011). Part of the challenge is that, in the absence of information about which variables to control for, it is difficult to draw much insight about any particular regression outcome in this context. A failure to reject the FIRE hypothesis could be consistent with FIRE being a good description of how expectations are formed, but it could also be consistent with FIRE being incorrect and the specific variable z being irrelevant for predicting x. A rejection of the FIRE hypothesis could be consistent with FIRE actually being untrue. Or, it could also be consistent with FIRE being true but sampling error leading to a false rejection. Thus, no matter what the outcome is of the regression, no one is likely to be convinced.

In Coibion and Gorodnichenko (2015a), we proposed a more specific test in the same spirit derived explicitly from models that deviate from full information. If individuals update their expectations infrequently or receive imprecise signals about the state of the economy, the average forecast error across agents should be predictable in a specific way:

$$x_{t+j} - F_t x_{t+j} = \alpha + \beta \times (F_t x_{t+j} - F_{t-1} x_{t+j}) + error,$$

namely, one should condition on the *forecast revision* about x. Intuitively, if we see people raise their forecasts on average, it would be because they received a noisy signal pointing toward higher values. But if those signals are imprecise, people would adjust their beliefs only partially upward, as we show more formally in Chapter 4, leading them to understate the ex post value of the variable on average. In other words, $\beta > 0$ when there is imperfect information or infrequent updating of information. We found that, for surveys in the U.S. and abroad, across forecasting horizons, across time and across variables, we could consistently reject the FIRE hypothesis of $\beta = 0$, and in a manner consistent with these alternative descriptions of how people form expectations. This result has been extended and built upon extensively since, and we discuss this literature in more detail in Chapter 4.

To better understand the predictability of forecast errors, it helps to think about the dynamics of beliefs conditional on a shock. Imagine that a shock to the economy were to permanently (for simplicity) raise inflation by 1 percentage point. Under FIRE, economic agents should immediately realize that a shock has occurred and understand its magnitude and implications for inflation. They would therefore immediately raise their forecasts of future inflation by the same 1 percentage point. The forecast error for all forecasts made after the shock happened would be zero. But now suppose instead that agents do not all immediately learn about the shock, or that they get some imprecise information about it. In that case, the average forecast will rise by less than 1 percentage point, since either some agents will not know about the shock and therefore not change their forecasts, or in the case of imprecise information, they will only raise their forecasts somewhat since they are not sure the shock has actually happened. After this shock, one would therefore expect to see inflation higher than what people were forecasting, but over time those forecasts would gradually converge up to actual inflation as all agents eventually learn about the shock.

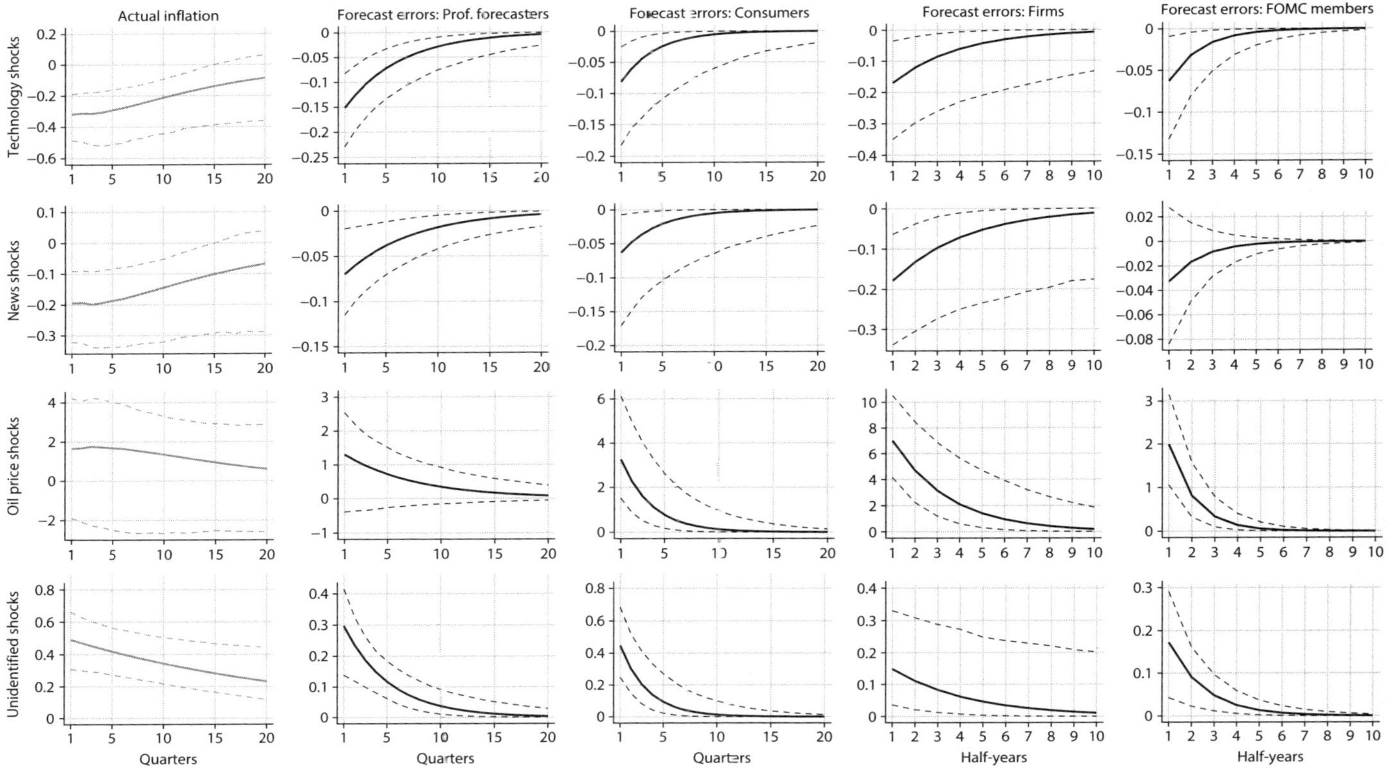

FIGURE 3.2. Impulse responses of actual and expected inflation to identified shocks by forecaster and shock type.
Notes: Solid lines are impulse responses. Dashed lines show 95% confidence bands.
Source: Coibion and Gorodnichenko (2012).

In Coibion and Gorodnichenko (2012), we tested this intuition using different kinds of "structural" shocks (technology, oil supply, and news shocks) for different types of forecasters (professionals, households, firms and central bankers). The main results of this exercise are plotted in Figure 3.2, which shows the impulse responses of inflation and forecast errors to each shock for each type of forecaster. Consider the technology shock first, which lowers inflation for some time before it returns to its original level (left column, first row). Forecast errors for firms, households and central bankers respond in the same manner: they are negative at first, then gradually converge to zero. The negative forecast errors indicate that forecasts do not fully decline along with inflation; in other words, they respond more gradually than they would under FIRE. This *underreaction* is symptomatic of survey forecasts and is exactly the pattern that one would expect if economic actors are not fully informed.

Fact 3: Uncertainty is often high and varies significantly over time.

Another characteristic of survey expectations is that they are often associated with high uncertainty. When making predictions about the future, households and managers are typically quite uncertain about the outlook. However, the amount of uncertainty they display varies both across individuals as well as over time.

The time variation in uncertainty was emphasized in Bloom (2009). In his seminal paper, Bloom showed that periods of high uncertainty in the U.S. commonly preceded or coincided with downturns, suggesting that high uncertainty could potentially be contributing to the downturns or even be their source. Early work following Bloom (2009) focused on financial measures of volatility and uncertainty, but spurred by this line of research, surveys have increasingly been used to measure economic uncertainty as well. The U.S. Survey of Business Uncertainty of the Federal Reserve Bank of Atlanta, running since 2014, for example, displayed a sharp increase in sales and employment uncertainty of U.S. firms during the COVID19 recession. The Decision Maker Panel in the U.K. similarly showed a sharp increase in uncertainty with the Brexit vote and its subsequent implementation.[1] This complements a wide range of evidence coming from other sources (Twitter/X sentiment, newspaper articles, etc.) that uncertainty is countercyclical.

1. Other non-survey measures of economic uncertainty also tend to rise sharply during downturns (Jurado, Ludvigson and Ng 2015, Bloom et al. 2018).

Across individuals and firms, there is also a lot of variation in perceived uncertainty. Low-income and less-educated U.S. households tend to report more uncertainty about their future income than do high-income or highly educated individuals (Ben-David et al. 2018). A more precarious financial situation, measured by the probability of defaulting on debt, is also associated with higher income uncertainty. With firms, Bloom et al. (2021) showed that better managed firms tend to make better forecasts and are more confident in their forecasts, displaying less uncertainty than less well managed firms. In Chapter 13, we return to how RCTs can be used to assess the extent to which this variation in uncertainty affects the economic decisions of both households and firms.

Fact 4: Economic expectations are (imperfectly) correlated.

To what extent can we treat different expectations interchangeably? If we know someone's inflation expectations, does that tell us everything we need to know about their other expectations? Are different expectations formed independently, so that each one needs to be measured separately? The answer is somewhere in between. The expectations that survey respondents report are generally correlated with one another, as one might expect, but not always very strongly and not always in the ways that one might expect.

Different Macroeconomic Expectations

It is common for surveys to ask respondents at least one question about inflation and at least one question about the broader macroeconomic outlook. These different questions can tell us something about the comovement, if any, that respondents perceive between inflation and the real economy. Figure 3.3 plots such a correlation for professional forecasters in the U.S. There is a clear positive correlation: forecasters who expect a higher rate of growth tend to expect higher inflation, as one might expect from movements along a Phillips curve if the economy is driven by demand-side shocks. Candia, Coibion and Gorodnichenko (2020) showed that this is true for professional forecasters in many advanced economies. Figure 3.3. also plots the same correlation for U.S. households. In this case, we see a striking *negative* correlation. Consumers who expect higher economic growth tend to expect lower inflation, whereas those who expect high inflation tend to expect low economic growth. Hence, at least unconditionally, households seem to hold a very different set of beliefs about the correlation of inflation with the real economy than do professionals. This "stagflationary" or supply-side view of inflation by households is well known

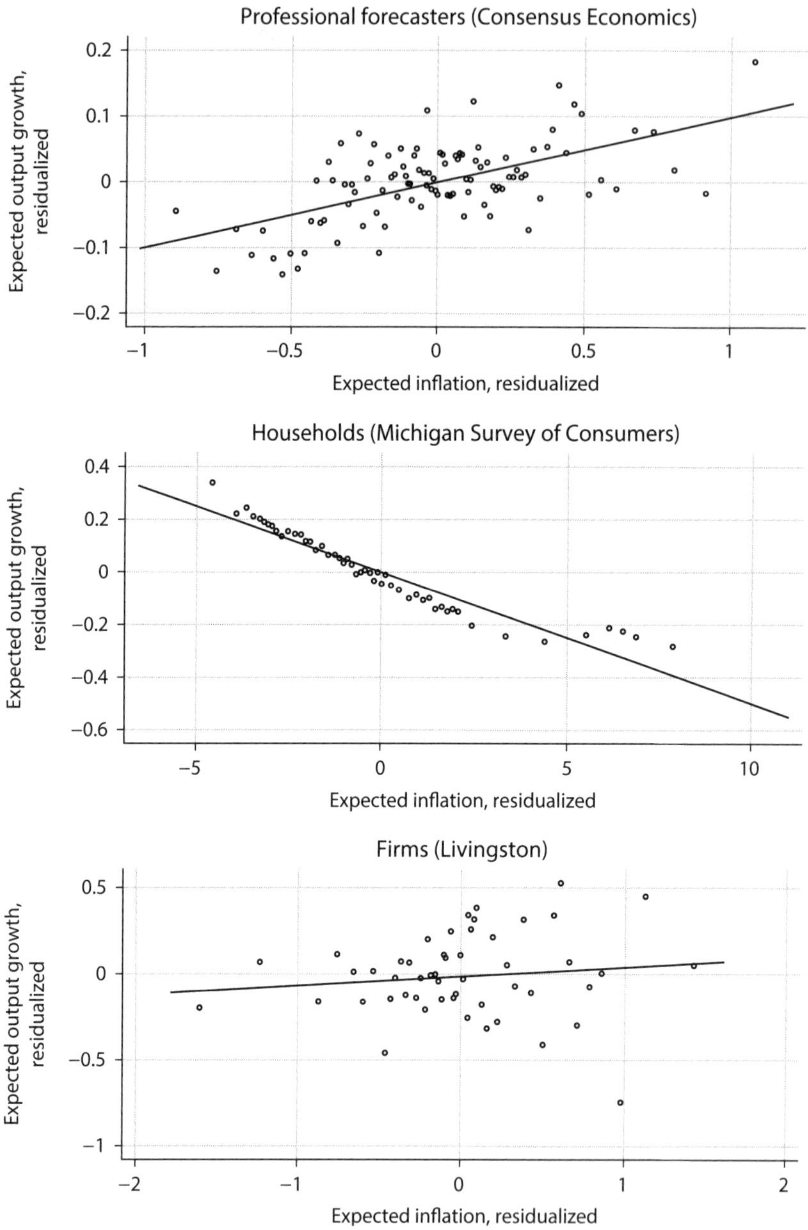

FIGURE 3.3. Joint distribution of one-year-ahead inflation and economic growth expectations.

Notes: The figure presents a binscatter plot and a linear fit.

Source: Candia, Coibion and Gorodnichenko (2020).

and is another striking feature of economic surveys (Kamdar 2019, Jain, Kostyshyna and Zhang 2024). It helps explain, for example, why a surge in inflation like that in 2021–23 could lead to a wave of pessimism about the economic outlook, even though standard labor market indicators pointed toward a strong recovery in the labor market during that same period. Firms in the U.S. seem to have a perception somewhere in between, as also shown in Figure 3.3. They display little clear correlation between economic growth forecasts and inflation forecasts.

Different Economic Actors

The difference in correlation of growth and inflation forecasts between firms and households is just one of many differences that arise when we compare economic expectations across different types of economic actors. Professional forecasters, financial market participants, households and firms often display different patterns in their economic expectations, and they should not be viewed as interchangeable. So it is important for surveys to target the relevant agents. Differences between households and professional forecasters can be dramatic at times. Firms tend to have views that are more informed than households, but closer to households than to professional forecasters. Financial market participants, while highly informed about economic developments, often hold economic views that deviate from the consensus opinion of professional forecasters. At times, surveys of one group can inform us about the expectations of others. For example, the Survey of Professional Forecasters includes independent professional forecasters but also economists working for large financial institutions, whose views may be closer to financial market participants'. Surveys of households include individuals with managerial responsibilities, whose expectations can be a proxy for those of firms (McClure et al. 2025). But as a general rule, researchers should be careful not to assume that surveys of one group will be representative of what all other economic actors expect.

Expectations and Uncertainty

How are reported forecasts and forecast uncertainty related, if at all? Consistent with the countercyclicality of uncertainty, it is not uncommon to observe that that when respondents expect bad economic conditions, their uncertainty tends to be higher. However, as shown in Figure 3.4, there is a V-shape to this relationship: those who expect very high economic growth also tend to have

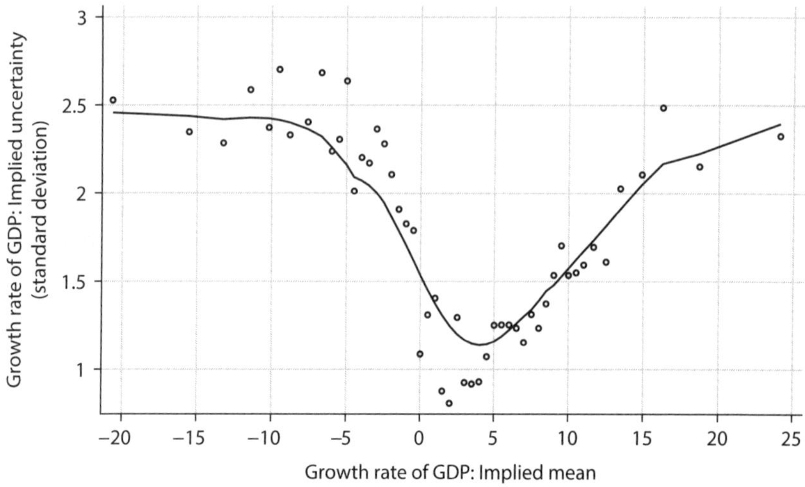

FIGURE 3.4. Joint distribution of macroeconomic expectations: 1st vs. 2nd moments.
Notes: The figure presents a binscatter plot and a nonparametric fit.
Source: Coibion et al. (2024).

more uncertainty. The V-shape in Figure 3.4 is for households in the Euro area but it seems to hold much more generally. Altig et al. (2022) documented a similar pattern for firms' uncertainty about their future sales: either very high or very low sales growth expectations were associated with more uncertainty, whereas those in the middle of the distribution displayed less uncertainty. The same V-shape pattern for sales growth expectations holds true with firms in New Zealand as well (Kumar, Gorodnichenko and Coibion 2023).

Higher-Order Expectations

Another type of expectation sometimes considered in surveys is a "higher-order" expectation, i.e., what the respondent thinks other respondents believe. In Coibion et al. (2021), for example, we asked firm managers in New Zealand to provide their higher-order expectations about inflation, i.e., what they thought other managers were predicting for inflation. These higher-order beliefs were strongly correlated with first-order beliefs, i.e., those respondents who expected higher inflation also tended to believe that other managers expected higher inflation. Consumers and firms in Germany also display the same pattern for higher-order inflation expectations (Kieren et al. 2025). Gorodnichenko and Yin (2024) document that retail investors have a high correlation between their first-order beliefs (that is, their own beliefs) and higher-order beliefs about future stock returns.

Micro and Macro Expectations

How strong is the link between what individuals expect for themselves and what they expect for the overall economy? Stronger than one might think. In general, both for households and firms, expectations about their own situation are positively correlated with what they expect for the overall economy. For example, firms expecting stronger growth in their own sales also tend to expect higher aggregate economic growth (Kumar, Gorodnichenko and Coibion 2023). Similarly for households: those expecting higher income growth for themselves generally expect a stronger economy and vice versa. The relationship is far from perfect, of course, and there can be many considerations that will weaken the connection between aggregate conditions and individual expectations, but overall, the link between the two is stronger than one might otherwise expect.

Fact 5: Inflation expectations are often "unanchored."

It is a tenet of modern central banking that one of its main objectives is to achieve and maintain "anchored" inflation expectations. The idea is that inflation expectations matter for price and wage decisions and if firms begin to expect inflation to be persistently high, then this will ultimately push inflation even higher. But what does it mean to have anchored expectations and are inflation expectations actually anchored? In Kumar et al. (2015), we proposed several different definitions of anchored expectations and we consider them here in turn.

Indicator 1: Forecasts Are Close to the Inflation Target

One way to assess if expectations are anchored is to check whether individuals' inflation forecasts are close to the inflation target of the central bank, especially for long-run forecasts. Even prior to the inflation surge of 2021–23, this was not the case in the U.S. and other advanced economies. Long-run inflation expectations of low- and mid-level managers in the U.S. were around 3.4% on average (McClure et al. 2025), well above 2.0%, and 3.7% for top executives surveyed in the Survey of Firms' Inflation Expectations (Candia, Coibion and Gorodnichenko 2024). For U.S. households, long-run inflation forecasts prior to the inflation surge were 3.0%, again well above the 2.0% target (Coibion, Gorodnichenko and Ulate 2019). The same was true for households in other advanced economies (Andrade, Gautier and Mengus 2023) and for firms (Kumar et al. 2015).

Indicator 2: Forecasts Are Not Too Dispersed

Even if the average long-run forecast were close to the inflation target, this could be because some people expect inflation to be well below the target while others expect it to be well above the target. This bimodal distribution would be hard to interpret as being consistent with anchored expectations. A second definition of anchored expectations is therefore that forecasts should be tightly distributed around the target. But as we have already discussed, disagreement about inflation is pervasive, both in the short run and the long run, so this definition of anchored expectations definitely does not apply to households or firms in advanced economies.

Indicator 3: Individuals Should Show Confidence in Their Inflation Forecasts

If survey respondents are extremely uncertain about their inflation forecast, one would again be hard-pressed to refer to these as "anchored," even if the average outcome they predicted were close to the target. As described earlier, uncertainty in forecasts tends to be high, and long-run inflation forecasts are no exception. Whether we look at households or firms, in the U.S. or other advanced economies, we consistently find high uncertainty in long-run inflation forecasts, again inconsistent with the notion of anchored inflation expectations.

Indicator 4: Individuals Make Small Forecast Revisions

If an expectation is "anchored," it should not be moving very much. Another simple definition of anchoring is therefore that forecast revisions, especially at longer horizons, are small. Given that many surveys of households and firms have a panel component, we can consider the magnitude of these forecast revisions over time. By any definition of "small," the average size of inflation forecast revisions for U.S. households and firms is *not* small. For example, for mid-level managers in the U.S., it is 3.6 percentage points over three months, which is quite large (McClure et al. 2025), and that magnitude is similar for U.S. households (Candia, Coibion and Gorodnichenko 2020). This is clearly at odds with inflation expectations being anchored.

Indicator 5: Little Comovement in Long- and Short-Run Expectations

A final metric for anchored expectations is whether changes in short-run inflation expectations translate into changes in longer-run inflation expectations. Intuitively, transitory shocks may move our beliefs about inflation over the next year, but if we believe the central bank will be successful in stabilizing inflation, our long-run forecasts should be largely unchanged. Again, the data are generally not supportive of this definition of anchored inflation expectations. Surveys of expectations generally display high correlations between changes in short-run and long-run inflation expectations. For example, the correlation between short-run and long-run inflation forecasts for U.S. CEOs is much higher than what would be expected given estimates of U.S. inflation persistence, a feature which is also true for households in the U.S. and other advanced economies (Candia, Coibion and Gorodnichenko 2024).

In short, regardless of what definition of anchoring we rely on, it is evident that the inflation expectations of households and firms in advanced economies are not consistent with the notion that they are fully anchored. While this may challenge a pillar of central bank wisdom, the lack of anchoring of expectations in advanced economies is likely a reflection of the success that central banks have had in these economies since the 1980s. With a long history of low and stable inflation, paying attention to inflation was not a primary consideration for households and firms for a long time, so it should not be surprising that their inflation expectations became more dispersed and detached over time. How the recent surge in inflation alters this situation and for how long remains to be seen.

Summary

These stylized facts are illustrative of what surveys can help achieve. The facts themselves may not seem surprising: people disagree, are uncertain, make predictable errors, form joint beliefs differently than do professionals, and do not have complete faith in central banks. Yet each fact is at odds with the simple macroeconomic models we typically work with. So, finding ways to systematically incorporate such features has been and remains an important line of research in macroeconomics.

4

Mapping Survey Expectations into Theory

HOW DO WE APPLY SURVEYS OF expectations or the resulting empirical stylized facts like the ones in Chapter 3 to macroeconomic models? In this chapter, we describe two specific applications of surveys that speak directly to theory. One is on the formation of expectations themselves. Any macroeconomic model must take a stand on how beliefs are formed, and surveys can provide important insights into this essential ingredient of our models. The second is on the use of expectations data from surveys to test structural relationships predicted by macroeconomic models. A famous example is the Phillips curve, which links nominal and real variables in typical business cycle models. Since Friedman (1968) and Phelps (1967), it has been well understood that the Phillips curve should incorporate expectations. We will focus on how the availability of expectations data from surveys helps identify and test the nature of the Phillips curve, as well as other structural relationships.

Surveys and the Expectations Formation Process

One of the stylized facts that emanates from surveys described in Chapter 3 is that forecast errors are predictable. We discussed in detail how forecasts tend to underreact to different structural shocks relative to what one would expect from the benchmark of full-information rational expectations (FIRE), where the agents understand the structure of the model (including the expectations process) and its governing parameters, as well as observe all shocks in real time. Indeed, the fact that people disagree about the future, the first stylized fact of expectations in Chapter 3, already rules out FIRE. But no one believes that FIRE is literally true, and the fact that a theory is not literally true is insufficient to reject it as a modeling framework. What we would like to know is whether deviations from the theory are *economically* important enough to warrant formalizing these departures and incorporating them into our workhorse models. In the case of expectations, we will show that the answer is a decisive yes. Deviations from FIRE are economically large and need to be incorporated into structural macroeconomic models.

In principle, there are many ways that one can deviate from FIRE. Some theories focus on departures from full information while others instead emphasize departures from rationality. In this chapter, we begin by considering models of imperfect information and show how these allow us to test and quantify departures from FIRE in a tractable way. But models of imperfect information with rationality also yield some testable predictions and, as we will see in this and subsequent chapters, some of these predictions are contradicted by the data, indicating that there may also be some deviations from rationality in practice.

Models of imperfect information

To quantify how important deviations from FIRE may be, it is necessary to start with models that allow for such departures. Here, we consider two simple and intuitive deviations from the full-information dimension of FIRE. One is the sticky information model pioneered by Mankiw and Reis (2002), which captures the notion that there are periods of time when we are not paying attention to economic conditions. In this setup, individuals in the economy sometimes hold full-information rational expectations about a macroeconomic variable x_t, and we denote such FIRE beliefs for individual i by $E_{it}x_{t+h}$, that is, expectations of person i at time t for variable x at some future time $t+h$. When an agent holds rational expectations in some period, they incorporate all of this information such that, ex post, any mistake in their forecast was unpredictable given time t information. Formally, $\varepsilon_{i,t+h|t} \equiv x_{t+h} - E_{it}x_{t+h}$, the forecast error for horizon h, is orthogonal to all information dated t and earlier, that is, $E[\varepsilon_{i,t+h|t}z_t] = 0$. In standard FIRE models, all agents have these expectations at all times.

The main assumption of the sticky information model is that individuals do not always update their beliefs. In periods without updating, they have no new information and so their beliefs are the same as in the previous period. When they update, they get FIRE. Denoting the forecast of individual i about variable x at some time $t+h$ as $F_{it}x_{t+h}$, this means that in periods when they update beliefs, their forecasts are $F_{it}x_{t+h} = E_{it}x_{t+h}$, the FIRE expectations from that period. But in periods when they do not update their beliefs, their forecasts are the FIRE expectations from the date of their *last* update. If this was k periods ago, then their forecasts are $F_{it}x_{t+h} = E_{i,t-k}x_{t+h}$.

Mankiw and Reis (2002) assumed that the updating of information happens according to a Poisson process, with probability $1 - \lambda$ of updating each period, so λ can be thought of as the degree of information rigidity. When it is equal to zero, everyone updates their beliefs every period and we are back in the FIRE environment. When $\lambda > 0$, then there is infrequent updating of information. In that case, the gradual response of forecasts to shocks that we described in Chapter 3, and which is shown in Coibion and Gorodnichenko (2012), will naturally follow, since, when a shock occurs, a fraction $1 - \lambda$ of people will adjust their beliefs to FIRE but a fraction λ will not change their beliefs at all, so the average belief will underreact. More formally, the *average* forecast across individuals at time t ($F_t x_{t+h}$) can be written as a weighted average of current and past FIRE expectations such that:

$$F_t x_{t+h} = (1-\lambda)\sum_{k=0}^{\infty} \lambda^k E_{t-k} x_{t+h} = (1-\lambda) E_t x_{t+h} + \lambda F_{t-1} x_{t+h}. \qquad (1)$$

The second equality implies that the average forecast at time t is a weighted average of the previous average forecast and the current FIRE belief. As long as there are information rigidities ($\lambda > 0$), average forecasts will under-respond to a structural shock. How much of an under-response there is depends on how large λ is. Reis (2006a, 2006b) studied the microfoundations of this approach and derived conditions under which this formulation can arise when households or firms face a fixed cost to acquiring new information each period.

A second model of imperfect information considers a different setting, where individuals update their beliefs every period but receive only limited information about the current state of the economy. This "noisy information" approach was famously applied to macroeconomics in the "island" model of Lucas (1972), but it has been studied in many other settings, including Kydland and Prescott (1982) and Woodford (2001). Heuristically, this model posits that economic agents extrapolate from their local conditions ("islands") and therefore local conditions shape expectations about aggregate variables, which is borne out in the data (e.g., D'Acunto et al. 2021, Andrade et al. 2022, Baumann et al. 2024, Coibion, Gorodnichenko and Weber 2025).

Formally, every individual receives a noisy signal about the economic variable x (for example, inflation) each period, denoted by s_{it} for individual i. This signal is equal to the true value x_t plus some noise (ε_{it}) such that $s_{it} = x_t + \varepsilon_{it}$. Because agents do not observe the exact value of x_t each period, they form a belief about it given by $F_{it}x_t$. Assuming they are Bayesians, this belief will be given by $F_{it}x_t = (1 - G) \times F_{i,t-1}x_t + G \times s_{it}$, where G is the Kalman gain (see Hamilton 1994). The gain parameter determines how much weight individuals place on the new information in forming their beliefs and is a function of how precise the signal is. As the variance of the noise in the signal goes to 0, the gain goes to 1. Assuming that x_t follows a simple autoregressive (AR) process $x_t = \rho x_{t-1} + v_t$, their beliefs about future values of x_t will be $F_{it}x_{t+h} = \rho^h F_{it}x_t$. The *average* forecast in this setting follows:

$$F_t x_{t+h} = G \times E_t x_{t+h} + (1 - G) \times F_{t-1} x_{t+h}. \qquad (2)$$

Note that this is the same dynamics for average beliefs as that in the sticky information model, except that the information rigidity is now characterized by $1 - G$. As with sticky information, a noisy information model can also replicate the underreaction of average forecasts to a structural shock documented in Coibion and Gorodnichenko (2012), because only partial weight is attached to the FIRE expectation. In this case, agents update their expectations all the time but do so slowly because they know that the signal s_{it} may be changing due to noise ε_{it} rather than a true innovation v_t.

Coibion and Gorodnichenko (2015a)

With both models predicting the same dynamics for the evolution of average forecasts, it follows that their predictions about the predictability of forecast errors will also be the same. In a 2015 paper, we showed that this predictability can be expressed in the following form:

$$x_{t+h} - F_t x_{t+h} = \alpha + \beta \times (F_t x_{t+h} - F_{t-1} x_{t+h}) + error, \qquad (3),$$

where α should be zero and *error* is the FIRE error from t to $t+h$, meaning that it is uncorrelated with all variables dated t and earlier. Under sticky information, $\beta = \lambda/(1 - \lambda)$, which is positive whenever $\lambda > 0$, whereas under noisy information, $\beta = (1 - G)/G$, which is positive whenever $1 - G > 0$. Hence, in both models, the prediction is that when forecasters revise their predictions for a variable upward between two periods, the subsequent forecast error should be positive on average, i.e., the average forecast is not moving up enough relative to FIRE.

This prediction can be tested empirically with survey forecasts, as long as those forecasts include revisions of a variable at a common horizon. It represents a very simple test of FIRE that has several advantages relative to traditional tests used in the literature. First, the relevant regressor, namely forecast revisions, is specified by the theory. Thus, we avoid data mining. Second, this specification nests not just FIRE but also alternative models of the expectations formation process. Third, estimates of β speak not just to whether we can reject FIRE statistically but also, because β maps into the degree of information rigidity, to whether those rejections should be thought of as economically significant.

Applying this to inflation forecasts from professional forecasters, firms and households, we found that estimates of β are generally close to 1 and statistically different from 0. Hence, we can strongly reject the null hypothesis of FIRE. Even more importantly, we can infer the implied degree of information rigidity. In the context of sticky information, our estimates imply that $\lambda \approx 1/2$, meaning that individuals update their beliefs every six months on average. Put into a sticky information model like Mankiw and Reis (2002), this magnitude of information rigidity predicts important macroeconomic differences relative to FIRE. The rejection of FIRE is therefore not just statistically significant but also economically significant. The same holds true in the case of the noisy information model.

Because this empirical specification is so simple and can be applied in different ways, we were able to explore a number of additional characteristics of information rigidities. First, using cross-country surveys of expectations, we showed that information rigidities are pervasive across countries. Second, using forecasts of different variables and horizons, we could explore the time variation in information rigidities. We found that during the Great Moderation period in the U.S. when macroeconomic volatility was relatively low, information rigidities increased as the volatility of the economy declined. This is what one expects from models of information rigidities: as volatility declines, the benefit to paying attention is lower, so the optimal degree of inattention should rise. We observe something similar over the course of business cycles. During recessions, individuals are more attentive to economic conditions than they are during recoveries. This fact points to state dependence in the expectations formation process, a feature at odds with the simplest versions of sticky and noisy information models but one that was explored in Gorodnichenko (2008).

Loungani, Stekler and Tamirisa (2013)

In a follow-up paper, Loungani, Stekler and Tamirisa estimated the same empirical specification as Coibion and Gorodnichenko (2015a) on a much broader panel of countries, but they also considered a related empirical specification based on Nordhaus (1987). Consider the sticky information model, for example, in which average forecasts evolve according to:

$$F_t x_{t+h} = (1-\lambda)\times E_t x_{t+h} + \lambda \times F_{t-1} x_{t+h}. \tag{4}$$

Taking the time difference, one can show that this yields

$$F_{t+1} x_{t+h} - F_t x_{t+h} = \lambda \times [F_t x_{t+h} - F_{t-1} x_{t+h}] + (1-\lambda)\times [E_{t+1} x_{t+h} - E_t x_{t+h}]. \tag{5}$$

The last term, $[E_{t+1} x_{t+h} - E_t x_{t+h}]$, is the revision in FIRE beliefs between t and $t+1$ that must be orthogonal to all information dated t and earlier. The other two terms are revisions in forecasts. Thus, one can estimate λ directly by regressing the average forecast revision from t to $t+1$ on the average forecast revision from time $t-1$ to t. The advantage of this specification relative to the one in Coibion and Gorodnichenko (2015a) is that it does not require data on ex post outcomes of x_t and can be applied using only survey data on expectations. This can be an advantage when there are many data releases for a given variable x_t and it may not be clear which is the relevant one to use to construct forecast errors. The disadvantage of this specification is that it requires three different forecasts of x_t over time for the same horizon, which is generally available only in surveys of professional forecasters. Applying both approaches to surveys of professional forecasters for 46 countries, Loungani, Stekler and Tamarisa (2013) found economically significant degrees of information rigidity across countries. They also confirmed that information rigidities are reduced during recessions relative to other periods, consistent with some state dependence in the expectations formation process. Additional evidence of state dependence was presented in Baker, McElroy and Sheng (2020), who showed that the degree of information rigidity declines sharply after unexpected natural disaster shocks.

Goldstein (2023)

Another closely related approach in the same spirit is developed in Goldstein (2023). Instead of focusing on average forecast revisions, Goldstein's approach focuses on individual deviations from the consensus forecast. Specifically, he proposed to estimate:

$$F_{it}x_{t+h} - F_t x_{t+h} = \alpha + \beta \times [F_{i,t-1}x_{t+h} - F_{t-1}x_{t+h}] + error. \tag{6}$$

Goldstein showed that under sticky information, $\beta = \lambda$, whereas under noisy information, $\beta = 1 - G$. Hence, this approach can also in principle directly recover the underlying degree of information rigidity. He emphasized that his approach has several advantages relative to that of Coibion and Gorodnichenko (2015a). First, his regression utilizes individual-level forecasts, not just consensus forecasts. The number of observations is therefore much larger, which can lead to more precise estimates of β. Second, like the specification proposed in Loungani, Stekler and Tamirisa (2013), this approach only relies on forecast data and does not require taking a stand on vintages to use for ex post outcomes. Third, and perhaps most importantly, this approach is immune to the inclusion of public information in the noisy information model. If agents receive not just private signals but also common signals, then one can show that the β estimated in Coibion and Gorodnichenko (2015a) will be biased downward: the true degree of information rigidity will be even higher than what is estimated. The approach in Goldstein (2023), because it focuses on deviations of individual forecasts from the mean, nets out common information and is therefore immune to this concern. Consistent with this intuition, Goldstein's estimates of information rigidity from his specification were generally higher than those implied only by mean forecasts. Thus, these results further support the potential importance of information rigidities in the expectations formation process.

Bordalo, Gennaioli, Ma and Shleifer (2020)

In focusing on individual expectations, Goldstein (2023) is one of many recent studies that have moved beyond predictions for mean forecasts and toward predictions that are expected to hold at the *individual* level. Perhaps the most well known in this spirit is an influential paper by Bordalo et al. (2020), in which they run the same regression as in Coibion and Gorodnichenko (2015a) but at the individual level:

$$x_{t+h} - F_{it}x_{t+h} = \alpha + \beta \times [F_{it}x_{t+h} - F_{i,t-1}x_{t+h}] + error. \tag{7}$$

Coibion and Gorodnichenko (2015a) had emphasized that their predictions should *not* be expected to hold at the individual level but only on average across forecasters. Why? Consider an individual in the noisy information model who receives a positive signal. They know this positive signal can reflect two possibilities. One is that the fundamental x has gone up, in which case they should raise their forecasts of future values of x. The second is that it is only noise in the signal and nothing has happened to x, in which case they should not raise their forecasts of future values of x. In choosing the optimal Kalman gain, individuals are balancing these two forces and raise their forecasts only somewhat, such that, on average, they are not making a predictable error. In other words, under noisy information, $\beta = 0$ when the regression is applied at the individual level. It is only across all individuals, where the individual noise washes out, that predictability should occur. But what Bordalo et al. (2020) show is that, for many variables, the estimated coefficient on individual forecast revisions is actually *negative*. On average, when forecasters raise their forecasts, the actual outcome ends up being lower than their forecast, a feature which they refer to as overreaction.

To explain this outcome, Bordalo et al. (2020) proposed a model of diagnostic expectations, building on earlier work by Gennaioli and Shleifer (2010) and Bordalo et al. (2016). In this context, individuals tend to put more weight on new information than they should, a deviation from rational expectations. Specifically, their belief about x can be written as:

$$F_{it}x_t = G \times \theta \times s_{it} + (1 - G \times \theta) \times F_{i,t-1}x_t, \tag{8}$$

where θ denotes the additional weight assigned to new information relative to what is optimal, as given by the Kalman gain. In this setup, the consensus-forecast regression of Coibion and Gorodnichenko (2015a) will estimate the combination $G \times \theta$ rather than just G, and the individual regressions of Bordalo et al. (2020) should identify a negative coefficient if $\theta > 0$. Intuitively, if individuals place more weight on new signals than what is implied by the Kalman gain, they will tend to raise their forecasts by more than they should when receiving a positive signal, and this will lead to negative predictability in the forecast error.

So, are individuals over- or underreacting to news? At the macro level, the key property is how forecasts respond to structural or fundamental shocks. This depends on the coefficient identified in consensus regressions of Coibion and Gorodnichenko (2015a) and replicated in Bordalo et al. (2020). In both cases, average forecasts are underreacting to fundamentals on average relative to FIRE, consistent with the impulse responses to specific structural shocks in Coibion and Gorodnichenko (2012). However, the results of Bordalo et al. (2020) suggest that imperfect information models are not sufficient to explain deviations from FIRE: departures from rationality are also needed. The "overreaction" that comes from diagnostic expectations means that there is less underreaction to fundamentals than would be the case from just imperfect information, as agents overrespond to news, but underreaction is still the key macroeconomic implication, as emphasized in Angeletos and Huo (2021).

Other interpretations have also been proposed for why the individual-level regressions of Bordalo et al. (2020) may yield $\beta < 0$ even if there is no overreaction. For example, if there is measurement error in expectations data, then these regressions will have a downward bias in their estimates of β, as emphasized in Juodis and Kucinskas (2023), leading to the appearance of overreaction even when there is none. Another interpretation is provided in Sung (2022). She introduced imperfect recall into a noisy information model. If individuals have noise in their memories, the consensus-forecast regressions of Coibion and Gorodnichenko (2015a) will underestimate the true degree of information rigidity in expectations and the individual-level regressions of Bordalo et al. (2020) will display negative estimates of β even though there is no overreaction to news. In a similar spirit, Ryngaert (2022) argues that one may need both information frictions and extrapolation to explain the data more fully.

Kohlhas and Walther (2021)

Another form of overreaction is explored in Kohlhas and Walther (2021). In addition to regressions of forecast errors on forecast revisions, they estimated specifications like

$$x_{t+h} - F_t x_{t+h} = \alpha + \beta \times x_t + error \tag{9}$$

at both the individual and the consensus levels. These specifications consistently led to negative estimates of β, so that when, for example, output rises, individuals tend to overpredict how high it will be in the future, which Kohlhas and Walther (2021) referred to as extrapolation. These two empirical findings—underreaction in Coibion and Gorodnichenko (2015a) regressions but extrapolation in Kohlhas and Walther (2021) regressions—cannot be simultaneously explained by simple imperfect information models or traditional models of extrapolation bias. Instead, Kohlhas and Walther (2021) proposed a new model of noisy information in which individuals have to choose which structural components they pay more attention to. Because information is noisy, their model displays underreaction in consensus regressions of forecast revisions. And if individuals choose to pay more attention to procyclical variables, then they become overoptimistic in booms (and vice versa in busts), which can explain the extrapolation results in their empirical analysis. Hence, Kohlhas and Walther (2021) could explain both sets of findings within a rational expectations framework through the endogenous allocation of attention to different imperfectly observed structural components, as in Sims (2003) and Mackowiak and Wiederholt (2009).

Building on this approach, Broer and Kohlhas (2024) estimated a similar specification, but one including a wide range of variables:

$$x_{t+h} - F_{it}x_{t+h} = \alpha + \beta \times \mathbf{Z}_t + error, \tag{10}$$

where **Z** denotes other macroeconomic variables or sources of information than just x. When they did so, they found that, above and beyond the overreaction to recent values of x documented in Kohlhas and Walthers (2021), individuals tend to both overreact to certain public pieces of information while simultaneously underreacting to others. Hence, a successful theory of expectations should be able to explain why individuals underreact to some pieces of public information while overreacting to others. Broer and Kohlhas (2024) proposed such a model by extending noisy information to allow individuals to be overly confident in the precision of their information, both relative to the truth and relative to the perception of others. The former generates the overreaction to news about the variable being forecasted (x), while the latter helps explain why different signals can lead to different patterns of over- and underreaction. This is because other signals reflect the decisions of others in the economy and therefore also their beliefs. Relative overconfidence induces individuals to view public signals as less precise and less responsive to new information, which can allow for underreaction to some of these signals. Again, departures from both rationality and full information appear necessary to explain the behavior of survey expectations.

Summary

The growing availability of survey data on expectations has led to an explosion of research into the nature of the expectations formation process. One clear result stands out: the predictability in forecast errors indicates a systematic and economically significant rejection of the FIRE assumption. How to interpret and model that rejection is a central area of ongoing research. Models of imperfect information and rational expectations can go a long way in explaining the behavior of average forecasts, but individual-level evidence is increasingly suggesting that deviations from rationality may also be needed. Whether this needs to be in the form of overextrapolation as in Angeletos, Huo and Sastry (2020), diagnostic expectations as in Bordalo et al. (2020), cognitive discounting as in Gabaix (2020) or other cognitive constraints remains to be determined. One potentially fruitful way of further distinguishing between models of expectations is to make more use of the systematic patterns of disagreement emphasized in Chapter 3 and in Mankiw, Reis and Wolfers (2004). Another is to focus on higher-order beliefs. By increasing the available facts about expectations, it will become easier to disentangle different models that can make similar predictions about first moments. Another avenue is to focus on experiments that provide information to survey respondents, which can yield clearer evidence on how beliefs respond to new information, which we delve into in the next part of the book.

Surveys and Structural Macroeconomic Relationships

Beyond providing direct evidence on how individuals form beliefs, surveys of expectations can also be invaluable in helping us understand the role of expectations in shaping macroeconomic outcomes. In later parts of the book, we will focus on causally identifying how expectations *affect* individual decisions. But even without making statements about causality, the existence of survey measures of expectations can already be of use in characterizing how macroeconomic outcomes are determined. In this section, we will focus on the

Phillips curve, the relationship between inflation and production/employment in the economy, but since expectations appear in most structural macroeconomic relationships, the idea applies much more broadly.

Expectations and the Phillips curve

In 1958, A.W. Phillips found that over decades in the U.K., wage inflation and unemployment were strongly negatively correlated. This correlation between price measures in the economy and indicators of economic activity like output or unemployment became known as the Phillips curve. While early Keynesian models treated this as a stable trade-off between unemployment and inflation that policymakers could choose between, the stagflationary experience of the 1970s and early 1980s made this view untenable. As shown in Figure 4.1 for the U.S., since the 1950s, the Phillips curve can be better characterized as a cloud, given the absence of any clear relationship between inflation and unemployment that can be seen there. Since the Phillips curve is at the heart of many business cycle models, the absence of any clear relationship in the data is the source of much derision toward macroeconomists by noneconomists and even some macroeconomists. The diagnosis for the Phillips curve has ranged from alive and well (Bob Gordon) to hibernating (Jerome Powell) to dead (Bob Hall) or murdered (Jim Bullard).

In contrast, we view macroeconomists' understanding of what underlies the Phillips cloud as one of the major achievements of modern macroeconomics, with survey measures of expectations being an important ingredient. At the heart of this are Friedman (1968) and Phelps (1967), who concurrently predicted that if policymakers tried to exploit the Phillips curve— as they did over the course of the 1960s—the correlation between inflation and unemployment would disappear, a prediction clearly borne out in Figure 4.1. Their intuition was that if policymakers pursued sustained expansionary policies that reduced inflation and lowered unemployment (a movement along the Phillips curve), workers would start expecting rising inflation in the future and demand higher wages as a result (the Friedman channel) to bring their real wages back up. Firms setting prices for extended durations would increasingly anticipate that any fixed price would depreciate more rapidly and so would raise prices by more (the Phelps channel). Both mechanisms imply that as the inflation expectations of workers and firms increase, *the Phillips curve shifts*. In the long run, unemployment will be unchanged and inflation will be

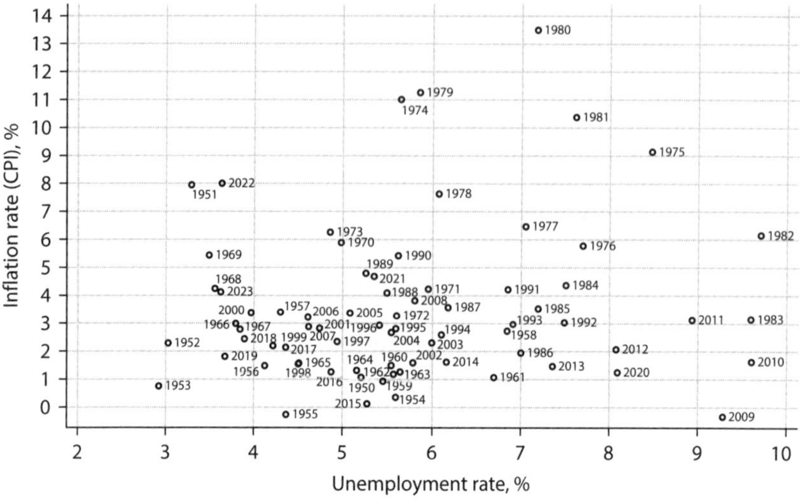

FIGURE 4.1. Joint distribution of inflation rate and unemployment rate for the U.S.

Notes: Own calculations. Annual data are from the U.S. Bureau of Labor Statistics.

persistently higher. The view that the position of the Phillips curve depends on inflation expectations is commonly referred to as an expectations-augmented Phillips curve, an insight that led to a Nobel Prize for Edmund Phelps.

Subsequent macroeconomic modeling has consistently confirmed the importance of expectations in thinking about the Phillips curve. While macroeconomists rarely agree on the exact nature of the Phillips curve, which depends on specific modeling assumptions, most models used by macroeconomists deliver some version of an expectations-augmented Phillips curve. We report in Table 4.1 the specific formulations of the Phillips curve postulated by different macroeconomic models and tested by previous studies (e.g., Zhang et al. 2008, Korenok et al. 2010, Coibion 2010, Afrouzi and Yang 2017). The most well known is the New Keynesian Phillips curve (NKPC),[1]

$$\pi_t = \beta E_t \pi_{t+1} + \kappa x_t + \varepsilon_t, \tag{11}$$

1. Detailed derivations of this expression can be found in Woodford (2003) and Galí (2015).

TABLE 4.1. Information structure and Phillips curve.

Information structure	Phillips curve
Full-information rational expectations with time-dependent pricing (Calvo 1983)	$\pi_t = \beta E_t[\pi_{t+1}] + b_1 x_t$
Full-information rational expectations with time-dependent pricing (Gertler and Leahy 2008)	$\pi_t = \beta E_t[\pi_{t+1}] + b_2 x_t$
Sticky prices and backward rule of thumb firms (Galí and Gertler 1999)	$\pi_t = (1 - b_4)\pi_{t-1} + b_4 E_t[\pi_{t+1}] + b_3 x_t$
Sticky information (Mankiw and Reis 2002)	$\pi_t = \bar{E}_{t-1}[\pi_t] + b_5 \bar{E}_{t-1}[\Delta y_t] + b_6 y_t$
Adaptive learning (Milani 2005)	$\pi_t = \hat{E}_t \pi_{t+1} + b_7 x_t$
Rational inattention (Afrouzi and Yang 2017)	$\pi_t = \bar{E}_{t-1}[\pi_t] + \bar{E}_{t-1}[\Delta y_t] + b_8 y_t + b_9(\bar{E}_t[\pi_{t+1} + \Delta y_{t+1}] - i_t)$

Notes: The table shows Phillips curves derived under various assumptions about how economic agents form expectations. Coefficients b vary across specifications and depend on structural parameters and details of information structure. π_t is inflation, x_t is output gap, y_t is output, and i_t is the nominal interest rate. E_t denotes full-information rational expectations given information available at time t. $\bar{E}_t$ denotes *average* expectations (not necessarily full information, but rationality is preserved) across agents. $\hat{E}_t$ denotes expectations when agents use information up to period t to learn about structural parameters in the economy. See Coibion, Gorodnichenko and Kamdar (2018) for more details.

which links inflation (π_t) to expected inflation $E_t\pi_{t+1}$, the output gap (x_t) and supply-side shocks (ε_t). β is the discount factor (which is close to 1), while $\kappa > 0$ denotes the slope of the Phillips curve. Consistent with Phillips (1958), higher levels of economic activity will tend to be associated with inflation, but this is conditional on the expected inflation and supply shocks. Other versions of the Phillips curve in Table 4.1 all include some measure of inflation expectations (although the timings of the expectations differ, depending on the model) and posit a positive link between the real economy and inflation conditional on those expectations.

Estimating these Phillips curves without data on expectations has been a challenge. The most common approach was pioneered by Galí and Gertler (1999) and consisted of imposing FIRE such that $E_t\pi_{t+1} = \pi_{t+1} + \eta_{t+1}$, where η_{t+1} is the FIRE expectations error that is uncorrelated with all information dated t and earlier, such that $E[\eta_{t+1}\mathbf{Z}_t] = 0$. Substituting out expectations from the Phillips curve using this expression and rearranging yields a moment condition for estimation by the generalized method of moments that does not require observing inflation expectations. They showed that using labor's share as the measure of economic activity (a proxy for marginal costs) yields reasonable estimates of κ, especially if the Phillips curve is augmented to include a lagged inflation term.

However, a number of issues have been raised with this type of estimate of the NKPC. First, it relies on imposing FIRE, which on its own can be strongly rejected empirically. Second, the resulting estimates are either insignificant or have the wrong sign when the measure of the real economy is a traditional output gap or an unemployment gap measure. Third, much of the predictive performance of the NKPC relies on the addition of an ad hoc lagged inflation term (Rudd and Whelan 2005). Fourth, estimates are sensitive to small variations in sample size, the inflation measure and other changes (Mavroeidis, Plagborg-Moller and Stock 2014). Fifth, the estimated NKPC appears inconsistent with inflation dynamics during the Great Recession, when the very low levels of economic activity would have predicted a disinflation that did not materialize, the "missing disinflation" puzzle. Finally, the NKPC has very limited out-of-sample explanatory power (Atkeson and Ohanian 2001).

Many of these problems disappear when we bring in survey expectations to estimate the NKPC. Roberts (1995) and Adam and Padula (2011) found that controlling for survey expectations eliminates much of the sensitivity to the measure of real activity used in the Phillips curve. The need for ad hoc lags in the Phillips curve is mitigated (Fuhrer 2017), estimates are more stable over time and across specifications, and out-of-sample forecasting performance improves (Coibion, Gorodnichenko and Kamdar 2018). Finally, if one conditions on households' expectations of inflation (which seem to be a better proxy for firms' expectations than professional forecasters), the "missing disinflation" puzzle also disappears (Coibion and Gorodnichenko 2015b).

Nor is this benefit to using survey measures of inflation expectations limited to the U.S. In Panel A of Figure 4.2, we plot the relationship between inflation and unemployment across 18 countries/regions for which survey data are available. As shown earlier for the U.S., this result can only be characterized as a cloud: there is no clear unconditional relationship between inflation and unemployment. However, once we condition on available survey measures of inflation expectations for households or firms (as available) for these same countries, we get Panel B of Figure 4.2, which shows an unambiguous negative relationship between the two. In other words, the structural Phillips curve is alive and well once we condition on real-time inflation expectations, even though inflation and real activity may look uncorrelated over time.

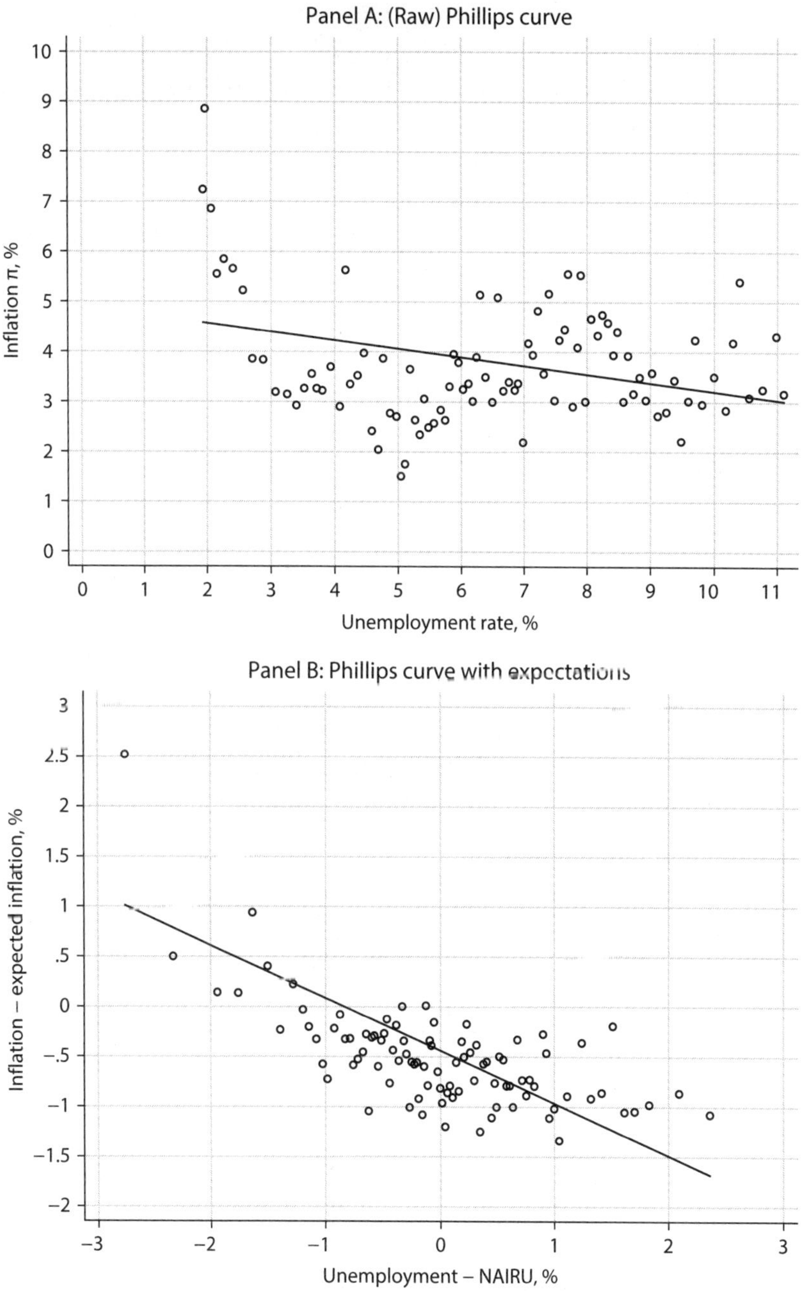

FIGURE 4.2. International evidence on the Phillips curve.
Notes: Each panel is a binscatter plot. Non-accelerating inflation rate of unemployment (NAIRU) is from the Organization for Economic Cooperation and Development (OECD). Actual unemployment and inflation are from the OECD. Expectations data are from various surveys. See Coibion, Gorodnichenko and Ulate (2019) for more details.

Other Applications

Applying survey forecasts to help estimate structural macroeconomic relationships is not limited to exploring the Phillips curve, of course. Another well-known application of survey forecasts is to the monetary policy rule. Because central bankers are well aware of the delayed effects of monetary policy on the economy, they must set interest rates in anticipation of future economic developments. To capture this formally, policy rules are now typically formulated in a forward-looking fashion, such as

$$r_t - r^* = \varphi_\pi \times [E_t \pi_{t+h} - \pi^*] + \varphi_y \times [E_t y_{t+h} - y^*], \tag{12}$$

in which the deviation of the interest rate r_t from its steady state r^* depends on how far expected inflation $E_t \pi_{t+h}$ is from the inflation target π^* and how far expected output $E_t y_{t+h}$ is from its steady state y^*. While these rules can be estimated after imposing FIRE in a manner analogous to that with the NKPC (see Clarida, Galí and Gertler 2000), one can also estimate the policy response function conditional on historical forecasts of inflation and output, as shown by Orphanides (2003) and Coibion and Gorodnichenko (2011b), and therefore without imposing the counterfactual assumption of FIRE.

The same could be done with consumption Euler equations, wage Phillips curves, and so on. Crump et al. (2022), for example, estimated consumption Euler equations using survey data from the New York Fed's Survey of Consumer Expectations and found much more precise estimates of the intertemporal elasticity of substitution with survey data than prior work. These results are consistent with the finding for German consumers (Dräger and Nghiem 2021). Similarly, Christelis et al. (2020) incorporated consumption uncertainty measured from a survey into an estimated Euler equation to identify the coefficient of relative prudence, which determines the strength of precautionary savings motives.

Another application is to estimated dynamic stochastic general equilibrium (DSGE) models. Rather than focusing on individual structural relationships, this approach focuses on estimating the entire model, either by matching impulse responses as in Christiano, Eichenbaum and Evans (2005) or through Bayesian methods as in Smets and Wouters (2003). Typically, this is done using observable macroeconomic variables, but this line of research increasingly adds survey measures of expectations as additional observables to discipline the expectations formation process in the model. Melosi (2017), for example, used this strategy to study the signaling effects of monetary policy. Smets, Warne and Wouters (2013) estimated a DSGE model of the Euro economy and assessed the extent to which augmenting it with survey forecasts helps with out-of-sample forecasting. Carvalho et al. (2023) estimated a sticky price model in which firms are uncertain about the long-run mean of inflation using survey measures of professional forecasters. Coibion and Gorodnichenko (2011a) focused on estimating the general equilibrium effects of strategic interactions between agents with different expectation formation processes. One limitation of these papers is their reliance on surveys of professional forecasters, who we know form expectations that differ significantly from those of households and firms. The scope of models of expectations formation considered in these papers is also limited relative to the wider range of frictions and biases considered in the literature on expectations formation. Both suggest we still have much to learn from applying expectations measures to estimated DSGE models.

Summary

Together, these applications illustrate some of the ways in which existing survey expectations can help guide and shape macroeconomic models. The most direct way is of course by helping us understand the nature of the expectations formation process. Significant progress has been made, especially in terms of documenting and quantifying departures from FIRE, but much more needs to be done to characterize what alternative model of expectations should replace it. Models of imperfect information can go a long way in explaining the underreaction of expectations that is pervasive in survey data, but there are features of the data that require going beyond these simple frameworks. Determining the importance of these additional moments will be necessary to assess whether the future benchmark model of expectations will need to embody departures from rationality in addition to deviations from full information.

Edward Prescott famously said that surveys cannot be used to test rational expectations because we can only test combinations of theories and observations: rationality is always defined within a specific framework. Finding deviations from rationality in the data could therefore indicate not that people are irrational but rather that the framework we are using is the wrong one. For example, biased forecasts could reflect irrationality or ambiguity aversion in preferences (Huo, Pedroni and Pei 2024). So these types of results should always be interpreted with care. Deviations from full information (such as disagreement about recent economic conditions), on the other hand, are clearer to establish, and the evidence for imperfect information is quite striking. But even in that case, some evidence for imperfect information such as persistence in forecast errors can alternatively be explained through models of full information with regime switches (Hajdini and Kurmann 2023).

Even without a well-defined alternative model, the use of survey expectations to estimate structural macroeconomic relationships illustrates some of their benefits by eliminating puzzles that might otherwise lead us to jettison entire model structures, such as the Phillips curve. But by themselves, these structural relationships do not address causality. Taking this next step requires being able to identify exogenous variation in beliefs, the topic to which we now turn.

PART II

Creating Exogenous Variation in Expectations

5

Designing Information Treatments

WHILE SURVEY MEASURES of expectations are very useful on their own, one natural limitation to their use is the fact that they are jointly determined with observable outcomes. This makes it difficult to identify the specific contribution of expectations to decision-making. To resolve this, one approach is for researchers to look for "natural experiments" that lead to clear exogenous variation in expectations, such as from close political elections (Jens 2017, Binder, Kamdar and Ryngaert 2024) or the Russian invasion of Ukraine (Gründler, Dräger, and Potrafke 2025). But this is often infeasible and, even when possible, it may be difficult to generalize a natural experiment to a different setting. An alternative approach is to directly *create* exogenous variation in beliefs through information treatments. In this chapter, we describe how randomized information treatments can be implemented and some pitfalls to avoid. In doing so, we build closely on the excellent overview of information treatment design by Haaland, Roth and Wohlfart (2023), to whom we refer the interested reader for more details on some of the topics described.

What Constitutes a Successful Information Treatment?

Information treatments entail providing different pieces of information to survey participants, with the goal of creating exogenous variation in beliefs. Typically, this is done by randomly allocating survey participants into either a control group or a treatment group. The former is not provided with information whereas the latter is, so that any subsequent difference in expectations or behavior can be attributed *causally* to the information provided. This randomized control trial (RCT) is akin to that used in medical research to assess the effects of medications, but in this case the "treatment" is information. One crucial element is the random allocation of participants to either control or trial groups, which ensures that being treated is uncorrelated with any attribute of individuals. But this is just a first step toward a successful information treatment. If the goal is to meaningfully change the economic expectations of agents, then several additional conditions must be satisfied.

Relevance of the information treatment

One imperative for a successful information treatment is that the provided information relates in some direct manner to the expectations of interest. For example, to change the inflation expectations of households, we could provide them with information about recent inflation; recent forecasts of future inflation from well-informed sources such as professional forecasters or the central bank; or the inflation target, if there is one, of the central bank. Information that is less relevant, such as an unemployment forecast or recent stock market returns, may fail to move expectations in a meaningful way.

Information must not be already known by survey participants

While it's important to provide information that is relevant, to successfully create changes in expectations, the information must also be new to the respondents. If we provide information that is known to the individuals, that information should already have been incorporated in their expectations, so being provided with the information again will not change their beliefs. For example, we once ran an information treatment on firms in Uruguay in which we told them about the central bank's inflation target. Because, as it turns out, most firms there already knew what the central bank's inflation target was, the information treatment failed to generate any meaningful revisions in inflation expectations (Weber et al. 2025).

Note that there is a tension between the first two conditions. If information is relevant to forming expectations about something, why wouldn't respondents already know it? A FIRE environment provides a useful benchmark: agents know all of the relevant information that can help predict economic outcomes, so there should be nothing that could be told to them in a survey that changes their expectations, and hence information treatments should always fail. Intuitively, the success of information treatments therefore relies on a form of imperfect information: there must be some available information that is relevant to forming expectations but not universally known to the subjects. But the fact that information is not already known does not necessarily mean that it is not potentially important for decision-making. For example, as academics, how well we will be able to live during our retirement years depends largely on how well our 401(k) accounts perform. This might suggest that we would be very well informed about stock returns. And yet, neither of us pays much attention to what happens in the stock market. When we have some extra free time, that time typically gets allocated to family, leisure, chores or work. Tracking the performance of the stock market would be far down the list. But if someone were to provide us with unsolicited information about recent market dynamics, it might lead us to change our portfolios. Since people cannot choose to be fully informed about everything given all the constraints that we face (both cognitive and in terms of time), this leaves room for information treatments to work even about information that matters for decision-making.

Information must be easy to comprehend

Another characteristic that can cause an information treatment to fail is that the conveyed message is not easily comprehensible to survey participants. If a treatment uses terminology that is unfamiliar, has complicated expressions or roundabout language, has excessive use of math or statistics, or is overly lengthy, respondents may fail to understand the content of the information, in which case the treatment will not lead to any meaningful impact on expectations. This can be particularly problematic when survey respondents have less education or expertise about the area they are being asked about. Formulating information treatments in a manner that is appropriate to the audience is therefore an important element to consider. An information treatment that is informative to a chief financial officer may not be appropriate for someone with a different background. For example, one of us recently did a conference presentation, not realizing that half the audience was going to be noneconomists. The initial slides consisted of equations for motivation, which made sense for a macroeconomist audience, but the presentation was met with glazed eyes from the noneconomists. This is precisely what information treatments should try to avoid. A number of papers have explored how different presentations of the same content can affect the ease with which it is processed. Combinations of audio and video, for example, can be particularly effective in moving inflation expectations relative to text, especially for those who are less informed about the economy (Ash et al. 2024).

The information source must be credible

Yet another reason why an information treatment could fail to change expectations is that respondents are skeptical about the source of the information. For example, telling someone who does not trust the Federal Reserve that the Fed's inflation target is 2% may provide them with information they did not have, but it could still fail to change their inflation expectations. Alternatively, if an individual believes that inflation statistics are manipulated by the government (as they were in Argentina; see Cavallo, Cruces and Perez-Truglia 2016), telling them what the most recent "official" inflation rate is may have a limited effect on their inflation expectations because they will think that the statistic is not informative about underlying inflation.

As we can see, there are many factors that can cause an information treatment to fail in terms of changing respondents' beliefs. It could be that the provided information is not perceived as relevant, it could be that the information is already known to respondents, it could be that they do not view the information as trust-worthy, or it could be that they simply do not understand the information provided. Each of these is a fundamentally different source of failure, so it is important to include questions in the survey that can help distinguish between these possible mechanisms. For example, we can include questions before the treatment that measure the respondents' prior knowledge about the information treatment. In the case of inflation, this could entail asking them what they thought the inflation rate had been over the previous 12 months (for an information treatment involving recent inflation) or what inflation rate they thought the central bank was trying to target (for an information treatment involving the inflation target of the central bank). In the context of interest rate changes, Knotek et al. (2024) found that survey respondents lowered their inflation expectations after being told about recent Fed interest rate increases *only* if they were not previously aware of these policy changes. To measure understanding, a survey can include questions that assess a respondent's prior understanding of statistics, probability, or economics. An alternative is to ask them immediately after the treatment whether they were already aware of this information. Through these additional types of questions, researchers can disentangle the various mechanisms that can lead to small effects of information treatments on economic expectations.

Anchoring and demand effects

These mechanisms are all pushing toward finding no effects of information treatments on beliefs. But if beliefs do in fact change, does that necessarily mean that the treatment was successful? Unfortunately, the answer is no, as there are other mechanisms that can lead to the appearance of a successful treatment effect even when in fact expectations did not really change. One such mechanism is anchoring. This psychological effect has been documented in Tversky and Kahneman (1974) and is based on the idea that if individuals are told about a specific number, that fact alone can shape their answers to subsequent questions even if that number is irrelevant.[1] In Coibion, Gorodnichenko and Weber (2022a), for example, we found that telling U.S. households that the population of the U.S. had grown by 2% over the previous two years reduced their inflation expectations, even though population growth should have no clear effect on inflation, a finding that is suggestive of anchoring to the 2% number. This is an example of a "placebo" treatment, i.e., a piece of irrelevant information that includes the same number as that provided in the other information treatment. While we found an effect of the placebo treatment on inflation expectations, it was very small compared to being told about the inflation target. Placebo treatments therefore allow researchers to rule out that the effect of a treatment is due to an anchoring effect, but they require an additional treatment group, which reduces the effective sample size for other groups. Additional strategies to minimize anchoring effects include measuring quantitative beliefs on a very different scale than what is used for the treatment and incorporating some qualitative measures of beliefs that are not sensitive to numerical anchoring (Haaland et al. 2023).

Another possible confounding mechanism is demand effects, which is that survey respondents realize what the survey is trying to do and try to please the researcher by providing answers consistent with this. For example, if a central bank runs a survey of inflation expectations and survey participants know this fact, the participants may do some research on inflation to provide "correct" answers that are consistent with the objectives of the central bank. There are several strategies used to try limit the scope of demand effects in

1. To be clear, the anchoring effect in survey responses is different from the anchoring of inflation expectations that is emphasized by central banks. The former is a psychological effect where a response or decision is influenced by a reference point ("anchor"). The latter is the insensitivity of inflation expectations to macroeconomic shocks.

contaminating information treatments. One is to use follow-up surveys to measure effects on beliefs, since individuals are unlikely to recall the prior survey's perceived purpose, especially if the two surveys do not appear similar (Haaland, Roth and Wohlfart 2023). Another is to mask the purpose of the survey by asking questions on unrelated topics first, although this can be costly in terms of using up valuable survey space (Facchini, Margalit and Nakata 2022). A third approach is to incorporate an explicit information treatment group that deliberately aims to induce a survey demand effect. Like the "placebo" treatment for anchoring, this is very useful for measuring the potential quantitative importance of this channel, but it requires an additional treatment group (de Quidt, Haushofer and Roth 2018). Fourth, we can ask questions that aim to assess what respondents perceive the purpose of the study to be, which can again help determine the potential importance of demand effects (Allcott and Taubinsky 2015, Bursztyn et al. 2023). Finally, minimizing in-person interactions between survey subjects and interviewers reduces the pressure to please the interviewers. As a result, phone and (especially) online surveys are less likely to have demand effects.

While anchoring and demand effects are commonly found to be small when explicitly tested for, this may not always be the case. It is therefore important for surveys and information treatments to be designed *ex ante* in such a way as to be able to rule out (or at least limit the size of) *ex post* that they are contaminating estimated treatment effects.

Ethical considerations

Suppose that you have designed an information treatment that can successfully change individuals' economic expectations while ruling out that such changes are driven by anchoring or demand effects. Should you implement it? A first step will be getting approval from an Institutional Review Board (IRB) responsible for ensuring that any study on human subjects is done subject to certain minimum criteria to protect participants. These criteria are generally easy to satisfy if information treatments are truthful and publicly available as well as entail minimal possible costs on participants, because this information (for example, an inflation report prepared by the statistical office) is already in the public domain and subjects are generally not excluded from access to this information. We view this bar as a little too low and we encourage researchers in this area to think carefully about their treatments. As we describe in subsequent chapters, successful information treatments often affect the decisions of households and firms. So it is imperative that information treatments not be deceptive in any way.

One commonly used metric to avoid deception is that the information provided should be truthful. While it would be incredibly interesting to run fictitious information treatments where some individuals are told the Fed is forecasting an inflation rate of 5% while others are told 0%, *this should not be done* as it can lead to wrong beliefs and poor choices. But information can be true and still be deceptive and potentially harmful. For example, it is truthful to tell someone "inflation in the U.S. was [X]% in the past," where X could be any number from −16% (June 1921) to 20% (June 1917), but few respondents would imagine that the provided number comes from more than 100 years ago. If they changed their beliefs thinking that the provided value was recent and then acted on those beliefs, this could make them significantly worse off. As Voltaire once said, "everything you say should be true, but not everything true should be said." Researchers should avoid, as much as possible, the use of truthful but misleading information treatments.

At what point should we consider information treatments to be misleading? One way to make this determination is for researchers to ask themselves whether they would provide the same information to someone that they were trying to inform. For example, in the case of academics, would you provide the same information to your students in the context of a lecture without qualifying the information? For central bankers, would they make the statement to a policymaker and expect it to help the policymaker make a better (or at least no worse) decision? Or, if your friends came to you and asked for your professional opinion about the topic, is this a piece of information that you would offer as relevant and informative? If so, then the information can be considered to be net positive. But if there is some doubt or a sense that the researcher, central banker or you would want to qualify the information or put it in a broader context before sharing it in these settings, they may be wading into a gray area, and it's likely time to redesign the information treatment.[2]

Another reason, above and beyond the desire to avoid anyone being hurt by participating in research studies, why researchers should try to always err on the side of safety is that it would take very few ill-designed studies that

2. The nature of some research projects may require providing incomplete or misleading information (e.g., to study the effect of fake news). These situations require a very careful cost-benefit analysis and, appropriately, the requirements from IRBs are much stricter.

cause harm to make an IRB approval become increasingly difficult and binding. Minimizing bureaucratic hurdles is important for this line of research, and it is in everyone's interest to stay away from the gray areas that could significantly move the standards required by IRBs.

Practical Considerations in Designing Information Treatments

When designing the information treatments, there are several questions that immediately come up. The first is, how many information treatments do we do. Second, should treatments be uniform across individuals or tailored to the individual respondent. Third, how do we treat, if at all, the control group.

Number of information treatments

Picking the number of treatments reflects a trade-off between the scope of the project and the size and limitations of the survey. The greater the number of treatments, the smaller will be the sample size for each treatment and the noisier are the results likely to be. A good rule of thumb when it comes to economic expectations is to have approximately 1,000 households per treatment arm in a household survey and 100–200 firms per treatment arm in a survey of firms.[3] Having multiple treatments, when possible, can help along a number of dimensions.

One important advantage of multiple information treatments is that they can help with identifying cross-learning, which is when information about one topic leads individuals to change their beliefs about different variables, all of which might matter for their decisions. Consider, for example, learning that inflation has been lower than expected in the previous year. This might lead an individual to revise their inflation expectations downward, but it could also lead to revisions in beliefs about the state of the real economy, future wage growth and the path of interest rates, among other things. To the extent that each of these channels could affect decisions like consumer spending, cross-learning would make it difficult to attribute changes in spending specifically to the revision in inflation expectations even if the treatment was about

3. The smaller number of firms than households needed reflects the fact that firm responses are typically of higher quality and subject to much less noise. Glennester and Takavarasha (2013) discuss formal power calculations to determine sample sizes.

inflation. By having information treatments that move different expectations by different relative amounts, one can disentangle these different channels, as we discuss in more detail in Chapter 10.

This logic applies to higher moments of expectations as well. In many cases, uncertainty about economic outcomes can affect decisions above and beyond expectations of first moments (Bloom 2009). The perceived skewness of the distribution could also be important. With multiple information treatments, we can induce different relative variation in first, second, or even third moments of beliefs, thereby allowing researchers to identify their relative effects. We used this strategy in Coibion et al. (2024) and Kumar et al. (2023), for example, to estimate how macroeconomic uncertainty affects the economic decisions of households and firms, respectively. Mikosch et al. (2024) also applied multiple treatments to quantify how uncertainty affects the demand for new information.

A third use of multiple treatment arms is to study the effects of different horizons in information treatments. In many settings, an optimal decision today depends on an entire expected *path* of future outcomes, not just those over a fixed horizon. One potential application is with forward guidance by a central bank, in which policymakers make statements about the future path of interest rates over potentially different horizons. In Coibion et al. (2023), for example, we used 22 different treatment arms about the past, the current, or the future path of either inflation or interest rates to assess how the horizon of the treatment affects household expectations.

A fourth possible use of different treatment arms is to assess the importance of the *source* of the information in affecting expectations. One illustrative example of how much the source of the information can matter is D'Acunto, Fuster and Weber (2021). Their goal was to determine how strongly people respond to Federal Reserve forecasts depending on how people perceive the representativeness of the Federal Reserve. They randomly assigned survey participants to one of three treatment arms. In each group, respondents were presented with the same forecast of unemployment from the Federal Open Market Committee (FOMC), but illustrated with a photo of a different FOMC member. One group was shown a photo of a Thomas Barkin (a White man), one of Raphael Bostic (a Black man) and one of Mary Daly (a White woman). They found that being shown these different images altered perceptions of how inclusive the Federal Reserve is. Studying the effect on unemployment expectations, they concluded that for women and Black survey participants, expectations respond more strongly to the FOMC forecast when that forecast is associated with a photo of an underrepresented group than when it is not, whereas no such effect exists for White male respondents. This is a striking example of how the source of the information can have important effects on how strongly expectations respond to the treatment.

A fifth possible use of multiple treatment arms is to allow for explicit measurement of anchoring or demand effects, as mentioned earlier. To control for possible anchoring effects, an additional treatment arm could include the same numerical value as in other treatments, but apply it to a context that is not relevant to the expectations being measured, thereby providing a pure anchoring effect. To control for possible demand effects, one could similarly include a treatment arm that explicitly provides guidance on what researchers are looking for. For example, de Quidt, Haushofer and Roth (2018) included a "weak" demand treatment arm that told participants, "We expect that participants who are shown these instructions will [work, invest, . . .] more/less than they normally would," and a "strong" demand treatment arm that went even further by telling participants, "You will do us a favor if you [work, invest, . . .] more/less than you normally would." They found very modest demand effects for the "weak" treatment arm but significantly larger effects for the "strong" treatment arm, indicating that while demand effects will typically be small, they can be important in certain cases.

Common versus personalized treatments

A second important choice that needs to be made with information treatments is whether a treatment should be common to all participants within the treatment group or whether the information should be more narrowly targeted to the individual. All of the examples of treatments described above are of the common type: everyone within a treatment group receives the exact same piece of information. But in principle, one can tailor the provided information to be specific to an individual. Providing more targeted information can make a treatment more powerful if it is seen as more relevant than an aggregate statistic.

A great example of this approach is Roth, Settele and Wohlfart (2022). They studied the importance of individuals' exposure to business cycle risk in determining how useful they perceived information about the aggregate economy to be. Individuals were assigned to one of two treatment groups, in which they received a tailored measure of their business cycle exposure. Specifically, they were shown visually how much the unemployment rate went up during the Great Recession for individuals like them, defined at a narrow level (census division of residence, five-year age brackets, educational attainment and three-digit occupation code). The two treatment groups differed in the source of the unemployment data, so that depending on which group they were assigned to, a given individual could get two different measures of business cycle exposure. The authors found that ex post perceived measures of business cycle risk were strongly affected by the treatments and led to large differences in willingness to get forecasts about the aggregate economy thereafter.

Another example of a tailored treatment is from Hvidberg, Kreiner and Stantcheva (2023). Their interest focused on how relative social positions affect beliefs about fairness and redistribution. They linked a survey of households in Denmark that tracks reference groups and beliefs about incomes of the reference groups with administrative data that precisely measures actual incomes of the relevant reference groups. The authors implemented a randomized information treatment in which those in the treatment group were shown where they ranked in the income distribution for different reference groups compared to where they thought they ranked, before asking them follow-up questions. Hvidberg, Kreiner and Stantcheva found that individuals who initially overestimated their position in the income distribution and then learned that they are worse off relative to their peers tended to take on more negative views about the fairness of income inequality.

Passive versus active control group

A third important choice to be made in the design of an information treatment is in terms of the control group. The most common approach to an RCT is to have a control group that receives no additional information of any kind and to which the treatment group(s) can be compared directly. However, other approaches can also be used. One is for the control group to include a "placebo" treatment, so that any difference between the treated and control group will be net of anchoring effects. This is the approach used in standard medical trials, for example, with the "placebo" being medicines with no pharmaceutical content. Another common approach is to use an "active" control group which also receives an information treatment analogous in form to that of the treatment group but different in size (see Haaland, Roth and Wohlfart 2023 for more on active control groups). A nice example of this approach is Roth and Wohlfart (2020), who allocated households in a survey to two treatment groups, each of which received a truthful professional forecast about the likelihood of a recession, but with one forecast significantly more pessimistic than the other. The authors then assessed how revisions in expectations affected the spending plans of respondents. Another application of this approach is Mikosch et al. (2024). Their goal was to assess how uncertainty about exchange rates affects households' and firms' information acquisition. Running parallel surveys of households and firms, they split each sample into two groups. Each group was provided a common forecast of the exchange rate but different truthful predictions about the uncertainty around the forecast. With this design, the authors could identify the effect of uncertainty on information acquisition net of beliefs about the level of the exchange rate.

Why have an active control group? The main advantage is that it can increase the range of variation in beliefs. In a standard treatment setup with a passive control group, most of the variation will come from individuals who initially have large misperceptions and then reduce those misperceptions when provided with true information. With an active control group, the entire distribution is used, with some individuals shifted either up or down depending on which treatment they receive, as in Roth and Wohlfart (2020). Because both groups get treated, an active control group can also net out demand and anchoring effects. However, there are several limitations to active control groups. For instance, the interpretation of results can sometimes be less immediate than when there is an untreated control group. This is particularly the case when the question of interest is precisely how receiving information changes beliefs (e.g., when studying the effects of policy communication), in which case it may be more helpful to have an untreated control group. It can also be less suitable to settings where multiple information treatments are to be applied, in which case a common passive control group is important for us to be able to compare across different treatment effects.

Summary

There are a lot of ways in which information treatments can go wrong. Survey participants can fail to respond to treatments because of irrelevance of the information, a lack of trust in its source or an inability to digest it, among other things. Or they can respond to information for the wrong reasons, such as psychological anchoring effects or experimenter demand effects. But avoiding these potential hurdles is quite feasible in most cases and, with careful design, can lead to exciting new sources of exogenous variation in beliefs.

6

Quantifying and Understanding the Effects of Information Treatments on Expectations

YOU'VE RUN A SURVEY with a carefully designed information treatment. What now? In this chapter, we describe different ways of analyzing the effectiveness of information treatments on expectations. As we will see, the simplest strategies can often miss much of the most interesting behavioral responses of individuals to new information, so some care must be taken in thinking through the best way to identify treatment effects. We also discuss some practical considerations that arise in working with survey data, such as noise in survey responses and extreme observations, as well as the external validity of this type of RCT.

How Should We Estimate the Effects of Treatments on Expectations?

There are three general approaches used to assess treatment effects on expectations. One focuses just on ex post beliefs and relies on "between" variation, that is, differences in the posterior beliefs across individuals. The second focuses on *revisions* in individual beliefs, which we can think of as "within" variation. The third also considers revisions in beliefs but takes into account that how your expectations respond to an information treatment should depend explicitly on what your prior belief was.

Average treatment effects ("between" variation)

Once we observe the posterior beliefs of individuals measured after information treatments, the simplest approach to measuring treatment effects is to assess whether there are systematic differences in the average expectations across control and treatment groups. This can be done by running a regression such as

$$posterior_i = \alpha + \sum_j \beta_j \times \mathbb{I}(i \in j) + error, \qquad (1)$$

projecting the posterior beliefs of individual i on indicator variables $\mathbb{I}(i \in j)$, which are equal to 1 if individual i is in treatment group j. Because each individual can be in only one group, if one of the indicator variables is equal to one, then other indicator variables must be equal to zero. For participants in the control group, they are assigned values equal to 0 for every indicator. Thus, α will identify the average posterior belief of respondents in the control group, whereas $\alpha + \beta_j$ identifies the average posterior belief of respondents in treatment group j. β_j therefore tells us whether the information led to a different *average* posterior belief for treated individuals relative to untreated individuals.

To appreciate how this approach works, Figure 6.1 plots the distribution of posterior inflation expectations of U.S. households in 2018Q2 from Coibion, Gorodnichenko and Weber (2022a). As we can see, the distribution of expectations for the control group is very dispersed, with an average expectation of 6.7%. The figure also plots the distribution of expectations for a treatment group that was told that the Federal Reserve was targeting an inflation rate of 2.0 percent. The distribution of their posteriors is shifted to the left, by approximately 1.5 percentage points, indicating that the treatment on average reduced the inflation expectations of households. Thus, the estimate of β is roughly 1.5 percentage points.

There are several features of specification (1) that are appealing. First, it is very easy to understand and provides an immediate and clear statistic for the average effect of information treatments. Second, no controls are necessary to run this specification since the random assignment of information treatments implies that the indicator variables are uncorrelated with other determinants of expectations. Although β is estimated consistently in equation (1), introducing controls to equation (1) can increase the precision of the estimates. Third, this specification does not require the measurement of prior beliefs on

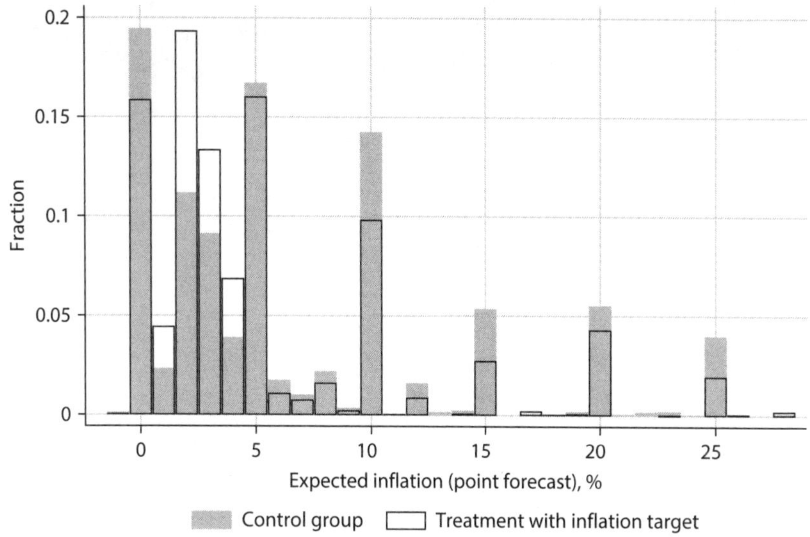

FIGURE 6.1. Distribution of inflation expectations by treatment status.
Source: Coibion, Gorodnichenko and Weber (2022a).

the part of survey participants. Given these advantages, this is a natural starting point for any analysis of treatment effects.

However, this should almost never be the stopping point! The reason is that this approach, while highly tractable, suffers from several important shortcomings that tend to mask much of the interesting variation that information treatments are likely to induce. First, as we discussed in Chapter 3, one of the most pervasive features of survey data on expectations is the disagreement that we observe in economic forecasts: the cross-sectional variance of posteriors can be very large and much of this variation will generally be unrelated to the information treatments. Because the treatments are orthogonal to these other sources of variation, this does not matter asymptotically, but in small samples including or excluding controls can be important for the estimates of β.

Second, estimates of the mean expectation across a group will tend to be very sensitive to the presence of outliers and extreme observations. For example, with inflation expectations, it is not uncommon in a survey to have a few individuals predict inflation of 20% or 50% over the next year. Whether 20% expected inflation or another higher expectation is reasonable or not can depend on the context, but one can certainly have situations where

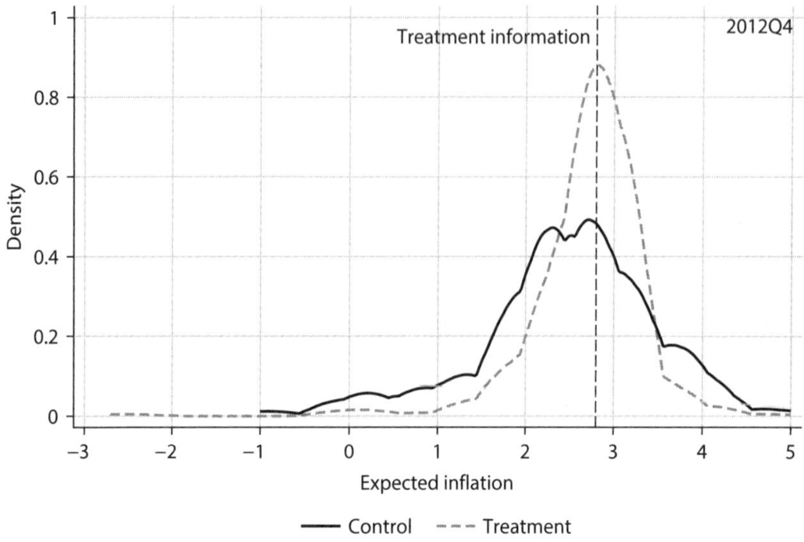

FIGURE 6.2. Distribution of inflation expectations for Italian firms in treatment and control groups.
Notes: The figure shows kernel densities for the distribution of inflation expectations. Data are for 2012Q4.
Source: Coibion, Gorodnichenko and Ropele (2020).

respondents have a sensible explanation for their high expectations. Just a few of these observations can significantly move the mean. Again, asymptotically this should not be an issue since we would expect similar proportions of extreme observations in the control and treatment groups, but small samples imply that these types of outliers can play a disproportionate role in estimating different means across groups. We discuss some strategies to address outliers a little later, but it should be noted that no matter how we address these, this approach is susceptible to extreme observations.

A third issue with relying on the "between" variation is more conceptual and reflects the fact that treatments may have a very powerful effect on individual beliefs but fail to be identified using this specification. Consider a simple setting where some individuals expect inflation to be zero over the next year while others expect it to be 4%. A subset of these individuals is told that the Federal Reserve is predicting an inflation rate of 2%. This would tend to lead those who initially expected zero inflation to raise their forecasts toward 2%, whereas those who initially thought it would be 4% will tend to reduce their forecasts toward 2%. In this case, the average forecast for the treatment group may be identical to that for the control group (both around 2%), so estimating equation (1) would yield no identifiable treatment effect, even though the treatment changed expectations in a systematic fashion.

This is not just a theoretical concern. Figure 6.2 reports the distribution of inflation expectations for Italian firms in treatment and control groups from Coibion, Gorodnichenko and Ropele (2020). Clearly, the distribution for the treated group is more concentrated around the provided signal. While the difference in the average across the groups is relatively small, this difference masks large movements on either side of the mean.

Average treatment effects on revisions ("within" variation)

Given that the initial beliefs of individuals seem to matter for what happens to their posterior beliefs, a natural second approach is to condition on those beliefs and therefore exploit the "within" variation of changes in beliefs rather than just focusing on the levels of posteriors. A natural specification in this context is to estimate

$$posterior_i - prior_i = \alpha + \sum_j \beta_j \times \mathbb{I}(i \in j) + error. \quad (2)$$

Relative to specification (1), the big advantage of this specification is that individuals' prior beliefs absorb much of the variation in beliefs that was observed in Figure 6.1 without needing to control for a wide range of observable characteristics of individuals that correlate with their expectations. As a result, one is more likely to estimate a precise average treatment effect in small samples than when using specification (1).

However, this approach also suffers from some drawbacks. The first is that it requires measures of both posterior and prior beliefs, which is more demanding in terms of survey space. Furthermore, measuring the same belief twice within a survey is not as innocuous as it sounds. Survey participants generally strongly dislike being asked the same question multiple times in a survey, so there is a risk of greater attrition and selection taking place in terms of who completes the survey. One solution to this is to measure priors and posteriors within the same survey using different question formulations. For example, one could measure the prior expectation using a distribution question in the style of the New York Fed's Survey of Consumer Expectations or following Altig et al. (2022), then later in the survey ask for a posterior belief using a point forecast. In practice, of course, survey space is limited, and every question comes with an opportunity cost, but measuring both priors and posterior beliefs can be an important advantage when it comes to estimating treatment effects with more precision. Furthermore, it reduces the need to measure a wide range of additional control variables relative to specification (1), which can save survey space.

Another drawback of this approach is that it still does not address the fact that some individuals may increase their forecasts in response to information while others may reduce their forecasts when presented with the same information, depending on their initial priors. While specification (2) can adequately measure the difference in the average size of revisions across treatment and control groups, it does not speak to the fact that many individuals in the treatment group are revising their beliefs in different directions. As a result, we could still be missing much of the treatment effect on beliefs.

Conditional treatment effects

The third approach to estimating treatment effects, and our favorite in most cases, identifies the effect of new information on beliefs *conditional on prior beliefs*. To do so, we can estimate the following specification:

$$\begin{aligned} posterior_i = \alpha + \sum\nolimits_j \beta_j \times \mathbb{I}(i \in j) + \delta \times prior_i \\ + \sum\nolimits_j \gamma_j \times \mathbb{I}(i \in j) \times prior_i + error. \end{aligned} \tag{3}$$

This specification is clearly not as simple to interpret as specifications (1) and (2) but actually speaks to treatment effects in a very direct and transparent manner. First, note that for the control group, the specification reduces to $posterior_i = \alpha + \delta \times prior_i$. Given that individuals in the control group do not receive new information, we would expect their posteriors to be the same as their priors, and therefore $\alpha = 0$ and $\delta = 1$. In Figure 6.3, we plot a binscatter of prior and posterior beliefs for the control group using the sample of U.S. households in the Nielsen Homescan Panel from Coibion, Gorodnichenko and Weber (2022a). We find that the estimated value of δ is close to but somewhat below 1, which reflects the fact that posteriors and priors are measured

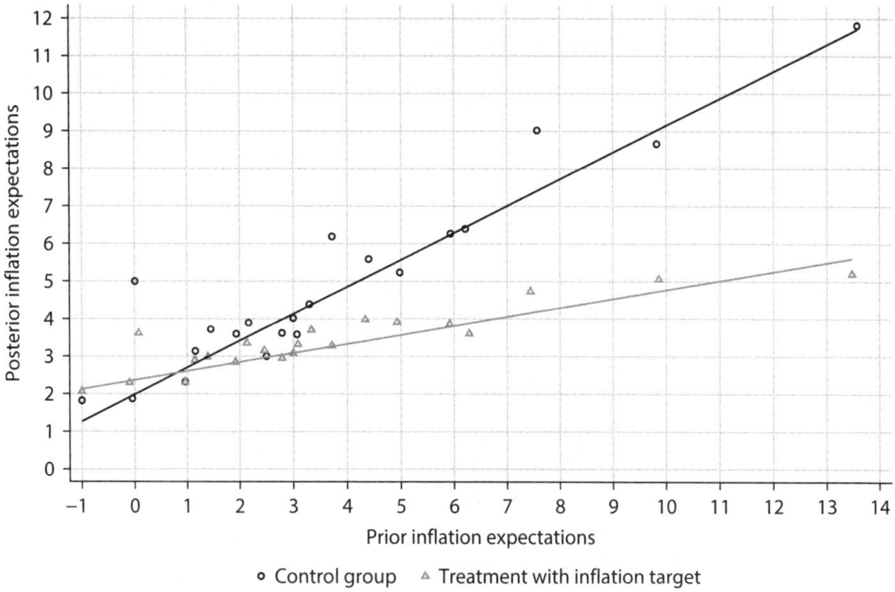

FIGURE 6.3. Joint distribution of prior and posterior inflation expectations by treatment status.

Notes: The figure presents binscatter plots for posterior vs. prior inflation expectations by treatment status. Solid lines show fitted linear relationships. See Coibion, Gorodnichenko and Weber (2022a) for more details.

using somewhat different questions, and measurement error in priors will tend to bias δ downward somewhat.

For treatment group j, specification (3) reduces to $posterior_i = (\alpha + \beta_j) + (\delta + \gamma_j) \times prior_i$. Hence, β_j captures shifts in the intercept linking posterior and prior beliefs for the treatment group relative to the control group, whereas γ_j captures changes in the slope. Suppose the information treatment were so powerful that all treated households set their posterior beliefs equal to the provided signal (such as the Fed's inflation forecast). In that case, we would estimate $\gamma_j = -1$ since posteriors would not depend on priors and β_j would be equal to the signal in treatment j (assuming $\alpha = 0$ and $\delta = 1$ for the control group). Now consider the opposite extreme in which the treatment has no effect on beliefs whatsoever, in which case posteriors are equal to priors just as for the control group. This would lead to estimates of $\gamma_j = \beta_j = 0$. Thus, in general, we should expect $\gamma_j \in [-1, 0]$: the difference in the slope of the treatment group relative to the control group should be negative, meaning that the posteriors of treated individuals do not rely as strongly on their priors as do posteriors of individuals in the control group. How much less they rely on the priors will speak to the size of the treatment effect. No treatment effect corresponds to $\gamma_j = 0$, and complete adoption of the treatment is given by $\gamma_j = -1$.

Consider this visually in Figure 6.3, which plots a binscatter relating posteriors and priors for the treatment group and the control group, where the treatment group was told that the Fed targets 2% inflation. We see that the slope of the line relating posteriors and priors for the treatment group is fairly flat, unlike for the control group. Individuals who initially predicted inflation of 10% on average revised their forecasts to around 5% when provided with the Fed's target. Individuals who initially predicted inflation of 1% raised their forecasts. Thus, specification (3) captures the upward *and* downward revisions of beliefs depending on where individuals' priors were and provides a clean metric of the effectiveness of the treatment, which is determined by γ_j. Furthermore, the visual representation of this specification provides a transparent and natural interpretation of how treatments affected beliefs *across the distribution*. Because we often need to use different questions to elicit priors and posteriors, δ may be different from 1. In this case, we recommend scaling γ_j by δ, that is, one can use γ_j / δ to measure the change in the slope.

Another advantage of this specification is that, like specification (2), it is largely insensitive to the inclusion of controls for individual characteristics. Even though individual characteristics tend to be important predictors of expectations, because specification (3) explicitly controls for prior beliefs, it already captures the role of these characteristics in shaping beliefs in the first place. The only meaningful source of variation between posteriors and priors should be the information treatment and measurement error, and since controls are uncorrelated with selection into treatments and measurement error, adding controls does not generally affect the results.

In short, specification (3) has several crucial advantages that make it a good benchmark to analyze the effects of information treatments on beliefs. It can measure the effects on beliefs even when the *average* effect is zero. It utilizes the entire distribution of beliefs to characterize the effects of new information. It can be visualized in a way that makes treatment effects transparent. And it is robust to whether controls are included or not. Given all these advantages, we recommend it as one of the most reliable and informative strategies to measure treatment effects.

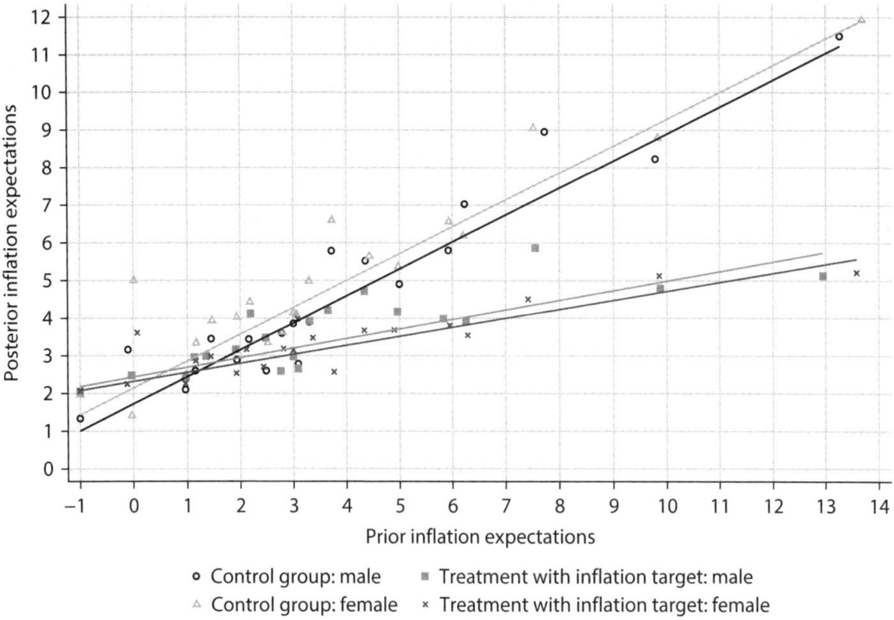

FIGURE 6.4. Joint distribution of prior and posterior inflation expectations by treatment status and demographics.
Notes: The figure presents binscatter plots for posterior vs. prior inflation expectations by treatment status and subsample. Solid lines show fitted linear relationships. See Coibion, Gorodnichenko and Weber (2022a) for more details.

Heterogeneous Treatment Effects

Should we expect treatment effects to be the same across individuals? We've already seen one possible caveat, namely that prior expectations are an important determinant of how beliefs respond to the provided information. But conditional on those priors, should we expect to see much variation in treatment effects above and beyond what is captured in priors?

Given specifications (1)–(3), it is straightforward to run the same specification on different subgroups of the population. For example, with households, one can compare different genders, different income brackets, different education levels, or different occupations to see if treatment effects vary across these dimensions. As shown in Figure 6.4 for the same U.S. households as before, we do not find any meaningful variation in the size of treatment effects by, for example, gender. This is not uncommon. Even though these characteristics can be very important in shaping economic expectations, their effect is embodied in individuals' prior expectations. Once one conditions on these, different individuals respond to the same information in a largely analogous manner.

There are two important caveats to this. The first is practical. Subsample splits naturally involve smaller sample sizes and larger standard errors. In many cases, it is not clear whether a failure to reject the null of equal treatment effects really reflects the fact that different individuals are responding in the same way or whether there is too much sampling uncertainty to identify different effects with precision. This is an important caveat to bear in mind when designing surveys with different treatment groups. Small sample sizes restrict not just the number of treatments that can be done but also the extent to which we can hope to study heterogeneity in treatment effects, which in many cases is of great interest.

The second caveat is that some factors can lead to systematic differences in terms of how people respond to information treatments, but those factors are often not easily captured with standard observable characteristics such as age and education. In general, and as described in Chapter 5, there are several characteristics that are important for how much a given information treatment causes an individual to change their beliefs, conditional on the initial level of those beliefs. To successfully change expectations, information treatments need to be relevant, credible, comprehensible and novel. These conditions may not be the same for everyone, and in those cases one should indeed expect to see different treatment effects.

For example, complicated information treatments may have little effect on those with limited cognitive skills but large effects on others. Treatments that originate from a specific source (e.g., the Federal Reserve, a specific politician) may have very limited effects on individuals who do not view this source as credible or reliable. This can be particularly important when studying the effect of communication from policymakers, as some may view the source as much less credible than others, leading to highly heterogeneous treatment effects. The novelty of the information can also differ, with some individuals already being familiar with the provided information and others not, also leading to heterogeneity in treatment effects.

Heterogeneity in treatment effects can be either a problem or a point of interest depending on the research question. When one is interested in how a specific piece of information affects beliefs, then having a subset of individuals dismiss the information because, for example, they already know it will induce a downward bias in estimated treatment effects. In this case, it is helpful to be able to identify those individuals and exclude them from the analysis. In other cases, the heterogeneity is itself a characteristic of the treatment effect that we want to study. For example, if one is interested in how policy communication from the president affects expectations, it is important to know to what extent some individuals may dismiss the information due to political ideology or bias, as this speaks to how effective this type of communication would actually be. Excluding individuals who are less responsive to the treatment in this case would yield a misleading estimate of the overall treatment effect.

Extreme Values and Outliers

Another reason why one might want to exclude certain observations is that they appear to be outliers. These are not uncommon in survey data, especially in online surveys where there may be "speeders," people who are racing through the survey to collect the reward without paying attention to the questions. But there are also people who may genuinely hold beliefs very different from the average belief, in which case there is no clear basis for excluding their answers. In general, how should one go about dealing with outliers and extreme observations?

One option is to try and eliminate obvious cases of "speeders" and others who are not taking the survey seriously. One can use simple strategies like dropping anyone who answered the survey in a very short period (say, less than one second per question; but one can use other thresholds). Another option is to explicitly include a question explaining that some participants do not read questions and, to verify that they are indeed paying attention, to ask them to provide a specific response to a subsequent question (Haaland, Roth and Wohlfart 2023).

A different strategy is to explicitly identify extreme values using a predetermined threshold. Values beyond the threshold can then be dropped ("censored") or capped at some value ("winsorized"). It is not uncommon for censoring or winsorizing to be applied to the top and bottom 1% of observations, with some researchers applying even more aggressive thresholds (2%, 5%). A disadvantage of censoring or winsorizing is that it may lead the researcher to treat different observations from a single respondent differently, with some responses winsorized and others not, which may give misleading estimates; if censoring, the number of observations may fall rapidly if one has to censor across many variables.

One strategy that can avoid some of these pitfalls is to use Huber (1964) robust regressions or similar methods that downplay influential observations. The Huber (1964) procedure reweights different observations based on an algorithm that assesses how much they move parameter estimates. Observations that seem to have undue weight will be downweighted to minimize their impact on results. This procedure has several advantages. First, while the researcher can choose a tuning parameter, there is much less leeway for a researcher to "experiment" with different approaches to yield a desired result. Second, outliers are identified not solely because they are extreme values but rather because their *correlation* with other observations is unusual. The outliers identified by Huber regressions may therefore differ quite a bit from those that would be picked out by censoring or winsorizing around some threshold. More generally, Huber regressions provide a tractable approach to dealing with outliers that minimizes the influence of the researcher.[1]

External Validity

When presenting research utilizing an RCT with an information treatment, one of the most common questions that will be asked is, "What if you ran the same experiment in a different place and at a different time, would you expect the same results to hold?" This is an excellent question about the external validity of the experiment and one that should never be dismissed.

There are at least three strategies for characterizing the external validity of an information experiment. The first is to utilize results on heterogeneous treatment effects to draw implications for what might happen in other settings. The absence of heterogeneity is at least suggestive that the results would also hold in other settings. If, instead, the results are being driven by a specific subset of the respondents, with the others responding differently, then this is suggestive that in a different context where the pool of respondents might be different, the results could vary in a predictable way. The second strategy is to use theory to infer how well the results could hold in other settings. Because information treatments can sometimes be mapped to theoretical models of expectations formation and these models may make predictions about the nature of expectations and when they change, the combination of theory and

1. The reader interested in learning more about robust methods in econometrics is referred to Maronna et al. (2019).

experiments can be used to speculate in an informed manner about other settings.

The third and most direct strategy is to try to answer the question directly by running identical information treatments in different settings or different periods. A prominent example of this is the insightful paper by Cavallo, Cruces and Perez-Truglia (2017). They applied a nearly identical information treatment in Argentina and the U.S. In both countries, households were surveyed about their inflation expectations and a randomized information treatment was done in which a subset of households was provided with information about recent inflation. In the U.S., the authors found that the information treatment had a very powerful effect on expectations, much like what is documented in Figure 6.3. In Argentina, in contrast, they found no meaningful effect of the information on inflation expectations. Cavallo, Cruces and Perez-Truglia (2017) argued that this most likely reflected the different attention that households paid to inflation. In the low-inflation U.S., households were inattentive to and uninformed about inflation, so providing them with recent inflation statistics could meaningfully affect their inflation expectations. In Argentina, where inflation was high and volatile, households were keeping track of inflation statistics and therefore the information treatments were not providing them with new information. This suggested that there were limits to the external validity of the information treatment experiment: clearly the results could differ significantly across countries.

In a recent paper (Weber et al. 2025), we extended this argument by studying very similar information treatments done across many countries, but also within countries over time. Consider, for example, the case of the U.S. Figure 6.3 documented that an information treatment involving the Fed's inflation target could have a very powerful effect on the inflation expectations of U.S. households, which is similar to the finding in Cavallo, Cruces and Perez-Truglia (2017). What happens if we could rerun a similar information treatment in the U.S. over time, especially as the inflation rate spiked in 2021–2022? Because we had been running repeated surveys of households in the Nielsen Homescan Panel and had included the same information treatment in a number of different waves, we were able to explore whether information treatments within a country varied as the inflation environment changed.

Figure 6.5 plots the estimated treatment effects, measured as γ_j / δ using specification (3), over the different survey waves that included some of the same information treatments. Prior to the inflation spike of 2021, we see that treatment effects were consistently large. Repeating the same experiment at

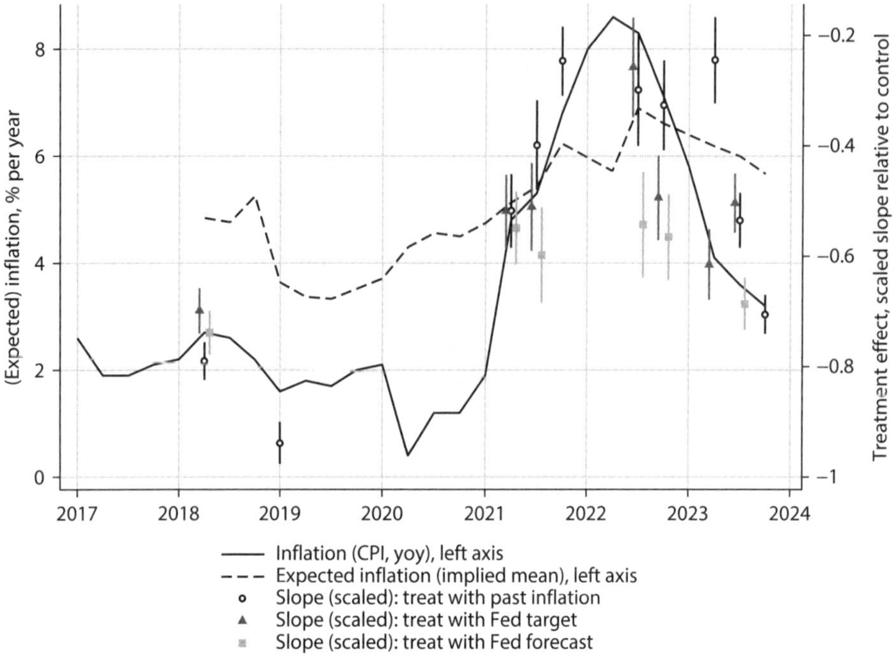

FIGURE 6.5. Treatment effects by survey wave.
Notes: The figure shows the time series of actual and expected inflation in the U.S. as well as estimated treatment effects (the scaled slopes) for various treatments across RCTs. The whiskers show the 90% confidence intervals.
Source: Weber et al. (2025).

different periods in which the economic environment was broadly comparable led to the same results, pointing toward external validity of the experiment. But when the inflation rate spiked, the estimated treatment effects fell sharply in absolute value: providing the same kind of information to U.S. households no longer seemed to have any meaningful effect on their expectations, much as Cavallo, Cruces and Perez-Truglia had found in Argentina!

The study provides evidence from other settings and other agents as well. Using data from the Business Inflation Expectations (BIE) survey, we also found that the effect of information treatments on U.S. firms fell in absolute value following the inflation surge, albeit with a lot more statistical uncertainty due to much smaller sample sizes. In the Euro area, the same patterns could be found for households, using repeated information treatments in the ECB's Consumer Expectations Survey, and for firms, using the fact that some firms were repeatedly provided with information in the Bank of Italy's Survey of

Income and Growth Expectations. In contrast, repeated information treatments in a country that had consistently low inflation (New Zealand) yielded consistently large treatment effects while repeated treatments in a country that had consistently high inflation (Uruguay) yielded consistently small treatment effects. In every case, low inflation environments were associated with large treatment effects while high inflation environments were associated with small treatment effects.

This corroborates the earlier findings of Cavallo, Cruces and Perez-Truglia (2017), demonstrating that the economic environment plays an important role in determining how information treatments may affect expectations. This is good news for the external validity of this approach in the sense that, as long as the economic environment is comparable, similar treatments in different countries or periods lead to very similar treatment effects. But when economic environments change, so do treatment effects.

Summary

Information treatments can provide a powerful tool to change the economic expectations of individuals in a way that is measurable, informative and often relevant for policy. While there are some practical issues that arise in their design, implementation and analysis, these are far from insurmountable. Furthermore, the results often seem to hold up well when replicated in other settings, as long as those settings are broadly comparable. Clearly different environments can lead to clearly different results. With these methodological points in mind, we now turn to some lessons that have been learned from the growing body of work applying randomized information treatments to the study of expectations and policy communication.

7

What Have Information Treatments Taught Us about Policy Communication?

INFORMATION TREATMENTS have been applied to many areas of economics to study how expectations respond to different pieces of information, but one of the most active areas of research involves the scope for policy communication to affect beliefs and ultimately the decisions of households and firms. In this chapter, we review some of the main findings from this literature, focusing in particular on monetary policy communication, which has been one of the most active areas of research, but also considering lessons for communication about fiscal policy, financial stability, the COVID19 pandemic and education policy.

Lessons about Monetary Policy Communication

Financial markets hang on every word uttered by central bankers around the world. A wrong sentence can lead to wild swings in asset prices, as during the "taper tantrum" initiated by then Fed Chair Bernanke's discussion of the possibility of reversing quantitative easing. Press conferences are often broadcast alongside tick-by-tick changes in stock markets, which seem to respond in real time to not just the language monetary policymakers use but even their tone and facial expressions (Gorodnichenko, Pham and Talavera 2022, Curti and Kazinnik 2023, Alexopoulos et al. 2024). In contrast, the response of households and firms to monetary policy decisions seems to be much more muted. For example, Lamla and Vinogradov (2019) studied changes in daily household measures of inflation expectations around U.S. monetary policy announcements and found no response. Even large policy changes often go unnoticed by households and firms. Only about a third of U.S. households were aware of the very large and rapid interest rate cuts made in March 2020 by the Federal Reserve in response to the COVID19 pandemic, despite widespread news coverage about them at the time (Binder 2020). When the Federal Reserve announced a major change in strategy in August 2020, switching to Flexible Average Inflation Targeting, that also went largely unnoticed by the U.S. public (Coibion et al. 2023). Things seem to be no better in Europe, where even some large policy changes by the ECB had no effect on the expectations of German firms (Enders, Hünnekes and Müller 2019). While recent work has been able to find that some households and firms respond to policy announcements at high frequency (see, e.g., Lewis, Makridis and Mertens 2020, Binder, Campbell and Ryngaert 2024, De Fiore, Lombardi and Schuffels 2019, and Yotzov et al. 2024), the main takeaway from this line of research remains the striking disconnect between how attentive financial markets are to monetary policy compared to how inattentive households and firms seem to be.

A by-product of this inattention is that when even simple messages about inflation or monetary policy do reach the public, they can have powerful effects on beliefs. In Chapter 6, for example, we described results from Coibion, Gorodnichenko and Weber (2022a) showing that when U.S. households learned about the Fed's inflation forecast or the inflation target in 2018, their inflation expectations declined by up to 2 percentage points on average. Binder and Rodrigue (2018) estimated a similar effect on long-run inflation expectations of U.S. households. This pattens holds for other advanced economies. For instance, Coibion, Gorodnichenko and Kumar (2018) found the same orders of magnitudes for firms in New Zealand, while Nghiem, Dalloul, and Dräger (2024) documented strong effects on inflation expectations from providing central bank forecasts to German households.

These large effects of information on the economic expectations of households and firms have several potential implications. One, related to economic theory, is that these point toward rejections of full-information rational expectations (FIRE), as we discuss in more detail in the next chapter. Another more practical implication is that there is scope for monetary policy communication to shape the expectations of households and firms in important ways. Given that central banks were constrained by the zero lower bound on nominal interest rates for much of the last 20 years, the power of these simple information treatments suggests that communication with the public—households and firms—could provide another arrow in the quiver of monetary policymakers as they attempt to stabilize economic conditions. To successfully communicate with the public, however, central banks need to be aware of a number of caveats that may hamper the success of their strategies (Coibion et al. 2020).

Reaching the public

Since central banks first deliberately began to try to communicate with the broader public in the 1990s, their recipe for doing so has been simple: release some form of communication and wait for the media to distribute it more broadly. While this approach is successful with financial markets, which anxiously await every central bank release or statement, it clearly leaves much to be desired for the general public. Why is this communication strategy so ineffective? First, the media primarily reports what will draw the public's attention (you never read about a plane that did not crash!), so other more pressing news such as celebrity weddings, sporting events or political scandals can easily crowd out news coverage of central bank decisions. Second, even if the news media report on the policy decisions, the coverage may have a limited impact because many individuals no longer rely on traditional news sources. Third, on the off chance that someone reads a news article about policy decisions, they may choose to disregard the information.

An example of the latter was shown in Coibion, Gorodnichenko and Weber (2022a). As discussed before, this paper studied the effect of providing news about recent inflation, the Federal Reserve's inflation target and the Fed's inflation forecast on the inflation expectations of households, documenting powerful effects of these treatments on beliefs. But we also included some other information treatments aiming to characterize how different forms of the same information might lead to larger or smaller effects on beliefs. One such treatment provided the entire FOMC statement for households to read, full of jargon and Fed-speak (Alan Greenspan, a former Fed Chair, once described it as "mumbling with great incoherence"). This treatment had the same effect on expectations as simpler treatments, although it was communicated in a much more complicated manner but also included far more information. Another treatment provided a news article covering that same policy statement from a national nonpartisan newspaper, *USA Today*, which used much more accessible language to describe the same information. Surprisingly, this information treatment had a much *smaller* effect on expectations than either the simple information treatments or the one providing the entire FOMC statement. The reason seemed to be that many individuals viewed newspapers as unreliable sources of information and therefore dismissed the information, consistent with the old quip from Mark Twain: "If you don't read the paper, you're uninformed. If you read the newspaper, you're misinformed."

If not through the traditional news media, then how are central banks supposed to reach the general public? One approach is through social media, which many individuals perceive as far more reliable than traditional news media. Indeed, many central banks now run active social media accounts, but these can reach only those individuals who actively choose to follow these accounts or adjacent feeds. The scope of this strategy can be increased by utilizing influencers and others with large social media followings, paying social media providers to expand coverage of messages from central banks, and using forms of communication (such as visuals) that are more likely to draw the attention of viewers (Haldane and McMahon 2018, Bholat et al. 2019). A creative implementation of this approach is from the Central Bank of Jamaica, which used reggae music to describe its inflation target. Another example is from the Federal Reserve Bank of Cleveland, which has developed animated videos that explain inflation and central banks. Yet another approach would be to follow the example of public health campaigns. Many governments have long and quite successful histories of public health information campaigns such as against smoking, relying on information campaigns using public billboards, magazine ads, and other media. Regardless of the approach, achieving the outcomes observed in information treatments requires being able to reach the general public without relying exclusively on traditional news coverage, a step that most central banks are far from successfully taking.

Communicating about targets or instruments

One immediate question that arises from thinking about how to communicate policy decisions is whether the communication should focus on what was decided (the "instrument") or what the policy aims to achieve (the "target"). In the case of central banking, the answer unambiguously is that central banks should focus on communicating about the target when it comes to the general public. Those who have studied the effects of information treatments involving information about interest rates have generally found little pass-through of this information into inflation expectations (Coibion et al. 2023) or house price expectations (Binder, Kuang, and Tang 2023). This is likely because many individuals do not have a clear understanding of how monetary policy decisions affect the real economy. Andre et al. (2022a) illustrated this most clearly when they asked households what they thought would happen after an unexpected increase in interest rates, which yielded widespread disagreement on whether inflation would rise or fall as well as on how unemployment and production would react. In contrast, statements about the intended aim of policy tend to be much more powerful (D'Acunto et al. 2020).

Is guidance about future policy effective?

Monetary policy has increasingly become about the communication of the expected future path of interest rates (Swanson 2021). This serves to minimize financial instability as well as to increase the power of monetary policy since statements about the future path of interest rates can have large immediate effects on long-term interest rates, which ultimately feed through into the decisions of households and firms. Is communication about future policies also powerful in shaping the expectations of households and firms? The answer seems to be largely no. In Coibion et al. (2023), for example, we used 18 different information treatments that provided paths of future interest rates and varied the horizon and levels of these projected paths. Despite the wide variation in interest rate paths across different treatments, there was little variation in how future interest rates affected households' expectations. Similar results emerge from experiments in the lab (Kryvtsov and Petersen 2021). While forward guidance can still be partly effective through its transmission via financial market variables, the strong theoretically predicted effect of communicating about future policies on the expectations of households and firms does not materialize in practice. To affect the beliefs of the general public, policymakers are likely to be better off focusing on statements that emphasize their commitment to returning the economy to targeted levels, rather than on extensive discussions of the future policy steps needed to achieve this objective.

One-time statements or communication campaigns?

To shape beliefs of households and firms, is it enough to surprise them with a new announcement, or do policymakers need to engage in a repeated communication campaign? The answer depends on the extent to which new information about inflation or monetary policy is retained by households and firm managers. Information treatments are exceptionally adept at answering this question when participants are repeatedly surveyed, allowing researchers to study how long new information is reflected in their beliefs. When it comes to monetary policy or inflation, the answer seems to be: not very long. For example, among U.S. households participating in the Nielsen Homescan Panel, the effects of information treatments about inflation and monetary policy are very large on impact, small after three months, and largely dissipated after six months. In other words, six months after the information treatment, one can no longer distinguish between the beliefs of the control and the treated households. Other information treatments that have studied the effects of monetary policy communication have found broadly similar timelines. For example, in Coibion, Gorodnichenko and Kumar (2018), we found that the effects of information treatments on firms in New Zealand had largely dissipated after six months, as was the case with firms in Italy in Coibion, Gorodnichenko and Ropele (2020).

The implication is that to successfully and persistently change the beliefs of households and firms, policymakers need to pursue communication *campaigns*, much like public health campaigns. Information needs to be seen repeatedly and regularly by the public for it to be fully incorporated into their beliefs in the long run. One-time policy announcements should not be expected to have more than a transitory impact, if any, on expectations and decisions. Repetition is the mother not only of learning, but also of communication.

Does one size fit all in communication with the public?

It is now well understood by most central banks that communicating with financial markets and communicating with the public are two different things requiring separate strategies. The Bank of England, for example, uses a layered approach to its communication that includes a visual summary targeted toward the general public as part of its more technical Inflation Report. But recent work has emphasized that, even within the general public, a multifaceted approach is likely to be more successful because of the vast heterogeneity in the understanding, the prior knowledge and the interest of the public when it comes to monetary policy.

In particular, there are three tiers that require differentiation. The first is in terms of reaching the target audience. As already discussed, there are individuals who will be easy to reach via *The Wall Street Journal*, but some will be more likely to access the news via social media, and others will require yet different modes. So there has to be a wide range of methods used to reach the general public. The second is in terms of who is cast as presenting the message. D'Acunto, Fuster and Weber (2021) documented that some individuals are more receptive to information coming from women, whereas others are more susceptible to information coming from minorities. Thus, it is helpful to have different messengers of the same information. The third is about the way in which the information is provided. Much as some students learn economic concepts better through visual methods, whereas others need to see the algebra, communication about monetary policy can be formulated in terms of figures, numbers, statements, or even songs. Employing different ways of presenting the same information is likely to be helpful in reaching a broader audience (Haldane, Macaulay, and McMahon 2021, Dräger and Nghiem 2023). For example, Ash et al. (2024) document how the combined use of both audio and visual media improves the transmission of central bank communications to less-informed households. Bholat et al. (2019) argue that simplifying messages can further improve transmission of central bank messaging, over and above the choice of medium. Varying how the message is promoted can therefore help policymakers reach a broader audience.

Be mindful of unintended consequences

Policy is not made in a vacuum, nor are economic variables independent objects. When policy aims to, say, "anchor" inflation expectations by telling households or firms about recent economic developments, the new information may change the underlying economic narrative that individuals perceive, leading them to change more than just their inflation expectations. This "cross-learning" is particularly relevant with macroeconomic information treatments. Because macroeconomic variables are driven by underlying forces that affect many outcomes jointly, changing the beliefs of an individual about one area may induce them to change their other economic expectations as well. And as emphasized in Andre et al. (2022a), households and firms may hold very different beliefs than experts about the way in which economic conditions evolve or the ways in which different macroeconomic variables respond to a common shock.

This is particularly clear in the case of inflation. While experts typically view inflation as positively correlated with economic activity, households around the world strongly associate inflation with bad economic times (Shiller 1997, Kamdar 2019, Stantcheva 2024). An example of this in the RCT setting can again be found in Coibion, Gorodnichenko and Weber (2022a), in which one information treatment was to provide U.S. households with the latest unemployment numbers. Because most households were overestimating the rate of unemployment, the treatment led them to lower their forecasts of unemployment. At the same time, they significantly *reduced* their inflation forecasts even though the treatments were only about unemployment.

Cross-learning can be an issue because how individuals ultimately respond to the new information will depend on all of the changes in their beliefs, not just the channel targeted by the treatment. For example, an information treatment could raise the inflation expectations of a consumer, leading them to spend more today in the anticipation of higher prices in the future (the intertemporal substitution channel); but if the same treatment also raises their beliefs about future unemployment risk, this force could lead them to reduce their spending today (an income effect channel), making the expected effect of the information treatment on spending a priori ambiguous (Candia 2024). Relatedly, higher inflation expectations can increase macroeconomic uncertainty, thus inhibiting consumer spending (Coibion et al. 2024). Cross-learning can blunt policy effectiveness in other ways. For instance, raising inflation expectations can lead the public to raise their expectations of nominal interest rates so that the net effect on the real interest rate is reduced, which would further diminish the stimulatory effects of higher inflation expectations (Coibion et al. 2023). To avoid counterproductive cross-learning effects, communication should be holistic and emphasize the broader message that policymakers are trying to achieve.

Summary of monetary policy communication lessons

Our takeaway from the extensive literature on monetary policy communication is that there is much promise for improvement in this area in the future, which could significantly help policymaking in times when it is otherwise constrained. But there are a number of practical challenges that need to be surmounted for this strategy to succeed. Developing a successful monetary policy communication campaign will not be feasible at the time it is most needed if the groundwork for it has not been laid ahead of time. It is therefore important for central banks to use non-crisis times to prepare themselves, and the public, for those occasions when communication tools could be most effectively used.

Lessons about Fiscal Policy Communication

In macroeconomic models, how fiscal policy is communicated can be just as important as how monetary policy is communicated. Indeed, whether it is monetary or fiscal policy that is the primary actor that serves to stabilize debt in the long run has been predicted to be a crucial determinant of macroeconomic dynamics (e.g., Leeper 2010). Fiscal decisions have implications beyond current levels of taxation and the provision of government benefits. Because government spending ultimately has to be paid for over time by individuals through taxes or monetization, beliefs about the future evolution of fiscal policy should be an important determinant of private saving behavior.

At the heart of fiscal policy is the government's intertemporal budget balance, which says that the present discounted value of current and future spending must equal the present discounted value of tax payments and interest payments on existing debt. Because debt, spending, taxes, interest rates and inflation are tied together through this intertemporal budget constraint, cross-learning should be at the heart of fiscal policy communication. When increases in current and future government spending are announced, individuals should anticipate that this spending will ultimately be paid for either by offsets in spending in the future, higher future taxes, higher future inflation or some combination thereof. The specific way in which they expect this spending to be paid for should in principle also affect their current decisions since, for example, an expectation of higher future taxes should lead them to start saving more today to pay for the future tax burden.

To what extent do individuals adjust their beliefs in response to fiscal policy conditions? Or maybe, to paraphrase President Ronald Reagan, are people not concerned about the fiscal deficit because it is big enough to take care of itself? Unlike with monetary policy communication, there is very limited existing evidence on how households or firms adjust their beliefs, if at all, to news about the fiscal outlook. One exception is Coibion, Gorodnichenko and Weber (2021), in which we applied fiscal information treatments to U.S. households. The paper focused on beliefs about the fiscal outlook over the next ten years, and how these beliefs changed in response to information about either current fiscal/monetary conditions or *future* fiscal conditions, thereby identifying the channels through which households expected fiscal balance to be sustained over time.

We applied six different information treatments. Two involved telling respondents about either the existing U.S. federal budget balance or the U.S.

government debt level. Another presented information about the current interest rate on government debt. The other three treatments were forward-looking in nature. One provided the Congressional Budget Office's (CBO's) projected inflation rate over the next ten years. Another treatment included the CBO's projected *change* in the size of the national debt over the next ten years. The final treatment told individuals the projected *level* of the national debt in ten years by the CBO. Respondents were then asked about their expectations about future spending, tax and debt levels in ten years relative to existing levels, as well as what they expected would be the inflation rate over the next ten years and what the interest rate would be in ten years.

Due to space constraints at the time, we elicited only posterior beliefs in the survey. As a result, we were restricted to estimating average treatment effects using specification (1) shown in Chapter 6. This greatly limited the set of questions that we could ultimately answer. This was a useful lesson for us about the choice of questions to include. Ex post, we regretted including some tangential questions and not eliciting priors instead.

In Table 7.1, we first report the average beliefs for these variables for the control group from Huber (1964) robust regressions. Untreated respondents on average expected an inflation rate of almost 4% in the next year but only 15% cumulative inflation over the next decade. In terms of fiscal beliefs, they expected both spending and revenues to rise relative to current levels, but for spending to increase by more, leading them to expect higher debt. When told about either the current deficit or the current government debt level, they did not, on average, change their beliefs about inflation or the fiscal outlook over the next ten years, indicating that this information was viewed as reflecting transitory budget factors that did not meaningfully affect the longer-run fiscal outlook.

When told about the CBO's projected inflation outlook, households revised their inflation expectations toward the treatment: they reduced their short-run inflation forecast but raised their long-run inflation forecast toward the CBO levels. Importantly, we did not find any change in expected fiscal indicators over the next ten years. This was notable because, under an active monetary policy regime, fiscal policy should be accommodating the change in monetary policy required to achieve this inflation rate, thereby leading to a changing fiscal balance. But individual expectations did not change in a way consistent with this type of regime.

In contrast, with the future fiscal outlook treatments (T4 and T6), there were more pronounced changes in both the fiscal and the inflation outlooks

TABLE 7.1. Treatment effects on levels of expected inflation and fiscal indicators.

	Inflation expectations		Fiscal indicators in 10 years			
	12-month ahead	10-year ahead, cumulative	Spending, % relative to current level	Revenue, % relative to current level	Debt, % relative to current level	Interest rate
	(1)	(2)	(3)	(4)	(5)	(6)
Control group	3.848***	15.361***	23.018***	13.660***	21.189***	7.490***
	(0.058)	(0.295)	(0.422)	(0.315)	(0.424)	(0.140)
Treatment effects relative to control						
T1 (current deficit)	0.035	−0.319	−0.821	0.296	0.788	−0.226
	(0.083)	(0.411)	(0.587)	(0.443)	(0.593)	(0.198)
T2 (current debt)	0.013	0.132	−0.043	0.453	0.399	0.218
	(0.083)	(0.419)	(0.599)	(0.448)	(0.598)	(0.200)
T3 (current interest rate)	−0.344***	−0.153	−0.290	0.370	0.630	−1.186***
	(0.077)	(0.416)	(0.589)	(0.450)	(0.597)	(0.186)
T4 (debt projection, change)	0.249***	1.018**	0.989*	0.070	2.503***	0.135
	(0.084)	(0.426)	(0.597)	(0.452)	(0.607)	(0.202)
T5 (inflation projection)	−0.366***	1.361***	0.948	0.396	0.531	0.022
	(0.079)	(0.416)	(0.597)	(0.446)	(0.602)	(0.200)
T6 (debt projection, level)	0.359***	1.284***	1.121*	1.699***	2.893***	0.410**
	(0.087)	(0.430)	(0.593)	(0.455)	(0.607)	(0.202)
Observations	21,217	19,741	23,795	23,377	23,414	22,936
R-squared	0.006	0.002	0.001	0.001	0.002	0.004

Notes: The table reports estimates of specification (1) in Chapter 6 for inflation expectations and fiscal indicators as the dependent variables. Inflation expectations are measured as point predictions. Coefficients for groups other than the control group are relative to the coefficient for the control group. All estimates are based on Huber (1964) robust regressions. Regressions use sampling weights. The samples for inflation expectation regressions are restricted to respondents reporting nonnegative inflation expectations in the pre-treatment responses. Robust standard errors are in parentheses. ***, **, and * denote statistical significance at 1, 5, and 10 percent levels. See Coibion, Gorodnichenko and Weber (2021) for more details.

for the future. When individuals learned that future debt levels were projected to be higher than what they expected, they raised their forecasts of the future debt levels toward the projection, but they also raised their expected levels of future spending, which indicates that they attributed the higher levels of projected debt to higher spending on the part of the government. In both cases, they also significantly increased their long-run inflation expectations, indicating that they expected part of the debt increase to be monetized over this period. This is what one would expect from a regime of fiscal dominance, where the central bank is forced to accommodate a changing fiscal outlook, consistent with Bianchi, Faccini and Melosi, (2023). Andrade et al. (2025) found similar results for European households.

This experiment is at best a first pass at identifying some of the ways in which expectations vary with the fiscal outlook, but it is already suggestive that this outlook can matter for more than just fiscal expectations. There are many interesting open questions that follow. For example, how important are wealth effects from changes in government debt (Barro 1974), how sensitive are decisions to fiscal expectations, how much is political ideology a factor in explaining observable differences in fiscal outlooks? Another more practical implication is to the use of sunset provisions in U.S. tax reforms, a strategy in which tax changes are slated to expire within ten years to minimize the number of votes required to pass them. If individuals are very forward-looking with respect to budget decisions, the use of such provisions may not be innocuous given their economic implications. Using a natural experiment, Bachmann et al. (2021) studied a related application in Germany when fiscal authorities passed a future increase in the value-added tax (VAT), which fueled an increase in inflation expectations prior to the tax increase being put in place and a concurrent increase in consumer spending. A better understanding of such open questions would allow economists to be able to think more carefully about a number of interesting topics, such as the design of fiscal communication strategies.

Lessons about Other Policy Communication

Of course, policymaking extends to many areas beyond monetary and fiscal issues, even in macroeconomics. We now consider two such areas to which information treatments have been applied: bank runs and the COVID19 pandemic.

Bank runs

The year 2023 was shaped by an unusual economic event in the U.S.: a run on a large traditional bank, Silicon Valley Bank (SVB), which caused widespread concern that the entire banking system could be at risk. This led to explicit statements by both the Federal Reserve and the president that the U.S. banking system was safe, in an attempt to forestall further withdrawals by individual and corporate depositors. Shortly after this experience, we ran a survey of U.S. households designed to study their confidence in the U.S. banking system, their knowledge about recent bank failures, and their sensitivity to policy communications implemented to alleviate the instability in the banking system, as described in Sandri et al. (2023).

Despite the survey being run shortly after the highly publicized failure of SVB, we found that most U.S. households were unaware of any distress in the banking system and broadly viewed it as quite safe. They tended to view their own bank as even safer than the broader banking system and furthermore expected some form of guarantee of their deposits in case of failure, generally even beyond the FDIC insurance limit. However, when told about the SVB failure in a randomized information treatment, retail depositors became more likely to withdraw their deposits.

In Sandri et al. (2023), we considered three communication interventions through information treatments to assess how much these interventions could offset the increased banking risk associated with learning about SVB's collapse. One was a description of the FDIC insurance on individual accounts. This communication about FDIC insurance effectively offset the higher perceived risk from the SVB collapse, as respondents who were told about the existence of FDIC insurance reduced their expected loss in case their bank failed. A second treatment involved being provided with the Federal Reserve's statement on the stability of the U.S. banking system. Like the FDIC treatment, receiving information about the Fed's communication offset the higher risk from the SVB failure, in this case by reducing the probability that depositors assigned to their bank failing in the future.

The third treatment came from President Biden, who had asserted that Americans should have confidence that the banking system was safe. In contrast to the other communications, this treatment had much less power on average in offsetting the perceived risk of bank failures. Why? We found that, among Biden's electoral base, the treatment was quite effective, just as effective as the Federal Reserve and FDIC statements. But amongst others, Biden's words held little comfort and failed to offset any of the greater perceived banking risk following SVB's collapse. This provides another illustration of how the source of the message can be important for the power of communication, particularly when it comes to messages from elected officials.

Communication during the COVID19 pandemic

The COVID19 pandemic provides another setting in which policymakers actively tried communicating with the public along a number of dimensions, providing guidance about health risks and precautions as well as about their economic policy responses to the crisis. The potential effectiveness of these policy communications was studied in Coibion, Gorodnichenko and Weber (2022b). In this paper, we used another survey wave of Nielsen Homescan panelists, conducted in April 2020 at the onset of the pandemic in the U.S., to assess how communication from policymakers about COVID19 and their responses to it affected beliefs during this unique time period.

The paper utilized one control group and nine treatment groups with roughly 1,500 respondents per treatment arm. One treatment involved providing information from the World Health Organization about the transmission risk of the virus, which was significantly lower than what most respondents believed at the time. As a result, this treatment generated an exogenous decrease in the perceived risk associated with the pandemic. When looking at respondents' economic expectations after the treatment, we found little difference relative to beliefs in the control group, indicating that individuals' economic expectations, both for the aggregate economy and for their own economic situation, were not very sensitive to their perceived pandemic risk. Because macroeconomic expectations worsened sharply during the pandemic overall, these results indicate that the increased pessimism about the outlook was not driven by the pandemic itself but likely by related policy actions like lockdowns and stay-at-home restrictions.

Another set of treatments involved providing a description of Congressional fiscal actions (e.g., stimulus checks), reductions in interest rates by the Federal Reserve, a combination of the two, or government recommendations regarding social distancing and the prevalence of shelter restrictions. These treatments were done individually or in combination with the health information about the transmission risk of the virus. These combinations allowed us to study the marginal effects of policy decisions, with and without the health information. In short, we found that none of the treatments had economically significant effects on either the macroeconomic or the microeconomic expectations of respondents.

How do we interpret the absence of treatment effects in this context? One possible explanation could be that respondents were already aware of the information. But in the case of the health information treatment (for which we could measure prior informedness), this was far from true. And it seems unlikely that respondents would be familiar with all the policy responses. Another interpretation could be that respondents were skeptical of the provided information and therefore ignored it when forming expectations; but since this is the same setting in which we had previously found large treatment effects in Coibion, Gorodnichenko and Weber (2022a), this seems unlikely as well. Instead, the most likely interpretation is "information" effects: learning about large policy responses made respondents think that conditions must be worse than they previously thought, yielding largely offsetting effects on expectations. While well known (and debated) in the context of monetary policy decisions (e.g. Nakamura and Steinsson 2018a, Bauer and Swanson 2023), these results suggest that information effects can be pervasive and avoiding them may require communications that more sharply separate underlying conditions and what policy responses are expected to achieve.

Summary

Information treatments are actively being used to study a variety of topics, with the potential effectiveness of policy communication being a particularly important application. Much has already been learned, especially with respect to monetary policymaking, but there continue to be open areas of research, especially when it comes to fiscal policy and financial stability. With the growing availability of surveys, especially ones that allow for the randomized provision of information, more progress is on the way.

8

Mapping Information Treatments into Theories of Learning

INFORMATION TREATMENTS can provide sharp evidence of changes in beliefs in response to new pieces of information. Can these changes in beliefs help us understand how to model the learning process of individuals? In this chapter, we focus on how one can map estimated information treatment effects into models of learning. We begin by focusing on Bayesian learning with an exogenous signal structure and describe some testable predictions that stem from this framework. While much can be explained within this simple framework, some key results in the literature cannot. We consider three such results in more detail and describe theoretical models that can better make sense of the results. A key takeaway is that it is important to model the endogenous nature of the information acquisition problem of economic agents to better understand the characteristics of estimated information treatment effects.

Simple Bayesian Learning

We begin by considering the Bayesian learning problem formalized in Cavallo, Cruces and Perez-Truglia (2017), who studied the updating of inflation expectations of households in the U.S. and Argentina. In their experiment, households in each country were provided with information about recent aggregate inflation π_t to assess how they update their beliefs about future inflation in response. The starting point is to imagine a continuum of households that hold prior beliefs about recent inflation given by π_{it}^{prior}, where i denotes the individual household and t denotes the time period. The uncertainty around that prior belief is given by σ_{it}^{prior}, which is the standard deviation of the distribution of subjective expectations for household i. For now, we take these prior beliefs as given.

Some agents are presented with a signal about underlying inflation, which is given by $s_t = \pi_t + \varepsilon_t$, where ε_t is a random variable that is normally distributed with mean zero and standard deviation σ_{st}, that is, $\varepsilon_t \sim N(0, \sigma_{st}^2)$. The inverse of the standard deviation squared can be thought of as the precision of the signal. When the standard deviation is zero, the signal is perfectly precise. If an agent updates its beliefs using Bayesian learning, its posterior belief about recent inflation π_{it}^{post} will be given by

$$\pi_{it}^{post} = \frac{(\sigma_{it}^{prior})^{-2}}{(\sigma_{it}^{prior})^{-2} + (\sigma_{st})^{-2}} \pi_{it}^{prior} + \frac{(\sigma_{st})^{-2}}{(\sigma_{it}^{prior})^{-2} + (\sigma_{st})^{-2}} s_t, \tag{1}$$

and their posterior uncertainty about that belief will be

$$(\sigma_{it}^{post})^2 = \frac{(\sigma_{it}^{prior})^2 (\sigma_{st})^2}{(\sigma_{it}^{prior})^2 + (\sigma_{st})^2}. \tag{2}$$

Noting that the coefficients in the first expression sum to 1, we can rewrite the belief updating rule as:

$$\pi_{it}^{post} = (1 - G_i) \times \pi_{it}^{prior} + G_i \times s_t, \tag{3}$$

where G is the Kalman gain given by $G_i = \frac{(\sigma_{st})^{-2}}{(\sigma_{it}^{prior})^{-2} + (\sigma_{st})^{-2}}$. Intuitively, the Kalman gain captures how much weight agents put on incoming information.

Equation (3) describes how agents' beliefs about recent inflation evolve in response to the signal. It states that their posterior belief is a weighted average of their prior belief and the signal provided to them. The weight they assign to the new information relative to their prior belief is increasing in the precision of the signal and increasing in their prior uncertainty. Thus, agents should tend to respond more to new information when that information is perceived as more precise and reliable, as well as when they are more uncertain initially about their prior beliefs.

To see how this relates directly to information treatment experiments, note that these experiments typically include a control group, to which no signal or information is provided, and a treatment group, to which a common signal is provided. For individuals who are in the control group, their posteriors should be equal to their priors: $\pi_{it}^{post} = \pi_{it}^{prior}$ if i is in the control group. Those in the treatment group update their beliefs according to (3). If we define an indicator variable $\mathbb{I}(i \in T)$ equal to 1 if an individual is in the treatment group and 0 otherwise, the updating rule can be written more generally as:

$$\pi_{it}^{post} = (1 - \mathbb{I}(i \in T)) \times \pi_{it}^{prior} + \mathbb{I}(i \in T) \times [(1-G) \times \pi_{it}^{prior} + G \times s_t]. \quad (4)$$

Or equivalently:

$$\pi_{it}^{post} = \pi_{it}^{prior} + G \times s_t \times \mathbb{I}(i \in T) - G \times \pi_{i,t}^{prior} \times \mathbb{I}(i \in T). \quad (5)$$

Recall that the preferred empirical specification described in Chapter 6 to estimate information treatment effects was given by:

$$posterior_i = \alpha + \delta \times prior_i + \beta \times \mathbb{I}(i \in T) + \gamma \times \mathbb{I}(i \in T) \times prior_i + error. \quad (6)$$

We can observe a clean mapping from the empirical specification to the theory, such that the predicted coefficients are as follows. First, α is the average difference between posteriors and priors of the control group, so it should be equal to zero. Second, $\delta = 1$ since for the control group, posteriors and priors should be the same. Third, $\beta = G \times s_t$ denotes the average level of the treatment that combines the weight assigned to new information (G) and the actual value of the signal provided in the treatment (s_t). Finally, we have $\gamma = -G$, which identifies (the negative of) the weight assigned to new information in the treatment group. Hence, estimating information treatments using specification (6) can recover the learning rate.

In practice, beliefs used in the estimation of (6) are commonly forward-looking expectations, not "nowcasts" or "backcasts." However, this does not generally pose any additional complications to the interpretation. To see this, suppose that, for example, forecasts are formed based on nowcasts such as $F_{it}\pi_{t+1} = \rho F_{it}\pi_t$, where ρ measures the persistence of inflation. If the signal is about current inflation, then equation (2) would become

$$F_{it}^{post} \pi_{t+1} = F_{it}^{prior} \pi_{t+1} + \left(\frac{G s_t}{\rho} \right) \times \mathbb{I}(i \in T) - G \times F_{it}\pi_{t+1} \times \mathbb{I}(i \in T). \quad (7)$$

The estimated γ would still identify the learning rate from the new information. Only the interpretation of the estimated β would change since it would now depend on the rate at which nowcasts map into forecasts, which is governed by ρ.

This clean mapping between learning rates and the estimated information treatment effect has been used extensively in the literature to characterize how rapidly new information is incorporated by individuals. Haaland, Roth and Wohlfart (2023) summarized learning rates from a wide range of papers and found that these differ enormously across studies, even for the same variable. For example, in the case of U.S. inflation, Armantier et al. (2016) estimated the household learning rate from treatments about professional forecasters of 0.39, whereas Cavallo, Cruces and Perez-Truglia (2017) concluded that the household learning rate from official inflation statistics was 0.84.

The simple learning model, while providing a transparent and tractable mapping to estimated treatment effects, implies that there are only two possible sources of variation in treatment effects: prior uncertainty and signal precision. Support for the first prediction is widespread but not universal. In the case of inflation expectations, Armantier et al. (2016), Cavallo, Cruces and Perez-Truglia (2017) and Coibion, Gorodnichenko and Kumar (2018) all found that more uncertain households and firms tend to respond more strongly to information about inflation than do those that are more confident in their beliefs. But in the case of housing prices (Armona et al. 2019) and labor market expectations (Conlon et al. 2018), no difference was found along this margin. Fuster et al. (2021)'s estimates even indicate that prior uncertainty is sometimes negatively related to learning. It is also difficult to explain large differences in learning rates across studies in terms of perceived precision or reliability of the signals. Some recent work has therefore considered additional forms of learning to help make sense of findings from estimated information treatments that are otherwise hard to reconcile with the simple model presented here.

Interpreting Variation in Treatment Effects across Inflation Environments

One factor that could be important in explaining differences in learning rates is the economic environment. In Weber et al. (2025), we explored how the inflation environment affects learning in information experiments. To do so, we combined very similar information treatments applied across time and countries. Figure 6.5 plotted the variation in information treatments found for U.S. households as the inflation rate went from being low and stable in the pre-COVID19 era to surging in 2021–2022. As the inflation rate rose, the estimated size of information treatments fell sharply in absolute value, indicating that U.S. households in 2022 were placing far less weight on provided information about recent inflation than they did in 2018 or 2019. This finding seems to hold more broadly: we documented similar variation in time for U.S. firms, as well as firms and households in the Euro area, over time. Furthermore, firms in Uruguay, which experienced consistently high inflation, never showed strong information treatment effects, whereas firms in New Zealand, over a long period during which inflation was consistently low, systematically responded very strongly to new information about inflation. These results are summarized in Figure 8.1.

In principle, many forces could be at work in explaining these different information treatment effects as the inflation environment changed. One is the volatility effect: if high inflation is volatile inflation, a rise in inflation could induce more attention on the part of agents, which could affect how they respond to treatments. A second force is that higher inflation affects either the benefit of information about inflation or the cost of acquiring information, either of which could alter the attentiveness of agents and their responses to new information. A third is that periods of higher inflation lead individuals to become less trusting of official statistics or the central bank, which could also potentially affect learning. Finally, higher inflation could alter the nature of the information that agents acquire, perhaps inducing them to rely less on available price signals and instead acquire public signals about aggregate conditions.

To formalize these potential channels, we consider a static rational inattention problem in the spirit of Sims (2003), in which individuals optimally decide what information about inflation to acquire. In this setting, agent i chooses signals S_i from a set of available Gaussian signals about π, denoted by S, and then rationally forms its posterior belief given the joint distribution of π and S_i, which is given by

$$\pi_i \equiv \mathbb{E}[\pi \mid S_i] = \mathrm{Cov}(\vec{S}_i', \pi) \,/\, \mathrm{Var}(\vec{S}_i)^{-1}\ \vec{S}_i, \tag{8}$$

where $\vec{S}_i \equiv \mathrm{vec}(S_i)$ is the vectorized version of the information set S_i. The rational inattention problem is determining what signals to acquire, subject to cognitive costs that limit the ability to process information. For example, households could theoretically process and track all of the prices that they face and pay in their daily lives, but because they face cognitive costs, in general they will choose to focus on a subset of the prices they encounter in their

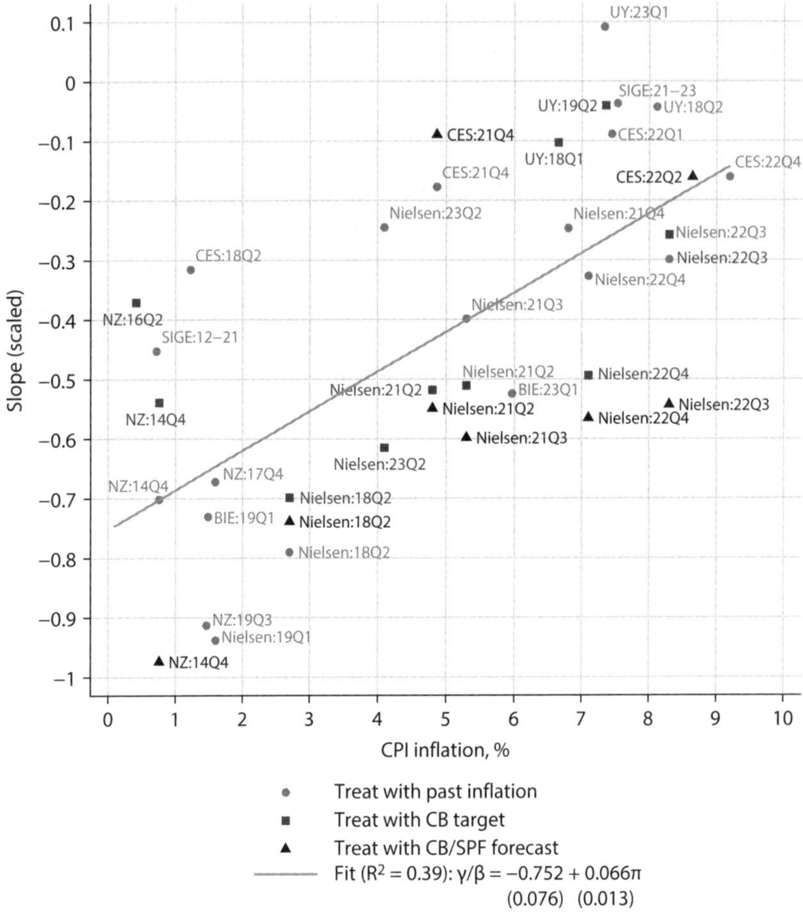

FIGURE 8.1. Inflation rate and the strength of the treatment effect.
Notes: The figure plots the estimated scaled slope effects vs. the annual rate of inflation at the time of the corresponding survey.
Source: Weber et al. (2025).

shopping experience to form inflation forecasts (D'Acunto et al. 2021, Coibion and Gorodnichenko 2015b). In addition to this standard rational inattention problem, we also allow for individuals to separately be able to purchase a preprocessed signal S_p, which is not subject to cognitive costs but comes at a fixed cost ϕ.[1] We think of this as the decision to acquire publicly available information about inflation.

1. Macroeconomic models are notorious for complexity and using nearly all Greek letters. So it is important to keep notation as intuitive as possible. For example, the

Given this setup, we can write the formal problem for these agents as follows:

$$\min\left\{\begin{array}{l}\phi+\min\limits_{S_p\subset S_i\subset\mathbb{S}}\left\{\frac{1}{2}B\mathrm{Var}(\pi\,|\,\vec{S}_i)+\omega I(\vec{S}_i;\pi\,|\,S_p)\right\},\\ \min\limits_{S_i\subset\mathbb{S}}\left\{\frac{1}{2}B\mathrm{Var}(\pi\,|\,\vec{S}_i)+\omega I(\vec{S}_i;\pi)\right\}\end{array}\right\}. \tag{9}$$

The second argument is where the agent chooses the signal structure $\vec{S}_i$ to minimize its uncertainty $\mathrm{Var}(\pi\,|\,\vec{S}_i)$ subject to the cost of processing information $\omega I(\vec{S}_i;\pi)$. As described in Maćkowiak, Matějka and Wiederholt (2023), the benefit of attention comes from the expectation of a quadratic loss under imperfect information, which reduces to the product of the uncertainty and the coefficient B summarizing the curvature of the payoff function. The cost of processing information is assumed to be linear in the reduction in entropy (i.e., distance) between the prior and the posterior distributions. The coefficient ω denotes the marginal cost of each unit of information that is processed. The first argument describes the rational inattention problem of the agent *if* they have chosen to first acquire (at the fixed cost ϕ) the preprocessed information denoted by $S_p=\pi+v_p$, where $v_p \sim N(0,\sigma^2_{v,p})$ is the noise in signal S_p and the noise is uncorrelated with π or S_i. The first min operator therefore represents the choice of whether or not to acquire S_p. When the fixed cost becomes very large ($\phi\to\infty$), then the agent never acquires S_p, and the problem reduces to the standard rational inattention decision.

For simplicity, we focus on the case when ω is sufficiently small so that agents always process some information, i.e., they never rely exclusively on preprocessed signal S_p or have an empty information set. In this case, agents will choose to acquire enough information such that

$$\mathrm{Var}(\pi\,|\,\vec{S}_i)=\frac{\omega}{B} \tag{10}$$

regardless of their choice over S_p (see Weber et al. 2025 for derivations). Hence, their uncertainty will depend exclusively on the cost-to-benefit ratio of acquiring new information at the margin. A larger benefit to acquiring information will lead them to choose to acquire more information and thereby reduce their uncertainty, as will be true when the cost of information falls. In contrast, a

Greek letter ϕ is pronounced in Greek as "fee." Hence, fixed costs (fees) are often denoted with ϕ.

change in the volatility of the inflation process itself will not affect the uncertainty of the agent.

The fact that the choice over S_p also does not matter indicates that the availability of the preprocessed signal does not ultimately change how confident the agent is. Instead, it acts as a substitute for some of the information that the agent would have acquired through their own signals. It therefore induces a *composition effect* in the information acquisition problem, but not a change in total information acquisition, which is governed by the overall uncertainty of the agent at the end of the problem. When will this composition effect materialize? The agent will choose to observe S_p if and only if its fixed cost is smaller than the cognitive cost of processing the same amount of information about inflation through other signals:

$$S_p \in S_i \Leftrightarrow \phi < \omega I(S_p, \pi). \tag{11}$$

If higher inflation is associated with either a reduction in the fixed cost of acquiring S_p ($\phi\downarrow$) or an increase in the informativeness of S_p about inflation $I(S_p, \pi)\uparrow$), then the agent will be more likely to acquire the preprocessed signal S_p. Changes in the inflation environment can therefore affect both the composition of acquired information and the overall level of information acquired by individuals.

How does this translate into estimated information treatment effects? Consider now many agents like the one above participating in a survey after having solved their optimal information acquisition problem. A subset of these agents will be presented with an information treatment in which they are given the signal S_p. They will then form a posterior belief about inflation given by:

$$\tilde{\pi}_i \equiv \mathbb{E}[\pi \,|\, S_i, S_p] = \pi_i + \frac{\operatorname{Cov}(S_p, \pi \,|\, \vec{S}_i)}{\operatorname{Var}(S_p \,|\, \vec{S}_i)}(S_p - \mathbb{E}[S_p \,|\, \vec{S}_i]). \tag{12}$$

If the agent has already seen S_p in the pre-treatment stage, then the posterior belief after the treatment will be the same as the pre-treatment belief: $\tilde{\pi}_i = \pi_i$, exactly as would be the case for the control group. Intuitively, in this case, the agent has not observed any new information and their belief should not move due to the treatment. In contrast, if S_p is not fully spanned by S_i, then we have

$$\begin{aligned} \tilde{\pi}_i &= \pi_i + \frac{\operatorname{Cov}(S_p, \pi \,|\, \vec{S}_i)}{\operatorname{Var}(S_p \,|\, \vec{S}_i)}(S_p - \mathbb{E}[S_p \,|\, \vec{S}_i]) \\ &= \pi_i + \frac{\operatorname{Var}(\pi \,|\, \vec{S}_i)}{\operatorname{Var}(\pi \,|\, \vec{S}_i) + \sigma^2_{v,p}}(S_p - \mathbb{E}[S_p \,|\, \vec{S}_i]). \end{aligned} \tag{13}$$

We can therefore rewrite the posterior belief of agents in the treatment group as being given by:

$$\tilde{\pi}_i = \pi_i + \frac{\text{Var}(\pi \mid \vec{S}_i)}{\text{Var}(\pi \mid \vec{S}_i) + \sigma^2_{v,p}} \times \mathbb{I}\{S_p \notin S_i\} \times (S_p - \pi_i), \tag{14}$$

where $\mathbb{I}\{S_p \notin S_i\}$ is an indicator variable for whether the agent chose to acquire signal S_p prior to participating in the survey. If we again define an indicator variable $\mathbb{I}(i \in T)$ equal to 1 if an individual is in the treatment group and 0 otherwise, we can rewrite posterior beliefs for any participant in the survey as:

$$\begin{aligned}\underbrace{\tilde{\pi}_i}_{\text{posterior}} &= \underbrace{1}_{\delta} \times \underbrace{\pi_i}_{\text{prior}} + \underbrace{\frac{\text{Var}(\pi \mid \vec{S}_i)}{\text{Var}(\pi \mid \vec{S}_i) + \sigma^2_{v,p}} \times \mathbb{I}\left\{S_p \notin S_i\right\}}_{\beta} \times S_p \times \mathbb{I}(i \in T) \\ &\quad \underbrace{- \frac{\text{Var}(\pi \mid \vec{S}_i)}{\text{Var}(\pi \mid \vec{S}_i) + \sigma^2_{v,p}} \times \mathbb{I}\left\{S_p \notin S_i\right\}}_{\gamma} \times \pi_i \times \mathbb{I}(i \in T),\end{aligned} \tag{15}$$

which maps directly into the same empirical specification as before.

There are two margins through which treatment effects can vary. The extensive margin reflects the fraction of respondents who have already acquired the information in the signal (i.e., for whom $S_p \in S_i$). The intensive margin captures the fact that, conditional on not knowing the signal ex ante (i.e., $S_p \notin S_i$), the strength of the response of the response to the signal will depend on the uncertainty of the agents going into the survey $(\text{Var}(\pi \mid \vec{S}_i))$ and the perceived precision/noise of the signal $(\sigma^2_{v,p})$.

Suppose, for example, that higher inflation is associated with more volatile inflation. In the model, more volatile inflation affects neither the total information acquisition of agents nor its composition. Thus, this mechanism would not affect the size of treatment effects according to the model. Another possible channel is one in which high inflation raises the value of information (B) or lowers the cost of information (ω) about inflation. This would lead agents to acquire more overall information and thereby reduce their uncertainty about inflation $(\text{Var}(\pi \mid \vec{S}_i))$, which in turn would make them respond less to information treatments along the intensive margin. However, as shown in Panel A of Figure 8.2, average uncertainty among U.S. households did not fall as the inflation rate rose, indicating that this channel could not be driving the change in estimated treatment effects documented in Figure 6.5.

Another possible channel is via the perceived noise in the signal $\sigma^2_{v,p}$. Noisier signals induce smaller treatment effects, again along the intensive margin. If higher inflation leads people to have less trust in the central bank, then information treatments about the inflation target or the FOMC's inflation forecast might be expected to have smaller effects on beliefs. Panel B of Figure 8.2 shows measures of trust in the Federal Reserve over time. While there was a decline in trust in 2021–2023, the figure reflects a return to pre-COVID19 levels and does not seem to be specific to trust in the Federal Reserve, and so does not provide a good explanation for the change in treatment effects in 2018–2022. Hence, it is difficult to explain the change in treatment effects through factors that operate along the intensive margin.

The extensive margin depends on the decision of whether or not to acquire the signal S_p prior to taking the survey. An increase in the share of people acquiring the signal would be predicted if higher inflation reduces the fixed cost of acquiring S_p ($\phi\downarrow$) or increases the informativeness of S_p about inflation ($I(S_p, \pi)\uparrow$). Consistent with this mechanism, Panel C of Figure 8.2 shows that Google searches about inflation rose sharply during the inflation surge. There was also a surge in news coverage of inflation, which could be interpreted as reducing the cost of acquiring information about aggregate inflation. Taken together, these results suggest that the most likely explanation for the reduced information treatment effects in times of high inflation is an information composition effect, as households become relatively more reliant on information from aggregate statistics and less reliant on other signals they observe, such as the prices in their daily shopping.

Interpreting Endogenous Choices over Information Acquisition

One unnatural feature of standard information treatment experiments is that researchers pre-select what information is given to people, whereas under normal circumstances individuals choose which pieces of information they collect. Fuster et al. (2021) explored this dimension of the information acquisition decision in a novel way. Focusing on housing prices, they devised an experiment in which respondents could choose from amongst three different pieces of information that they could access. The experiment also provided a metric for how much participants would be willing to pay, if at all, for their preferred

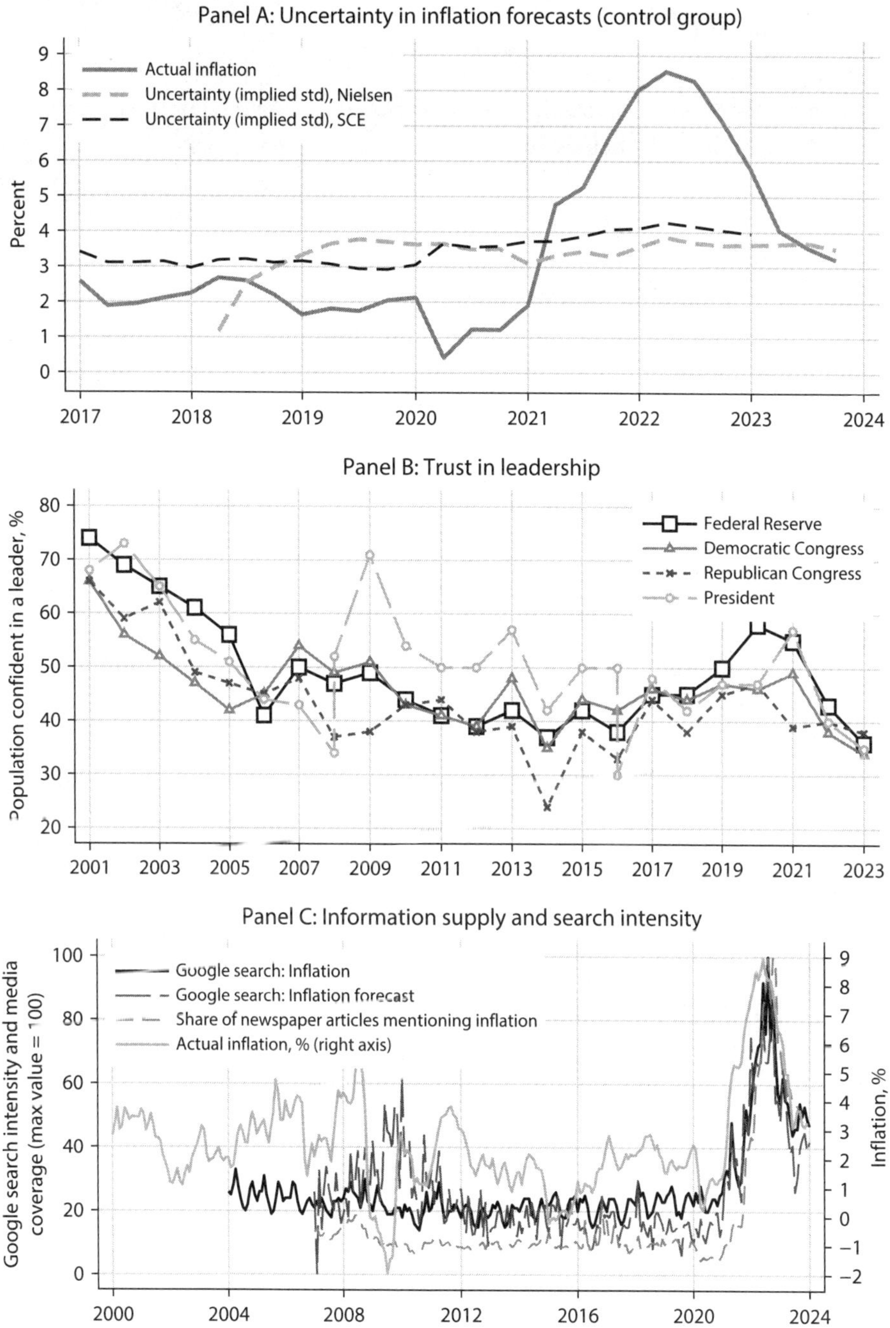

FIGURE 8.2. Properties of beliefs and media coverage in the U.S.
Notes: Panel A plots the time series of uncertainty (standard deviation implied by subjective probability distributions) in households' inflation expectations in the New York Fed's Survey of Consumer Expectations (SCE) and in the Nielsen Homescan Panel. Panel B plots the time series of the share of U.S. population having trust in the leader of a government institution (Gallup). Panel C plots the time series of search intensity (Google Trends) for "inflation" and "inflation forecasts." Each search intensity is normalized so that the maximum value in the reported sample is equal to 100. See Weber et al. (2025) for more details.

choice. Fuster et al. (2021) then assessed how receiving the information affected respondents' beliefs about housing prices. They reached three key findings.

First, respondents chose different pieces of information, and their ranking over different choices was correlated with their abilities: higher ability individuals successfully ranked more informative options higher than did lower ability individuals. Second, respondents who were more uncertain about future house prices generally were willing to pay *less* for information about housing prices and responded less to new information, contrary to what standard learning models would predict. Third, a lower cost of information did not lead to a decrease in the dispersion of beliefs, again at odds with what standard models would predict.

To explain these findings, Fuster et al. (2021) also turned to a rational inattention model, but they incorporated the cognitive costs of processing information at the time when the information treatments were being processed.[2] Specifically, individuals first have a prior over the fundamental θ (future housing price growth) given by mean μ_i and variance $\sigma^2_{i,\theta}$, where subscript i indicates that these may differ across individuals. There are three possible sources of information indexed by $j \in \{1,2,3\}$, each of which is a noisy signal about the fundamental: $x_j = \theta + \varepsilon_j$, with ε_j being normally distributed with mean zero and perceived variance $\sigma^2_{\varepsilon,j}$. When agents receive the signal x_j, paying attention to it is modeled as a noisy signal $s_{ij} = x_j + \psi_i$, where ψ_i is mean-zero noise with variance $\sigma^2_{i,\psi}$ that arises due to limited attention. Variance $\sigma^2_{i,\psi}$ will be a *choice* variable in the information acquisition problem. That is, individuals choose how much precision they would like to have in a signal. Conditional on choosing signal j and variance $\sigma^2_{i,\psi}$, agents form a posterior belief about the fundamental given by

$$E[\theta \mid s_{ij}] = \mu_i + \frac{\sigma^2_{i,\theta}}{\sigma^2_{i,\theta} + \sigma^2_{\varepsilon,j} + \sigma^2_{i,\psi}}[\theta + \varepsilon_j + \psi_i - \mu_i], \tag{16}$$

2. In the previous section, we described the case where people are deciding how much information to acquire prior to taking the survey (Weber et al. 2025). Fuster et al. (2021) focus on the information processing and acquisition problem when people are taking the survey and receiving the treatment. Mackowiak and Wiederholt (2024) consider the joint decision about acquiring and processing information prior to as well as during the survey.

such that the weight on the new information is increasing in the perceived precision of the information and the attention allocated to processing the signal. The posterior variance is

$$\sigma^2_{\theta|s_{ij}} = \frac{1}{\dfrac{1}{\sigma^2_{i,\theta}} + \dfrac{1}{\sigma^2_{\varepsilon,j} + \sigma^2_{i,\psi}}}. \tag{17}$$

The agent receives a payoff $-B\times(\theta - E[\theta|s_{ij}])^2$. In other words, the payoff is decreasing in and is proportional to the squared prediction error.

The objective of the agent can then be written as maximizing the payoff net of the costs of acquiring and processing information:

$$-B\times\sigma^2_{\theta|s_{ij}} - \phi\times\mathbb{I}(i\in Buy) - \frac{\omega}{2}\times\ln\left(1+\frac{\sigma^2_{\varepsilon,j}}{\sigma^2_{i,\psi}}\right), \tag{18}$$

where I $(i\in Buy)$ is an indicator equal to 1 if information is acquired at cost c and the final term captures the cost of paying attention to the provided signal, which is formulated in terms of the reduction in uncertainty about the received signal. The fixed cost to processing any information means some agents may choose not to process any information at all.

The optimal information choice involves the selection of j that maximizes the return for individual i (j_i^*) and implies a willingness to pay (WTP) for information given by:

$$WTP_i = \max\left\{0, \left(\frac{\sigma^2_{i,\theta}}{\sigma^2_{i,\theta}+\sigma^2_{\varepsilon,j_i^*}} - \frac{\omega}{2\times B\times\sigma^2_{i,\theta}}\right) - \frac{\omega}{2}\times\ln\left(\frac{2\times B\times\sigma^2_{i,\theta}}{\omega}\,\frac{\sigma^2_{i,\theta}}{\sigma^2_{i,\theta}+\sigma^2_{\varepsilon,j_i^*}}\right)\right\}. \tag{19}$$

This solution implies that some agents will place a value of 0 on new information, which can explain why some survey participants chose not to take any of the provided signals. This will occur for individuals who see little value in information (low B) or have a high cost of processing information (high ω).

In addition, Fuster et al. (2021) showed that the weight on information provided in treatments will be given by:

$$E[\theta | s_{ij}] = \mu_i + \alpha_i [\theta + \varepsilon_{j_i^*} + \psi_i - \mu_i], \quad (20)$$

where $\alpha_i = \max\left\{0, \frac{\sigma_{i,\theta}^2}{\sigma_{i,\theta}^2 + \sigma_{\varepsilon, j_i^*}^2} - \frac{\omega}{2 \times B \times \sigma_{i,\theta}^2}\right\}$ and j_i^* indicates the chosen signal. Some agents will have $\alpha_i = 0$ and therefore place no weight on the information because the value of the new information is too low for respondents to bother processing it.

Another implication of the model is that higher prior uncertainty is not necessarily associated with stronger responses to the new information. This is because in general, we would expect those individuals who value information less (low B) or have a high cost of processing information (high ω) to be the ones who are more uncertain a priori. As a result, one can get the otherwise counterintuitive finding that it is individuals with the least a priori uncertainty who value the information the highest and respond the most strongly to it, a pattern completely at odds with the simple learning model first presented in this chapter.

A third implication of the model worth highlighting is that if the cost of information declines, disagreement among agents may rise rather than fall. This is because a low cost of information would lead to more information acquisition and beliefs that gradually get closer to the truth. However, in this setting, agents can acquire different signals from one another, so disagreement may rise due to these different information sources. Even conditional on choosing the same signal, there is idiosyncratic (cognitive) noise in the processed signal and differential signal weights $\alpha(i)$, both of which induce more disagreement when agents increase the weight they place on this common signal.

Interpreting Information Updating about Higher-Order Beliefs

A third example of an information experiment that finds results at odds with the standard learning model is Coibion et al. (2021). In this paper, we studied how firms in New Zealand formed expectations about aggregate inflation, but also beliefs about the *beliefs* of other firms, their higher-order forecasts ("I think you think . . ."). Specifically, we studied how their inflation expectations changed when provided with information about either the average forecast of other firms in New Zealand or the average belief about what other firms were forecasting for inflation in New Zealand. Practically, this was implemented by first measuring the inflation expectations of firms in the control group ("first-order expectations") and the expectations of what other firms were predicting for inflation on average ("second-order expectations"). The average values of each were then used in the information treatment arms. The striking finding was that providing firms with the average second-order belief of other firms led to much larger changes in inflation expectations than did providing them with the average first-order beliefs of firms.

To see why this is a puzzle, consider a setting in which each firm $i \in [0,1]$ chooses to set its optimal price, p_i, as a linear combination of its expectation of a fundamental, m, and its expectation of the aggregate price level in the economy, $\overline{p}$:

$$p_i = (1-\eta)\, E_i[m] + \eta E_i[\overline{p}], \tag{21}$$

where parameter $\eta \in (0,1)$ describes the degree of complementarity in pricing. Because the price level is equal to the average price $\overline{p} \equiv \int_0^1 p_j dj$, manager i can obtain:

$$p_i = (1-\eta) E_i[m] + \eta E_i\left[\int_0^1 p_j\, dj\right]. \tag{22}$$

This equation indicates that a firm's optimal price depends on its belief about the fundamental and its belief about what prices other firms will be charging.

Define the average expectation in the economy for variable m as $\overline{E}[m] \equiv \left[\int_0^1 E_j(m) dj\right]$ and let $E_i[\overline{E}[m]]$ be the expectation of manager i about the average expectation in the economy. In a similar spirit, $E_i[\overline{p}]$ is the first-order ("own") expectation about the price level, $E_i[\overline{E}[\overline{p}]]$ is a higher-order expectation about the price level in the sense that this is the expectation of manager i about what other managers think about the price level. We can iterate these expectations to the kth higher order recursively ("I think you think I think you think. . . ." iterations done k times): $\overline{E}^k[X] \equiv \left[\int_0^1 E_j(\overline{E}^{k-1}[X]) dj\right]$.

Using the definition of the price level and repeated substitutions in equation (22), we find:

$$p_i = (1-\eta)E_i[m] + \eta(1-\eta)E_i[\overline{E}[m]] + \eta^2(1-\eta)E_i[\overline{E}^2[m]] + \cdots. \quad (23)$$

The optimal price of firm i therefore depends not just on its own belief about the fundamental but also what it thinks other firms believe about the fundamental, and so on.

Now suppose that firms have access to two types of information to form beliefs. One is a public signal observed by all firms: $y = m + \varepsilon$, where $\varepsilon \sim N(0, \kappa_y^{-1})$. In addition, each firm i also receives its own private signal about m : $x_i = m + v_i$ with $v_i \sim N(0, \kappa_x^{-1})$, where ε and v_i are uncorrelated and v_i is independent and identically distributed across managers. κ_x and κ_y capture the precision of each type of signal. Firms weigh their signals according to the relative noise in each to obtain an individual expectation of m:

$$E_i[m] = \frac{\kappa_y}{\kappa} y + \frac{\kappa_x}{\kappa} x_i = (1-\delta)y + \delta x_i, \quad (24)$$

where $\kappa = \kappa_x + \kappa_y$, and, for ease of notation, $\frac{\kappa_x}{\kappa}$ and $\frac{\kappa_y}{\kappa}$ are denoted by δ and $1-\delta$, respectively. If the private signal is more precise than the public signal, then the firm places relatively more weight on the private signal in forming beliefs about the fundamental. After repeated substitutions of equation (24) into equation (23), one can derive the optimal price as a function of observed signals:

$$p_i = \chi_y y + \chi_x x_i, \quad (25)$$

where $\chi_y \equiv \frac{1-\delta}{(1-\eta)\delta + (1-\delta)}$ and $\chi_x \equiv \frac{(1-\eta)\delta}{(1-\eta)\delta + (1-\delta)}$ with $\chi_y + \chi_x = 1$. The intuition is straightforward: the public signal has a higher weight when it is more precise or when firms care relatively more about the prices of other firms (strategic complementarity), because the public signal is common across firms. Their beliefs about other firms' prices are then formed accordingly, e.g., for first- and second-order beliefs about aggregate prices:

$$E_i[\overline{p}] = \chi_y y + \chi_x((1-\delta)y + \delta x_i) = (1-\chi_x\delta)y + \chi_x\delta x_i, \qquad (26)$$

$$E_i\left[\overline{E}[\overline{p}]\right] = \chi_y y + \chi_x[(1-\delta^2)y + \delta^2 x_i] = (1-\chi_x\delta^2)y + \chi_x\delta^2 x_i. \qquad (27)$$

In the empirical application, firms in New Zealand received one of several treatments, which included being told the average first-order belief of firms about inflation and being told the average second-order belief of firms about inflation. The key empirical finding was that being told the latter led to much larger revisions in the inflation expectations of treated firms than being told the former.

To map this result into the theoretical model, we assume that each information treatment is perceived as a noisy signal about the beliefs of other firms. For example, for the treatment involving the average beliefs of firms about inflation, we interpret this as providing a signal for $\overline{E}[\overline{p}]$ given by $s_B = \overline{E}[\overline{p}] + \xi_B$, where $\xi_B \sim N(0, \kappa_B^{-1})$ and ξ_B is uncorrelated with noise ε and v_i. For the treatment involving the average belief of firms about what other firms think inflation is, the signal is given by $\tilde{s}_C = \phi_x\delta^2 m + \xi_C$ with $\xi_C \sim N(0, \kappa_C^{-1})$.

After a lot of algebra, one can show that, in response to a new signal, firms will update their beliefs as follows:

$$\begin{aligned} E_i^{Post}\begin{bmatrix} \overline{p} \\ \overline{E}[\overline{p}] \end{bmatrix} &= GH\begin{bmatrix} \chi_y \\ \chi_y + \chi_x(1-\delta) \end{bmatrix} y \\ &\quad + (1-GH)E_i^{Pre}\begin{bmatrix} \overline{p} \\ \overline{E}[\overline{p}] \end{bmatrix} + \begin{bmatrix} \chi_x \\ \delta\chi_x \end{bmatrix} G\tilde{s}. \end{aligned} \qquad (28)$$

In the case of the signal about the average belief of firms about inflation, the Kalman gain G is given by:

$$G_B = \delta\kappa^{-1}\chi_x\delta(\kappa_B^{-1} + (\chi_x\delta)^2\delta\kappa^{-1})^{-1}, \qquad (29)$$

where κ is the precision of the prior $E_i(m \mid x_i, y)$. In the case of the signal about the higher-order belief of other firms about inflation, G is instead given by:

$$G_C = \delta\kappa^{-1}\chi_x\delta^2(\kappa_C^{-1} + (\chi_x\delta^2)^2\delta\kappa^{-1})^{-1}. \qquad (30)$$

For the same signal precision ($\kappa_C^{-1} = \kappa_B^{-1}$), we would therefore have $G_B > G_C$: beliefs should respond more strongly to the signal about firms' first-order beliefs than to the signal about their higher-order beliefs, the opposite of what we observe empirically. To match the amount by which firms' beliefs respond to higher-order beliefs relative to first-order beliefs, we would need the signal about higher-order beliefs to be about ten times more precise than the signal about first-order beliefs, which seems a priori implausible. Hence, the fact that firms respond so much to the treatment about higher-order beliefs seems inconsistent with the simple noisy information model. In the paper, we explored possible deviations from the baseline noisy information model to determine how to possibly explain the result. But ultimately it is quite difficult to explain this feature of the data without introducing some departures from rationality in addition to the departures from full information.

Summary

Keynes once famously said that "when the facts change, I change my mind. What do you do, sir?" Information treatments build on this intuition by providing new facts to survey respondents and characterizing the extent to which this new information leads them to change their beliefs. These results can be compared to the predictions of models of the expectations formation process in ways that allow us to refine our understanding of how people form their economic beliefs. One important takeaway from this early literature on information treatments is that incorporating the *endogenous* nature of information acquisition is both quantitatively and qualitatively important. The degree to which individuals acquire information about a topic depends on their incentives to do so as well as the costs of acquiring that information, both in absolute terms as well as in relative ones. But as the economic environment changes, so do these incentives and costs, leading people to alter how attentive they are.

An implication of models with endogenous information acquisition is that central banks should be cautious in claiming success for their communications policies when their citizens appear well informed about monetary policy and inflation. Households in Argentina know much more about inflation and what their central bank is doing than do households in the U.S. But this is clearly not a reflection of successful communications by the Central Bank of Argentina; instead, it is a reflection of their *policy failure*. Similarly, when Americans seemed to become more well informed about inflation and the Fed's inflation target in the early 2020s, this was not due to better communications by the Fed but rather due to the inflation spike. Good monetary policy will induce individuals to become *less* attentive and informed. Good communication policies will therefore need to significantly lower the costs of acquiring information about inflation and monetary policy if they want to keep their population well-informed about monetary policy even under normal circumstances.

Ultimately, the main reason we are interested in understanding how economic expectations are formed is that we think that these expectations matter for the economic decisions taken by individuals and firms. The evidence we have described so far has focused only on how beliefs are formed, not on how these beliefs affect decisions. In the next few chapters, we turn to this key question and describe how the same RCT methods can also be used to determine the extent to which expectations actually shape economic decisions.

PART III

Characterizing the Effects of Subjective Expectations on Economic Decisions

9

Measuring Decisions and Outcomes

ULTIMATELY, WE CARE about economic expectations primarily because we believe they shape economic decisions. Assessing how they do so, however, is a major challenge. We have covered how to measure expectations and how to use randomized information treatments to create new and exogenous variation in those beliefs. It's time to turn to the key question of characterizing how (and even whether!) expectations affect decisions. The first step to doing so is to have measures of those decisions. In general, there are three ways of linking expectations and decisions. The first is by matching survey data with external sources of information on economic outcomes. The second is by measuring outcomes through subsequent survey waves. The third, typically used when neither of the first two ways are available, is by using measures of planned actions from the survey in lieu of ex post decisions. In this chapter, we discuss all three strategies and the broader ability to match surveys of expectations with external sources of information.

When External Information on Decisions Is Available

The ideal scenario for studying the relationship between expectations and decisions is when survey data can be matched to external (administrative) data on outcomes. Due to anonymity requirements of most surveys, this is often infeasible. However, there are a number of exceptions to this, for both household and firm surveys, that are worth emphasizing and highlighting, as these represent unique settings for research purposes.

On the household side, researchers have found settings where surveys can be matched to external information on spending, income and assets, as well as portfolio investments. For measuring spending, the most well-known case is the Nielsen Homescan Panel in the U.S., in which participants track all of their retail purchases. As explored in D'Acunto et al. (2021) and Coibion, Gorodnichenko and Weber (2022a), researchers can run surveys of expectations of these households and match the resulting measures of economic expectations to actual spending outcomes of households. The Nielsen measures of spending are high-quality and high-frequency, but are typically available only with a lag of one or more years and cover only a subset of household spending (primarily food and household products). Another setting that may allow researchers to observe actual spending of consumers is through data from financial institutions. Galashin, Kanz and Perez-Truglia (2020), for example, were able to access credit card spending data from a Malaysian commercial bank and combine it with a survey of the bank's clients. This type of data from a financial institution allows for very high-frequency measures of spending that can cover a broad range of spending, but a limitation is that the specific payment type covered by the bank may represent only a subset of household spending (e.g., if they use cash or credit/debit cards from different institutions). The increasing reliance of consumers on digital payments is likely to open new possibilities of this type, but access to the data will depend on the willingness of financial institutions to share their proprietary information and run surveys on their clients.

In some countries, household surveys can be matched to administrative data on income and assets, as discussed in Chapter 2. For example, Vellekoop and Widerholt (2019) combined income and wealth data from national statistical agencies in the Netherlands with the Dutch National Bank Household Survey. The existence of a wealth tax means that tax authorities have an estimate of the total financial wealth of individuals, and the presence of a property tax also allows tax authorities to measure the value of personal real-estate holdings. The administrative data also includes measures of mortgage debt, but not other liabilities such as credit card debt. Similarly, in Denmark, Caplin et al. (2023) linked survey data from the Copenhagen Life Panel Survey to administrative data collected by the Danish government on all citizens, which includes demographic information as well as annual data on household income and wealth. Since many countries collect detailed information on individuals for taxes, unemployment insurance, and other government policies, there is the possibility that surveys may increasingly be linked to such administrative data.

Another notable example of a household survey being linked to external data is Giglio et al. (2021). They ran repeated surveys of Vanguard's retail investors and were able to link survey responses to respondents' investment holdings and transactions at Vanguard, a large financial firm. Like credit card spending data, this data from Vanguard provided high-quality and high-frequency information on the investment decisions of retail investors, combined with data on their economic expectations. As in the case of credit card data, the limitation of this approach is that investors may have accounts at multiple financial institutions and therefore we may observe only a subset of investors' portfolio decisions. Nonetheless, this setting allowed these researchers to provide an unprecedented perspective on the link between the expectations of investors and their financial decisions, as we describe in Chapter 15.

There are also many cases in which firm surveys can be matched to external data. One particularly notable case is the Italian Survey of Inflation and Growth Expectations (SIGE) of firms. As shown in Coibion, Gorodnichenko and Ropele (2020), this survey can be matched to several external administrative datasets. One is the Central Credit Register, which provides information on loan applications as well as loan balances and utilization of firms. A second is the National Social Security Institute, which collects administrative data from employers on pension contributions to their employees. This provides, for each worker in a firm, data on gross take-home pay, the occupational category, and the type of labor contract. A third is the Company Accounts Data Service, one of the major credit rating agencies in Europe. This data source provides information on income and profits of firms, as well as detailed balance sheet information. Jointly, these data sources provide a very comprehensive source of data on Italian firms that can be matched to the SIGE.

There are other contexts in which firm surveys can be matched to external data sources. For example, the Survey on the Access to Finance of Enterprises (SAFE), which measures inflation expectations of firms in the Euro area, can be linked to Orbis data, which provides extensive information on sales, employment and balance sheets of firms. Tanaka et al. (2021) connected survey data from the Japanese Annual Survey on Corporate Behavior (ASCB), which includes forecasts of real GDP for Japan, to accounting data on participating firms. Delgado et al. (2024) combined a monthly survey of Colombian managers with administrative data on the export and import decisions of those firms. Bloom et al. (2019) described surveys of U.S. manufacturers implemented in conjunction with the Census Bureau for which responses could be matched to other census datasets, such as those of the Census of Manufactures and Business R&D and Innovation Survey, as well as to patent applications from the U.S. Patent and Trademark Office. Gennaioli, Ma and Shleifer (2016) tied survey responses from the Duke survey of Chief Financial Officers to Compustat data on their firms' income statements and balance sheets.

At times, researchers can themselves create external information on firms that can then be matched to survey data. For example, in Kumar et al. (2025), we scraped online prices of New Zealand firms on a daily basis for an extended period prior to and after surveying these firms. The scraped online prices provide an external source of information on firms' prices, which can then be combined with the survey data on expectations and an information treatment to assess how expectations affect prices.

Thus, it is not impossible to find settings in which surveys can be matched to external sources of information. But it is not common either. And finding settings in which information treatments can also be applied within those surveys is even less frequent. When these three key ingredients are present (surveys, the ability to run information treatments, and external data on decisions), we have the ideal setting to study the causal effects of expectations on decisions. But given how uncommon this is, it is important to also understand other strategies that can be used when external data on decisions is not readily available.

When External Information on Decisions Is Unavailable

In the absence of external data on decisions, there are two primary approaches used by researchers to assess the decision-making of survey respondents. When it is possible to run multiple survey waves with the same participants over time, one approach is to ask them in subsequent waves to report on their decisions over recent periods. When multiple survey waves are not feasible, then the primary alternative approach is to ask respondents about their planned decisions for the future as part of the survey.

<u>Self Reported Plans for the Future</u>: In many cases, researchers have the ability to run only a single survey, either because the cost of multiple surveys is prohibitive or because it is a preexisting survey that relies on repeated cross-sections with a limited or no panel dimension. In this case, the only way to assess whether beliefs affect decisions is by measuring the latter through what participants report they are *planning* to do.

A very nice illustration of this approach is the study by Roth and Wohlfart (2020). They were interested in how beliefs about the macroeconomic outlook affect household decisions. They ran an information experiment in which participants were provided with different professional forecasts of the likelihood of a recession over the next six months. In addition to considering how respondents revised their beliefs about the economic outlook, their job prospects and their expected income, Roth and Wohlfart included questions about respondents' future spending plans, such as whether they would change their spending on food. This allowed the authors to show causally that when individuals become more pessimistic about the economic outlook, they plan to reduce their spending on nondurable goods in the future. Another example of using self-reported spending plans is Crump et al. (2022). They relied on questions in the New York Fed's Survey of Consumer Expectations (SCE) about respondents' expected consumption growth over the next 12 months to estimate consumption Euler equations[1] and identify the intertemporal elasticity of substitution. Surveys like the New York Fed's SCE or the ECB's Consumer Expectations Survey often include questions about expected changes in overall spending, but also about large discrete decisions, such as the planned purchase of a house or a car.

Sometimes, household surveys do not explicitly ask for individuals' plans but instead ask a more general question such as, "Is now a good time or a bad time to buy . . . ?" The Michigan Survey of Consumers, for example, has asked this question for decades and it has been the basis for a long line of research. For instance, Bachmann, Berg and Sims (2015) used these questions to assess how inflation expectations correlate with perceptions about whether now is a good time or a bad time to purchase durable goods. This type of question can also be helpful because some decisions, like buying a house, are taken only infrequently by individuals, and so we would observe very few people in a survey who are actually planning to buy a house in the near future. Another advantage of this formulation is that it is sometimes followed by questions that seek to assess *why* respondents answer the way they do, for example, because interest rates are high/low, because prices are expected to rise/fall, etc. However, because these questions tend to be qualitative in nature and do not speak

1. The consumption Euler equation is the optimality condition for how households should allocate consumption over time to maximize their welfare. For example, the standard log-linearized Euler equation is $c_t = E_t c_{t+1} - \frac{1}{\sigma}(i_t - E_t \pi_{t+1})$, where c, i, π denote consumption, the nominal interest rate, and the inflation rate, respectively, and $\frac{1}{\sigma}$ is the intertemporal elasticity of substitution. That is, consumption today depends on expected consumption tomorrow and the real interest rate $r_t \equiv i_t - E_t \pi_{t+1}$, as well as how willing households are to move consumption from one period to another.

directly to what a specific respondent plans to do, they are much less commonly included in modern household surveys than more targeted questions about individuals' planned decisions.

Another way to deal with decisions that are only infrequently made is to ask a hypothetical scenario question. For example, in Coibion et al. (2024), we asked households after an information treatment how they would allocate a windfall gain of $10,000 across different types of financial assets. Because households do not often reallocate their financial portfolios, identifying how these portfolios respond to beliefs can be a challenge, especially when the reallocations are small. Furthermore, the hypothetical question focuses on marginal investments, whereas questions about overall portfolio allocations would identify average investment allocations. Another complication with actual portfolios is that many households hold little or no financial investments, so there is nothing for them to reallocate. The hypothetical question gets around these limitations. Of course, it does not speak as clearly to what individuals will actually do, but it can provide a useful complementary piece of information for understanding the effect of beliefs on decisions. We discuss the use of hypothetical questions in much detail in Chapter 11.

Questions about planned decisions are also frequently used in surveys of firms. For example, the Italian SIGE asks firms about their expected price changes over the next 12 months. The Atlanta Fed's survey of chief financial officers asks firms about their expected price, wage, and employment changes for the current and next calendar years. Surveys of New Zealand firms described in Coibion, Gorodnichenko and Kumar (2018) included questions about firms' expected future price, wage, employment and investment decisions. The ECB's SAFE survey similarly includes questions about expected price, wage and employment changes (Baumann et al. 2024). Kumar, Gorodnichenko and Coibion (2023) went much further and asked firms about their plans for opening new foreign markets, investing in new technologies, starting new product lines, and engaging in advertising decisions, among other things. In principle, there are few limits (other than precious survey space) as to what future plans firms can be asked about in a survey.

<u>Ex Post Self-Reported Decisions</u>: The other way to assess decisions made by economic agents through a survey is by simply going back to them in subsequent surveys and asking them directly about what they have been up to. Surveys with a panel dimension typically include such retrospective questions. For example, the New York Fed's SCE survey includes questions about recent

consumption growth as well as questions about whether respondents purchased large durable goods, such as a house or a car. Coibion, Gorodnichenko and Weber (2020b) asked households to report how they spent stimulus checks from the government during the COVID19 crisis. Surveys also sometimes ask about labor search decisions (e.g., did you search for a new job?), purchases of financial assets (e.g., did you buy cryptocurrency?), and so on. Surveys may even be combined with job offers to perform a task (Baek and Yaremko 2022).

Some surveys of firms follow a similar practice and ask firms about their recent decisions. For example, the Atlanta Fed's CFO survey asks firms to report on their recent pricing decisions, employment decisions and wage-setting decisions. The ECB's SAFE asks similar follow-up questions. Because firm surveys are typically quite short to prevent panel attrition, the range of outcomes observable in these surveys is typically much more limited than in household surveys. Through the use of special modules or separate occasional surveys of firms, additional margins of adjustment can still be explored. For example, we asked firms in Kumar, Gorodnichenko and Coibion (2023) about their recent advertising investments, and whether they had adopted any new technologies or opened new product lines, as well as whether they had recently entered new foreign markets.

Comparing External Information, Plans and Self-Reported Ex Post Decisions

As a general rule, having external sources of data on outcomes is ideal, especially when that data is from administrative sources. Assessing how much better the external data actually is requires having multiple sources of data, which is uncommon. However, there are a couple of settings that allow us to compare how different forms of data sources on economic decisions stack up.

One is the Nielsen surveys of households described in Coibion, Gorodnichenko and Weber (2022a). Nielsen, a marketing company, asks households participating in their panel to track their daily spending on certain categories of goods, providing detailed and high-quality data on household spending. The surveys of households that we used included questions asking households to provide estimates of how much money they had spent, on a monthly basis, on different categories of goods, including categories that closely overlapped with those measured through scanned purchases. As a result, this setting

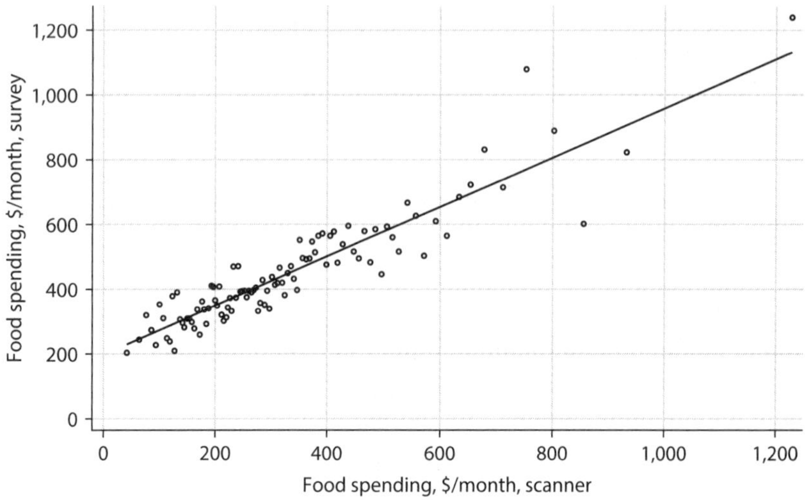

FIGURE 9.1. Joint distribution of self-reported spending and spending reported in the Nielsen Homescan Panel.
Notes: The figure shows a binscatter plot of food spending according to scanner data vs. food spending reported in a survey. See Coibion, Gorodnichenko and Weber (2022a) for more details.

allows us to compare self-reported answers from the survey to the scanner-based spending measures from Nielsen for the same households over the same period.

Figure 9.1 presents a binscatter of these two measures of spending on common categories of goods, primarily food and other retail consumer goods. Overall, we can see that the two measures line up closely on average. The slope of the line linking the two is close to 1, indicating that across different income/spending levels, self-reported spending from the survey follows actual spending measures from scanned purchases. In other words, the average survey respondent provides a valid estimate of their actual spending, such that, at least when it comes to consumer spending, self-reported measures line up closely with actual spending on average.

However, while correct on average, self-reported measures tend to be much noisier than actual spending measures. One way to see this is in Figure 9.2, which plots the distribution of actual (scanner) spending by households in Nielsen as well as the distribution of self-reported spending. The distribution of actual spending is smooth, with a long right tail of individuals who spend significantly more than the average. The distribution of self-reported

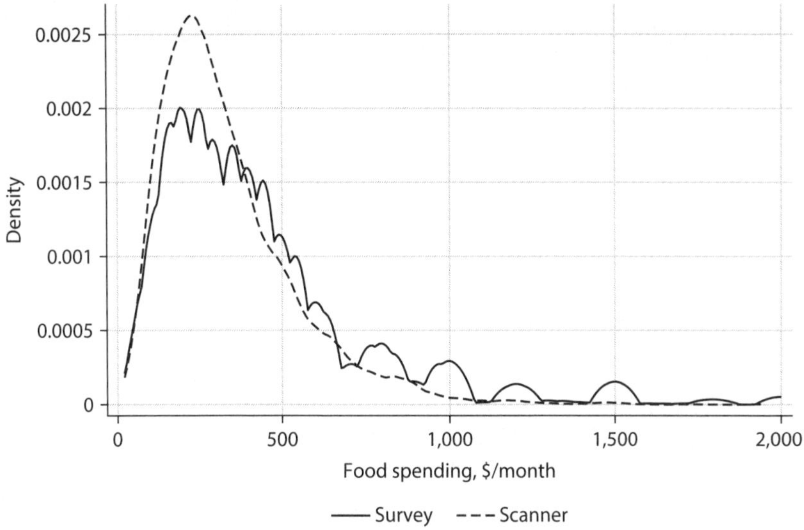

FIGURE 9.2. Distribution of self-reported spending and spending reported in the Nielsen Homescan Panel.
Notes: The figure shows kernel densities for the distribution of food spending according to scanner data and food spending reported in a survey. See Coibion, Gorodnichenko and Weber (2022a) for more details.

spending, on the other hand, is quite different. First, it is shifted toward the right, indicating that households are overstating their spending on specific categories of goods on average. Second, there is lumping that takes place around round numbers, like $1,000 or $1,500, per month. This rounding is typical of self-reported data and, because the underlying data is smooth, indicates that there is more measurement error in self-reported data than in the "true" data. This feature appears to be quite pervasive in household self-reported measures of decisions: rounding is omnipresent and the measurement error exceeds what can be found in administrative or other high-quality data. This does not mean that self-reported data is not useful, but rather that large numbers of observations may be needed to cut through the additional noise that is introduced in self-reported measures.

What about self-reported data on planned decisions? There are again a few settings in which data on both planned decisions and ex post decisions are available and can therefore be used to assess their relative merits. One such setting is in the surveys of firms in New Zealand described in Coibion, Gorodnichenko and Kumar (2018). We asked firms a number of questions about

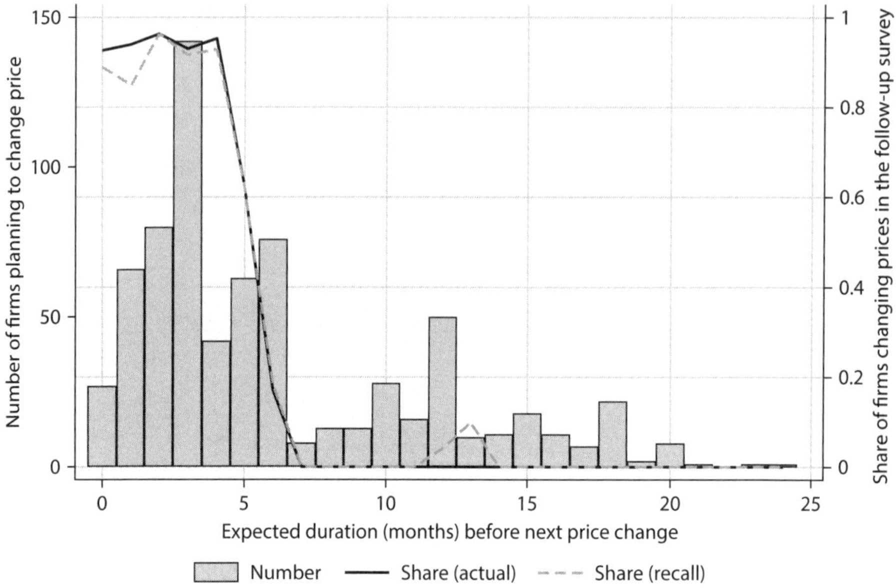

FIGURE 9.3. Distribution of New Zealand firms' expectations and actions. *Source:* Coibion, Gorodnichenko and Kumar (2018).

their planned actions over the next three months, including about their prices. They were first asked when they expected to change their prices next (in months), as well as by how much. In a follow-up wave three months later, the same firms were asked whether they had changed their prices, and by how much. This approach allowed us to characterize how well-planned price changes aligned with ex post reported decisions on price changes.

Figure 9.3 provides a comparison of the timing of price changes. On the *x*-axis, firms are classified based on how many months they expected before their next price change. The lines represent what fraction of firms, in each bin, actually changed their prices in the next three months. The results are striking. For firms that initially reported that they planned to change prices within the next three months, around 90–95% subsequently did. Of firms that initially stated that they did not expect to change their prices for six or more months, almost none did. Hence, at least in terms of their plans with respect to the *timing* of their price changes, self-reported plans lined up quite closely with ex post decisions.

In Figure 9.4, we consider how good measures of self-reported price changes were relative to ex post price changes for those firms that changed

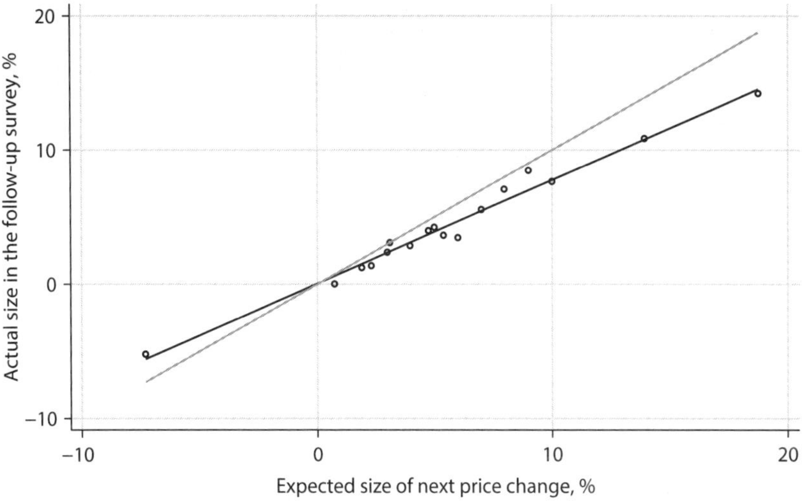

FIGURE 9.4. Joint distribution of self-reported price changes and ex post price changes for firms in New Zealand.
Notes: The figure presents a binscatter plot for expected size of price changes vs. actual size of price changes. The darker line is the fitted linear relationship. The lighter line is the 45-degree line. See Coibion, Gorodnichenko and Kumar (2018) for more details.

their prices between the initial and follow-up waves. Again, we see a striking positive correlation in the binscatter: firms who initially said they would raise their prices by 5% or 10% on average changed their prices by 5% or 10%, respectively. While there is quite a bit of variation in terms of what firms actually did, as one might expect given the unique conditions that can affect any particular firm, the important takeaway is that self-reported planned price changes appear to be a good proxy for what firms actually do ex post. Yotzov et al. (2024) found a very similar result for firms' expected and ex post price changes in the British Decision Makers Panel survey of firms.

Together, these results indicate that both self-reported plans and self-reported ex post decisions from surveys generally seem to do a good job of capturing the actual decisions that households and firms make. Hence, when external sources of data on decisions are not available, asking respondents to tell us about their decisions within a survey is a reasonable way to proceed. Indeed, in many cases it is the only way to proceed. But researchers should bear in mind the additional measurement error associated with such measures.

Summary

To assess how beliefs affect decisions, there is no getting around the fact that researchers will need measures of what respondents actually did. In some cases, it is possible to match surveys to external sources on decisions, and, as a general rule, this can be extremely useful. But often, this is infeasible, or external data does not capture all of the relevant decisions that researchers may be interested in. In those cases, asking respondents to tell us about their planned decisions or, in subsequent waves, to tell us what they have done is typically the only way to measure decisions. Fortunately, the available data suggests that these self-reported measures are good on average, but depending on the quality of survey responses, it may take a lot of observations for these average effects to kick in. So once again, large survey samples may be necessary to help cut through measurement error in survey data.

10

Quantifying the Effects of Beliefs on Decisions

WITH SURVEY MEASURES of expectations in the bag, an information treatment that has created exogenous variation in beliefs, and subsequent measures of decisions, it's now time to quantify how changes in beliefs affect decisions. In this chapter, we describe different strategies to estimate the pass-through of beliefs into actions and discuss challenges that can (and likely will) arise during this critical step.

Approach 1: The Two-Step Reduced-Form Approach

The most direct way to quantify how decisions are affected by new information provided in an RCT is by simply projecting ex post decisions on an indicator variable for treatment groups. For example, letting $Y_{i,t+h}$ denote decisions of agent i in $h=0,\ldots,H$ periods after the treatment, one could run a simple cross-sectional regression such as:

$$Y_{i,t+h} = \alpha^{(h)} + \beta^{(h)} \times \mathbb{I}_t(i \in T) + \delta^{(h)} \times \boldsymbol{X}_{it} + error \qquad (1)$$

where $\mathbb{I}_t(i \in T)$ is an indicator variable equal to 1 if agent i was in the treatment group at time t or 0 otherwise, and $\boldsymbol{X}$ denotes individual controls measured prior to the treatment. Coefficient $\beta^{(h)}$ will therefore measure the *average* effect of being provided with the information in the treatment relative to those in the control group who were not provided with the information.

This approach is simple and transparent and therefore provides a natural starting point to the analysis. In Coibion, Gorodnichenko and Kumar (2018), for example, we used this approach to estimate how much information treatments about recent inflation or the central bank's target altered the decisions of firms in New Zealand after six months. We first split firms into two groups, the "informed" and the "uninformed," based on whether or not their prior inflation expectations were close to 2%. Focusing on the "uninformed," firms whose inflation expectations fell on average in response to the information treatment, we found that treated firms significantly reduced their employment and investment compared to untreated firms, by 2–3% on average. In contrast, the effect on prices was small and that on wages effectively zero. Because treatments are randomly assigned, this type of analysis can provide decisive evidence that information treatments affect economic decisions.

The same approach can be applied in the case of an active control group (i.e., where both groups receive a treatment). In such a case, $\mathbb{I}_t(i \in T)$ would be an indicator variable equal to 1 if agent i was in the "high" treatment group and 0 if it was in the "low" treatment group. The coefficient $\beta^{(h)}$ would then capture the effect of the difference in information on ex post decisions. Chopra, Roth and Wohlfart (2025) used this approach to estimate how information about future home price growth (either high or low forecasts) affects subsequent spending decisions of renters and borrowers, as described in more detail in Chapter 16.

While transparent and tractable, there are at least two potential limitations to this approach. First, while it provides a clear estimate of the effect of the information treatment on decisions, this is often not the metric that we are most interested in. For example, in Coibion, Gorodnichenko and Kumar (2018), the question that we wanted to answer was how the inflation expectations of firms affect their economic decisions. The fact that the information moved both inflation expectations and decisions indicates that there is a connection between the two but it does not provide a quantitative metric of the pass-through of expectations into decisions. To measure this pass-through, one needs to first estimate the average effect of treatments on expectations through a specification such as the following:

$$F_{it}^{post}\pi_{t+1} = \psi + \theta \times \mathbb{I}_t(i \in T) + \eta \times \boldsymbol{X}_{it} + error, \qquad (2)$$

where $F_{it}^{post}\pi_{t+1}$ denotes the post-treatment forecast of inflation of agent i. The coefficient θ captures the average effect of the treatment on expectations, in this case of inflation. The pass-through of expectations into decisions $\gamma^{(h)}$ is then given by the ratio of the two coefficients: $\gamma^{(h)} = \beta^{(h)} \ / \ \theta$. For firms' inflation expectations, we found in Coibion, Gorodnichenko and Kumar (2018) that information treatments reduced the inflation expectations of uninformed firms by about 1 percentage point on average ($\theta \approx -1$), implying pass-through rates of inflation expectations into employment of around 3 and into investment of around 2, considerable responses. As we will see in Chapter 12, this type of elasticity of decisions to expectations may be more informative about underlying mechanisms and theory than reduced-form estimates of how treatments affect decisions. While these key elasticities can be recovered through this approach, doing so requires following an indirect two-step procedure.

The second potential disadvantage of this approach is that it requires the information treatments to have strong *average* effects on beliefs and decisions. In many cases, information treatments can be successful in moving expectations and decisions, but their *average* effects can be zero, as discussed in Chapter 6. Recall that if two individuals initially believe inflation will be 0% and 4% respectively, a treatment that the Federal Reserve targets an inflation rate of 2% will tend to move both inflation expectations toward 2%, say, to 1% and 3%. While the treatment is successful in moving expectations, its average effect on expectations is zero, and we would expect the average effect on decisions to therefore also be zero, even if the pass-through of expectations is nonzero. This two-step approach would therefore provide a misleading interpretation of the link between expectations and decisions.

There are cases, however, when estimating equation (1) can be sufficient, such as when one is interested in measuring the average effect of a treatment on an action or belief for which the treatment should have an effect in only one direction. For example, in Coibion, Gorodnichenko and Ropele (2020), we wanted to determine whether being *repeatedly* provided with information about publicly available information about inflation allowed firms to earn higher profits on average. We discuss the specific setting in more detail in Chapter 12, but, in short, Italian firms participating in the Italian SIGE survey were randomly allocated to one of two groups, one of which repeatedly received the most recent inflation numbers through the survey whereas the other group was not provided with the information during the survey (but could have accessed it themselves separately since the information was publicly available). Importantly, firms stayed in each group for years. Prior to this randomization, all firms in the survey had been receiving the information about inflation through the survey question formulation. Thus, we could estimate a panel version of equation (1) with profits of each firm as the dependent variable. We found that firms continuously receiving the information about inflation *ended up earning higher profits* (measured using financial data from administrative sources) relative to firms that did not get this information, even though these two groups of firms earned the same profits on average when they were all initially getting the same information through the survey. We viewed this result as providing some of the most decisive and simplest evidence that firms do not utilize all available information (i.e., they have imperfect information); but, consistent with rational inattention motives, the change in profits from this extra information was small.

Approach 2: The One-Step Instrumental Variable Approach

An alternative approach to estimating expectational pass-throughs is to effectively combine the two steps into one, while simultaneously incorporating the differential response of expectations across firms to the treatment and exploiting it. As proposed in Coibion et al. (2023) to assess how consumers' inflation expectations affect their spending decisions, this approach consists of estimating the following specification by instrumental variables:

$$Y_{i,t+h} = \xi^{(h)} + \gamma^{(h)} \times F_{it}^{post} \pi_{t+1} + \rho^{(h)} \times F_{it}^{prior} \pi_{t+1} + \mu^{(h)} \times \boldsymbol{X}_{it} + error \quad (3)$$

where, again, $F_{it}^{post} \pi_{t+1}$ denotes the posterior expectation after the treatment while $F_{it}^{prior} \pi_{t+1}$ denotes the prior expectation before the treatment. Note that in this specification, the pass-through of expectations into decisions $\gamma^{(h)}$ is directly estimated. By controlling for prior beliefs, the specification is effectively focusing on the individual revisions in beliefs generated around the treatment. Finally, to pin down the exogenous variation in beliefs stemming from treatments, one instruments for posterior beliefs through the first stage regression described in Chapter 6:

$$\begin{aligned} F_{it}^{post} \pi_{t+1} = b_0 + b_1 \times \mathbb{I}_t(i \in T) + b_2 \times F_{it}^{prior} \pi_{t+1} + \\ b_3 \times \mathbb{I}_t(i \in T) \times F_{it}^{prior} \pi_{t+1} + error, \end{aligned} \quad (4)$$

which conditions on prior beliefs, and therefore captures the link between posteriors and priors conditional on receiving treatments or not.

This approach resolves both potential issues from the reduced-form strategy. First, it directly recovers the pass-through of beliefs into decisions, which is generally what we are interested in. Second, it does not rely only on average effects but instead exploits the fact that individuals may be changing their beliefs in different directions depending on their priors. Examples of this approach being used include Coibion et al. (2023) and Coibion, Gorodnichenko and Weber (2022a), both studying how inflation expectations affect ex post household spending decisions. In each case, we found large negative effects of inflation expectations on durable goods purchases, while in the latter we also found sharp positive effects on nondurable goods spending. Dräger, Lamla and Pfajfar (2023) found similar results using information treatments in the Bundesbank's survey of households. Together, these establish a strong causal link between households' inflation expectations and their subsequent spending decisions.

However, despite the clear causal link that can be established using this approach, it (like all methods) is not foolproof and suffers from some potential limitations, some practical and some conceptual. We now describe some of these and how (or whether) they can be dealt with.

Unobservables and Planned Decisions

In many cases, there is little reason to expect that a particular expectation plays a major role in accounting for specific decisions. This is especially true when using an RCT to generate exogenous variation in beliefs: doing so requires providing information to respondents that they don't know, which can only work if the expectation is not too important in driving their decisions. For beliefs that have the most immediate effects on decisions, we would expect agents to be initially well informed, making it difficult to change those beliefs through an information treatment. For example, in the papers described above, we would not expect inflation expectations to be a primary determinant of household spending or firms' employment decisions. This makes them well suited to an RCT treatment, since it is relatively easy to provide information that changes households' or firms' inflation expectations.

One implication of this feature is that most of the cross-sectional variation in decisions we observe should therefore not be accounted for by the expectation we are studying. As a result, it may be difficult to identify the marginal effect of expectations on decisions in small samples. One solution is to include a wide range of control variables, which can help soak up some of the variation, but there are limits to how many controls one can observe. Researchers often used fixed effects to control for heterogeneity, but this is not an option in

TABLE 10.1. Effect of inflation expectations on durable goods spending decisions.

	Actual spending	
	1st follow-up wave	2nd follow-up wave
	(1)	(2)
Panel A. Control for spending plans		
Posterior inflation expectations	−1.472***	−1.743***
	(0.263)	(0.403)
Observations	11,080	9,755
R-squared	0.06	0.08
1st stage F-stat	110.6	86.54
Panel B. No control for spending plans		
Posterior inflation expectations	−1.725***	−2.039***
	(0.277)	(0.437)
Observations	11,080	9,755
R-squared	−0.004	0.014
1st stage F-stat	110.5	86.62

Notes: The table reports estimates from regressing ex post durable goods spending measures (extensive margin) on household inflation expectations and household controls. Inflation expectations are instrumented using information treatments. Panel A includes a control for any intended purchase of durable goods reported in the first wave of the survey. Panel B does not include a control for any intended purchase of durable goods reported in the first wave of the survey. Household controls include gender of the respondent, age and age squared of the respondent, presence and number of children, education of household head (a set of indicator variables), log household income, and household size. Robust standard errors are in parentheses. ***, **, and * denote statistical significance at 1, 5, and 10 percent levels. For each regression, we use Huber (1964) regressions in the first stage and jackknife procedures in the second stage, as described in Coibion, Georgarakos, Gorodnichenko and van Rooij (2023). See Coibion, Gorodnichenko and Weber (2022a) for more details.

typical RCT settings, where treatment status is not changing over time. Another solution, and one that is particularly useful in this setting, is to measure *planned decisions prior to the treatment.* For example, for firms, one could ask about how they expect to change their employment or prices over the next few months. For households, one can ask about how much they expect to spend on nondurables in future months or whether they expect to make a large durable goods purchase. These measures of planned decisions should capture all of the relevant observable and unobservable characteristics that matter for the decision immediately prior to the treatment. In other words, we can compress heterogeneity into one sufficient statistic (i.e., the planned action) that we can use as a control to better identify the effect of expectations on ex post decisions. Effectively, controlling for prior plans means that we are using ex post forecast errors as dependent variables.

In Table 10.1, we present estimates of the effect of inflation expectations on subsequent U.S. households' durable goods purchases from Coibion, Gorodnichenko and Weber (2022a), both controlling (Panel A) and not controlling (Panel B) for prior plans to buy a durable good. We can see that the control adds nontrivial explanatory power (comparing the R^2 in each) and that this allows us to estimate the effect of inflation expectations on durable goods purchases with more precision: for example, in the second follow-up wave, standard errors are 10% smaller when we control for prior plans.

Heterogeneity in the Importance of Expectations for Decisions and Selection

Another issue that may arise is that there is heterogeneity in the importance of expectations for decisions. Suppose, for example, that we have two groups of firms, one of which thinks that inflation is important and incorporates it into its decision-making, whereas the second group does not. We would therefore expect the second group to be quite inattentive to inflation and to have expectations that are far from those of more informed firms. Consider what this would mean for the estimation approach proposed here. There is one group of firms for whom expectations do affect decisions, but because those firms will be well informed to start with, we may not be able to generate any meaningful exogenous variation in their expectations. Without exogenous variation in their beliefs, we will not be able to identify the effect of expectations on their decisions.

Firms in the second group, on the other hand, begin quite uninformed, so we would expect the information treatments to be successful in moving their expectations. Hence, they will provide a source of identification for linking decisions and beliefs. But, for this group of firms, inflation expectations do not affect decisions. As a result, estimates of equation (3) will point toward a conclusion that firms' inflation expectations do not affect their decisions, even though for the first group of firms this may not be the case. When this type of heterogeneity exists, our estimates will provide a *lower bound* on how much beliefs matter for firms.

A similar effect can arise not from firms being of fundamentally different types, but simply through the endogenous acquisition of information, as formalized in Afrouzi, Flynn and Yang (2024). Consider a decision like buying a house, for which inflation expectations should be an important determinant due to their role in the real interest rate. Because this decision is made infrequently, individuals will have an incentive to acquire a lot of information about inflation when they are close to buying a house, but may have little incentive to do so the rest of the time, when they are not in the housing market. In such a setting, our approach will again tend to underestimate the importance of expectations for decisions. The RCT will successfully generate exogenous variation in the inflation expectations of those who are not in the housing market (since they will tend to be uninformed and responsive to treatments), which will yield estimates of expectations on decisions of close to zero. In contrast, it will be difficult to generate any variation in expectations for those individuals who are actively in the housing market, since they are more informed to start with. So, even though expectations would play an important role for the decision of some agents in this environment, our approach would tend to significantly understate this role.

This type of example is not just a theoretical thought exercise, but is likely to be quite relevant and common. For example, when we found a large effect of inflation expectations on firms' decisions in New Zealand, this was specifically for the subset of firms that were initially uninformed about inflation. For those that were well informed to start with, the RCT generated little variation in expectations and there was little variation in their ex post decisions too. Yet, these firms tended to be the ones that reported that inflation was important to their decisions when directly asked, so the effect of expectations on decisions was likely even higher for them than for uninformed firms. Because identification was only possible for the latter group, however, the resulting estimates were likely a lower bound for the role of expectations in shaping decisions across all firms, something we did not realize at the time.

There are some ways to check for and address this concern, beyond noting that estimates may be a lower bound. One possibility, as in Coibion, Gorodnichenko and Kumar (2018), is to split the sample and assess whether the results are different for different subgroups, especially based on their initial knowledge. However, given limited survey sizes and the need to already split the survey into treatment groups, doing subsample analysis is not always feasible or informative. Another option is to employ hypothetical scenario questions, as described in more detail in the next chapter. Hypothetical questions about how individuals would act if they held different beliefs are not subject to the same concerns and can help indicate whether there really is underlying heterogeneity in pass-through of expectations into decisions.

Note, however, that this kind of heterogeneity is not an issue when the question of interest is how much policy communication might affect economic outcomes. In that case, the relevant metric is how much an information treatment passes through into decisions, not the overall pass-through of expectations into decisions. Because well-informed individuals and firms would likely be unaffected by the policy communication (unless it were somehow very new), the effect of the policy would be limited to the less informed. The importance of this type of heterogeneity or selection therefore depends on the question that we are trying to answer empirically.

Separating Different Expectational Channels

When we estimate equation (4), we are implicitly attributing all of the variation in ex post decisions that is correlated with the expectations variable to that single expectation. Is this reasonable? For example, if high inflation tends to be volatile inflation, those who expect higher inflation should also tend to be more uncertain about future inflation. Or if people believe that high inflation is associated with worse economic outcomes, they might expect their income to be lower as well when they raise their inflation expectations. Either mechanism— higher inflation expectations being associated with more uncertainty or an expectation of lower income—could affect subsequent decisions, such as those of consumer spending, above and beyond the traditional intertemporal substitution channel that macroeconomists typically focus on. Effectively, equation (3) estimates the *total* effect of a change in expectations, which may operate through various channels. If one is interested in how a policy communication strategy affects overall outcomes, then the total effect may be the relevant statistic. But if one would like to understand the different channels through which expectations affect outcomes, say, to map the estimates into underlying structural parameters, then it could be helpful to separate the total effect into the direct and the indirect (e.g., operating through changes in other expectations) effects of a change in expectation.

There are at least two ways to address potential indirect effects of expectations. The first is to assess whether information treatments affect more than the expectation that one is interested in. For example, in Coibion,

Gorodnichenko and Kumar (2018), we found that information treatments regarding recent inflation rates or the central bank's inflation target had sharp effects on the inflation expectations of uninformed firms but did not have any corresponding effects on other expectations, such as for unemployment. When we can rule out other expectational channels in this way, we can be more confident that the estimated coefficient on a given expectation identifies the direct effect of that expectation on decisions.

However, in many cases, this will not be the case, since people tend to form beliefs about economic outcomes jointly. In Coibion, Gorodnichenko and Weber (2022a), for example, U.S. households that lowered their inflation expectations when provided with information about recent inflation tended to also lower their expectations of future unemployment. The resulting estimates of equation (3) should then reflect both intertemporal and expected income effects from treatments. In Coibion, Gorodnichenko and Ropele (2020), firms in Italy tended to become more pessimistic about the economic outlook when they had higher inflation expectations, leading them to reduce their employment and investment. When the ECB was at the effective lower bound, this effect reversed, and higher inflation expectations were associated with more optimism about the economic outlook, leading firms to *increase* their employment and investment. This highlights the importance of measuring many different expectations in surveys, above and beyond the ones that are expected to be directly affected by information treatments.

When different expectations are highly correlated but we would like to separately identify their causal effects on decisions, one solution is to generate exogenous variation in each form of expectation that we would like to identify the effect of. Effectively, we therefore need multiple information treatments. Treatments do not need to move only one expectation at a time, but they do need to induce different *relative* changes in expectations. For example, if we are trying to separate the effect of first and second moments of expectations (mean forecast versus uncertainty), then we need one treatment that moves mean forecasts more relative to uncertainty than another treatment. We implemented this type of approach in Georgarakos et al. (2024), using different treatments that aimed to affect both mean inflation forecast and inflation uncertainty of European households. One treatment provided information about the mean inflation forecast of professional forecasters, a second treatment provided information about the spread between the most optimistic and pessimistic professional forecasters, and a third treatment included both pieces of information. As shown in Figure 10.1, these treatments *all* affected both the mean forecast and inflation uncertainty of households. Importantly, the proportion by which they affected them differed across treatments. This is what is needed to deliver identification.

With these treatments, we then estimated the following regression:

$$Y_{i,t+h} = \xi^{(h)} + \gamma^{(h)} \times F_{it}^{post} \pi_{t+1} + \phi^{(h)} \times \sigma_{it,\pi}^{post} + \rho^{(h)} \times F_{it}^{post} \pi_{t+1} + \tau^{(h)} \times \sigma_{it,\pi}^{prior} + \mu^{(h)} \times \boldsymbol{X}_{it} + error, \quad (5)$$

where $\sigma_{it,\pi}^{post}$ and $\sigma_{it,\pi}^{prior}$ are the posterior and the prior inflation uncertainties of household i at time t. Posterior expectations of both first and second moments were included in the specification so that we could separately measure their effects on decisions. We then instrumented for both $F_{it}^{post} \pi_{t+1}$ and $\sigma_{it,\pi}^{post}$, using priors, treatment indicators, and interactions of each. As shown in Table 10.2 for durable goods purchases, we found strong negative effects of inflation uncertainty on durable goods purchases but positive effects from mean inflation expectations when we separately identified the two channels. When we controlled only for inflation forecasts (and therefore integrated the uncertainty channel into the coefficient on inflation expectations), we recovered the same negative overall effects of inflation expectations on durable goods spending as in Coibion, Gorodnichenko and Weber (2022a). So the total effect of inflation expectations on durable goods spending appears to be negative, but this is because the negative indirect effect through uncertainty dominates the positive direct effect of inflation expectations. The latter positive effect can only be identified once we are able to control for the associated changes in inflation uncertainty. The same empirical strategy to separate the effects of inflation expectations from inflation uncertainty on household spending decisions was also used by Kostyshyna and Petersen (2024) in Canada, Fischer et al. (2024) in the United Kingdom, and Aktug and Atesagaoglu (2024) in Turkey.

This kind of decomposition can only be recovered with multiple information treatments and multiple measures of expectations. Doing so is therefore quite demanding in terms of survey size, for both the number of respondents and the length of the survey. One alternative, discussed in more detail in the next chapter, is to ask respondents hypothetical scenario questions that try to decompose the total estimated effects into their underlying channels. While this does not lend itself to easily getting quantitative causal effects, it can shed light on underlying mechanisms at work and can help subsequent studies identify which channels to focus on.

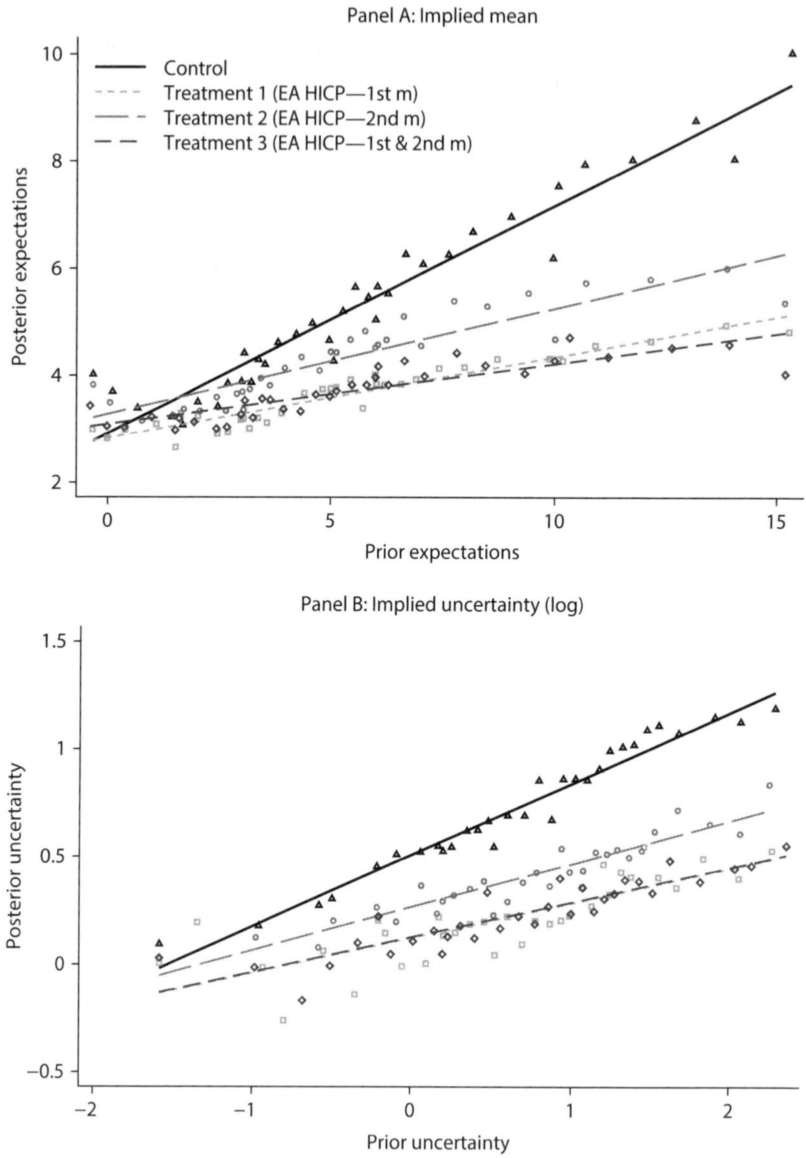

FIGURE 10.1. Treatment effects on inflation expectations, 1st and 2nd moments. *Notes:* The figure reports binscatter plots of prior vs. posterior beliefs about inflation expectations in the Euro area as well as the fitted linear relationships. See Georgarakos et al. (2024) for more details.

TABLE 10.2. Effect of inflation uncertainty on purchases of durable goods.

	Dependent variable: Indicator variable for whether a durable good is purchased.					
	Home	Durable	Car	Holiday package	Luxury items	Other
	(1)	(2)	(3)	(4)	(5)	(6)
Posterior mean	0.421	4.812***	0.483	1.934	0.539*	0.451
	(0.268)	(1.369)	(0.315)	(1.578)	(0.283)	(0.863)
100×log(Posterior uncertainty)	−0.025**	−0.230***	−0.024*	−0.091	−0.021**	−0.055*
	(0.010)	(0.057)	(0.013)	(0.065)	(0.011)	(0.034)
Observations	11,514	11,506	11,502	11,512	11,519	11,483
R-squared	0.002	-0.041	-0.001	0.100	0.022	0.036
1st stage F-stat (mean)	118.4	113.8	117.6	114.8	118	112.7
1st stage F-stat (uncertainty)	100.5	99.29	99.10	100.7	101.9	101.2
KP Wald test	10.63	9.532	10.34	10.51	10.48	10.19

Notes: The table reports IV estimated coefficients on posterior beliefs about inflation in specification (5). The first stage is given by specification (4). The dependent variables take values 0 (no purchase is made) and 100 (a purchase is made). Heteroskedasticity robust standard errors are reported in parentheses. ***, **, and * denote statistical significance at 1, 5, and 10 percent levels. See Georgarakos, Gorodnichenko, Coibion and Kenny (2024) for more details.

Other Practical Considerations

When estimating how expectations affect decisions through an RCT strategy, other issues may arise in practice that are worth briefly discussing.

Horizon of actions: Ideally, one would like to trace out the dynamic response of decisions to a change in expectations, which would require measuring the decisions of firms over time after the treatment. While this may be feasible when external information is available, it will be more difficult to do when follow-up surveys are used to measure outcomes. Unless there is an existing panel dimension to the survey, a researcher will need to take a stand on the amount of time between the treatment and the follow-up surveys. If the horizon is too short, agents may not have time to respond. If the horizon is too long, the effects of the treatment may be drowned out by all the other sources of variation that arise over the time sample, making the estimates too imprecise to be of use. In practice, horizons of three to six months seem to strike the right balance, but this can depend on the type of decision. For example, in Coibion, Gorodnichenko and Ropele (2020), we found that inflation expectations had transitory effects on prices that dissipated within three months, whereas the effects on employment and investment were still growing over a year after the treatment. In general, the nature of the treatment, the type of expectation and the specific outcomes considered will affect what type of horizon is most relevant.

State dependence: One limitation of the RCT approach has to do with how to generalize a treatment implemented in one place at one moment in time to a different setting. Only repeated evidence over different periods and different settings will help establish the generality (or not) of any result. Thinking about the mapping from empirical estimates to underlying parameters can also help one make inferences about whether results would hold elsewhere. If estimated coefficients map cleanly into a structural parameter, then one might expect this estimate to be reproduced systematically in other settings. If instead the estimated coefficients map into a reduced-form parameter that is, for example, a function of underlying shocks or a combination of different effects, then those coefficients are likely to vary with economic conditions. In Coibion, Gorodnichenko and Ropele (2020), for example, higher inflation expectations led firms to reduce employment in normal times, but the effect was reversed during the period when interest rates in Italy were at the effective lower bound.

We argued that this was because, in normal times, Italian firms attribute inflation to supply-side factors, so higher inflation is associated with lower demand, which leads firms to reduce their employment. But when interest rates are at zero, they may become more optimistic about the economic outlook when they expect higher inflation, leading firms to hire more employees. Because the estimated elasticity of employment to inflation expectations captures different channels, and some of these channels are state-dependent, the resulting estimates should be expected to be time-varying as well. State dependence in the effects of inflation expectations on consumer spending has also been documented (Candia 2024).

Nonlinearities: While the issue of nonlinear effects is not specific to this methodology, because the applications are to individual or firm-level outcomes and the changes in expectations are experimentally induced, asymmetries and nonlinearities may be particularly important. For example, consider discrete outcomes like durable goods purchases. Small changes in expectations may be insufficient to induce any visible reaction on purchases of cars or houses in small samples, whereas larger changes could induce significant changes in purchases. Similarly, firms may be more wary of cutting prices than raising them, so experiments that lead firms to, say, raise their inflation expectations may lead to larger estimates than those in which most firms reduce their expectations. Within a given experiment, limited sample sizes can make this type of asymmetry or nonlinearity difficult to detect.

Measurement error: Surveys are notoriously prone to measurement error. This is an unavoidable feature of working with this type of data. And with self-reported survey measures of decisions, there is noise on both the left-hand and the right-hand sides of the regressions, as well as in the instruments. So how can we cut through this noise to get estimates of any precision? First, large sample sizes play a crucial role here. Working with very large surveys, like those done by Nielsen or by the ECB, makes a big difference, especially for household data. Every effort should be made to maximize sample sizes, which makes it imperative to keep the length of surveys limited and of a level of difficulty that does not make people abandon them midway. Another strategy is to invest in improving the quality of responses. For example, in-person/phone interviews tend to have better quality than online surveys. Because the former is much more expensive than the latter, there is a trade-off between sample size and quality of survey responses. Surveys that are run by government agencies or established, reputable survey firms can improve the quality of responses too. One can also offer incentives (e.g., lottery tickets, mugs, coupons) to survey respondents to improve the quality. Finally, well-crafted survey questions (clear and short questions, calibrated options, consistency checks, etc.) help reduce noise too.

Another way to reduce the effects of measurement error from surveys is by measuring decisions via external sources of information, when possible. To see how much of a difference this can make, Table 10.3 presents estimates from Coibion, Gorodnichenko and Weber (2022a) for the effects of inflation expectations on households on their ex post spending, where the latter is measured either via Nielsen scanned data or as self-reported by households. As discussed in the previous chapter, the latter tend to be noisier estimates than the former. How much of a difference does this make in practice? The standard errors of the estimates using the external measures of spending are less than half those from self-reported data! That represents a very large increase in precision from having access to external data on decisions. The latter, of course, may have additional issues (e.g., less frequent measurement, definitions that are incompatible with the survey, etc.), but as a general rule, they can bring a lot of value to this estimation strategy.

A third strategy to address the noise in survey data is to use methods that deal with outliers. For example, Huber (1964) robust regressions provide one way to systematically identify and downplay the role of outliers. Jackknife procedures can also help identify influential observations.[1] When implementing our instrumental variable (IV) strategy, we recommend using Huber regressions for the first stage and jackknife procedures for the second stage to minimize the role of outliers in both dimensions, as done in Coibion et al. (2023), for example.

Survey respondents and their responsibilities: In the treatment stage, information is provided to the survey respondent and the change in their expectations is subsequently compared to decisions to quantify the pass-through from expectations into decisions. This assumes that the respondent can make the decisions that the researcher is interested in. In some cases, especially in complex organizations, this may not be the case. For example, firm surveys typically

1. In a nutshell, jackknife is a cross-validation technique in statistics where one estimates the coefficient of interest by dropping one observation at a time to assess how the estimate for the full sample depends on a particular observation.

TABLE 10.3. Effect of inflation expectations on spending decisions.

Dep. var. is indicated in the title of the panel	100 × log (actual spending), horizon, month	
	1st follow-up wave	2nd follow-up wave
	(1)	(2)
Panel A. Total spending, survey		
Posterior inflation expectations	1.826***	1.015
	(0.690)	(0.638)
Observations	6,459	6,570
R-squared	0.414	0.414
1st stage F-stat	46.97	60.06
Panel B. Total spending, scanner		
Posterior inflation expectations	0.950***	0.864**
	(0.286)	(0.336)
Observations	13,170	13,132
R-squared	0.751	0.696
1st stage F-stat	134.8	128.1
Panel C. Spending on food items, survey		
Posterior inflation expectations	1.299*	0.873
	(0.775)	(0.640)
Observations	6,626	6,748
R-squared	0.460	0.473
1st stage F-stat	50.36	63.81
Panel D. Spending on food items, scanner		
Posterior inflation expectations	0.568**	0.237
	(0.266)	(0.313)
Observations	13,170	13,136
R-squared	0.773	0.708
1st stage F-stat	136.3	132.8

Notes: The table reports estimates from regressing spending measures (indicated by each panel) on household inflation expectations and household controls. Inflation expectations are instrumented using information treatments. Dependent variables are as follows: Panel A is total monthly spending reported by households in the follow-up waves of the survey, Panel B is total spending measured in Nielsen scanner data, Panels C and D are total spending on food as measured in survey and scanner data, respectively. Panels A–D include controls for past spending levels. Household controls include gender of the respondent, age and age squared of the respondent, presence and number of children, education of household head (a set of indicator variables), log household income, and household size. Robust standard errors are in parentheses. ***, **, and * denote statistical significance at 1, 5, and 10 percent levels. For each regression, we use Huber (1964) regressions in the first stage and jackknife procedures in the second stage, as described in Coibion, Georgarakos, Gorodnichenko and van Rooij (2023). See Coibion, Gorodnichenko and Weber (2022a) for more details.

target CEOs or CFOs. While these individuals are in charge of some decisions, much of what is decided by a firm is done at lower levels of management. CEOs, for example, may not be directly involved in pricing decisions or wage-setting decisions within the firm. Changing their inflation or demand expectations could therefore have no effect on these outcomes because they are not involved in making those decisions. And yet, the relevant decision-makers' expectations of inflation or economic activity could still matter. But to the extent that the information treatment does not reach those particular individuals within the firm, we would find no pass-through of expectations into decisions even where such a pass-through exists. This is less of a concern with smaller firms, where the top manager or owner is likely to be very involved in the majority of decisions made within the firm, but for larger firms, this issue can be quite important. To the extent that some of the information treatments go to respondents who are not responsible for certain decisions, our approach will tend to underestimate the pass-through of beliefs into decisions. One potential solution is to identify the role of respondents within a firm, as done in McClure et al. (2025) and Savignac et al. (2024). This can help assess whether treatment effects on decisions vary depending on the role of the respondent, but doing so successfully would require much larger samples of firms than are currently available. In the absence of this type of evidence, it's important to bear in mind this limitation, which will tend to bias downward estimates of expectational pass-through into decisions.

Multiple hypothesis testing and preregistration: One fortunate outcome of being able to run longer surveys or matching surveys to external data is that it may allow for having many different outcomes that one can study. For example, in Coibion, Gorodnichenko and Ropele (2020), because the Italian SIGE survey could be matched to several administrative datasets, we were able to observe outcomes on different types of employment, balance sheet decisions, credit utilization and other outcomes beyond those self-reported in the survey. With many possible outcomes, it may become necessary to adjust p-values to reflect the many statistical tests being run. One way to do this is to use Romano and Wolf (2016) or similar corrections to obtain correct p-values. Another approach to dealing with the fact that there may be multiple potential outcomes is to preregister experiments and be clear ex ante about which outcomes will be the focus of the study. Doing so is becoming increasingly common and helps reduce the risk of researchers "data-mining" and justifying significant results ex post.

However, insisting that *all* results be preregistered would be counterproductive. Mike Tyson once said, "Everybody has a plan until they get punched in the face." Receiving your newly run survey data is often just like getting punched in the face. Unforeseen responses and issues are more the rule than the exception when it comes to experiments with expectations, and rare will be the study where one can blindly follow a preregistration plan. Sometimes, unexpected results require researchers to examine questions or topics that are outside their original research idea. In other cases, researchers may not know at the time of the RCT design what external sources they may be able to match the data to. The reality of scientific discovery is that much of it is accidental (e.g., penicillin, radioactivity, Viagra, microwave), and researchers should have the liberty to pursue unexpected results as they arise. But when research deviates from preregistered plans or is not preregistered at all (we confess we almost never remember to do this ourselves), it is important for researchers to justify their empirical choices with as much clarity as possible. And subsequent work that follows up on "accidental" discoveries should take advantage of preregistration plans to verify that earlier findings hold up to repeated experiments.

Summary

The increasing availability of survey data, combined with the ability to run information treatments, has led to the possibility of assessing the role of expectations in driving decisions in new ways. This very exciting area of research is already providing new evidence that can shape theory and policy. In this chapter, we have focused on inflation expectations and the extent to which these causally affect both household and firm decisions. RCTs from many research teams have provided decisive and novel evidence that inflation expectations do in fact shape the decisions of households and firms, along many margins. In the case of households, for example, inflation expectations have been found to causally impact durable goods purchases, spending on nondurables and services, portfolio allocations, and labor search decisions. For firms, inflation expectations affect prices, employment, and investment, among other margins, and ultimately affect profits. While the precise channels through which these effects occur need to be further flushed out, being able to make causal statements about the effects of inflation expectations represents important progress relative to where we were just a few years ago.

But this is only a small subset of what can be done. There are many expectations that should affect decisions much more directly and powerfully than inflation expectations. In subsequent chapters, we will discuss other questions that are being addressed with RCTs in surveys. But before doing so, we want to consider whether there are alternative strategies that can yield similar results as well as how these types of estimates can be used to speak to theoretical models.

11

Alternative and Complementary Approaches to RCTs

THE EMPIRICAL STRATEGY described in this book is conceptually simple but is not so easy to implement in practice. It requires combining multiple waves of large-scale surveys, external information on decisions, and information treatments that generate sufficiently strong changes in beliefs. In trying to do so, a lot of things can go wrong. While potentially very powerful in illuminating the link between expectations and decisions, this type of research is both expensive and time-consuming, and requires access to survey resources that may not be open to many researchers. Are there alternative approaches to achieve similar outcomes that are not so resource- and time-intensive? To our knowledge, there exists one strategy that may achieve a similar outcome at a fraction of the cost: hypothetical scenario questions, sometimes referred to as "vignettes" or "strategic surveys." In this chapter, we discuss how these questions can identify concepts similar to those through RCTs, and their potential advantages, existing applications and examples.

Hypothetical Questions as a Substitute for RCTs

Conceptually, the approach described in this book is meant to identify answers to questions like the following: "If an economic agent were to expect that [some future economic variable] were higher by 1 percentage point, then by how much would they tend to [increase/decrease] their [decision] today as a result?" Our empirical strategy consists of measuring beliefs through surveys, using information treatments to change those beliefs, then using measures of ex post decisions to assess to what extent beliefs affect decisions. What if we simply asked economic agents how they would react to the same thought exercise? In principle, there is nothing stopping us from asking a survey participant: "If you expected [some future economic variable] to be 1 percentage point higher over the next [period], by how much would this affect your [decision]?" This question, if answered truthfully and precisely by respondents, could yield the same answer as the more roundabout RCT strategy we have described.

If this were the case, hypothetical questions would have several very appealing properties to make them an alternative to RCTs. Firstly, and most importantly, because they are self-contained, they eliminate the need to both use information treatments and either have multiple survey waves or external information on decisions. Instead, they can be implemented within a single survey wave and, because the same question can be asked to everyone in the survey (since we are not splitting the survey into different control/treatment groups), sample sizes do not need to be as large. These are very important advantages. As described in earlier chapters, implementing information treatments cannot be done in many surveys and doing so requires large samples. Similarly, running multiple survey waves can be expensive and matching to external data is often impossible. These constraints could limit the ability of many researchers to independently apply RCT methods, especially students and junior researchers. By eliminating many of the practical limitations that exist with large-scale RCTs, hypothetical questions would facilitate entry into this area, increase competition among researchers, and raise the rate of progress in this line of work.

There would be other advantages to hypothetical questions as well. One would be that they would yield answers much more rapidly, since they can be implemented in a single survey wave and do not require researchers to wait and see how people or firms actually change their behavior thereafter. This can be particularly important for using these questions to address policy topics in real time. Another advantage is that hypotheticals can easily be used to test for nonlinear or asymmetric effects. Nonlinear effects can be detected by randomly giving some respondents a small change in beliefs (e.g., 1%) while giving other respondents larger changes (e.g., 5% or 10%). Asymmetric effects can similarly be tested by giving some respondents an increase in beliefs about a variable while others are given a decrease in beliefs about the same variable. A third possible benefit is that hypotheticals can be used to separately identify partial versus total effects of changes in beliefs. This could be done by giving a random subset of participants a version of the hypothetical that explicitly rules out any change in beliefs other than for a single variable (e.g., "Suppose you thought inflation was going to be 1 percentage point higher than you currently believe, but all of your other economic expectations were unchanged . . .”), whereas others would be asked for a change in the same belief without specifying anything about other beliefs. The latter would identify the total effect of the change in expectations, whereas the former would identify the partial effect. Yet another potential benefit is that hypotheticals may work better than RCTs to measure some discrete outcomes (e.g., buying a home) that are only infrequently observed in surveys or for which only very large changes in beliefs would lead to discernable variation in outcomes.

Therefore, hypothetical questions hold the promise of identifying the same concepts as RCTs but in a much more direct and cost-effective manner. If they were proven to be effective, this could significantly augment the scope of research questions that we could answer through surveys. The question then is, do they work?

Hypothetical Questions: Do They Work?

The most systematic attempt to assess how well hypothetical questions work is a recent paper by Colarieti, Mei and Stantcheva (2024). They designed a number of different hypothetical questions in a survey of households that were meant to identify the same conceptual objects as those studied in previous research using other methods, which they referred to as “cross-validation.” For example, one hypothetical question asked individuals by how much they would reduce their spending if they lost their jobs. The resulting implied marginal propensity to consume from the hypothetical was very close to what had been previously estimated in Patterson (2023) using an alternative empirical strategy. This was just the first of several cross-validations that the authors did. Others included measuring the consumption response to expected income shocks or the consumption response to changes in mortgage payments, among others. In each case, the authors concluded that the hypotheticals were very successful in closely replicating the estimates found in other studies using different empirical methods. Pilossoph and Ryngaert (2024) asked survey respondents how likely they would be to search for work under different hypothetical inflation scenarios, and compared the results to the effect of inflation expectations on job search intensity they had estimated in another survey. They concluded that the hypothetical question yielded similar qualitative results as their other empirical evidence. In a similar spirit, in Coibion, Gorodnichenko and Weber (2022b), we compared how survey participants reported having used their COVID19 stimulus payments to hypothetical responses from participants who did not receive a stimulus check about how they would have used the funds had they received them. We found that the hypothetical questions yielded responses very similar to the non-hypothetical ones. Colarieti, Mei and Stantcheva (2024) cautioned, however, that hypotheticals would likely only work well when individuals were asked about decisions and scenarios they faced frequently. Asking about what they would do if they won a lottery, for example, would be less likely to yield the same answers as to what people actually did in that situation. In addition, while Colarieti, Mei and Stantcheva (2024) provided useful cross-validations, none of them was a direct comparison to evidence from RCTs of the type described here.

Other studies have provided more isolated evidence on the extent to which hypotheticals identify the same effects as RCTs. In Coibion, Gorodnichenko and Kumar (2018), where we studied how firms in New Zealand responded to changes in their inflation expectations using an RCT, our main conclusions were that, as firms' inflation expectations rose, they tended to raise their employment and investment, with little change in prices or wages. However, prior to running the RCTs, we had also asked firms in the survey how they would hypothetically react if they expected inflation to be higher in the future, in terms of prices, employment, investment and wages. While possible answers were only qualitative in nature (e.g. "very likely to raise prices"), this still provided a setting in which an RCT can be compared directly to a hypothetical question, something we did not realize might be worth pointing out at the time. Strikingly, and consistent with the results in Colarieti, Mei and Stantcheva (2024), responses to the hypotheticals for employment and investment indicated that firms would respond strongly to a change in their inflation expectations, but that their prices and wages would respond little, as subsequently found in the RCT.

Another example that provides a clear comparison of an RCT-based estimation and hypothetical questions is in Kumar, Gorodnichenko and Coibion (2023), in which we studied how macroeconomic uncertainty affects firms' decisions, as we describe in more detail in Chapter 13. An information treatment served to generate exogenous variation in uncertainty across firms, and a follow-up survey allowed us to track how decisions evolved. The RCT estimates made clear that higher uncertainty leads firms to significantly reduce their employment and investment, as well as make adjustments along other margins. In the first survey wave, we had also included a hypothetical question in which firms were asked how higher (or lower, for some firms) uncertainty might affect their decisions along many of the same dimensions. Potential answers were in qualitative form, so the quantitative results could not be directly compared to those of the RCTs. However, qualitatively, the RCT results lined up very closely with those of the hypothetical questions. In terms of the sign of how firms respond to uncertainty, only one dimension was at odds across the two approaches (how profit margins would adjust), whereas the results for all other firm decisions were consistent between the two approaches. Again, while one cannot compare the quantitative magnitudes in this case, the qualitative results were quite close, thus corroborating the results of Colarieti, Mei and Stantcheva (2024).

Hence, the available evidence so far is supportive of the notion that hypotheticals can be used to identify similar behavioral responses as what can be estimated using other methods such as RCTs. But it's not a slam dunk by any means, and there remain many potential caveats that one should bear in mind. First, as emphasized by Colarieti, Mei and Stantcheva (2024), hypotheticals are unlikely to work well when they involve scenarios that are far from typical ones for respondents. This can limit the scope of applications, as when analyzing rare policy changes. Second, while we have qualitative comparisons of RCTs and hypotheticals, quantitative ones are still missing. Third, while RCTs clearly identify partial equilibrium responses, hypotheticals do not clearly differentiate between partial and general equilibrium effects. To the extent that most individuals appear to engage in relatively low levels of higher-order thinking, this issue may not be quantitatively important, but that remains to be determined. Fourth, hypotheticals assume that respondents can quickly decide how they would act under different circumstances whereas in an RCT, where subsequent decisions are measured over long periods (e.g., three to six months), respondents have time to process their new beliefs and think carefully about how to change their behavior. Hopefully future research will be able to shed more systematic light on the settings and circumstances under which we can safely expect hypothetical questions to work as well as RCT experiments.

Hypothetical Questions: Existing Applications

Hypotheticals are not new to surveys. They have long been used, for example, to measure the risk tolerance of individuals and other underlying parameters, especially in household surveys (e.g., Barsky et al. (1997) use hypothetical questions to elicit risk tolerance). Firm surveys have more recently also begun to use hypotheticals to measure parameters that matter for economic models. For example, in Coibion, Gorodnichenko and Kumar (2018), we posed a hypothetical that asked firms by how much they would change their prices if they could do so immediately and costlessly, then asked them by how much their profits would change if they did so. The ratio of these two responses provided a measure of the steepness of the profit function of firms, an object previously unexplored. At the time, we used this measure to show that firms with larger slopes of the profit function (and who therefore should value information more) tend to be more informed than firms with smaller slopes of the profit function. Afrouzi (2024) used hypothetical questions to identify the degree of strategic complementarity in price setting. He did so with a three-part hypothetical, asking firms to imagine that if prices in the economy went up in the economy, a) by how much would their competitors raise their prices, b) by how much would they raise their price(s), and c) by how much would they raise their prices if their competitors did not change their prices at all. This combination of quantitative responses jointly provides a direct estimate of a parameter that is otherwise very difficult to pin down.

Hypotheticals have also been used in macro-labor to identify hard-to-measure variables. For example, Davis and Krolikowski (2025) ran surveys of individuals receiving unemployment insurance and asked them how much of their prior wage they would have been prepared to sacrifice to avoid being laid off. They found that many people would have accepted large pay cuts: one third would have been willing to see their wages decline by as much as 25% to keep their jobs. Because these questions measure an unobservable counterfactual, their paper illustrates how hypothetical questions can be used to study features of the economy that no other methods can easily identify.

In a similar spirit, we surveyed consumers across 13 advanced economies to see how much individuals report they would be willing to pay (WTP) in terms of their lifetime consumption to eliminate either economic volatility or inflation (Georgarakos et al. 2025). Macroeconomists have long been interested in measuring the costs of business cycles and inflation, as well as quantifying how large the gains could be to consumers from eliminating them. The consensus view based on standard macroeconomic models (Lucas 2003 provides an extensive review of this topic) is that households should not be willing to sacrifice much to eliminate business cycles and that inflation is much more costly. Our surveys yielded results strongly at odds with this consensus view: consumers across the globe reported that they would be willing to sacrifice around 5–6% of their yearly consumption to eliminate business cycles, almost identical to what they would be willing to give up to bring inflation to their desired target level.

A skeptic might say that these responses are nothing more than hypothetical numbers thrown out by people participating in a survey, with little bearing on whether they would actually sacrifice anything for the purposes of eliminating business cycles or inflation. But we think there are several reasons not to be too dismissive. One is that careful meta-studies comparing hypothetical and real WTPs when both measures are available for either public (e.g., Carson et al. 1996, Murphy et al. 2005) or private (e.g., Schmidt and Bijmolt 2020) goods have found that the hypothetical WTP tends to overstate the real WTP by only about 20–30% on average, and for many cases these measures are closely aligned and highly correlated. Carson et al. (1996) documented that hypothetical WTP overstated real WTP by a factor of 2 or more only in 3% of the studies. Thus, even if direct surveys may overstate WTP somewhat, we can still gauge the order of magnitude and debias survey-based WTPs to obtain more accurate estimates.

A second reason not to be too dismissive is that much of the cross-sectional variation that we observe, across both countries and individuals, is consistent with what theory would suggest. For example, Panel A of Figure 11.1 plots the average WTP for different countries relative to a measure of their recent economic volatility (how much unemployment increased during the pandemic relative to prior levels). People living in countries with higher macroeconomic volatility report a higher WTP to eliminate that volatility. In the cross-section of individuals (Panel B of Figure 11.1), we also observe that people who are more uncertain about the macroeconomic outlook are willing to pay more to eliminate the uncertainty, consistent with theory. Also in line with theoretical predictions is the fact that respondents whose income and consumption are more tied to aggregate business cycles report a higher WTP to eliminate those cycles. We find similar patterns when it comes to the WTP to eliminate inflation. People who live in countries that have had historically higher inflation are willing to pay more to reduce inflation to their target level (Panel A of Figure 11.2) as are those who are more uncertain about what inflation will be in the future (Panel B of Figure 11.2). Both patterns are again consistent with what theory would predict. So if the derivatives in the survey are correct, the levels may be as well.

Another unexpected finding from this paper, beyond the sheer size of how much people would be willing to sacrifice to eliminate business cycles, is that the two measures of WTP—to eliminate business cycles and to bring inflation

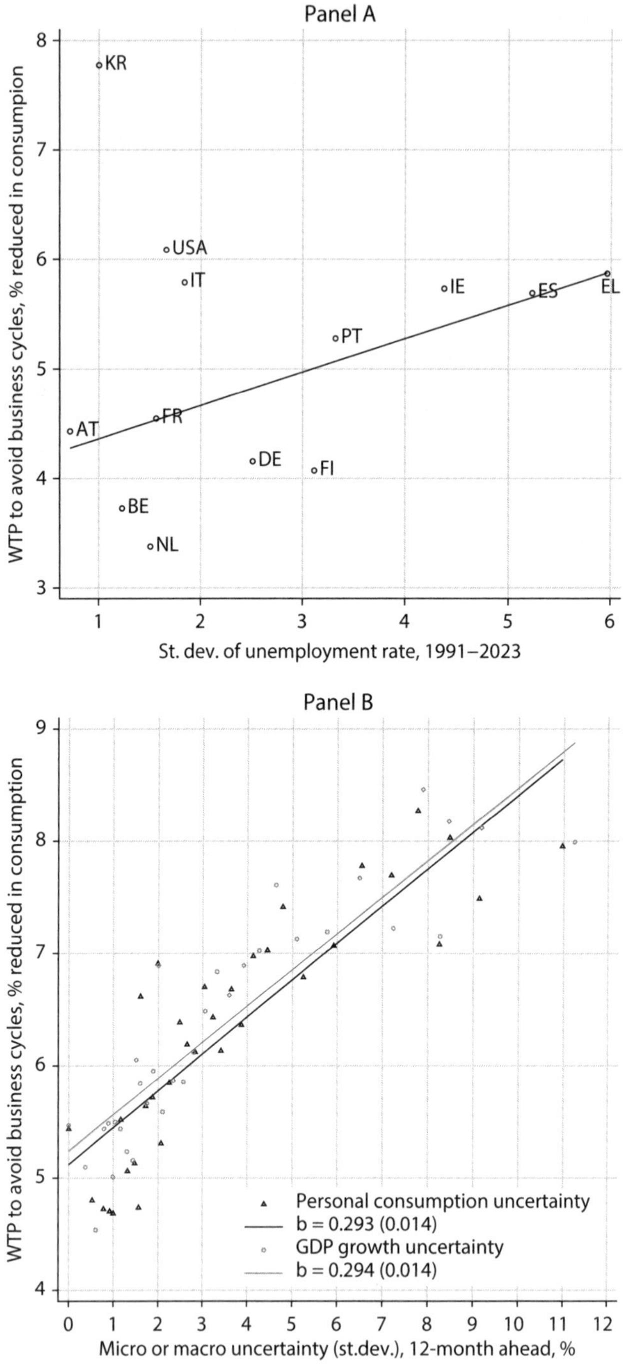

FIGURE 11.1. Determinants of the willingness to pay (WTP) to eliminate business cycles.

Notes: Data for horizontal axes in Panel A are from the World Bank. Panel B is a binscatter plot of willingness to pay (WTP) to avoid business cycles vs. uncertainty about the growth rate of GDP or uncertainty about the growth rate of personal (household-level) consumption. For Panel B, b reports the slope of the fitted linear relationship, and values in parentheses are the corresponding robust standard errors.

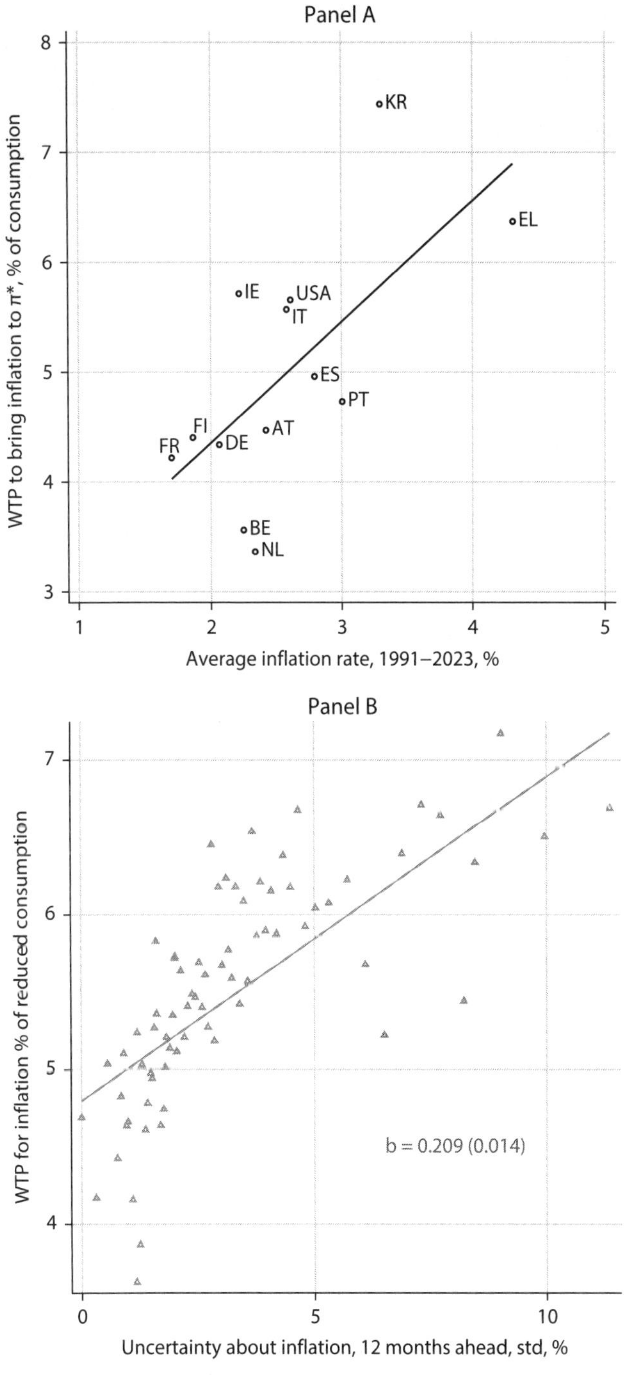

FIGURE 11.2. Historical inflation and the willingness to pay (WTP) to reduce inflation.

Notes: Data for the horizontal axis in Panel A are from the World Bank. Panel B shows binscatter plots of willingness to pay (WTP) to bring expected inflation levels to desired levels vs. uncertainty in the one-year-ahead inflation forecast (standard deviation implied by the reported subjective probability distribution).

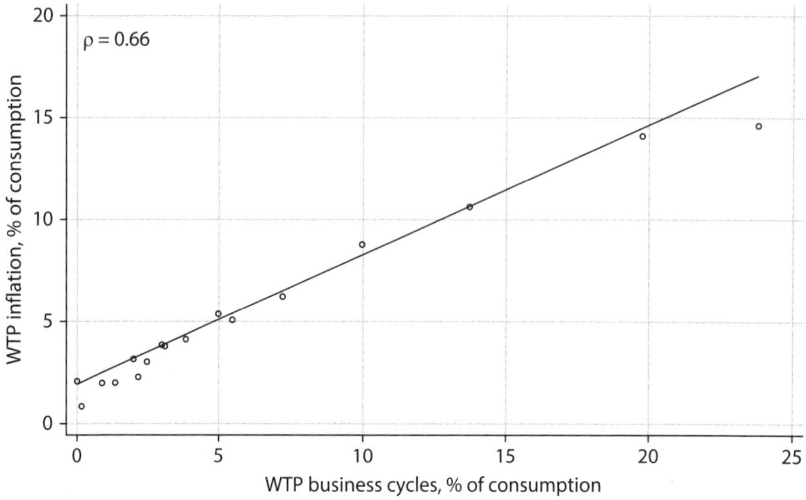

FIGURE 11.3. Willingness to pay (WTP) to eliminate business cycles vs. WTP to reduce inflation.
Notes: The figure shows a binscatter plot of willingness to pay (WTP; measured in % of consumption) to avoid business cycles vs. WTP (measured in % of consumption) to bring inflation from expected to desired levels. ρ shows the correlation between the WTPs.

to a desired level—are highly correlated. Figure 11.3 plots a binscatter of the two measures of WTP pooled across all countries: there is a striking large positive correlation between the two, a feature that holds within each country as well as across countries. Even though macroeconomists view the long-run level of inflation and economic volatility as largely separate things, this is not how consumers perceive them, leading to a strong correlation between their willingness to pay for them.

Because survey respondents were randomly provided with different formulations of the question measuring their WTPs to eliminate business cycles, which provided different pieces of information about their countries' volatility, our surveys incorporate an RCT element along with the hypothetical questions. We can then use this exogenous source of variation in the WTP for business cycles to better understand the source of the positive unconditional correlation between the two measures of WTP. Specifically, we regress WTP for inflation on the WTP for business cycles, and instrument for the latter using our information treatments. The IV estimates indicate a causal effect running from WTP for business cycles to the WTP for inflation. The coefficient, however, is only half the size of the OLS coefficient, indicating that there is either causality running in the opposite direction too or another source of variation induces common movements in the two types of WTP. This logic suggests that the reported WTPs likely refer to the combined effects of inflation and business cycles rather than ceteris paribus scenarios. Because our models frequently deliver strict delineations between real, nominal and financial forces, the resulting calculations of welfare costs of business cycles reflect these delineations. Consumers, to the extent that they may view these mechanisms as more tightly connected, may therefore be taking a much more holistic view of what eliminating business cycles means.

A particularly creative use of hypothetical questions is in Andre et al. (2022a). In a survey sent to both U.S. households and economic experts, they asked each respondent how they thought different types of shocks would affect the aggregate economy. For example, how would an increase in oil prices affect unemployment and inflation? They did this for several different types of economic shocks. They documented two particularly striking findings. One was that households often disagreed significantly about how different shocks would affect the economy, indicating that individuals often hold very different beliefs about how the economy functions, a feature at odds with standard macroeconomic models. A second was that for some shocks, the average beliefs of households and experts were completely different. For example, after an increase in interest rates by the central bank, experts tended to predict that inflation would decline whereas households tended to predict that it would rise. This paper, through its use of hypothetical scenarios, was able to document that disagreement about the economic outlook is likely to be pervasive even when everyone has the same information about the state of the economy, because they use different models to forecast how any given shock will affect economic outcomes.

In a similar spirit, researchers at the Federal Reserve Bank of New York have increasingly applied hypotheticals to their Survey of Consumer Expectations, in the absence of being able to run RCTs in that survey, to study how expectations might respond to different forces. In one such application, Armantier et al. (2022) used hypothetical questions to assess how learning that inflation has been higher than expected might affect the short-run and long-run inflation expectations of households, an exercise conceptually similar to that of the RCTs applied in Coibion, Gorodnichenko and Weber (2022a), but using hypotheticals. They concluded that the response of long-run expectations to such revisions in beliefs about recent inflation would be limited, indicating that inflation expectations of U.S. households are fairly anchored. In another application, Aidala et al. (2024) considered how hypothetical changes in gasoline prices would affect inflation expectations of U.S. households. Contrary to prior evidence using time series (e.g., Coibion and Gorodnichenko 2015b), their results pointed toward a limited pass-through of gas prices into inflation expectations. So, this represents one example in which the evidence from hypotheticals is less in line with prior empirical evidence, although it is difficult to make a clear quantitative statement as to how large the differences are in practice or if they reflect the methodological differences or changing inflation environments.

These papers do not directly address the question of how inflation expectations might in turn affect decisions. This question is taken up through hypotheticals in two recent papers: one by Jiang et al. (2024) and the other by Indarte et al. (2024). In the former, respondents were presented with a scenario in which their short-run inflation expectations were higher but their long-run inflation expectations were unchanged. A second specification of the hypothetical instead asked respondents about long-lived changes in their inflation expectations. In each case, respondents faced follow-up questions about how this would impact their other economic expectations, such as for how much their income will grow or what will happen to unemployment. Finally, respondents were asked about how their consumption over the next few months could be expected to change relative to what they were otherwise planning. Their main result was that, for most households, the difference in expected inflation would not lead to any change in their consumption decisions, a finding at odds with the RCT evidence in Coibion, Gorodnichenko and Weber (2022a) and Georgarakos et al. (2024). In contrast, Indarte et al. (2024) posed a hypothetical question about how respondents' current savings choices would change if they were to anticipate higher inflation in the future. In their survey of U.S. households, around 60 percent reported that they would decrease their savings. Both surveys were run at a similar time, when inflation in the U.S. was high. Given their very similar approaches but different results, more work will be needed to understand how to reconcile these two findings.

A second novel characteristic of Jiang et al. (2024) is that they showed that hypothetical scenario questions can be used to discern between the different mechanisms that can account for changes in consumption. They did so in two ways. One was through open-ended questions, in which they simply asked respondents to explain their answers in their own words. A second was by proposing specific mechanisms through which inflation might affect spending and asking respondents to pick from among these. Households were far from unanimous in the mechanisms they emphasized, but the majority appealed to some combination of lack of relevance to their decisions, a fixed budget and liquidity constraints in accounting for their lack of consumption adjustment. Others justified reducing their consumption because of wealth effects and fixed incomes, while some explained that they would raise their consumption because of the belief that future prices would be higher.

Summary

Hypotheticals hold a lot of promise for allowing us to answer new economic questions. In some cases, they can take the place of RCTs, which can be particularly useful, since RCTs are expensive, time-consuming and difficult to successfully implement. Existing evidence suggests that hypotheticals often (but not always) yield similar results as RCTs, indicating that the two approaches have significant overlap.

Indeed, rather than viewing them as substitutes, our preference is to view them as complements. Researchers applying RCT strategies should consider systematically including hypothetical questions in parallel. Not only would this provide more evidence on how the approaches compare, hypothetical scenario questions can shed light on more margins of adjustment than may be feasible in RCTs, thereby expanding the scope of the research project. And as illustrated in Jiang et al. (2024), they can also be used to help identify mechanisms at work in the RCT. Combining RCTs and hypothetical questions therefore holds a lot of promise in moving this line of research forward. Finally, hypothetical questions can be used to provide real-time analysis of how different policy actions or communications might affect firms and households. This could be particularly useful in times of crisis, when new policies or communications are being considered for whose effectiveness there is no historical evidence. The more systematic use of hypothetical scenario questions could therefore help policymakers make better decisions.

12

Mapping Expectational Pass-throughs to Theory and Applications

SO YOU'VE RUN a careful RCT that generated meaningful variation in beliefs and found empirically that those changes in beliefs had (or did not have!) a subsequent effect on decisions. Terrific! You excitedly go present this paper and are immediately asked about how this compares to theoretical predictions for the pass-through of expectations into outcomes. You mumble something in response about providing micro evidence for macro predictions and maybe relate your estimates to some aggregate relationships that have expectations terms of them, such as a Phillips curve. This could be a good starting point, but, really, what is the connection between these RCT-based estimates of expectational pass-throughs and the typical macroeconomic models that we know and love? In this chapter, we consider some pitfalls in thinking about expectations pass-throughs from standard models and discuss how instead to compare RCT-based estimates to theoretical predictions. We then develop one illustrative application to theory that shows how the estimates can be informative for quantitative macroeconomic questions. But, obviously, this approach can be useful in other contexts (see, e.g., Hajdini et al. 2023).

How Not to Think about Expectations Pass-through

Werning (2022) develops a wonderful illustration showing how using aggregate equilibrium relationships from macroeconomic models may be problematic for discussing the role of expectations in shaping decisions. He begins with the New Keynesian Phillips Curve (NKPC), which in its most famous form is typically expressed as

$$\pi_t = \beta E_t \pi_{t+1} + \kappa x_t, \tag{1}$$

and relates current inflation π_t to expected future inflation $E_t \pi_{t+1}$ and the current output gap x_t. This aggregate relationship, which follows from the assumption that firms update their prices infrequently, as in Calvo (1983),[1] combined with some assumptions about the rest of the model, has become the starting point for much of the monetary policy analysis in recent decades due to its tractability as well as its intuitive appeal. The NKPC captures both the traditional Keynesian Phillips curve logic (inflation will tend to be high when the economy is running hot and low when the economy is underperforming), since the coefficient $\kappa > 0$, as well as the Friedman (1968) and Phelps (1967) predictions that if inflation expectations start increasing, this will lead firms and workers to build this into their decisions, which ultimately can lead to more inflation.

The NKPC seems to make a very clear prediction about expectations pass-through into prices: if inflation expectations rise 1 percentage point, then inflation will rise almost one for one (since the discount factor β is close to 1). This seems to suggest a large potential role for inflation expectations in driving inflation dynamics and has been one of the justifications that central bankers use to explain their focus on "anchoring" inflation expectations. Since the slope of the Phillips curve κ is not very large empirically, even strong economic activity will not affect inflation much if inflation expectations do not change, i.e., remain anchored.

But Werning (2022) points out that if we iterate the NKPC forward, we can rewrite it just as correctly as

$$\pi_t = \kappa \sum_{j=0}^{\infty} \beta^j E_t x_{t+j}. \tag{2}$$

This equation states that current inflation depends on the current and future expected output gaps. Since inflation expectations do not appear in this expression, the implied pass-through of inflation expectations would now appear

1. In a nutshell, Calvo pricing posits that the timing of price adjustment is random and not related to how far actual prices are from desired prices. While this pricing may be the optimal strategy for firms under certain conditions, the main appeal of this modelling device is simple aggregation of heterogenous firms rather than the realism of its assumptions.

to be zero! Clearly, both statements about the pass-through of inflation expectations into actual inflation cannot be right at the same time.

What explains this black magic? As Werning (2022) makes clear, by the time we derive the NKPC shown above, we have made a number of assumptions about expectations that impose a straitjacket, such that:

$$E_t\pi_{t+1} = \kappa \sum_{j=1}^{\infty} \beta^j E_t x_{t+j}. \tag{3}$$

According to the standard theory, inflation expectations are inextricably linked to beliefs about the future path of the output gap. Changing one is identical to changing the other. But when we run an RCT that affects the inflation expectations of firms, there is nothing restricting their inflation expectations from changing in line with their beliefs about the future output gap. If their inflation expectations change but their beliefs about future output do not, what is the relevant predicted pass-through from the model: 0 or 1?

Another example of confusion that stems from relying on aggregate relationships from a macro model is in terms of which horizon of expectations should matter. Again, the NKPC in its traditional form seems to make a clear prediction: it is short-run inflation expectations of firms that matter for inflation determination, not long-run expectations. But Hazell et al. (2022) show that the NKPC can be rewritten instead as:

$$\pi_t = E_t\pi_{t+T} + \kappa \sum_{j=0}^{T} \beta^j E_t x_{t+j}, \tag{4}$$

which now relates current inflation to expectations of current and future output growth as well as *long-run* inflation expectations π_{t+T}. In this formulation, it is the long-run inflation expectations of firms that appear to matter for their pricing decisions, not their short-run expectations. So if policymakers want to anchor inflation expectations to stabilize inflation, should they focus on short-term or long-term expectations? If short-term inflation expectations rise but long-term expectations do not, does the model predict that current inflation will rise as well? The answer in the model is again that the nature of the assumptions that deliver these equivalent expressions imposes a straitjacket on inflation expectations that makes the two equations equivalent. But what if we do an RCT that ends up moving short-run and long-run inflation expectations in a way that is at odds with the restrictions imposed within the model? What is the relevant model prediction to compare our estimates to?

The answer to the latter is, neither. By the time we get to the aggregate relationships described above, the modeling restrictions that have been imposed make the thought experiment coming from the RCT an ill-defined one. Expectations are fully endogenous with respect to macroeconomic conditions and to each other within the model. The aggregate relationships reflect this endogeneity of beliefs and all of the associated restrictions imposed on their joint formation. It does not make sense to use aggregated relationships like the NKPC to answer questions that violate the restrictions that are embodied in it.

How to Think about Expectations Pass-through

If we cannot compare our RCT-based estimates to aggregate equilibrium relationships from our macro models, what should we do? Werning (2022) proposes a more targeted approach that focuses on individual agents and how their own decisions vary contemporaneously with their beliefs, *taking the latter as given*, which he refers as a "temporary equilibrium." The advantage is that this does not require imposing any restrictions on how expectations are formed and provides a framework that is more comparable to that of the RCT, but it limits our ability to consider dynamics or general equilibrium without imposing additional assumptions.

Consider the problem of a firm with sticky prices, as in Calvo (1983), which must set a price. Letting λ be the probability that a firm cannot reset its price each period, the log-linearized optimal reset price p_t^* of firms at time t is

$$p_t^* - \overline{p}_{t-1} = (1-\beta\lambda)E_{t-1}\sum_{s=1}^{\infty}(\beta\lambda)^s(\overline{p}_{t+s} - \overline{p}_t) + a_t,$$

where following Werning (2022) we assume expectations for time t decisions are using information from the previous period (i.e., firms cannot simultaneously observe prices of other firms) and denote the average level of prices at time t with $\overline{p}_t$. The term a_t captures all of the non-inflation expectations component of the reset price decision, namely, current and future expected real marginal costs. The other component of the optimal reset price depends on expected cumulative inflation between today and each future period, discounted by the probability that the firm is not able to change its price before then. This expected cumulative future inflation matters because, since the firm knows it may have the same price in future periods, it must take into account that its relative price will fall in the future as other firms raise their prices. The more a price-resetting firm expects other firms to raise prices in the future, the more it needs to raise its price today in anticipation. This is the direct channel through which inflation expectations affect price setting decisions in the model.

Again following Werning (2022), assume for simplicity that expected inflation is the same for all future periods and is given by π^e. Then the optimal relative reset price can be written as

$$p_t^* - \bar{p}_{t-1} = \left(\frac{1}{1-\beta\lambda}\right)\pi^e + a_t. \tag{6}$$

Note that this expression now makes a clear prediction for the pass-through of inflation expectations into prices for an individual firm: if its inflation expectations rise by 1 percentage point (holding everything else constant), a firm will raise its price by *more* than 1 percentage point, if able to do so that period. The firm overshoots because it knows it will likely keep its price the same for some time. For example, if $\lambda \approx 1/2$ at the quarterly frequency (firms change their prices every six months on average), $\left(\frac{1}{1-\beta\lambda}\right) \approx 2$.

The average change in prices across all firms, however, will be smaller since a fraction λ of firms are not changing their price at all. Averaged across firms, aggregate prices will evolve according to:

$$\pi_t = \left(\frac{1-\lambda}{1-\beta\lambda}\right)\pi^e + (1-\lambda)a_t. \tag{7}$$

This now makes a prediction about expectations pass-through into average prices that is closer to what we can estimate in an RCT. Specifically, the model predicts that if inflation expectations rise by 1 percentage point and nothing else changes (i.e. a_t is constant), then prices will rise by $\left(\frac{1-\lambda}{1-\beta\lambda}\right)$ on average. Since β is very close to 1, the implied pass-through into the price of an average firm is close to (but below) 1. Werning (2022) also considers alternative price setting formulations, such as the Taylor (1980) price setting (the pass-through of inflation expectations into prices is then ½) and menu cost models (the pass-through of inflation expectations into prices can vary but is generally positive and small). Hence, theoretical models of price-setting support the notion of a positive pass-through from inflation expectations, but the specific magnitude depends on the nature of price-setting and the underlying parameters.

How well do these predictions line up with RCT estimates? An important caveat in comparing the two is that the Werning (2022) approach isolates the direct effect of expectations on decisions while shutting down indirect effects. The indirect effect would be a change in inflation expectations also leading firms to revise their beliefs about current or future real marginal costs (a_t). In Coibion, Gorodnichenko and Kumar (2018), using firms in New Zealand, the information treatments that led firms to reduce their inflation expectations on average did *not* generate any particular change in other macroeconomic expectations, suggesting that it is reasonable to assume that $\frac{\partial a_t}{\partial \pi^e} \approx 0$ in that setting. The estimated pass-through of expectations into prices was small: an approximately 0.10 percentage point decline in prices for each 1 percentage point decline in inflation expectations. This is consistent with the predictions of menu cost models considered in Werning (2022).

However, the fact that other macroeconomic expectations did not respond to the information treatments in our New Zealand RCT is not a general result. In the information treatments involving recent inflation being provided to firms in Italy described in Coibion, Gorodnichenko and Ropele (2020), firms that raised their inflation expectations tended to significantly lower their views about future economic growth and the their own outlook. Even though one might expect this change in expectations to put downward pressure on prices, the estimated total effect from inflation expectations on prices was, if anything, larger than in New Zealand, pointing to a contemporaneous pass-through of approximately 0.2. And during the period of the effective lower bound in Italy, during which firms associated higher inflation with better economic outcomes for their firm and the country, the estimated pass-through was even higher, almost 0.7. In an experiment run on firms in Switzerland, Abberger et al. (2024) estimated a modestly higher pass-through of 0.3–0.4. However, when Akarsu, Aktug and Torun (2024) did a similar RCT in Turkey, where inflation was very high, their estimate of the pass-through of inflation expectations into prices was significantly higher, well above 0.5.

In short, the evidence from these available RCTs on the degree to which inflation expectations map into firms' prices is consistent with standard models of price-setting behavior in that higher inflation expectations lead to increases in prices. Because empirical estimates may include some indirect effects, as well as because of the statistical uncertainty around the estimates, it is difficult to use the estimates to strongly distinguish between models of price-setting. Instead, we view the broad consistency between theoretical predictions and the estimated magnitudes as vindicating the usefulness of both and highlighting how theory can complement this empirical strategy. However, this is but a starting point in terms of assessing how expectations affect decisions, given the range of different expectations and channels through which they affect many different economic decisions. We therefore expect that a lot of future research will be needed to more systematically assess the strength and relevance of these different channels underlying the economic decisions that form the backbone of macroeconomic models and dynamics.

Why Expectational Pass-through Coefficients Are Important

Besides validating and quantifying theoretical predictions about how expectations affect decisions, do causal estimates of expectations pass-through help us address any new theoretical or quantitative questions? The answer would obviously depend on the context, but here we would like to provide one illustration of how these estimates can help us with a quantitative economic model. The idea builds on the results described above, showing that firms' inflation expectations pass through into their prices with values that are broadly in line with standard pricing models. If that's the case, then otherwise identical firms who hold different inflation expectations will tend to set different prices. In standard macroeconomic models, price dispersion is a source of misallocation and leads to less aggregate production and consumption than would otherwise be the case, so there is a loss in welfare associated with this dispersion. By generating greater price dispersion, larger disagreement by firms about inflation should therefore be associated with worse economic outcomes.

Why is this potentially important? Empirically, there is a strong positive relationship between the level of inflation and the amount of disagreement about inflation expectations. Periods of high inflation tend to be periods when people disagree more about the inflation outlook. This was documented

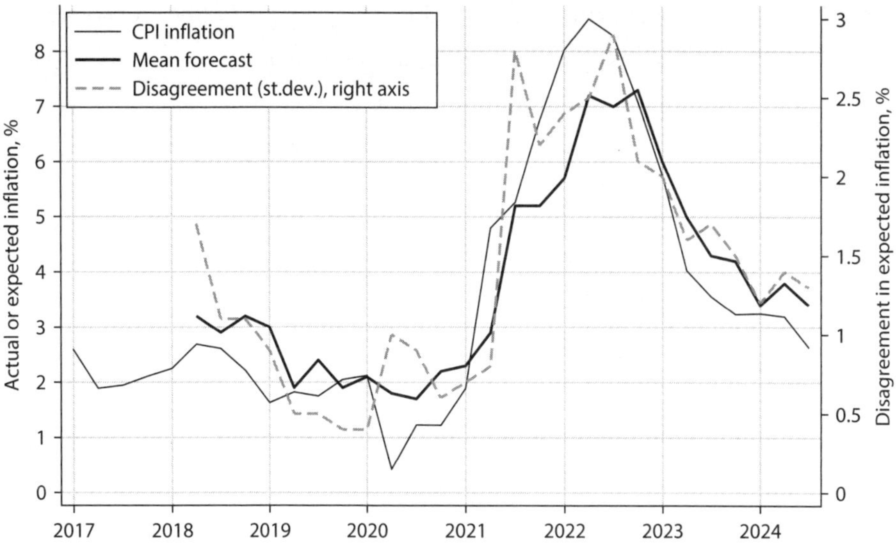

FIGURE 12.1. Firms' inflation expectations, U.S.
Source: Survey of Firms' Inflation Expectations (SoFIE), Federal Reserve Bank of Cleveland. See Candia, Coibion and Gorodnichenko (2024) for more details.

extensively by Mankiw, Reis and Wolfers (2004) for U.S. households and professional forecasters. In Figure 12.1, we plot how disagreement about future inflation among U.S. firms evolved as the U.S. inflation rate first rose and then fell from 2021 through 2024. Consistent with the earlier evidence of Mankiw, Reis and Wolfers (2004), firms in the U.S. began to disagree much more systematically about future inflation as the inflation rate rose, with the cross-sectional standard deviation of disagreement rising by a factor of 4. If we believe the argument above that high disagreement about inflation has welfare costs through price dispersion, then this period of high inflation would have imposed additional costs to society through this channel, above and beyond the usual costs of inflation that macroeconomists have long studied.

How large would the costs associated with this disagreement channel be? This is the question we tried to address in Ropele, Gorodnichenko and Coibion (2024), using a quantitative macroeconomic model that embodies the expectations channel described above and is disciplined through additional evidence from RCTs. For simplicity, we again assume Calvo (1983) pricing and begin with the pricing equation from Werning (2022):

$$p_{it}^{*} - \overline{p}_{t-1} = \frac{1}{1-\beta\lambda}\pi_{it}^{e} + a_{it}, \tag{8}$$

where i,t index firms and time, β is the discount factor, $1-\lambda$ is the probability of price resets, $\overline{p}_t$ is approximately the average price (that is, $\overline{p}_t = \int_0^1 p_{it} di$), and a_{it} collects terms that do not depend on inflation expectations (e.g., future real marginal costs). As before, we assume inflation expectations are the same across horizons for a given firm i at time t.

Heterogeneity in inflation expectations across firms implies that there is also heterogeneity in prices across firms. The cross-sectional dispersion in prices at time t is given by:

$$\begin{aligned} var_i(p_{it}) &\equiv \Delta_t \\ &= \lambda \Delta_{t-1} + (1-\lambda)\left(\frac{1}{1-\beta\lambda}\right)^2 var_i(\pi_{it}^e) + 2\frac{1-\lambda}{1-\beta\lambda} cov_i(\pi_{it}^e, a_{it}) \\ &+ (1-\lambda)\left\{\frac{1}{1-\beta\lambda}\overline{\pi}_t^e + \overline{a}_t\right\}^2 + (1-\lambda) var_i(a_{it}) - \overline{\pi}_t^2, \end{aligned} \tag{9}$$

where $\overline{\pi}_t \equiv \overline{p}_t - \overline{p}_{t-1}$ and $\overline{\pi}_t^e$ is average inflation expectations across firms. The first term in the expression above reflects the presence of sticky prices: since not all prices change, price dispersion in each period depends in part on price dispersion in the previous period. Given that prices depend on inflation expectations and all other factors included in a_{it}, the dispersion in prices across firms will also depend in part on the amount of disagreement in inflation expectations $var_i(\pi_{it}^e)$, the cross-sectional variance in a_{it}, and the covariance between the two $(cov_i(\pi_{it}^e, a_{it}))$. Holding all else constant, more disagreement across firms about future inflation raises price dispersion on impact as well as dynamically.

Unfortunately, because prices are difficult to compare across products, economists can rarely measure price dispersion directly. Instead, the misallocation that is induced by firms setting different prices is typically measured through how differently firms utilize inputs. For example, suppose all firms are hiring from the same labor market and facing the same wage. Then, they should all be hiring workers until the marginal revenue product of labor is equal to that wage. But if a firm has a price that is low relative to its competitors, then its demand will be high and it will need to hire additional workers to meet that demand, pushing the marginal revenue product below the wage. The extent to which marginal products of inputs differ across firms will thus vary with price dispersion.

To see this more formally, assume that the demand function for a variety produced by firm $i \in [0,1]$ is given by $Y_{it} = Y_t \left(\frac{P_{it}}{\overline{P}_t} \right)^{-\sigma}$, where i,t index firms and time, Y_{it} is output, P_{it} is the price of variety i, and $\overline{P}_t$ is the price level. The production function is $Y_{it} = Z_t K_{it}^{\alpha} L_{it}^{1-\alpha}$, where Z_t is the level of technology that is common across firms, L_{it} is the labor input, and K_{it} is the capital input. We assume that capital is a quasi-fixed factor that is set to the optimal "steady-state" level $\overline{K}$.

After a lot of algebra and using lower-case letters to denote logs of the corresponding variables (e.g., $l_{it} \equiv \log(L_{it})$), we can show that the cross-sectional dispersion of log marginal revenue products for labor and capital are given by

$$var_i(mrpl_{it}) = \left[(1-\alpha)\left(1-\frac{1}{\sigma}\right) - 1 \right]^2 var_i(l_{it}), \tag{10}$$

$$var_i(mrpk_{it}) = \left[(1-\alpha)\left(1-\frac{1}{\sigma}\right) \right]^2 var_i(l_{it}). \tag{11}$$

The dispersion in the marginal revenue products of labor and capital depends on the dispersion of the labor input across firms, effectively capturing the extent to which different firms are "too big" or "too small." This, in turn, depends on the extent to which their prices differ, and there is a direct mapping from dispersion in prices to dispersion in labor inputs:

$$var_i(l_{it}) = \left(\frac{\sigma}{1-\alpha} \right)^2 var_i(p_{it}). \tag{12}$$

It follows immediately that dispersions in marginal products of both labor and capital are related to the dispersion in prices:

$$var_i(mrpl_{it}) = \left[(1-\alpha)\left(1-\frac{1}{\sigma}\right) - 1 \right]^2 \left(\frac{\sigma}{1-\alpha} \right)^2 var_i(p_{it}), \tag{13}$$

$$var_i(mrpk_{it}) = \left[(1-\alpha)\left(1-\frac{1}{\sigma}\right) \right]^2 \left(\frac{\sigma}{1-\alpha} \right)^2 var_i(p_{it}). \tag{14}$$

As we discuss in the paper, it is also useful to compute the cross-sectional dispersion in the difference of marginal revenue products:

$$var_i(mrpk_{it} - mrpl_{it}) = var_i(l_{it}) = \left(\frac{\sigma}{1-\alpha}\right)^2 var_i(p_{it}). \tag{15}$$

These three particular measures of cross-sectional dispersion in marginal products, (13) – (15), are helpful because they relate directly to the total efficiency loss in the economy from misallocation. Specifically, following Hsieh and Klenow (2009) with the identifying assumption of no distortions in labor, we can derive the following expression for aggregate total factor productivity (TFP) effects from the dispersion of marginal revenue products:[2]

$$\begin{aligned} TFP = &-\left\{\frac{\sigma(1-\alpha)}{2} + \frac{\sigma(1+\alpha)\sigma}{2}\right\} \times var_i(mrpk_{it} - mrpl_{it}) \\ &- \frac{\sigma(1+\alpha)}{2} \times var_i(mrpl_{it}) + \frac{\sigma\alpha}{2} var_i(mrpk_{it}). \end{aligned} \tag{16}$$

Thus, this model delivers a clear mapping from disagreement about inflation expectations into aggregate TFP losses via the associated price dispersion that can be measured through the cross-sectional dispersion in marginal revenue products of inputs.

To quantify the effect of a change in disagreement about inflation on TFP, one could at this stage simply choose some parameter values to plug into the model and go from inflation disagreement to TFP losses, taking the model at face value. In Ropele, Gorodnichenko and Coibion (2024), however, we decided to take a less structural approach and discipline some of the pass-through from disagreement about inflation into misallocation through empirical estimates. The idea was to directly estimate the pass-through from disagreement about future inflation into dispersion of marginal revenue products, essentially asking the empirical question: does higher disagreement about inflation lead to more misallocation and, if so, by how much? The reason for doing this is that the model makes many assumptions in moving from disagreement about inflation to dispersion in marginal products that are clear simplifications, such as Calvo pricing. An empirical estimate allows us to abstract from these

2. See Gorodnichenko et al. (2018) for derivations.

assumptions and then compare our estimates to what the model would predict.

Doing so is not trivial, however. First, we need a survey that measures inflation expectations of firms. Second, we need a source of exogenous variation in beliefs, specifically in disagreement across firms. Third, we need to be able to measure marginal revenue products of inputs of firms. Fortunately, this is feasible using the SIGE survey of firms in Italy. The survey includes inflation expectations on a quarterly basis, which meets the first criterion. Due to the provision of information about inflation to a randomly selected subset of firms, it provides exogenous variation in disagreement. Third, it can be matched to external data sources that allow for the measurement of marginal revenue products of firms.

As discussed in Chapter 2, the SIGE is a quarterly business survey conducted by the Bank of Italy since December 1999. The sample is stratified by three *sectors* of economic activity (industry, nonfinancial private services and construction), four geographical *areas* (North-West, North-East, Centre, South and Islands) and three classes of size in terms of number of *employees* (50–199, 200–999, 1,000 and over). In the years preceding the COVID19 pandemic, each wave saw the participation of about 1,050 firms (400 in industry, 450 in nonfinancial private services and 200 in construction). Sampling weights are provided to ensure that the distribution of firms in the sample represents the distribution of firms in the reference population.

In each wave, firms are asked about their inflation expectations, but the way this has been done has evolved over time in a very unique way. Since the third quarter of 2012 the SIGE fielded two versions of the question, eliciting annual inflation expectations at various horizons: next six months, next year, next two years, and (since the fist quarter of 2014) years 3 to 4. Because expectations are highly correlated across horizons, we focus on one-year-ahead forecasts. Approximately one-third of the sample received the following question about inflation expectations:

> What do you think consumer price inflation in Italy, measured by the 12-month change in the Harmonized Index of Consumer Prices, will be . . . ?

while the rest of the sample had:

> In [previous month], consumer price inflation measured by the 12-month change in the Harmonized Index of Consumer Prices was [X.X]% in Italy and [Y.Y]% in the Euro area. What do you think it will be in Italy . . . ?

We took the first subsample as the control group (no provision of information) and the second subsample as the treatment group (provision of information). Before the third quarter of 2012, all firms received the second formulation of the question so that all firms were in the treatment group. Which version of the question a firm receives as of the third quarter of 2012 was determined via randomization. Once assigned to a group, a firm generally stays in that group for a number of survey waves. Assignment was randomly redrawn in the fourth quarter of 2012 and then again in the second quarter of 2017. Coibion, Gorodnichenko and Ropele (2020) verified that assignment is not predicted by the observable characteristics of firms.

Figure 12.2 summarizes the properties of inflation expectations for the two groups. The average inflation expectations (Panel A) and disagreement (cross-sectional standard deviation of expectations, Panel B) are similar across treatment and control groups before the third quarter of 2012 since both were being provided with the same information, but a clear divergence becomes visible after the third quarter of 2012, when their information sets differed. The average expectation of the treatment group follows actual inflation (i.e., the provided signal) much more closely than the average expectation of the control group. We also observe that the disagreement in inflation expectations is considerably smaller for the treatment group than for the control group. This difference in disagreement across the two groups of firms is at the heart of our empirical strategy.

The next step consisted of creating multiple groups ("cells") of firms based on geography, industry and size (our baseline had 36 groups but we explored other groupings) for firms in the control group (who did not receive information about inflation) and, separately, for firms in the treatment group (who received information about inflation each quarter). For each group of firms, we measured the disagreement in inflation expectations as well as the dispersion in marginal revenue products of inputs. We then measured the difference in dispersion and disagreement between firms in the treatment and control groups, for each group of firms. Specifically, the outcome variable for misallocation for input $X \equiv \{K, L\}$ was given by

$$y_{j,t}^{MRPX} \equiv std_{j,t}^{treatment}\left(\log(MPRX_{i\in j,t})\right) - std_{j,t}^{control}\left(\log(MPRX_{i\in j,t})\right),$$

where i, j, t index firms, cells, and time. Thus, $y_{j,t}^{MRPX}$ measured the difference in the dispersion of marginal revenue products for input X between control

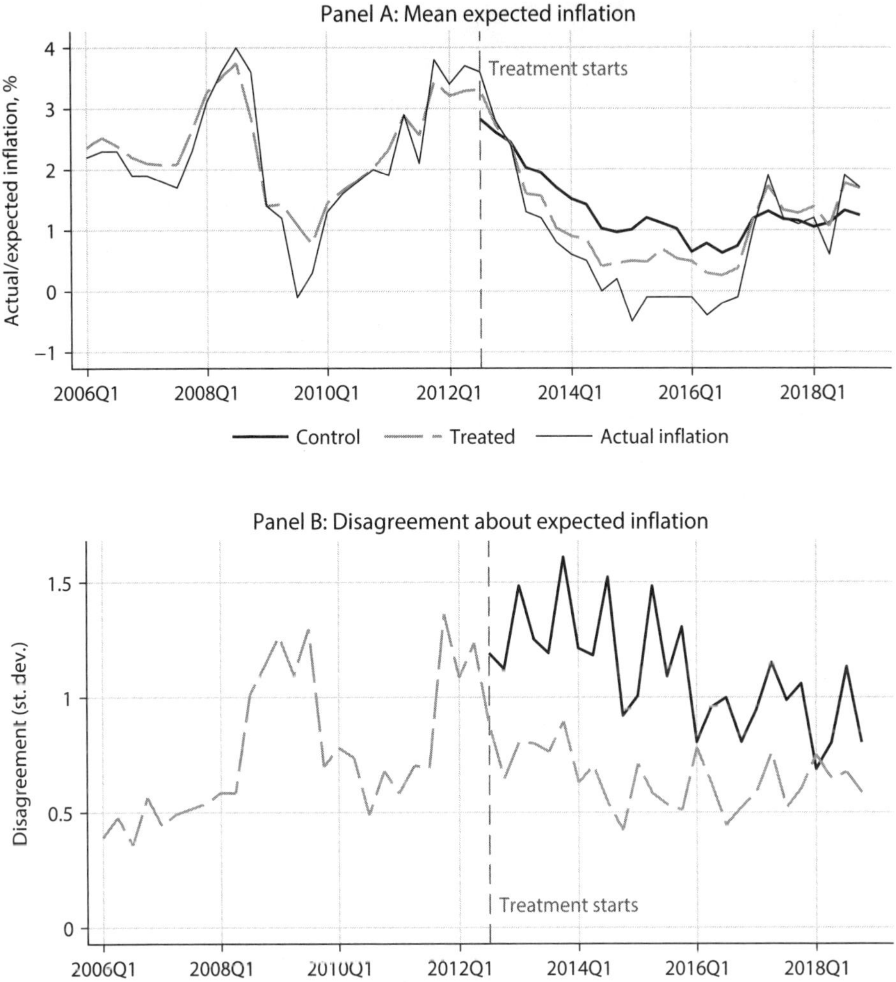

FIGURE 12.2. Firms' inflation expectations, Italy.
Source: Coibion, Gorodnichenko and Ropele (2020).

and treatment groups within a cell in a given period. The key regressor in our context was the difference in dispersion of one-year-ahead inflation expectations $F_{i\in j,t}\pi^{1y}$ for treated and control firms within a cell-time unit:

$$x_{j,t} \equiv std_{j,t}^{treatment}(F_{i\in j,t}\pi^{1y}) - std_{j,t}^{control}(F_{i\in j,t}\pi^{1y}).$$

We estimated the following equation on the data for 2012Q3–2019Q4:

$$y_{j,t+h}^{MRPX} = c_j^{(h)} + \tau_t^{(h)} + \sum_{k=0}^{4} \beta_k^{(h)} \times x_{j,t-k} + \sum_{k=1}^{4} \rho_k^{(h)} \times y_{j,t-k}^{MRPX} + error, \quad (17)$$

where c_j and τ_t are cell and time fixed effects. By varying h from 0 to H, we estimated the impulse response $\left\{\hat{\beta}_0^{(h)}\right\}_{h=0}^{H}$ of the outcome variable y at horizon $t+h$ to a shock in x in period t. This is the local projection approach developed in Jorda (2005). Because variation in $x_{j,t}$ comes from randomization, we could estimate specification (1) by OLS.[3] This regression effectively asked whether differences in disagreement about inflation across firms translate into differences in the dispersion of marginal products of input across those firms.

The answer, as shown in Panels A–C of Figure 12.3, is, yes. Regardless of the exact way in which we grouped firms, we found systematic evidence that when firms disagree more about inflation, this leads to more dispersion in the marginal revenue products of their inputs, and therefore more misallocation, as predicted by the theory. Furthermore, the quantitative magnitudes of the empirical estimates are broadly in line with what the basic model described above predicts. In the data, for example, the average responses across horizons are 7.0 (standard error 3.5) for $\log(MRPK)$ and 4.6 (standard error 2.5) for $\log(MRPL)$. For plausible calibrations of this model, the sensitivity of the (cross-sectional) standard deviation of the marginal revenue products of labor to the (cross-sectional) standard deviation of inflation expectations varies from 2 to 10, broadly in agreement with the empirical estimates. The equivalent elasticities for the marginal revenue products of capital dispersion and the ratio of capital-to-labor dispersions are predicted to be slightly higher but still close to what we estimated. Hence, there is again broad consistency between

3. One can think about this specification as a version of the Wald estimator, that is, an instrumental variable regression where the instrument is an indicator variable equal to 1 for the treatment group and 0 for the control group. In other words, the first stage is similar to specifications (1) and (2) in Chapter 6. Our discussion in that chapter emphasized that specifications (1) and (2) can be problematic because information treatments can increase or decrease the posterior depending on where the treatment signal is relative to the prior. However, when we work with disagreement, standard theory makes an unambiguous prediction: agents should have less disagreement after observing a common signal. In other words, the treatment unambiguously reduces disagreement, and thus one can use a version of specification (1) or (2). This is consistent with the evidence reported in Panel B of Figure 12.2.

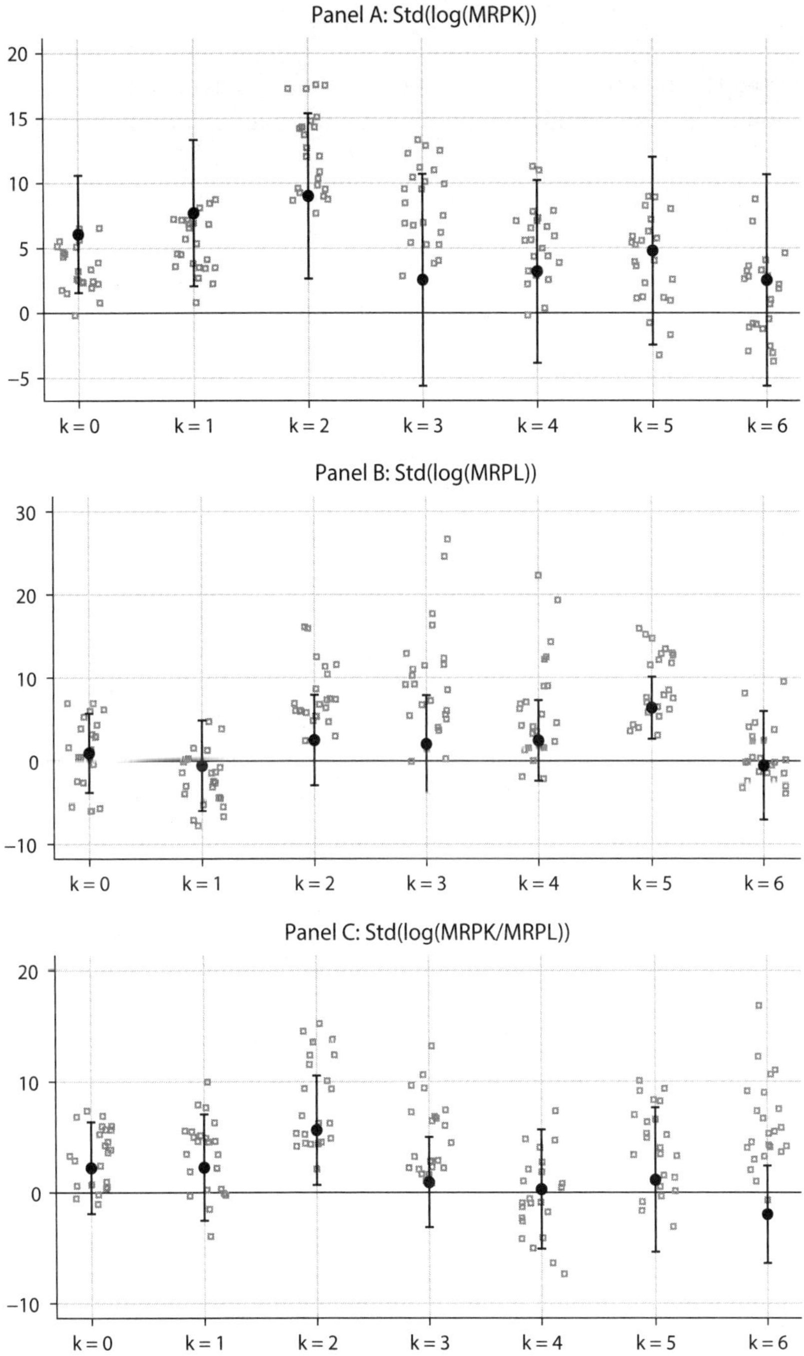

FIGURE 12.3. Responses of cross-section dispersion of marginal revenue products to information treatments, Italy.

Notes: The figure plots impulse responses of cross-sectional dispersion of marginal products to changes in the cross-sectional dispersion of inflation expectations. The baseline estimate is given by solid circles. The whiskers show the 90% confidence intervals. Empty squares show estimates for alternative definitions of cells. See Ropele, Gorodnichenko and Coibion (2024) for more details.

the implied pass-through of expectations into the actions of firms across theory and empirics, but this time measured using a mapping from dispersion in beliefs to dispersion in input choices and, therefore, misallocation.

Because the theory provides a clear mapping from marginal revenue products into TFP losses and the empirics provide a mapping from disagreement about inflation into dispersion in marginal revenue products, we could do two interesting quantitative exercises. The first asks the following question: suppose that all the firms in Italy were provided with information about recent inflation, as in the treatment group every quarter in the SIGE; by how much would misallocation decline? We think of this as providing a measure of potential gains from improved communication by the central bank. If all firms in Italy were provided with the basic information treatment involving recent inflation, inflation disagreement would decline and would therefore create aggregate TFP gains. The specific magnitude depends on parameters. When the elasticity of substitution is high ($\sigma = 10$), this policy intervention improves aggregate TFP by around ½ percentage point. The gain is 0.16% for a more conservative $\sigma = 3$. These results suggest that successful policy communication can improve the allocation of resources by shrinking cross-sectional disagreement in inflation expectations, but achieving such a gain in practice would require a communication strategy that successfully reached all firms in the economy, a difficult task. In a similar spirit, Drenik and Perez (2020) studied the time when Argentinian authorities manipulated inflation statistics and therefore made them *less* informative (the opposite of good communication). As firms' beliefs about inflation became more dispersed, price dispersion increased, leading to large welfare losses.

The second experiment goes back to Figure 12.1: given that the inflation surge of 2021–2022 was accompanied by a large increase in disagreement about inflation, how much of a loss did this inflation spike cause through the expectations channel into prices? To quantify this, we took into account the fact that, with higher inflation, firms will change prices more often, thereby reducing the pass-through of expectations into marginal revenue products by around one-third. Despite this reduction in pass-through, we estimated a 2.2 percent reduction in aggregate TFP for a conservative value of $\sigma = 3$, with other calibrations leading to even larger estimated losses. In other words, our estimates combined with the theoretical model imply that the inflation surge was likely very costly in terms of welfare. Just this one channel that we focus on already predicts large effects from the inflation surge, and there are many other channels through which inflation reduces welfare.

Summary

Empirical estimates based on RCT variation are clean and credible. But they don't answer everything. In most cases, it takes a combination of empirics and theory to answer an economic question. The RCT-based estimates that we have emphasized can be extremely powerful in testing and quantifying expectational channels. But they are even more powerful when combined with theoretical models to answer questions that empirics alone never can. The mapping from one to the other is not always straightforward, and there is much more work to do in thinking through how these estimates speak to theoretical models. But we hope this section has illustrated that doing so is feasible and potentially very useful.

PART IV

Applications

13

How Does Economic Uncertainty Affect the Decisions of Households and Firms?

MACROECONOMISTS DON'T AGREE on where recessions come from. Real Business Cycle models of the 1980s emphasized technology shocks, but we rarely observe the kind of large technological regress that would be necessary to explain a recession, much less a depression.[1] New Keynesian models of the 1990s and 2000s emphasized monetary and other demand shocks, but none have been found to be quantitatively important enough to explain most downturns. Since macroeconomists are nothing if not persistent, however, these early failures have not stopped research on business cycles. If traditional technology shocks don't work, maybe investment-specific technology shocks would (Fisher 2006), or perhaps it could be news about future technology (Barsky and Sims 2011). We have considered confidence shocks (Enders, Kleemann and Muller 2021), financial shocks (Caldara et al. 2016), commodity price shocks; you name it, we've tried it. But the punchline of 50+ years of business cycle research is that we still very much struggle to explain most business cycle fluctuations.

One of the most promising avenues macroeconomists have come up with to break this morass was by Nick Bloom in his 2009 seminal paper. He

1. Lucas (1994) wrote: "Imagine trying to rewrite the Great Contraction chapter of *A Monetary History* with shocks of this kind playing the role Friedman and Schwartz assign to monetary contractions. What technological or psychological events could have induced such behavior in a large, diversified economy? How could such events have gone unremarked at the time, and remain invisible even to hindsight?"

proposed a new source of business cycle fluctuations that had previously been largely left untouched by the macroeconomics profession: changes in uncertainty. In this paper, he made the first case for uncertainty shocks as a plausible source of business cycles. First, he showed that there have been large changes in uncertainty historically associated with wars (the Persian Gulf War), financial events (the 1987 stock market crash), political crises (the assassination of U.S. President John Kennedy), and so on. Second, he showed that, empirically, these types of events were on average followed by sharp economic contractions. Third, he wrote down a model that formalized how changes in uncertainty could lead to a "wait and see" effect that could rationalize the downturns following large uncertainty shocks. Since then, a large literature has built on his work, expanding our ability to measure uncertainty and to quantify how uncertainty affects economic outcomes. Here, we review some of this prior work and illustrate how RCT-based methods were used to help further this important literature.

Measuring Uncertainty

The original Bloom (2009) measure of economic uncertainty was a simple one, essentially capturing high-frequency volatility in stock markets. But stock markets can be volatile for all sorts of reasons, and those different reasons need not all have the same economic effects. So a lot of subsequent work concentrated on coming up with measures of economic uncertainty that were more targeted.

One paper that focused on measuring uncertainty of firms specifically was Bloom et al. (2018). They used detailed data on manufacturing firms from the Census Bureau to measure productivity changes at the level of the establishment/firm. What they were then able to show was that, during recessions, there was significantly more volatility in ex post productivity changes across firms. So if managers had been anticipating ahead of time this higher volatility in shocks to their firms, then they should have been more uncertain ex ante and this uncertainty would have lined up well with recessions. This is not limited to productivity changes. Bloom et al. (2018) show that many other measures of volatility across firms are significantly higher during recessions, such as output growth and stock price changes. In short, recessions are periods in which firm outcomes become much more dispersed than in normal times, consistent with there being an increase in volatility.

Other work focused on measuring different forms of uncertainty. For example, Jurado, Ludvigson and Ng (2015) estimated the common component of historical expected volatility across a wide range of macroeconomic variables, thereby creating a time series of macroeconomic uncertainty that differs quite a bit from the original Bloom (2009) measure. In follow-up work, Ludvigson, Ma and Ng (2021) separated financial uncertainty from macroeconomic uncertainty, again using the common variation in expected volatility across many different variables (either macroeconomic or financial). Baker, Bloom and Davis (2016) instead focused on measuring economic policy uncertainty. Their primary way of doing so was tracking the number of newspaper articles over time that included key words like "uncertainty" as well as words identifying policy, such as "fiscal," "monetary," etc. Again, the resulting measure looks quite different from the original Bloom (2009) measure. Hassan et al. (2019) created measures of firms' perceptions of political risk from discussions held during earnings calls. Aruoba et al. (2024) used the Chilean riots of 2019 as a quasi-natural experiment to separate the effects of ex ante uncertainty on prices from those stemming from ex post volatility. Gambetti et al. (2023) differentiated between changes in uncertainty that are associated with less disagreement ("agreed uncertainty") and those that are associated with more disagreement ("disagreed uncertainty"). One implication from these papers is that there are many different forms of economic uncertainty that are topic-specific and, while there are some common elements among them, they often behave quite differently over time.

Another approach to measuring uncertainty has been to rely on surveys. Survey measures can be useful because they are better suited to capturing "ex ante" uncertainty than many of the previously discussed measures, which, as emphasized in Aruoba et al. (2024), are often measures of "ex post" volatility instead. Long-running surveys like the Michigan Survey of Consumers typically have not included questions that are explicitly designed to measure uncertainty. However, researchers have nonetheless found some ways to try and quantify this concept using the available questions from the survey. One such approach is to rely on the cross-sectional disagreements in forecasts as a proxy for uncertainty, as considered, for example, in Bachmann, Elstner and Sims (2013). However, since forecasters can and often do confidently disagree with one another, and respondents making the same forecast can all be very uncertain in making that same forecast, uncertainty and disagreement are conceptually distinct, even though the evidence in Bachmann, Elstner and Sims (2013) suggests the two are correlated. Another approach has been to use the amount of rounding to large integers (e.g. 5%, 10%) in survey responses to proxy for uncertainty in forecasts (Binder 2017).

More recent surveys have begun to include questions that explicitly measure uncertainty. For example, the New York Fed's Survey of Consumer Expectations (SCE) and the ECB's Consumer Expectations Survey (CES) both include distribution questions in which respondents are presented with different bins and are then asked to assign probabilities to those bins. The Manski (2004) question of asking respondents for a minimum and a maximum value also provides a metric for measuring uncertainty. Likely the best formulation comes from Altig et al. (2022), who first proposed asking respondents to provide different possible scenario outcomes (e.g., what would be high inflation for the next 12 months?), and then asking them to assign probabilities to those outcomes. As discussed in Chapter 1, this question formulation avoids biasing respondents in any way through a choice of bins presented to them and is more flexible over time as economic conditions change and desirable bin ranges vary. We compared the performance of these different question formulations in Boctor et al. (2024).

These direct survey measures have been used to quantify uncertainty about a wide range of topics. Surveys of firms typically focus on one or two measures of uncertainty, such as uncertainty about their future sales or employment growth. This is what is done, for example, in the Federal Reserve Bank of Atlanta's Survey of Business Uncertainty or the Decision Maker Panel in the U.K. Because firm surveys must be kept very short to ensure continued participation of busy managers, and distribution questions are demanding to answer, it is generally infeasible to include more than one or two of these measures per survey. Despite the difficulty of measuring firm expectations, researchers have been able to run cross-country studies of firm-level uncertainty. Avalos et al. (2024), for example, surveyed 31,000 managers across 41 countries.

In contrast, household surveys now commonly ask questions that cover a broader range of areas for which uncertainty is measured. For example, the New York Fed's SCE measures uncertainty about aggregate topics such as inflation but also individual-specific outcomes such as expected income growth for the household. The ECB's CES similarly provides quantitative uncertainty measures for several different macroeconomic and respondent-specific outcomes. Having multiple uncertainty measures within a survey is useful because it can help us learn about the joint distribution of beliefs that respondents form.

In short, there have been remarkable developments in the measurement of uncertainty since Bloom (2009). We have time series of measures of different forms of uncertainty going back for years, as well as an extensive set of shorter time series of survey measures of expectations that cover a wide range of areas. These measures have already been useful in helping economists understand how beliefs are formed. But they have also been useful in helping us assess how uncertainty can affect individual and aggregate outcomes, a topic to which we now turn.

Non-experimental Evidence on the Effects of Uncertainty

Understanding the effects of uncertainty on economic decisions is difficult. As we have seen, uncertainty is highly correlated with other expectations. Identifying the effects of uncertainty on decisions and outcomes therefore requires being able to separate the uncertainty from the consequences of other changes that are happening at the same time. Fortunately, a lot of progress in this has been made in recent years.

Early attempts to identify the effects of changes in uncertainty almost exclusively relied on statistical identification based on timing assumptions. For example, Bloom (2009) ran a monthly vector autogression (VAR) with uncertainty ordered last. Implicitly, this approach assumes that uncertainty can respond within a month to other sources of variation but that other economic outcomes (such as production, prices, stock markets) cannot. Most other early work on measuring different forms of uncertainty followed similar strategies. The main limitation of this approach is that large uncertainty events of the type identified by Bloom (2009), such as the 1987 stock market crash or the 9/11 terrorist attacks, are unlikely to satisfy these restrictions: the level and uncertainty in stock prices would be expected to respond pretty much immediately and simultaneously to the event.

Researchers have pursued two strategies to overcome this identification challenge. Both are conceptually similar. One, which we describe in detail in the next section, relies on randomized information treatments in surveys to generate different relative changes in the first and the second moments of expectations, i.e., some treatments have relatively larger effects on the mean of expectations while other treatments have relatively larger effects on uncertainty. By creating these different relative changes in beliefs, we are able to separate the effects of both types of beliefs on decisions, as described earlier in Chapter 10. The other strategy uses differential exposure to economic shocks to effectively recover from observable data how beliefs would have changed in their absence, isolating the first from the second moments.

There are two particularly notable examples of this strategy. The first is Alfaro, Bloom and Lin (2024). They focused on identifying how uncertainty affects the economic decisions of firms. They did so by studying large public U.S. firms for whom data on outcomes and decisions can be observed in the Compustat database. They linked these data on firm-level investment, employment and sales (among other outcomes) to stock price information of the firms. The stock price speaks to the expected future profitability of a firm, and therefore incorporates first moments. The high-frequency volatility in stock prices was taken as the main proxy for uncertainty, although they also used options-based prices, which capture market uncertainty about future stock prices. To separate the effects of the first and the second moments, they made use of the differential effect of oil prices and exchange rates on the volatility of firms. The idea is as follows. We want to compare a firm in the airline industry, whose profitability will tend to depend negatively on oil prices, and a firm in the oil sector, whose profitability will rise with oil prices. In terms of the first moment effects of oil price changes, these two firms therefore have a negative correlation. But volatility in oil prices will affect both firms negatively relative to a firm that has little exposure to oil prices. These different relative exposures of firms to first and second moment changes in oil prices (and exchange rates) provide the key identification of the paper.

Armed with this identifying variation, the authors were able to assess how changes in both the first and the second moments of expectations affected subsequent firm-level outcomes. The results indicated that higher uncertainty about firms' future profitability leads them to reduce their investment and their employment over the next few quarters, and they tend to experience lower sales as a result. Thus, a rise in uncertainty has a clear contractionary effect on firms. In addition to this, the authors documented that the effects were particularly strong for credit-constrained firms.

The approach in Alfaro, Bloom and Lin (2024) is an excellent example of how to use quasi-experimental variation to study the ways in which uncertainty affects individual firms' decisions. However, it does not tell us what happens at the level of the aggregate economy, which would also capture how households, financial markets and policymakers respond, as well as the general equilibrium interaction of their responses. This question is tackled by Baker, Bloom and Terry (2024), who used cross-country data to assess the macroeconomic implications of changes in uncertainty. Their approach was conceptually similar to that of Alfaro, Bloom and Lin (2024), but with a different source of identifying variation. Specifically, they took historical data on macroeconomic outcomes for a wide range of countries and regressed them on average stock price changes (again to capture the effect of the mean of expected growth) as well as the volatility of stock prices over the preceding year (to proxy for uncertainty). Instead of relying on oil and exchange rate variation, however, they used the history of natural disasters and coups in the countries to separate the effects of the first and the second moments. Natural disasters have clear negative effects on the level of economic activity and raise volatility: recoveries can be fast or slow depending on the policy responses and the type of damage inflicted by the disaster. Political revolutions also tend to increase economic volatility, but their effects on average growth are less negative. Some political transitions lead to faster growth whereas others lead to slower growth. Thus, these two types of shocks affect average expected growth and the volatility in growth differently, allowing the authors to separately assess their respective effects on economic activity. Their main finding was a clear negative causal effect of volatility on growth: high uncertainty has a large negative *aggregate* effect on economic activity.

Jointly, these papers make a strong case that uncertainty has pronounced negative effects on firms' employment and investment decisions, effects that ultimately lead to contractions in the overall economy. These conclusions are based on identification strategies that explicitly aim to control for the potential correlation of uncertainty with other economic expectations, and thereby isolate the role of uncertainty in affecting outcomes even though beliefs and decisions are being determined jointly.

RCT-Based Evidence on the Effects of Uncertainty

What we like about these papers is that they really illustrate that much can be learned *without* running RCTs. With an inspired design for an identification strategy, one can tease out causality, even at the aggregate level. But for those of us who are not clever enough to be able to find such clean identification strategies in every context, there is always the brute force strategy of *creating* our own identifying variation in beliefs. If nothing else, this can serve as a useful check on results coming from quasi-experimental variation. And in cases where such quasi-experimental variation is unavailable, it may be all we have. So we'll describe parallel efforts to characterize the effects of uncertainty on firms and households using RCT methods.

In doing so, we rely on two papers that applied similar methodologies to identify the effects of macroeconomic uncertainty in surveys of households (Coibion et al. 2024) and firms (Kumar et al. 2023). For firms, the setting is a sequence of two surveys run in New Zealand in 2021 and 2022. For households, it is the ECB's monthly Consumer Expectations Survey, in which an RCT focusing on uncertainty was run in August 2020. In each case, there was an initial survey wave in which prior beliefs and plans were measured before an RCT was implemented. There were then follow-up waves that measured outcomes and decisions (one for New Zealand firms, three for Euro area households). We will focus primarily on the design and implementation of the New Zealand survey of firms but emphasize that the household survey followed an almost identical strategy, albeit focusing on households and their decisions. These two papers represent a direct application of the strategies described in the first three parts of the book, but whereas in previous chapters we concentrated primarily on inflation expectations, this application is to uncertainty about macroeconomic outcomes. Hopefully it helps illustrate that the RCT methods described here are potentially suitable to many questions.

The starting point as always is measuring initial beliefs and plans in a survey. For firms, we implemented a survey of around 4,000 firms from June through October 2021. Because our focus was on how macroeconomic uncertainty affects the decisions of firms, we included distributional questions about macroeconomic outcomes. Our main one involved future GDP growth in the New Zealand economy, and to measure prior beliefs we used the Manski (2004) min-max formulation:

> Now we'd like you to think about what you perceive as the most pessimistic and most optimistic economic outlooks for New Zealand over the next 6 months. What do you think the lowest annualized GDP growth rate might be for this time period and what do you think the highest might be? (please provide an answer as % per year).
>
> Lowest growth rate: .... % per year
> Highest growth rate: .... % per year
>
> You said that the lowest value is XXX and the highest value is YYY. The midpoint of this range is ZZZ= [(min+max)/2] % per year. What is the

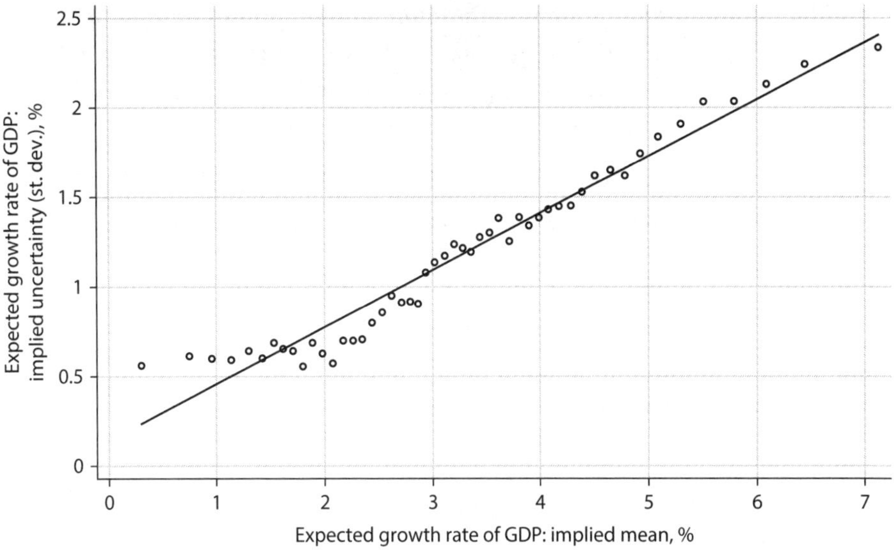

FIGURE 13.1. Joint distribution of economic growth expectations, 1st and 2nd moments, New Zealand.
Notes: The figure shows a binscatter plot between the first (implied mean) and second (implied standard deviation) moments of firms' one-year-ahead expectations for the growth rate of GDP. The line shows the fitted relationship. See Kumar, Gorodnichenko and Coibion (2023) for more details.

probability that the growth rate of the economy exceeds this midpoint at an annualized rate over the next six months?

. . . . %

Similar questions were asked about aggregate inflation as well as expected sales growth for the firm. From these we could measure average expected GDP growth, inflation and sales as well as the corresponding uncertainty around each of those beliefs. Figure 13.1 shows that there is a strong cross-sectional correlation between mean forecasts of GDP growth and the associated uncertainty around those forecasts, making it necessary to identify exogenous variation in those beliefs to assess how they affect decisions. Households in the Euro area surveys were asked equivalent questions about GDP growth in their country. These questions provide the "prior" beliefs for the empirical analysis.

Later in the same survey, *after* the information treatments, respondents were again asked about their expectations for GDP growth and other outcomes, this time to measure their "posterior" beliefs. To avoid asking the same question twice, we used the Altig et al. (2022) formulation:

> What do you think the growth rate of the New Zealand economy will be over the next twelve months in each of the following scenarios:
>
> Your most pessimistic outlook: % per year
> Your somewhat pessimistic outlook: % per year
> Your middle-of-the-road outlook: % per year
> Your somewhat optimistic outlook: % per year
> Your most optimistic outlook: % per year

Once firms had provided these five different forecast values, they were asked the follow-up question:

> Now, please tell us what probability you would assign to each of the five outlooks you just described. The probabilities should sum to 100.
>
> Probability that your most pessimistic outlook comes true: %
> Probability that your somewhat pessimistic outlook comes true: %
> Probability that your middle-of-the-road outlook comes true: %
> Probability that your somewhat optimistic outlook comes true: %
> Probability that your most optimistic outlook comes true: %

Households in the Euro area survey were given a simplified three-bin version of this question. For firms in New Zealand, we asked the same question for expected inflation and sales growth.

The heart of the experiment was the information treatment, designed to induce different relative variation in mean forecasts of GDP growth and the associated uncertainty around those forecasts. To do so, we randomly assigned respondents into one of four groups. One, the control group, received no information. Each of the other three groups was provided with a piece of information about the macroeconomic outlook.

The first treatment group received professional forecasts for the growth rate of New Zealand:

> We are going to give you information from a group of leading experts about the economy. The average prediction among professional forecasters is that New Zealand's GDP will grow 4% in 2021.

The second treatment group received different information about the New Zealand economy: the dispersion in growth forecasts of professional forecasters. Specifically, it was told

> We are going to give you information from a group of leading experts about the economy. These professional forecasters are quite uncertain about the outlook for the New Zealand economy. The difference between their optimistic forecast and pessimistic forecast is approximately 3.1 percentage points for the 2021 GDP growth rate.

This treatment describes the magnitude of the *difference* between the most optimistic forecaster and the most pessimistic forecaster, and does not include any information about the level of their forecast, to minimize the effect on first moments. Even though the treatment was designed to affect uncertainty, we did not actually provide information about the uncertainty in professional forecasts, but, rather, provided information about the disagreement among professionals. This was done because we were concerned that traditional measures of uncertainty in macroeconomic forecasts such as the confidence interval around point forecasts might not mean much to noneconomists, thereby leading to small treatment effects. The difference between optimistic and pessimistic forecasts, on the other hand, was simpler and, because it was presented shortly after firms were themselves asked to provide minimum and maximum values for GDP growth rates, it was immediately comparable to their own answers. The third treatment group received both pieces of information combined:

> We are going to give you information from a group of leading experts about the economy. The average prediction among professional forecasters is that New Zealand's GDP will grow 4% in 2021. They are quite uncertain about the economic outlook for the New Zealand economy. The difference between their optimistic forecast and pessimistic forecast is approximately 3.1 percentage points for the 2021 growth rate.

For households in the Euro area, the information treatments were comparable, but expressed in terms of growth in the Euro area or their specific country.

The effects of the two types of treatment on respondents' average expectation for GDP growth and their uncertainty about future GDP growth are shown in Panels A and B of Figure 13.2, respectively. In each panel, we plot firms' posterior beliefs (vertical axis) compared to their prior beliefs (horizontal axis), with each dot representing an average across approximately 50 respondents. For the control group, posteriors and priors line up closely, both for the first moment (expected GDP growth over next 12 months) and the second moment (uncertainty about future GDP growth). For the treatment groups, we can immediately see that all three treatments had powerful effects on both the first and the second moments of beliefs. The first treatment had very large effects on first moments, with most respondents moving their forecasts close to 4%, regardless of their prior belief. Strikingly, this treatment also had very large effects on the uncertainty in forecasts: respondents became much more confident in their GDP forecasts after being told what the average professional forecaster was predicting. The second information treatment, in contrast, had much smaller effects on first moments, but also smaller effects on second moments. Telling firms by how much professional forecasters disagreed about future GDP growth led them to become somewhat more confident about their own forecasts, but not nearly as much as when told about the level of the average professional forecast. The third treatment, which combined both pieces of information, yielded results in between the two other treatments. Thus, we can see that the information treatments induced different *relative* changes in the first and the second moments of respondents' beliefs, which, as discussed in chapter 10, is exactly what is needed to allow us to identify the differential effects of each type of belief on decisions.

To assess the effects of each type of expectation on decision k, we followed the approach proposed in Chapter 10 and estimated

$$action_i^k - plan_i^k = \alpha_1 \times Post_i^{mean} + \beta_1 \times Post_i^{uncert} + Controls_i + error, \quad (1)$$

which regresses the "surprise" decisions taken by firm i following the first wave on its posterior first and second moments from the end of the first wave and a number of firm controls, including its prior expectations for both the first and the second moments. The two posterior beliefs were instrumented for using indicator variables for each treatment group and interactions of these indicator variables with prior beliefs, again as described in Chapter 10. For some outcome variables, plans were not measured in the first wave, and in those cases we used either the change in decisions between the first and the follow-up wave (when available) or just the outcome in the follow-up wave.

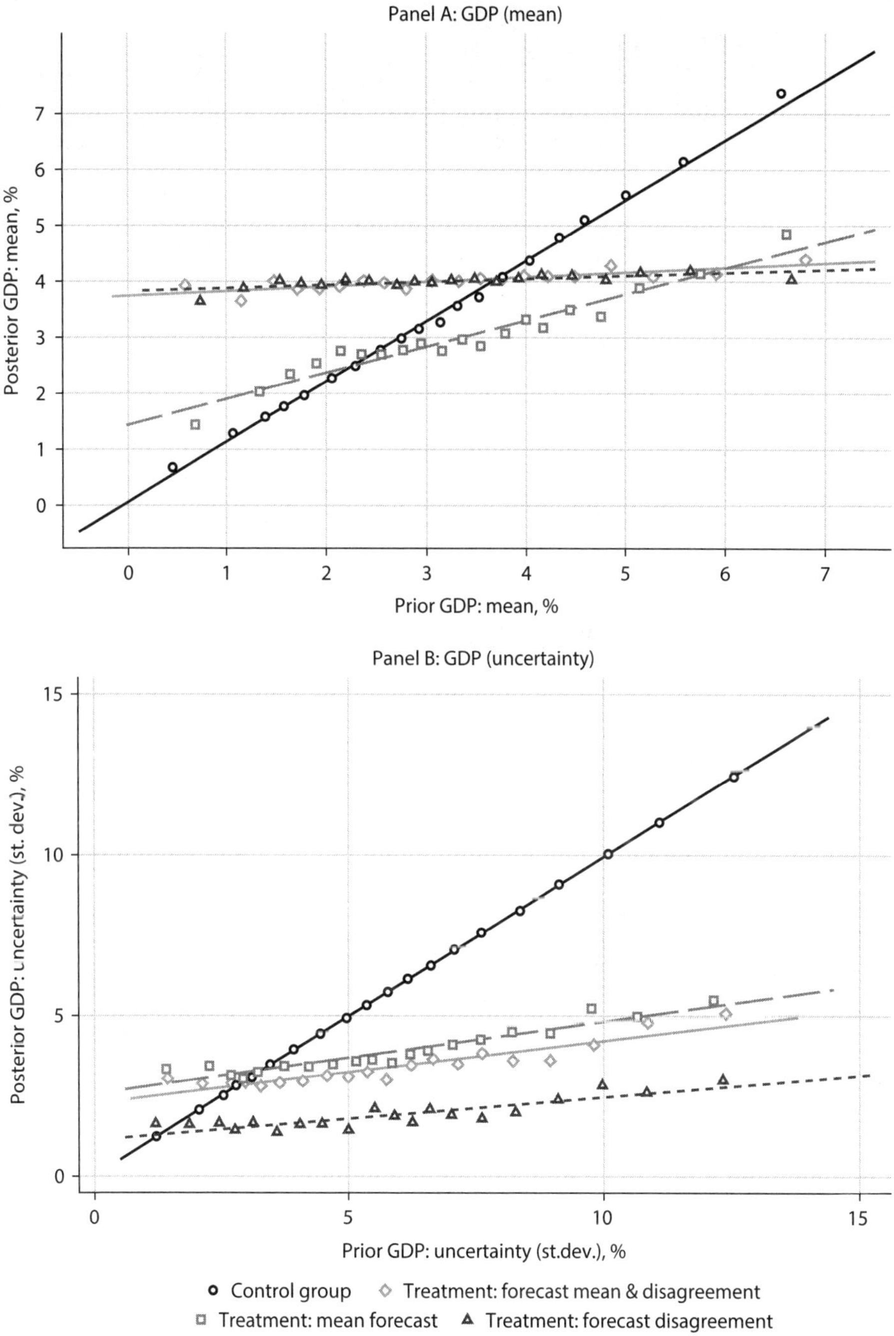

FIGURE 13.2. Treatment effects on firms' expectations for the growth rate of GDP in New Zealand.

Notes: The figure shows binscatter plots for prior vs. posterior expectations about the growth rate of GDP. The lines show the fitted relationships. See Kumar, Gorodnichenko and Coibion (2023) for more details.

TABLE 13.1. Effects of uncertainty on firms' decisions relative to plans.

	Dependent variable: Change relative to plan						
	Price	Employment	Capital stock	Wages	Advert. budget	R&D budget	Profit margin
	(1)	(2)	(3)	(4)	(5)	(6)	(7)
Posterior mean	−0.057***	−0.077	−0.024	−0.008	0.036	0.016**	−0.060***
	(0.017)	(0.105)	(0.015)	(0.009)	(0.023)	(0.008)	(0.016)
Posterior uncertainty	−0.106***	−0.618***	−0.075***	0.003	0.110***	0.000	0.009**
	(0.006)	(0.045)	(0.007)	(0.003)	(0.009)	(0.003)	(0.004)
Observations	2,020	2,020	2,020	2,020	2,020	2,020	2,020
1st stage F stat: post. mean	438.2	438.2	438.2	438.2	438.2	438.2	438.2
1st stage F stat: post. var	437.8	437.8	437.8	437.8	437.8	437.8	437.8

Notes: The table reports instrumental variable estimates of specification (1) for outcome variables indicated in column headers. Prior beliefs (1st and 2nd moments) are included but not reported. Robust standard errors are reported in parentheses. ***, **, and * denote statistical significance at 1, 5, and 10 percent levels. See Kumar, Gorodnichenko and Coibion (2023) for more details.

We report estimated outcomes for some variables in Table 13.1. The estimated coefficients on posterior uncertainty are generally statistically different from zero, indicating that we could reject the null hypothesis that uncertainty has no effect on firm decisions. Higher macroeconomic uncertainty leads firms to cut prices and reduce their employment and investment, but increase their spending on advertising. Along other dimensions not shown in Table 13.1, we also found that as macroeconomic uncertainty increases, firms tend to become less likely to adopt new technologies or open new facilities, and they value information more, especially information about the aggregate economy. In the case of households, higher macroeconomic uncertainty induces them to reduce their spending on nondurable goods and services, as well as become less likely to engage in large durable goods purchases. Thus, these results support the notion that higher uncertainty leads to a reduction in economic activity from both firms and households, consistent with the mechanism proposed in Bloom (2009).

There are additional features of these results worth noting here. First, we also included a hypothetical question about how firms would change their behavior if they became more or less uncertain about the future aggregate economic outlook. As discussed in Chapter 11, the results from the hypothetical questions largely confirm those from the RCT, thereby helping to validate the use of these questions. In addition, the hypothetical included additional margins of adjustment, such as increasing cash reserves or making fewer longer-term plans, that were not in the RCT due to survey space constraints, illustrating how these questions can also help expand the scope of topics that can be addressed.

The second point worth noting is the quantitative magnitude of the estimates. The closest point of comparison is Alfaro, Bloom and Lin (2024), discussed earlier. Their estimates indicated that a two standard deviation increase in uncertainty leads to a 0.18 standard deviation drop in investment across all firms and a 0.09 standard deviation drop in employment. In contrast, our estimates imply that a two standard deviation increase in uncertainty yields a 0.61 standard deviation decrease in investment and a 0.77 standard deviation decrease in employment. We therefore estimated much larger effects of uncertainty along these margins. These differences could stem from several sources. Probably the most relevant source is the difference in the types of firms considered: large U.S. publicly traded firms in Alfaro, Bloom and Lin (2024) versus the much smaller private companies in New Zealand in our survey. Why might this matter? Alfaro, Bloom and Lin emphasized that the effects of uncertainty are larger for firms that are more financially constrained. Since on average small firms in New Zealand are much more likely to be financially constrained than large publicly traded firms in the U.S., this may go some way in reconciling our much larger estimated effects. While there are no direct measures of financial constraints in our survey, financial constraints are often proxied by firm size (Gertler and Gilchrist 1994). Consistent with the argument by Alfaro, Bloom and Lin (2024), we found that smaller firms, which are likely to be financially constrained, responded much more in terms of employment to uncertainty than did larger firms in New Zealand.

Summary

Jointly, these papers paint a picture of a world in which economic uncertainty is important. From Baker, Bloom and Terry (2024), we know that exogenous changes in uncertainty affect macroeconomic outcomes. From Alfaro, Bloom and Lin (2024) and the RCT papers described above, we know that changes in uncertainty have direct effects on firms and households, much as theory predicts they would. But there is much more to learn. We do not, for example, have comparable causal estimates of how uncertainty affects financial markets. We also do not know exactly how different forms of uncertainty matter for decisions. Nor do we really understand the extent to which higher moments may matter. While there is therefore much that we remain uncertain about, we can be confident that this topic will generate much more research in future years.

14

How Do Expectations Affect Individual Portfolio Decisions?

INDIVIDUALS MAKE MANY important financial decisions: how much to save and borrow, how to allocate those savings across different types of financial assets, and how to choose between different forms of debt (credit card, mortgage, etc.). Most of these decisions should depend on expectations. For example, when deciding which financial assets to hold, individual investors would likely consider not only how liquid different assets are but also what rate of return they expect the asset to generate and how risky those assets are likely to be, among other factors. To what extent do these expectations actually matter for the financial decisions that individuals make? An extensive literature in behavioral finance has explored some of these questions, with recent work focusing on surveys that measure what returns people expect for different assets, as well as how these beliefs are related to their asset holding positions. Even more recent work has begun to use information treatments to study how investors change their beliefs in the face of new information, as well as how those beliefs about expected returns shape their actual financial decisions. In this chapter, we describe some of this ongoing line of research, focusing in particular on new research utilizing surveys and RCTs.

Individual Expectations about Asset Prices and Returns

Financial economists have long been interested in how individual investors make decisions about which assets to hold. The resulting field of behavioral finance has uncovered a wide range of ways in which individual investment decisions deviate from what standard theory would predict. Recent work in this field focuses on the beliefs of investors about past and expected future asset returns in an attempt to gauge whether puzzles about investment decisions reflect the beliefs of investors or the constraints that they face. For example, infrequent adjustment of portfolios could reflect an infrequent adjustment of beliefs about future returns—say, for example, because investors do not continuously follow market conditions—or financial costs to trading, which induce people to change portfolios only when the desired changes are large enough to justify the costs of adjusting their holdings.

To quantify the role of expectations about future asset returns in explaining financial decisions, it is necessary to first measure these beliefs. One paper that does so for a range of different financial assets is Weber et al. (2023). In it, we used repeated surveys of U.S. households participating in the Nielsen Homescan Panel to quantify expectations about future asset price returns. One survey wave in 2022Q3 used the following question:

> We would like to know how you think different assets might evolve over the next year. There is no right or wrong answer to this. For each of the following assets, please tell us what you think is the most likely rate of return over the next twelve months, as well as the lowest and highest rates of return that we might see over twelve months.

	Lowest rate of return	Most likely rate of return	Highest rate of return	I don't know
US Stocks	%	%	%	[]
US Bonds	%	%	%	[]
US Savings Account	%	%	%	[]
Cryptocurrency	%	%	%	[]
Gold	%	%	%	[]
US Housing	%	%	%	[]

Note that the question asks not only for an expected return but also a range of returns (from lowest to highest), which provides a measure of perceived riskiness of different assets. It also provides respondents with the ability to select "I don't know" as an option.

The first pattern that came out of this question was the striking unwillingness of respondents to even hazard a guess about future returns of many assets. For example, for stock returns, about 68% of respondents were unwilling to provide an answer. Even amongst those who held stocks in their portfolio, the share willing to provide an expected return was just above half (53%). For other risky assets, the fraction of people willing to provide an expected return was even lower, reaching just 16% for cryptocurrencies. By itself, this unwillingness on the part of many individuals to provide expected returns suggests a general lack of confidence about and knowledge of financial asset returns.

A second pattern that emerges from measures of expected returns of financial assets is how dispersed they are across individuals. For example, in this survey, the average expected return for stocks over the next 12 months was 9%, with a standard deviation of 7% amongst those owning stocks. Similar results hold when we focus on wealthy investors. One particularly striking paper in this literature is by Giglio et al. (2021). They were able to run surveys on a large panel of wealthy individual investors who invested through Vanguard, one of the largest asset management companies in the world. In their survey of wealthy investors, the standard deviation of expected returns for stocks over the next 12 months was 6%, almost identical to what we found with households in the Nielsen panel.

These differences in beliefs are not limited to stock returns. We found broadly similar degrees of disagreement across asset types. Furthermore, disagreement across asset classes tends to be systematic across individuals. Individuals who are optimistic about future stock returns also tend to be optimistic about future bond, gold and cryptocurrency returns, and vice versa for pessimists. These differences do not reflect different views about future inflation, which could mechanically induce a positive correlation in expected nominal returns across assets. Instead, the degree to which different individuals are optimistic or pessimistic about the common component of future financial returns is largely independent of what they expect will happen to inflation.

Explaining these differences in beliefs is not easy, however. A natural source of variation in beliefs might be demographics. For example, if people of different ages have lived through different rates of stock returns over their lives, they might extrapolate these experiences into their expectations of future returns. Consistent with this hypothesis, Malmendier and Nagel (2011) showed that those who have lived through dramatic events like the Great Depression have beliefs that are heavily shaped by the experience. But in general, while some demographic characteristics are statistically correlated with expectations, their combined explanatory power is quite weak (Giglio et al. 2021).

Expected Returns and Asset Holdings

Are these differences in beliefs across individuals related to their financial portfolios? The answer seems to be a resounding yes! When Giglio et al.

TABLE 14.1. Relative explanatory power of observables and expectations for share of asset in portfolio.

	R^2 of asset holding coming from	
	Observables	Expected returns and risk
Asset	(1)	(2)
Panel A. Actual portfolio holdings		
Crypto	0.08	0.11
Gold	0.08	0.06
Bonds	0.18	0.04
Stocks	0.22	0.14
Panel B. Desired portfolio holdings		
Crypto	0.06	0.17
Gold	0.07	0.08
Bonds	0.05	0.03
Stocks	0.25	0.14

Notes: The table reports R^2 from regressing the share of each type of asset in an individual's financial portfolio on either individual observables in the first column or on expected returns and perceived risk for all asset classes in the second column. The sample period is 2021Q3. The list of observables includes gender, income, education, race, homeownership, spending, employment status, political leanings, stimulus check payments, and financial wealth. See Weber, Candia, Coibion and Gorodnichenko (2023) for more details.

(2021) regressed individuals' equity share in their portfolio on their expected stock returns and additional controls, they found a robust and strong positive correlation. They estimated a coefficient of 0.6; that is, for every 1 percentage point higher expected return, individuals tend to increase the share of stocks in their portfolio holdings by around 0.6 percentage points. Given the wide dispersion in beliefs about stock returns already documented, this result indicates that differences in beliefs about stock returns can explain an important share of the heterogeneity in stock holdings across individuals.

In Weber et al. (2023), we similarly regressed portfolio shares for different assets on the expected returns of individuals for those assets as well as their perceived riskiness. The respective contribution of expected returns and perceived riskiness of the asset in terms of R^2 is presented in Table 14.1, relative to the contribution coming from observable characteristics of individuals like age, income, etc. As in Giglio et al. (2021), these results suggest an

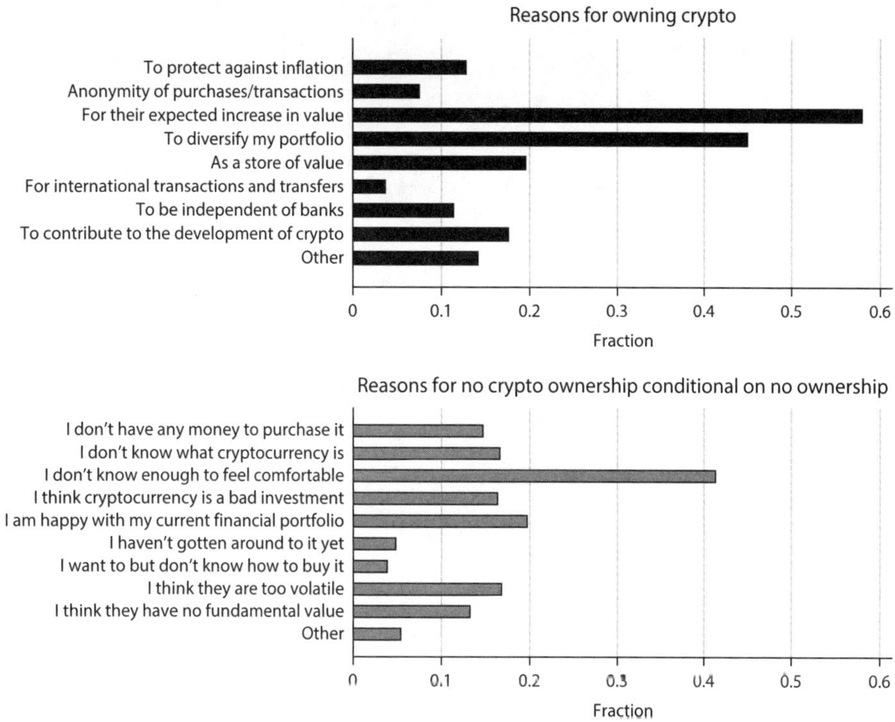

FIGURE 14.1. Reasons why individuals do and do not own cryptocurrency. *Source:* Weber, Canda, Coibion, and Gorodnichenko (2023).

important role for differences in beliefs for stock holdings, but also for holdings of other financial assets. The relative importance of beliefs for cryptocurrency holdings is, in particular, significantly higher than the combined contribution of all observable characteristics. This is consistent with more qualitative evidence as well. For example, when people are asked why they choose to own or not own a new risky asset such as cryptocurrency, they emphasize their knowledge of and beliefs about this asset as the most important factors. Figure 14.1 plots results from asking this type of question to U.S. households. Among those who hold cryptocurrency, they claim to do so primarily because they expect high returns on this asset. Other reasons include more standard ones such as for diversification, value preservation, or a hedge against inflation. Those who choose not to hold cryptocurrency emphasize a lack of knowledge, consistent with the low willingness to hazard a guess about possible returns, or a negative view about the potential returns of the asset.

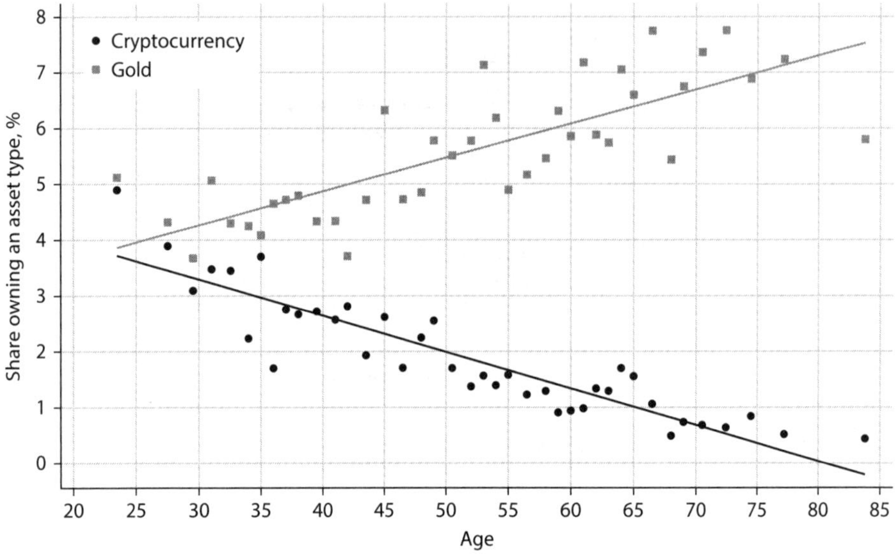

FIGURE 14.2. Gold and crypto ownership by age.
Notes: The figure shows binscatter plots of asset ownership vs. age. The lines show the fitted relationships. See Weber, Candia, Coibion and Gorodnichenko (2023) for more details.

Observing beliefs is also important because it can help identify key mechanisms at play behind people's asset holding decisions. For example, Figure 14.2 plots a remarkable pattern: older households systematically hold more gold and less cryptocurrency. Clearly, age is highly correlated with financial holdings. Why is this true? One explanation could be that younger individuals have a longer investment horizon and are therefore more willing to hold a high-risk high-return asset than older individuals, consistent with standard investment advice. But we found that the correlation between age and cryptocurrency holdings disappears once we control for expectations of future returns. Older people are less likely than younger ones to hold cryptocurrency, primarily because they think it will yield lower returns and it is not a good inflation hedge. Thus, it is much more the difference in beliefs about the properties of the asset between the old and the young that accounts for their different investment decisions rather than their different investment horizons.

While we can therefore observe strong correlations between beliefs about asset returns and asset holdings, it is not clear that these correlations are causal. For example, it could be that as we own an asset for longer periods, we learn that it is less risky than we initially thought. This would lead to the appearance of people being more likely to own an asset they perceive as safer, even though it is the act of ownership that is causing the change in beliefs rather than the converse. Breaking through this identification challenge requires strategies in which there are exogenous changes in beliefs that can then be linked to subsequent asset holding decisions.

Experimental Evidence on the Causal Effects of Beliefs on Desired Portfolio Allocations

How does new information about financial asset returns affect beliefs and decisions? Beutel and Weber (2023) made one elegant attempt to address this question in the context of stock market returns. They used two of the Bundesbank household surveys, with an RCT implemented in the first one. Prior to and after the information treatments, households were asked about their expectations of future stock market returns.

The main information treatments consisted of different pieces of information that may relate to expectations about future stock returns. One treatment provided respondents with information on the historical rate of return on stocks in Germany. A second showed information about stock returns over the last year only. These two treatments were therefore entirely backward looking and focused on historical changes in stock prices. The third treatment told households about earnings growth over the last 12 months. To the extent that stock prices should be tied to expected future earnings of companies, this treatment was about a fundamental determinant of stock prices, but a backward-looking one. The fourth treatment provided the price-earnings ratio of the German stock index at the time and informed respondents that this level was high by historical standards. In conventional finance models, this would tend to predict lower than average returns in the future, since prices were excessively high relative to fundamentals. The fifth treatment informed households by how much experts were predicting the stock market to increase over the next 12 months. Finally, the authors also provided a placebo treatment with information unrelated to asset prices.

The survey included questions that measured respondents' prior beliefs about each of the pieces of information in the treatments. This provided the authors a natural measure of how informed respondents initially were about these facts. Broadly speaking, Beutel and Weber concluded that households were overall quite uninformed about stock prices and returns. The only metric

TABLE 14.2. Information treatments.

Treatment	July 2021 wave	August 2022 wave
T2	Over the last 12 months, the inflation rate in the U.S. (as measured by the Consumer Price Index) averaged 5.8%.	Over the last 12 months, the inflation rate in the U.S. (as measured by the Consumer Price Index) averaged 8.5%.
T3	The inflation rate that the Federal Reserve tries to achieve on average is 2% per year.	The inflation rate that the Federal Reserve tries to achieve on average is 2% per year.
T4	The U.S. Federal Open Market Committee (which sets short-term interest rates) forecasts a 2.1% inflation rate in 2022.	The U.S. Federal Open Market Committee (which sets short-term interest rates) forecasts a 2.6% inflation rate in 2023.
T5	Over the last two years, the inflation rate in the U.S. (as measured by the Consumer Price Index) averaged 2.9% per year.	Over the last two years, the inflation rate in the U.S. (as measured by the Consumer Price Index) averaged 6.7% per year.
T6	The value of a Bitcoin has increased by 4,611% in the last 5 years.	The value of a Bitcoin has increased by 674% in the last 5 years.
T7	The U.S. stock market (as measured by the S&P 500) has increased by exactly 100% in the last 5 years.	The U.S. stock market (as measured by the S&P 500) has increased by 59% in the last 5 years.
T8	The value of a Bitcoin has increased by 4,611% in the last 5 years and the U.S. stock market (as measured by the S&P 500) has increased by exactly 100% over the same period.	The value of a Bitcoin has increased by 674% in the last 5 years and the U.S. stock market (as measured by the S&P 500) has increased by 59% over the same period.

T9	The value of a Bitcoin has increased by 244% in the last 12 months.	The value of a Bitcoin has fallen by 43% in the last 12 months.
T10	The U.S. stock market (as measured by the S&P 500) has increased by 34% in the last 12 months.	The U.S. stock market (as measured by the S&P 500) has fallen by 12% in the last 12 months.
T11	The value of a Bitcoin has increased by 244% in the last 12 months and the U.S. stock market (as measured by the S&P 500) has increased by 34% over the same period.	The value of a Bitcoin has fallen by 43% in the last 12 months and the U.S. stock market (as measured by the S&P 500) has fallen by 12% over the same period.
T12	The value of a Bitcoin has increased by 244% in the last 12 months but fell as much as 23% in just one month during that time.	The value of a Bitcoin has fallen by 43% in the last 12 months but increased as much as 33% in just one month during that time.
T13	The value of the U.S. stock market (as measured by the S&P 500) has increased by 34% in the last 12 months but fell as much as 1% in just one month during that time.	The value of the U.S. stock market (as measured by the S&P 500) has fallen by 12% in the last 12 months but increased as much as 5% in just one month during that time.
T14	n.a.	The value of a Bitcoin fell by 43% in the last 12 months but increased as much as 33% in just one month during that time. The U.S. stock market (as measured by the S&P 500) fell by 12% in the last 12 months but rose as much as 5% in just one month during that time.
T15	Picture with time series of Bitcoin price.	Picture with time series of Bitcoin price.
T16	Picture with time series of S&P 500 price.	Picture with time series of S&P 500 price.
T17	Picture with time series of Bitcoin price and S&P 500 price.	Picture with time series of Bitcoin price and S&P 500 price.
T18	Picture with time series of Monthly Percentage Return on Bitcoin and U.S. Stocks.	Picture with time series of Monthly Percentage Return on Bitcoin and U.S. Stocks.

Source: Weber, Candia, Coibion and Gorodnichenko (2023).

that respondents got correct on average was the long-term return of German stocks. In contrast, respondents significantly underestimated stock returns over the previous year as well as the decline in earnings. They also underestimated the price-earnings ratio at the time of the survey. Consistent with earlier evidence, Beutel and Weber (2023)'s survey displayed widespread heterogeneity in beliefs across respondents, most of which could not be explained by demographic information about them.

The information treatments were successful in changing respondents' beliefs about future stock returns. The effects of expert forecasts were particularly powerful, feeding almost one for one into respondents' beliefs about future returns. Positive information about past returns led people to expect higher future returns, pointing to extrapolative beliefs. Strikingly, when respondents learned that the price to earnings ratio was higher than they thought, they tended to expect higher future stock returns rather than, as theory would predict, lower stock returns. This type of belief can explain why we sometimes see wild stock price swings: as prices rise relative to earnings, people expect prices to rise further, leading them to purchase more stocks, causing prices to keep rising. Overall, these results point toward beliefs that are at odds with underlying fundamental dynamics.

Beutel and Weber (2023) then related these exogenous changes in beliefs to desired portfolio holdings. While they were not able to measure actual portfolios, their survey included a hypothetical investment allocation question in which respondents reported how they would assign windfall income across different financial assets. The advantage of this hypothetical approach is that it abstracts from adjustment costs and frictions that may lead to only limited adjustment in the actual portfolios of individuals in the short run. But because these frictions are of course relevant to decision-making, the hypothetical portfolio allocation should provide an upper bound on the pass-through of beliefs into financial decisions. Hence, the interpretation of results is more nuanced.

When Beutel and Weber (2023) ran the same regression as Giglio et al. (2021) of equity shares on expected returns, they found a very similar low pass-through of beliefs into decisions. Justifying such a low pass-through would require individuals to be far more risk-averse than they actually seem to be, a common puzzle in finance. However, once Beutel and Weber (2023) took into account the exogenous variation in expected returns created by their information treatments, the estimated pass-through of financial beliefs into portfolio decisions increased significantly. The resulting estimate was consistent with a much more reasonable degree of risk-aversion on the part of respondents. Note that this is not because Beutel and Weber (2023) were using a desired portfolio allocation, since running the same specification as Giglio et al. (2021) on this alternative measure yielded results comparable to the original ones. Instead, it was their ability to exploit the exogenous variation in beliefs generated through their information treatments that accounts for their much higher estimated pass-through, again illustrating the power of RCTs in identifying how beliefs shape decisions.

Experimental Evidence on the Causal Effects of Beliefs on Actual Portfolio Decisions

While it is useful to observe that beliefs about returns affect desired portfolio allocations, one would still like confirmation that these beliefs translate into *actual* portfolio decisions. Unfortunately, establishing such a finding requires a combination of surveys with information treatments and either external information on investment decisions (as in Giglio et al. 2021) or follow-up surveys to measure ex post portfolio allocations of respondents. While such settings are uncommon, there are at least two papers that provide results in this spirit.

One, Weber et al. (2023), studied how information about past returns affects ex post purchases of cryptocurrency by individuals. In two different Nielsen Homescan household surveys, we put in place a number of different information treatments related to asset returns. In 2021Q3, respondents were assigned to one of 18 different groups, one of which was a control group. Four groups received information about inflation (Table 14.2). As in Beutel and Weber (2023), one treatment group was told about stock returns over the last year and another group about returns over the last five years. Two other treatment groups received equivalent information regarding returns on bitcoin. Individuals in two treatment groups were provided with information about both stocks and bitcoin returns, either over five years or over the last year. Two other groups were told about stock and bitcoin returns over the last year, but also about the largest drop in prices over that time period. Finally, some groups were presented with visual evidence of returns on either stocks or bitcoin over recent years. All treatments about asset prices involved information about past price changes, which were publicly available information to anyone at the time.

In a follow-up survey, respondents were asked whether they owned any cryptocurrency, as they had been prior to the information treatment. We were therefore able to assess whether receiving information about past returns made individuals more or less likely to own any cryptocurrency. The survey also included a similar question as in Beutel and Weber (2023) about the ideal portfolio allocation. Using the latter question, we found broadly similar evidence as in Beutel and Weber (2023), except for the case of bitcoin returns: information treatments that provided positive news about past bitcoin returns tended to increase the desired share of portfolios going to cryptocurrency as well as to other high-risk assets like gold, with a corresponding decline in the desired equity share. However, most of the information treatments did not lead in subsequent waves to identifiable changes in the probability of a household owning cryptocurrency. There was only one treatment that had this effect: being told that returns to bitcoin over the last year were 244% led respondents to become 2 percentage points more likely to own cryptocurrency in the following quarter. But because of small sample sizes due to the very large number of treatments and the low share of people owning cryptocurrency during this period, it was generally difficult to identify significant changes in actual asset ownership due to these information treatments. Had we used a smaller number of targeted treatments, we likely would have been much more successful in identifying the effect of expected returns on asset purchasing decisions.

The second paper that provides a clear causal link from expectations to actual portfolio decisions is Georgarakos et al. (2024). In this paper, which we discussed in part in Chapter 10, we applied information treatments to European households that led to changes in their inflation expectations *and* their inflation uncertainty. Because the ECB's CES survey includes occasional questions asking respondents to describe the allocation of their financial portfolio across multiple asset classes, we were able to assess how both inflation expectations and inflation uncertainty affected households' *actual* financial portfolios. The key finding was that, as households became more uncertain about future inflation, they tended to allocate more of their portfolio into their highly liquid checking and savings accounts and less into very illiquid retirement accounts. Higher inflation expectations tended to move portfolios in the opposite direction. Thus, changing inflation conditions can also lead to portfolio reallocations by households.

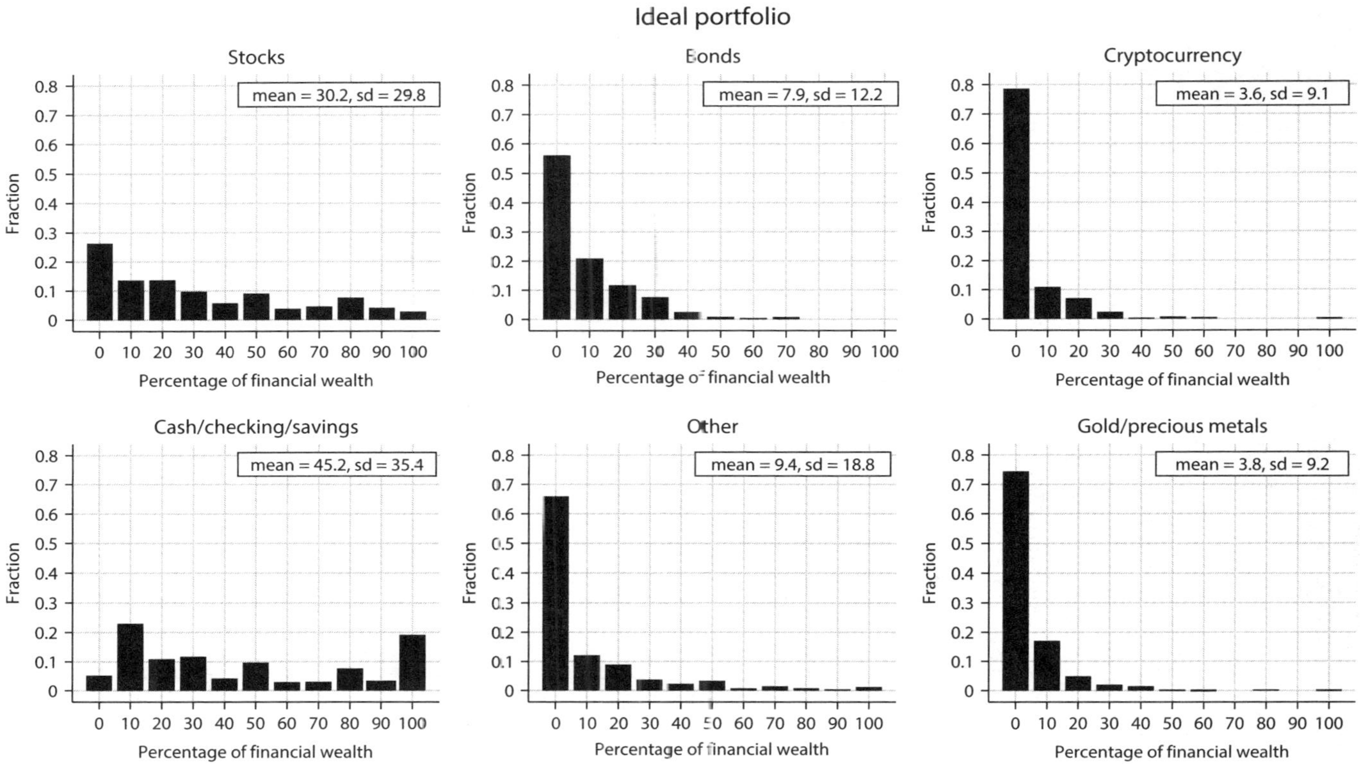

FIGURE 14.3. Desired portfolios.
Source: Weber, Candia, Coibion and Gorodnichenko (2023).

Experimental Evidence on the Effects of Expectations on Banking Choices

A surprising property of desired portfolio allocations discussed in the aforementioned papers is the large share of their portfolios that many individuals want to hold in cash and other liquid assets. Figure 14.3, for example, plots the distribution of desired portfolios across different assets. Two things stand out. First, there are some assets that very few respondents are interested in holding. Gold, cryptocurrency and even bonds are not commonly a desired component of individual portfolios. Second, cash and stocks are the main desired types of assets, with close to half of the population wanting to hold more than half of their portfolios in cash and equivalent liquid savings. With such a strong desire for holding large stocks of liquid assets, it becomes important to understand how individuals choose which institutions to place those liquid assets in and how readily they might be willing to reallocate these assets either to other banks or into other forms of savings.

One paper that tackles this question is Sandri et al. (2023). In it, we considered how perceptions about the stability of the banking system and consumers' own banks affect their willingness to withdraw their deposits and alter their financial portfolio. We did so using a survey of U.S. households implemented shortly after the collapse of the Silicon Valley Bank (SVB), at a time when banking distress was heavily covered in the media. Despite this intense news coverage, few Americans were aware of the SVB collapse and most were quite confident in the stability of the banking system and even more so in their own bank. Furthermore, even in the event of a collapse of their own bank, individuals seemed confident that they would recover their deposits.

To assess in a causal framework how the perceived riskiness of the banking system might affect their banking decisions, we implemented several information treatments to randomly selected survey participants. One treatment group was provided information about SVB's collapse. Three other treatment groups were provided information about the Federal Deposit Insurance Corporation (FDIC) deposit insurance or about public assurances from either the Federal Reserve chairman or President Biden about the stability of the banking system. The survey also collected information on people's propensity to withdraw money from banks—which we refer to as the "propensity to run"—before and after the treatments. Specifically, respondents were asked:

> Q6: How likely are you to withdraw some of your deposits in the next 12 months because of concerns that your bank may fail?

Answers were on a ten-point scale, ranging from "not at all likely" (1) to "extremely likely" (10). As shown in Figure 14.4, the propensity to run among respondents (prior to treatments) was higher for those who perceived a greater risk of their bank failing in the future or who expected to recover a smaller fraction of their deposits if such a failure occurred.

What happens when people become more likely to run on their bank? To determine this, we first needed to create exogenous variation in the propensity to run. We did so by utilizing the information treatments. These treatments had strong average effects on the propensity to run, conditional on respondents not being informed about the treatments in the first place. Figure 14.5 shows the treatment effects visually, depending on whether or not respondents were initially aware of the provided information. For example, in Panel A, we plot the average treatment effect of being told about the SVB collapse on respondents who initially were or were not aware of the SVB failure. As expected, the treatment did not have an effect on the beliefs of those who already knew about the run on SVB. But for those who did not, the treatment significantly raised their propensity to run. Through additional questions, we were able to show that this effect happens through two channels. First, information about the SVB collapse led individuals to perceive their own bank as riskier. Second, it made respondents believe that they were likely to recover a smaller fraction of their deposits if their bank did fail. Jointly, these two effects implied that when they learned about the SVB collapse, consumers perceived an increase in their expected potential loss from holding bank deposits of approximately 1–1.5% of their deposits.

The other three treatments, which focused on different policy responses, all tended to reduce the propensity to run amongst those who were unaware of the information provided. The FDIC treatment had a larger effect on the beliefs of people who did not know about FDIC insurance or those who underestimated the amount of deposits subject to insurance (Panel B). For the Fed treatment (Panel C), there was a similar differential effect from the Fed's reassurance about the stability of the banking system. Strikingly, Panel D presents a more nuanced response to the president's reassurance. In that case, there was a strong impact on beliefs of Democrats who had no prior knowledge of the treatment, whereas there was no effect on Republicans, even

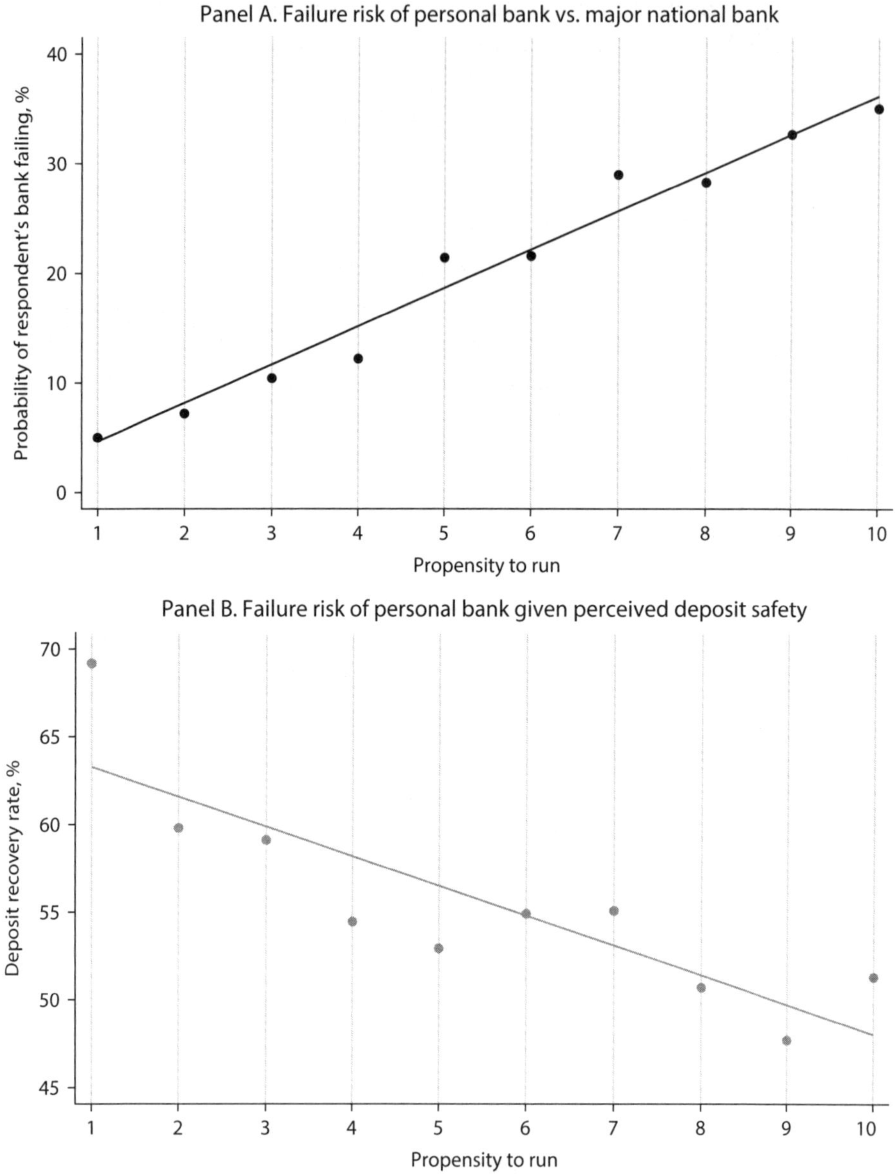

FIGURE 14.4. Propensity to run on a bank.
Notes: Panel A presents a binscatter for questions about the subjective estimate of propensity to run (1 [not at all likely] to 10 [extremely likely] scale) and the subjective probability of failure for the respondent's personal bank. Panel B presents a binscatter for questions about the subjective estimate of propensity to run (1 [not at all likely] to 10 [extremely likely] scale) and the subjective estimate of how much money (deposit) is going be recovered if the respondent's personal bank fails. See Sandri et al. (2024) for more details.

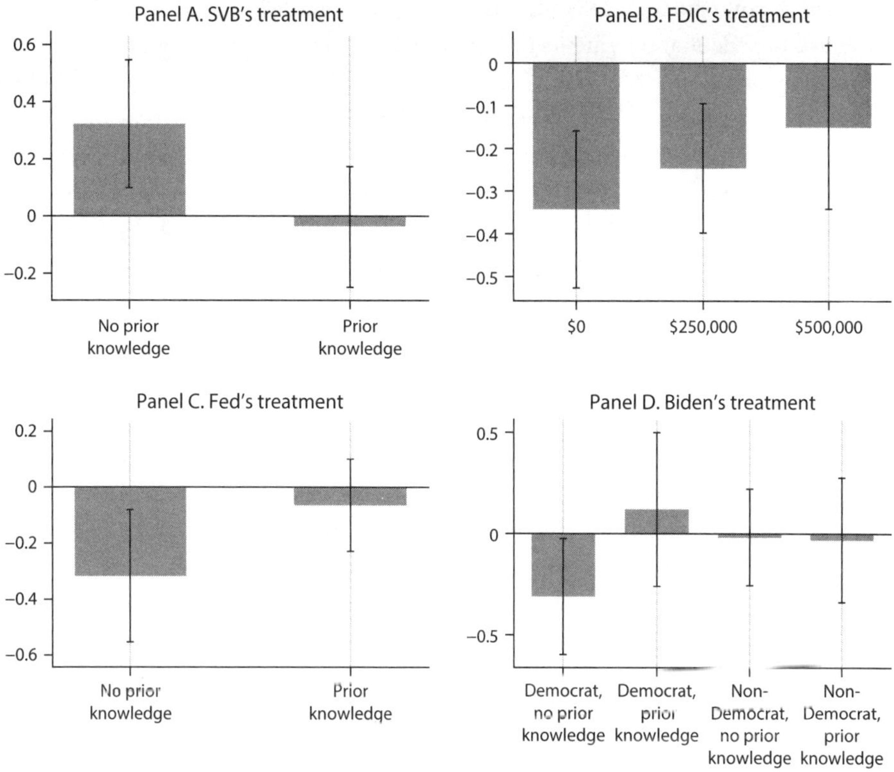

FIGURE 14.5. Treatment effects on respondents' propensity to run on their banks.
Notes: The figure visualizes the treatment effects with the bars showing the point estimates and the whiskers showing the 90 percent confidence intervals. See Sandri et al. (2024) for more details.

among those who were unaware of the information before. Clearly, messages from politicians differ in their impact, depending on the preferences of the audience.

So while all three policy messages tended to reduce the propensity to run, they did so through different channels. In the case of the FDIC treatment, this happened by reducing households' expected loss on deposits conditional on their bank failing. In the case of the Federal Reserve statement about a stable banking system, the effect operated instead by reducing the probability that households assigned to their bank failing in the near future. This suggests that public communication by the Fed and information about deposit insurance may be powerful tools to contain the risk of panic-induced bank runs. In contrast, presidential statements have a more limited reach, affecting only their electoral base.

We also considered whether fears about banking risk affected individuals' portfolio choices. First, we examined respondents' answers to hypothetical questions in the spirit of those described in Chapter 11: what share of deposits would they withdraw if their bank faced a certain probability of failing, and how they would allocate these funds across different assets? Second, we asked survey participants after the information treatments how they would allocate a monetary windfall. The two approaches yielded consistent results. People reacted to heightened bank risk by withdrawing funds from their primary banks, partially relocating them to other banks, and increasing their cash holdings, with a smaller fraction of the funds being used to purchase other financial assets. Using elasticities from either approach, we estimated that learning about the SVB collapse would lead households to withdraw around 2–3% of their deposits from their primary bank. With only about a third of the U.S. population aware of the SVB collapse, these magnitudes are remarkably in line with actual deposit outflows from the U.S. banking sector in the days following SVB's collapse, equal to about 0.7%.

Summary

Together, the evidence is strongly suggestive that individuals' beliefs causally influence their financial decisions. Whether it is expectations of future returns or the perceived riskiness of the assets, whether it is for stocks, cryptocurrency or savings accounts, expectations seem to play a crucial role in determining investment decisions. Still, while strong, this evidence is not as conclusive as in some other settings. For example, whereas we could observe ex post spending decisions of households or employment decisions of firms when studying the role of inflation expectations in Chapter 10, in this case we are relying primarily on questions about desired portfolios to measure outcomes. Ideally, we would be able to combine external information on investment decisions with surveys of beliefs and information treatments to shock those beliefs. Giglio et al. (2021) have done the former two whereas Beutel and Weber (2023), Weber et al. (2023) and Sandri et al. (2023) have done the latter two. One can also study how economic agents manage their debt in response to changes in expectations (Ropele, Gorodnichenko and Coibion 2022).

Another limitation is that the analysis is restricted to retail investors. Asset prices are increasingly determined by large asset management companies that often rely on algorithmic investment strategies, making it difficult to determine the role of expectations. There is sparse data on what investment decisions they make, no data that we know of on their expectations, and little hope of implementing information treatments for these very informed practitioners. As a result, it would likely be difficult to implement the kind of strategy described here with professional investors. But perhaps some clever researchers can find a way to do it. The returns to doing so would be high.

15

How Do Beliefs about Peers Shape Decisions?

We are all social creatures. As such, how we view ourselves relative to our peers is thought to matter for how we act and for our well-being. An extensive literature has studied the extent to which our perceived relative status affects our political opinions, consumption decisions and overall happiness. But doing so is challenging. How do we define peers? What are the metrics along which we compare ourselves to them? Does this actually affect any of our decisions or is it something that just changes how we perceive ourselves? In this chapter, we will review some of the existing work in this area. As we will see, there is already a very rich literature on peer effects that has thought carefully about identification and causality. Despite this, we view the strategy described in this book as well suited for making further progress in the area of peer effects, and we will describe some early attempts to do so.

Measuring Perceived Relative Standings

The first challenge with peer effects involves defining who is a peer and measuring beliefs about peer comparisons. A particularly notable paper in this regard is Hvidberg, Kreiner and Stantcheva (2023). They focused on Denmark, where they were able to match a survey of households to administrative data on incomes of the broader population. This allowed them to compare, using different definitions of peers, the beliefs of individuals about how their peers were doing financially with the actual distribution of income of their peers. For example, they asked respondents about large reference groups (e.g., same birth cohort, same gender) as well as much narrower ones (neighbors, coworkers). Respondents provided estimates of the income distribution for each reference group as well as of where they ranked relative to others in each group. With detailed data on actual incomes by age, region, employer, etc., the authors could construct the actual income distribution for each reference group.

They found two startling facts. First, on average, respondents were able to identify the median of the income distribution of different groups. People therefore not only understand that some groups make more money than others, but, on average, can also correctly identify by how much. Second, this masks an important bias underneath the average. Specifically, the authors documented what they called a "center bias." Those at the upper end of the distribution overestimated how much others made and therefore underestimated how high they were in the income distribution. For those at the bottom end of the distribution, the effect was reversed: they tended to underestimate how much others were making, leading them to think they were closer to the middle of the distribution than was the case. Thus, individuals seem to consistently believe that they are closer to the average than they actually are. And the further away from the center of the distribution people are, the worse this misperception becomes. For example, those at the 95th percentile of the distribution in Denmark overestimated what it takes to be in the top 5% of their age cohort by 50 percent!

These biases are worse for certain reference groups. In particular, as the reference group becomes narrower and closer to an individual's coworkers, the "center bias" gets more pronounced. For example, Hvidberg et al. (2023) found that respondents were better at predicting where they ranked relative to their former classmates than where they ranked relative to their coworkers. Some characteristics of the individual could also help predict how biased their views were. One was whether their spouse was a high earner. Danes with a high-income spouse tended to overstate where they are in the income distribution. Perhaps even more strikingly, those who owned expensive houses or cars relative to their neighbors were particularly susceptible to thinking that they were doing better relative to their peers than was actually the case.

We wrote a related paper with coauthors (van Rooij et al. 2024) focusing on the Netherlands, where it is also possible to connect survey data with detailed administrative information on the universe of Dutch households. In that survey, we asked respondents how much they thought their peers earned on average, without specifying exactly the peer group:

> How much do you think was the average net annual income of households that you associate frequently with, such as friends, neighbors, acquaintances, or people at work in 2019?

The advantage of being open-ended about the peers is that it is up to the respondent to define for themselves what is their most relevant peer group, which may differ across individuals. The downside of this approach is that we cannot determine how right or wrong respondents are in this respect since we do not know exactly what peer group they are comparing themselves to. A similar question was asked about how indebted they thought their peers were. This question is potentially useful because, like income, debt could be another metric along which individuals compare themselves to others.

We plot the resulting distributions of perceived relative positions in income and debt of Dutch respondents in Figure 15.1. Panel A shows the distribution of perceived relative income standings. On average, respondents perceived their peers as earning slightly more money than they did, but there is a thick left tail, meaning that we were more likely to find someone who believed that their peers were making far more relative to them than the converse. Panel B shows the equivalent distribution for perceived debt levels. In this case, people tended to think others were slightly more indebted than they themselves were. Again, there is a thick left tail, indicating that we were more likely to find someone who believed others were far more indebted than they themselves were than the converse. A binscatter in Panel C shows the correlation between the two perceived rankings. Interestingly, those who thought they earned more than their peers also tended to think they were more indebted than their peers, and vice versa.

Figure 15.2 shows how respondents' perceptions about their peers changed with their income level (Panel A) and their debt (Panel B). As we look at higher and higher income respondents, we can see in Panel A that their perceptions of their peers' incomes increased on average but by less than the increase in the income of the respondents. On average, respondents with higher *absolute* income thought that they also had higher *relative* income. With debt levels, we observe a similar pattern: respondents with more debt tended to believe that their peers also held more debt, but the increase was less than one for one, so on average respondents with higher absolute debt levels tended to think they had more relative debt.

In general, people's beliefs about where they stand in the income distribution are likely to be correlated with their opinions about how motivating income differences may be, how fair the income distribution is, and the role for redistribution. We plot some examples of these types of correlations in Figure 15.3, for both perceived relative income and debt standings from Dutch

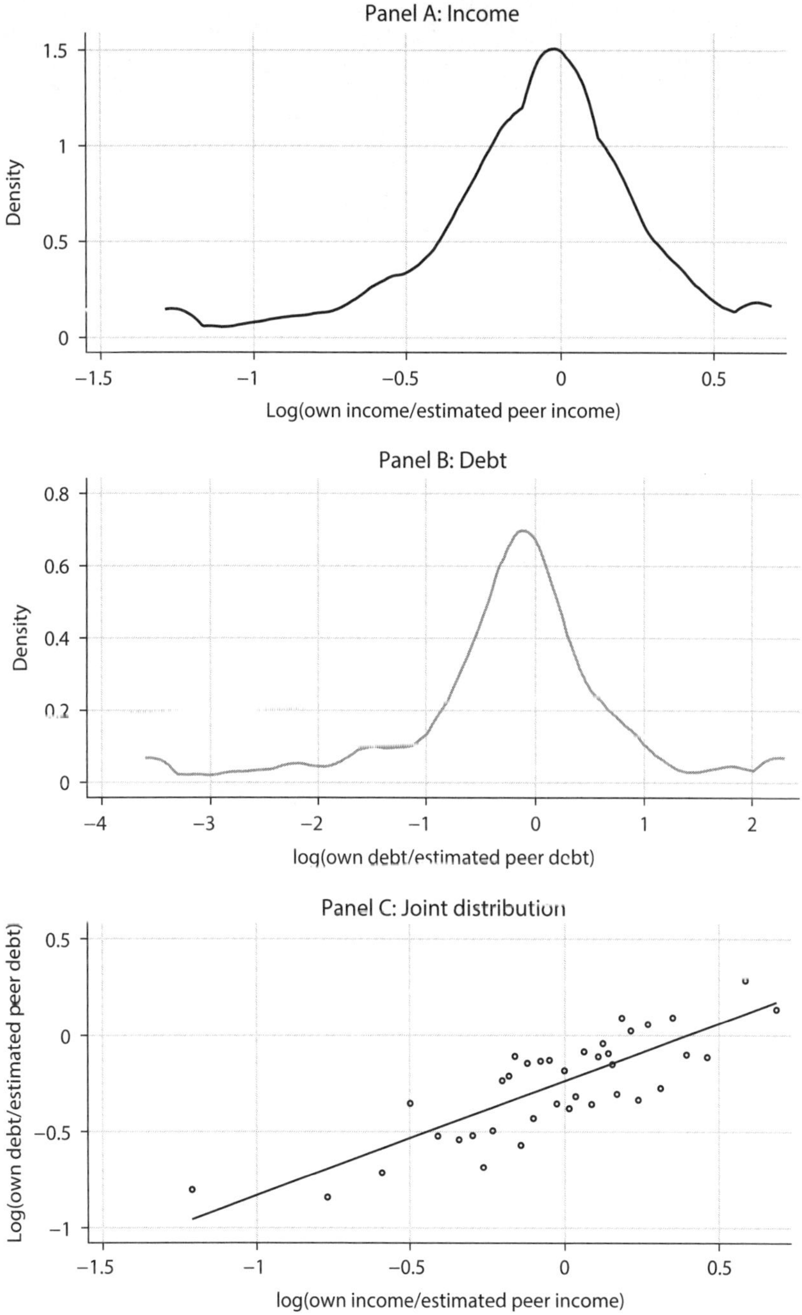

FIGURE 15.1. Distributions of perceived standings relative to peers.
Source: Panels A and B show kernel densities. Panel C is a binscatter plot. See van Rooij et al. (2023) for more details.

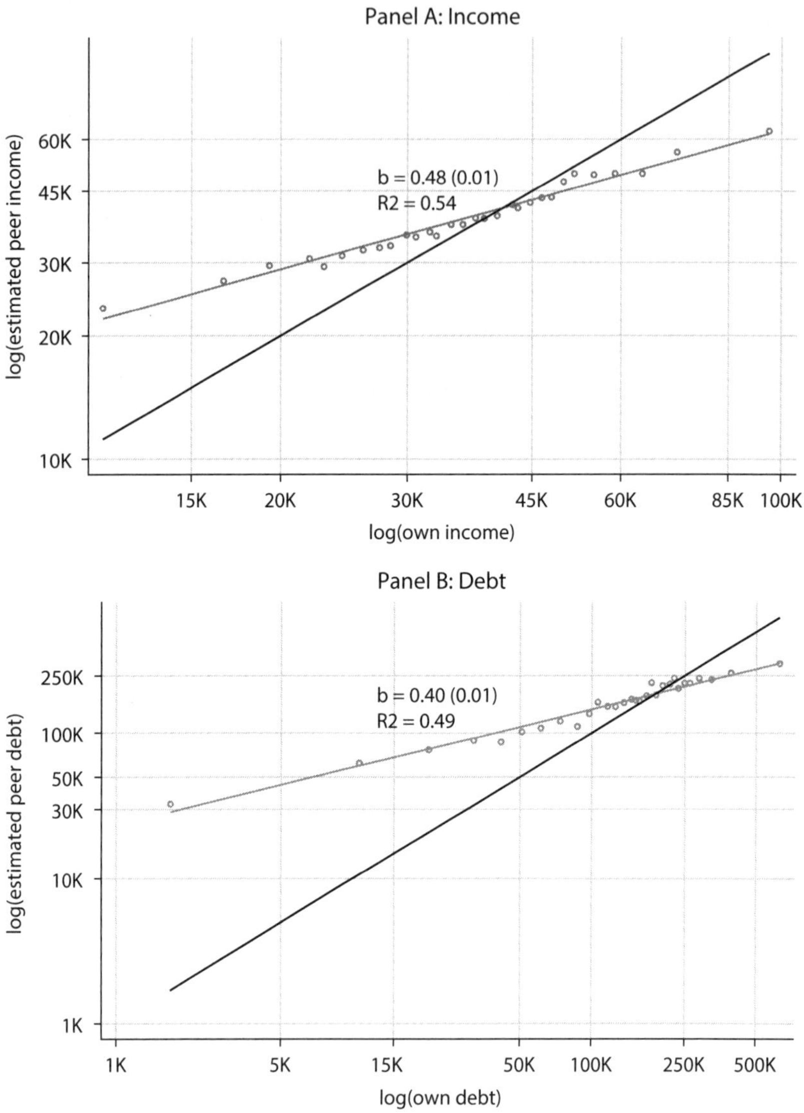

FIGURE 15.2. Perceived peer income and debt vs. own income and debt. *Notes:* The figures show binscatter plots of own expected income (debt) vs. perceived peer expected income (debt). All variables are measured before treatments (priors). The solid black line is the 45° line. See van Rooij et al. (2023) for more details.

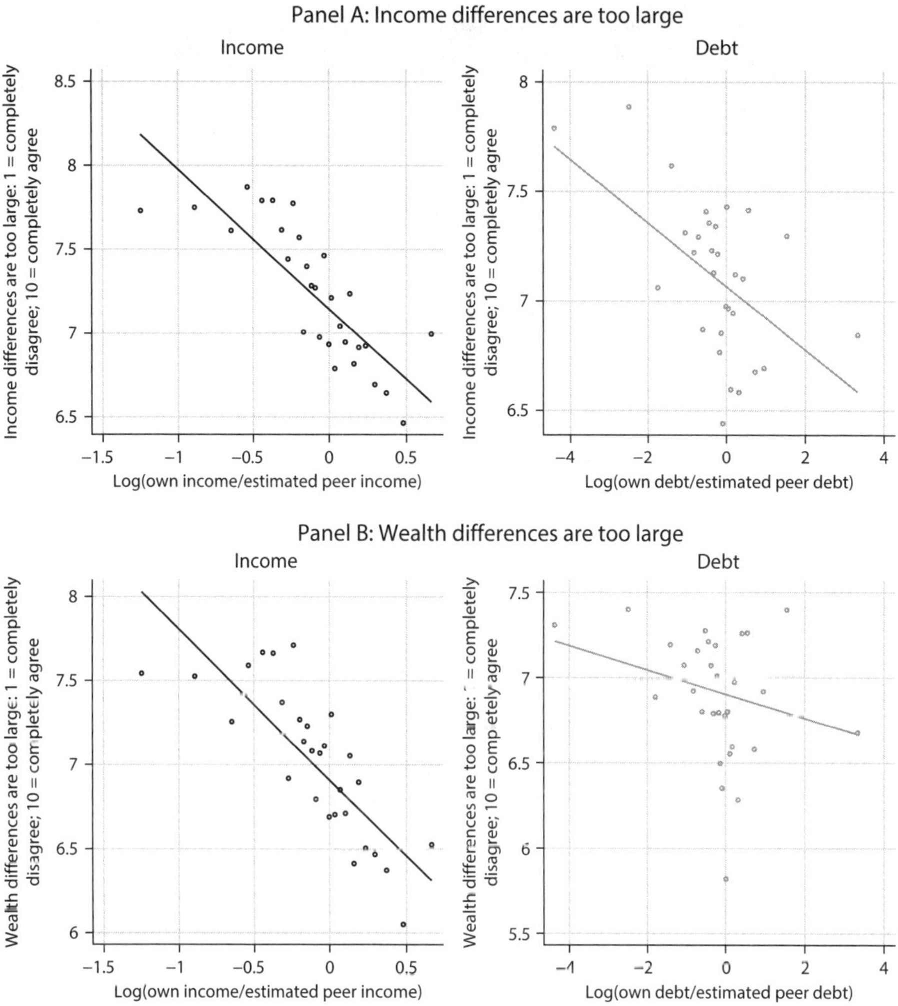

FIGURE 15.3. Joint distribution of perceived standings relative to peers and views on equity and redistribution.

Notes: The figures show binscatter plots of various beliefs vs. relative expected income or debt. See van Rooij et al. (2023) for more details.

survey respondents. There are striking patterns that are immediately visible. For example, people who believed they earn more than their peers were much less likely to think that income or wealth differences are too large (Panels A and B) or that policy should strive to make incomes more equal across people (Panel C). Instead, they were more likely to believe that income differences

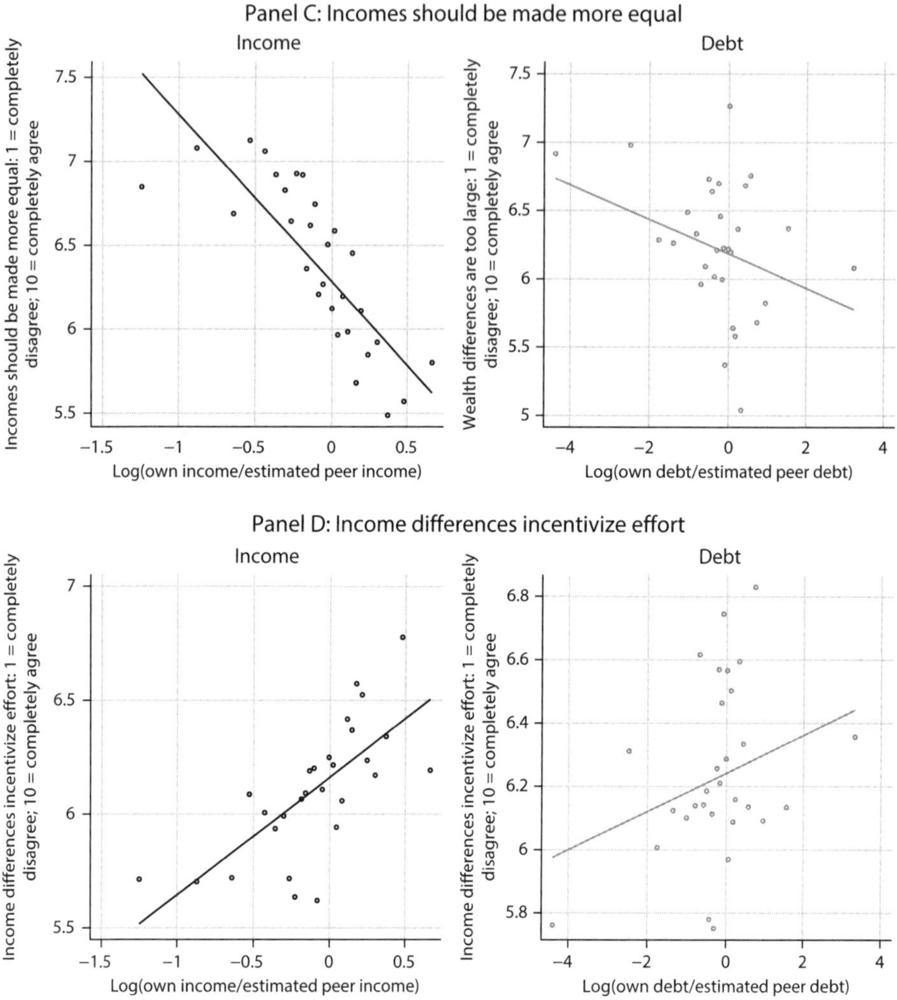

FIGURE 15.3. (*Continued*)

are a good motivation for people to work harder (Panel D) and that this hard work will tend to be rewarded (Panel E). People who believed they earn more than their peers were also much less likely to think that success is a matter of luck instead of hard work. Like Ferrer-i-Carbonell (2005) and Luttmer (2005), we found that people who believed they earn more than others tended to be happier, consistent with the idea that happiness may not be just about our

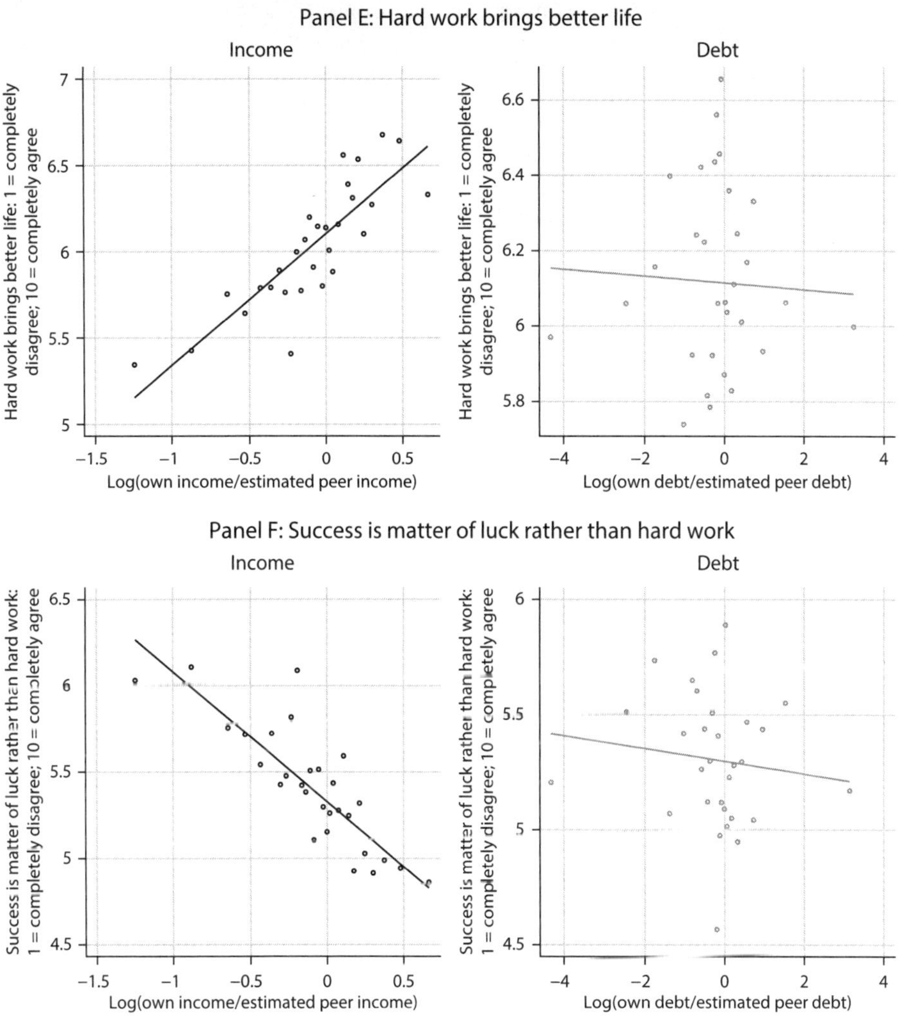

FIGURE 15.3. (*Continued*)

overall income and consumption but more about how we think we're doing relative to our peers.

Obviously, none of this evidence is causal. Perhaps people who think that hard work will be rewarded then work harder than others and end up in the upper end of the income distribution. Similarly, if one thinks that success is a matter of luck, then there may be little reason for them to work hard, so we

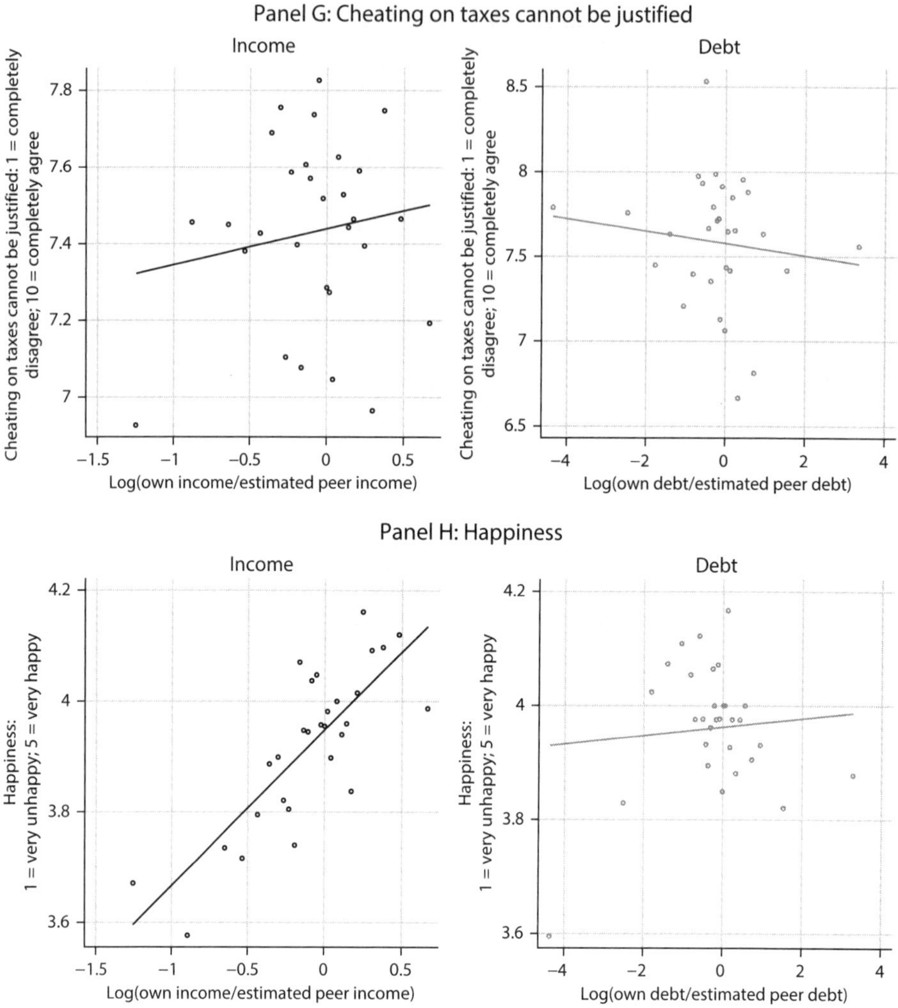

FIGURE 15.3. (*Continued*)

could end up seeing people who believe success is due to luck finishing up on the low end of the income distribution due to lower work effort. These correlations do not establish any causation. But if we are interested in understanding the extent to which peer effects affect outcomes, such as work effort, spending, and so on, we need a way to break through this identification challenge so that we can infer in which direction causality runs.

Creating Exogenous Variation in Perceived Relative Standings

One way to achieve causal identification is to create new variation in people's beliefs about their relative positions through an information treatment. This is the strategy we implemented in van Rooij et al. (2024). As mentioned earlier, the Dutch survey used in this paper can be complemented by external administrative data on actual income and debt of Dutch households. Because the administrative data includes information on the age, marital status, address, and so on of the respondents, it was possible for us to define peer groups for each individual in the survey in a fairly detailed manner. As a result, information treatments could be tailored to each individual respondent in the survey, which is a unique feature of this paper.

The identification strategy worked like this. As is typically done, respondents were randomly assigned to either a control group or one of several treatment groups. In this case, there were two treatment groups, which differed in terms of whether respondents would get information about the income of their peers or about the debt of their peers. In the case of the income treatment, we provided the average income of Dutch individuals that were within the same age group, that had the same general education level, and that had a similar living situation with a partner. In the case of debt, we provided the average debt level of Dutch individuals with the same characteristics as for income, but also the same housing characteristic, i.e., whether they owned their home or rented. Both pieces of information are publicly available from the Dutch Statistical Office. Within each of the two treatment groups, there were many different values or signals being provided about peers' income or debt levels given the heterogeneity in individual characteristics of respondents.

To see whether and how these treatments affected beliefs about peers, we first present visual representations of treatment effects in Figure 15.4. In Panel A, we compare posterior beliefs of individuals about their peers' income levels against their priors about peers' incomes for different groups of individuals. For the control group that received no information, we would expect posteriors to equal priors on average since the respondents did not receive information in between providing their priors and their posteriors. Indeed, that is exactly what we observe. For the treatment groups, we see that the relationship between posteriors and priors is much flatter. This indicates that survey respondents were placing some weight on the information that was provided to

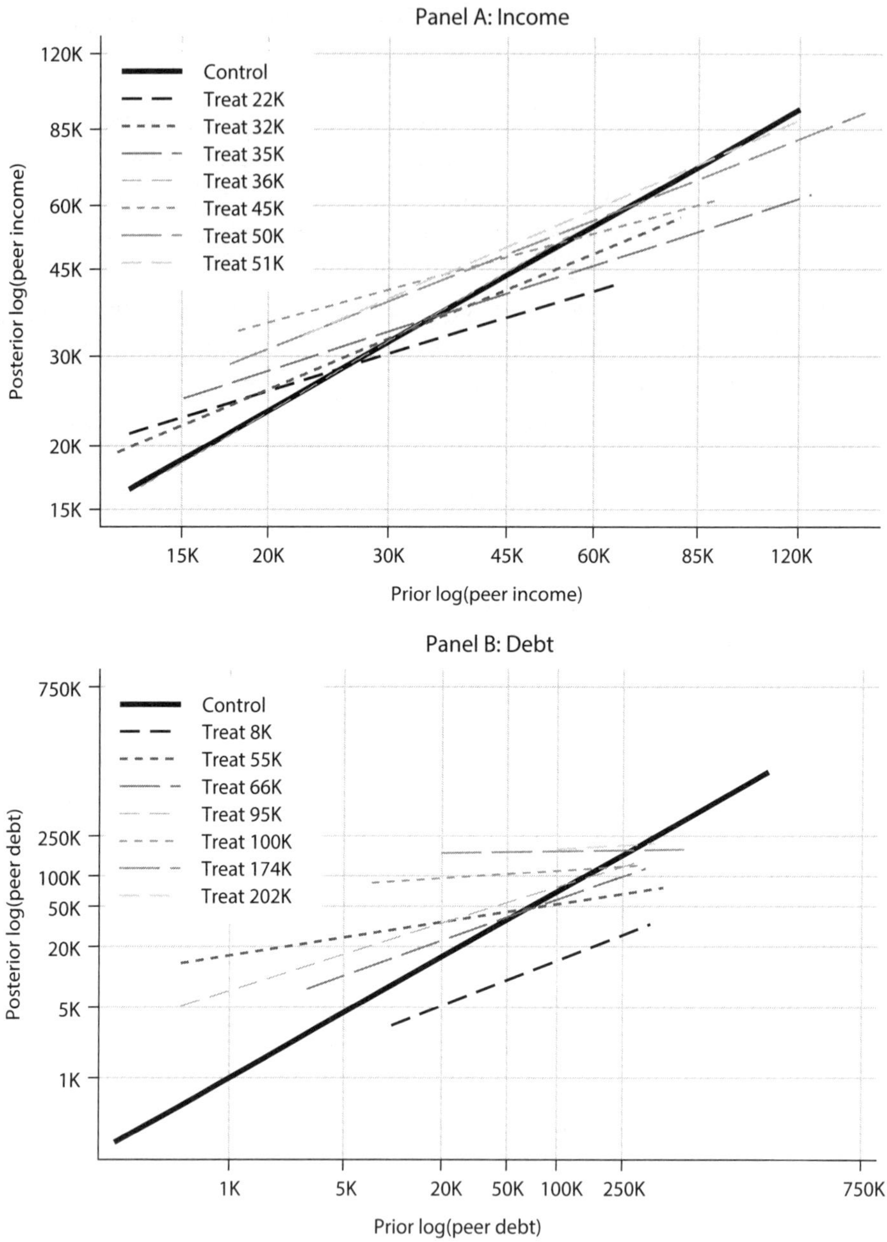

FIGURE 15.4. Effects of information treatments on perceived income and debt of peers.

Notes: The figures show fitted linear relationships between posterior and prior beliefs about peer expected income or debt for the control group (solid, thick, black line) and selected treatment groups. See van Rooij et al. (2023) for more details.

them, and therefore changed their beliefs about where they stood in either the income or the debt distributions.

This did not have to be the case. When respondents were asked about the income or the debt of their peers, it was left up to them to decide for themselves who they considered their peers to be in answering the question. When we provided the information treatment, we made clear that the provided information was for people of their age, marital status and education level. If the respondents defined their peers in a very different manner, then they would tend to dismiss the information as irrelevant in thinking about their relative position compared to their peers. The fact that they did change their beliefs about where they stood compared to their peers indicates that they viewed the provided information as at least partially speaking to their peer group.

Another notable feature of having respondent-specific treatments is that it introduced a new testable restriction from Bayesian learning. To see this, note that we estimated the following empirical specification, which follows the one proposed in Chapter 10 closely except that it now includes an interaction term between the treatment indicator and the value of the signal provided to the respondent ($TreatmentSignal_i$):

$$\begin{aligned} Posterior_i = a_0 + a_1 \times Prior_i + a_2 \times \ Prior_i \times \mathbb{I}(i \in T) + \\ a_3 \times \mathbb{I}(i \in T) \times TreatmentSignal_i + error, \end{aligned} \tag{1}$$

where $\mathbb{I}(i \in T)$ is an indicator variable equal to 1 if individual i is in the treatment group and 0 otherwise. To appreciate why this term is added to our baseline empirical specification, recall that under Bayesian updating, we have:

$$Posterior_i = (1-G) \times Prior_i + G \times Signal_i = Prior_i - G \times Prior_i + G \times Signal_i, \tag{2}$$

where $G > 0$ for the treatment group when the signal is at least somewhat informative. If the signal varies across individuals, then it is important to capture this variation in our empirical specification. Effectively, different values of the signal shift the relationship between the posterior and the prior up and down, exactly as shown in Figure 15.4, but leave the slope unchanged. For the control group, our empirical specification predicts that $a_1 = 1$ while $a_2 = a_3 = 0$ whereas within treatment groups we have $a_1 = 1$, $a_2 = -G$, $a_3 = G$. Thus, a testable prediction from Bayesian updating is that $a_2 + a_3 = 0$. In fact, when we estimated this specification using the information treatments described here and shown visually in Figure 15.4, we found that we could not reject this additional prediction.

In short, the information treatments worked well in creating variation in the beliefs of respondents about their relative standings in either the income or the debt distribution. Because this variation was randomly assigned, we did not need to worry about it being caused by other factors. As a result, we could use it to assess how changes in individuals' beliefs about their relative standing affected their decisions and beliefs along many different margins.

Perceived Relative Standings and Beliefs about Redistribution

With a clear source of exogenous variation in the perceived relative standings of individuals, we began by characterizing how these perceptions shape beliefs about the income distribution. To do so, we relied on the following empirical specification:

$$Belief_i^{Post} = b_1 \times \log\left(\frac{Own\ Income_i^{post}}{Peer\ Income_i^{post}}\right) + b_2 \times \log\left(\frac{Own\ Income_i^{prior}}{Peer\ Income_i^{prior}}\right) + Controls_i + error, \quad (3)$$

where $Belief_i^{Post}$ is the belief about inequality or fairness of respondent i measured in the follow-up wave and b_1 is the coefficient of interest. We instrumented for the posterior belief about an individual's perceived relative income standing using an information treatment indicator variable and its interaction with the individual's prior belief about their relative income standing as well as an interaction of the treatment with the specific signal value, as described in equation (1). Even though our information treatments did not necessarily correspond to peers as defined subjectively by a respondent, our instrumental variable approach still correctly identified the causal effect b_1 for the appropriate peer group because the posterior beliefs of respondents were reported for that group and the posterior beliefs were affected by the treatments (i.e., the first stage was strong).

The results indicated that many—but not all—of the correlations between perceived income standings and beliefs about redistribution shown in Figure 15.4 were in fact causal. When a person thinks they make more money relative to their peers, they become less likely to believe that the income and wealth distributions are too unequal. In turn, this also leads them to become less likely to think that incomes should be made more equal. This finding therefore points to an important causal link between where individuals perceive themselves in the income distribution and their belief in the need for income redistribution, a point that had been ambiguous in prior research. For example, Cruces et al. (2013) had found a similar result whereas Hoy and Mager (2021) concluded the opposite, Fehr, Mollerstrom and Perez-Truglia (2022) found no link in the context of global inequality and Kuziemko et al. (2015) found little effect for a range of redistributive polices (top income tariffs, minimum wages, food stamps) but a larger effect for estate taxes.

Why are those who perceive themselves as making more money than their peers opposed to trying to make the income distribution more equal? We found that one causal effect of having a high perceived income rank is that people became more likely to believe that income differences are incentivizing, that is, harder work results in higher income. However, despite the strong unconditional correlation between income rank and belief that hard work pays off or that success is due to working, we did not find any causal effect of higher perceived ranking on these views. So these seem to be likely examples of reverse causality. Believing that hard work pays off or that success is not due to luck is self-fulfilling: it induces more effort and leads people to end up, if not necessarily actually doing better, then at a minimum perceiving themselves as doing well relative to their peers. Another example of a noncausal relationship is the one between perceived debt levels and beliefs about redistribution or the rewards to work. While we can see relatively clear correlations between respondents' perceived relative debt levels and their beliefs about redistribution in Figure 15.4, we found that none of these seem to be caused by people's relative debt levels. In other words, when someone learns that their debt is higher than they thought relative to their peers, it does not lead them to change their beliefs about the fairness of their income or wealth distribution.

Perceived Relative Standings and Employment Decisions

A famous paper by Berkeley economists David Card, Alexandre Mas, Enrico Moretti, and Emannuel Saez (2012) studied what happens when workers are given the ability to see what their coworkers are earning. In their paper, this possibility was randomly assigned only to some workers at the University of California (where else would the researchers experiment on their colleagues?), thereby giving the authors the ability to estimate the causal effects of knowing peers' incomes in terms of job satisfaction and search. They found striking results: for workers who earned less than the median, the ability to find out what others were earning (and likely realizing that others were getting more) led to a significant decrease in job satisfaction and a rise in the time they spent searching for a new job. In contrast, for those who were earning more than the median (or who therefore likely learned they were making more than most of their colleagues), there was no detectable change in job satisfaction or time spent searching for a new job. Their results suggested that peer effects may be important but are asymmetric: knowing we are doing worse than others makes us worse off, but knowing we are doing better than others does not have the same kind of effect on our job satisfaction. A clear implication for those interested in improving workplace climate is to not disclose detailed compensation within a firm (many public universities continue to publish these data, but changing such policies is of course above our pay grade). However, the design of the study did not let the authors determine whether there were differences in actual job outcomes, such as people switching jobs. In a different study, Jaeger et al. (2024) showed that German workers tend to think that jobs in other firms would pay much closer to their own wage than is actually the case, i.e., they systematically underestimate the potential return on switching jobs. When some randomly selected workers were told about wages in other firms, they reported that they planned to increase their willingness to search for a new job and raise their wage demands.

In van Rooij et al. (2024), the presence of multiple survey waves allowed us to assess whether changes in perceived relative incomes affect job market outcomes. We focused on the extensive margin of people moving from being employed to not working, and vice versa. Using the same approach as before, we could estimate the causal effect of changes in perceived relative income and debt on employment outcomes in subsequent months. Across all respondents, there was no strong link between perceived income or debt ranking and subsequent employment outcomes. However, precisely as suggested by Card et al. (2012), we found that among those who received bad news in the income treatment (i.e., those who learned that their peers were earning more than they thought), there was a large increase in subsequent employment, consistent with them searching harder for work. We also asked respondents in the follow-up wave about how much income they expected to make in the future, and again found a similar pattern: those who received bad news in the income treatment significantly raised their income expectations thereafter, consistent with their searching more for better jobs after realizing their peers were doing better than they expected.

Together, these results therefore paint a fairly cohesive picture of how peer effects translate into job satisfaction and job search decisions. When people learn that their peers earn more than they thought, they become less satisfied with their positions, search for new work more intensively, and ultimately are more likely to be employed (if initially unemployed) and expecting to make more money. In contrast, there is no such effect present for those who think they are doing better than their peers. As long as we think we are above average, our job satisfaction appears to be ample.

Perceived Relative Standings and Spending Decisions

If we care about how we compare to our peers (and especially if what we care about is how they perceive us), then one solution to realizing we are not doing so well is to try to do better, such as by getting a better job and increasing our income, which the previous evidence supports. Another option is to convince other people that we are doing better than we really are. This is where "conspicuous consumption" comes in. Fancy cars, clothes and watches, for example, can give others the illusion that we are making more than we actually are, thereby raising our social status. Or if we see others purchasing fancy cars, we may feel the need to do the same, the "keeping up with the Joneses" effect. But how strong are these effects? Do they really matter for consumption?

There already exists some evidence supporting the existence of "keeping up with the Joneses." For example, Bertrand and Morse (2016) studied whether rising incomes at the top of the income distribution in the U.S. led those at the bottom of the distribution to spend more than they otherwise would have. They argued that this is indeed the case, especially for conspicuous categories of goods like cars. Agarwal et al. (2020) studied what happens to bankruptcies in neighborhoods where lottery winners live. They found that the presence of lottery winners in a neighborhood, who likely engage in visible and conspicuous purchases, leads to a rise in bankruptcies in surrounding areas, as neighbors borrow excessively to try to keep up appearances relative to their newly enriched neighbors (never win a lottery if you love your neighbors!).

In van Rooij et al. (2024), our follow-up surveys included questions about spending, as did the initial waves, which allowed us to assess to what extent changes in perceived relative rankings affect spending decisions in a clear causal framework. The survey tracked two forms of spending: "regular" spending on nondurable goods and on services as well as larger purchases of durable goods. We found that when people believed their peers earned more money, they became more likely to purchase large durable goods in subsequent months and spent more on them when they did, but at the same time they tended to reduce their spending on nondurable goods and services. Qualitatively, these results are therefore consistent with the notion that "keeping up with the Joneses" induces households to increase their spending on the most visible and conspicuous items, which are generally durables, when their peers seem to get richer, consistent with the earlier evidence in Bertrand and Morse (2016) and Agarwal et al. (2020).

However, the implied overall effect on total spending was actually quite small. For example, for the median household, the increase in durable goods spending corresponded to an extra €13 while the decrease in nondurable goods spending at the median was €15, so the net effect was a decline of €2 per month. This corresponded to a 0.2% decline in total spending when a respondent learned that their peers earn 1% more than they thought previously. For comparison, in macroeconomic models where "keeping up with the Joneses" mechanisms are used and estimated, they typically involve a pass-through of the consumption of others (which should be closely tied to income) into overall spending of 60–90% (see Havranek, Rusnak and Sokolova (2017) for a meta study). We also did not find any pass-through into borrowing decisions. Therefore, our combined results suggest that while there is some *reallocative* "keeping up with the Joneses" effect on spending (that is, buy some more flashy durables and reduce regular spending to compensate), its implication in terms of aggregate spending appears to be quite small.

Perceived Relative Standings and Happiness

There is a large body of literature studying the link between income and happiness. An early contribution by Easterlin (1974)—and later supported by Deaton (2008) and others—emphasized what became known as the Easterlin Paradox: the fact that higher income people within a country tend to be happier than lower income people, but average happiness within a country does not increase with overall income, at least beyond a certain threshold level of income. One explanation could be the relative income hypothesis, the notion that happiness depends on how our income compares to that of our peers instead of on its overall level. Much of the literature has focused on the correlation between income and happiness, with some evidence pointing toward positive correlations between relative income and happiness (e.g., Ferrer-i-Carbonell 2005, Luttmer 2005), while other papers have found weaker correlations (Stevenson and Wolfers 2008).

A major challenge in this area, as in many others, is establishing causality, since there are so many possible confounding factors that could be correlated with income and happiness. One suggestive result is from Natali et al. (2018), who studied the effect of large cash transfers to women in poor households. They found that these monetary transfers not only increased happiness, but also that the amount of the increase was most strongly correlated with changes in the women's perceived relative poverty rather than with changes in their actual consumption. Pischke (2011) used industry wage differentials to try to identify exogenous variation in income and found evidence suggesting that higher income leads to greater happiness.

Because the Dutch survey in van Rooij et al. (2024) generated exogenous variation in people's perceptions of their relative income standings as well as their measures of happiness in subsequent months, it provided a unique setting to assess whether the correlation between perceived income and happiness is causal. We found that it very much seems to be. Those with higher perceived income relative to their peers due to the information treatment were significantly happier two months later than comparable individuals with lower perceived relative income. Strikingly, our estimates using information treatments as instruments were three times larger than OLS estimates or unconditional correlations, and the resulting coefficient implied that relative income levels could account for a significant share of the observable variation in happiness in the data. In contrast, we found no such effect when it comes to perceived debt standings. So it really does seem to be relative income that matters.

But as was the case with job satisfaction, these effects do not apply across the board. Instead, the positive link between relative income and happiness occurred only for those who thought they were below average. For those in the lower end of the income distribution, moving up toward the average improves happiness, but once individuals think they are above average, there is little scope for their getting happier by becoming richer relative to their peers. In short, happiness is maximized in NPR's fictional Lake Wobegon, where everyone is above average.

Summary

Peer comparisons are a perfect application of the methods described here. They involve a belief (how we compare to others along some dimension) and decisions (spending, job search) that may be impacted by the belief, or even other beliefs (for example, the need for redistribution or for individual well-being). These beliefs need to be measured with surveys, and information treatments can serve to create variation in those beliefs that is unrelated to other factors, variation that is very difficult to find otherwise. With this variation, we can then estimate the pass-through from perceived relative standings into decisions, a quantitative metric that can be used to calibrate models with peer effects.

Of course, peer effects are much broader than simply income or debt comparisons of the types considered in this chapter (recall the Ice Bucket Challenge that went viral in the summer of 2014). And even in this limited context, many of the results described remained very imprecise because of limited sample sizes, measurement error in beliefs and self-reported outcomes, among other things. So the study of peer effects is still in its early stages and each research paper likely opens more questions than it answers. But with the growing ability to create exogenous variation in people's perceptions of their standing relative to peers, we have an unprecedented opportunity to learn about how and when these effects manifest themselves. And, ultimately, this type of knowledge may teach us how to find happiness from within instead of by comparison to others.

16

Expected Home Prices and Household Decisions

Home prices play a special role in the economy. Since for most people, their home will be the largest financial investment of their life, what happens to the price of that asset can play an enormous role in affecting their wealth accumulation. In turn, this can influence their spending and saving, their other investment decisions, or even their choices about whether to work and in what capacity, among many other margins. For example, high housing prices can make a home serve as collateral for entrepreneurs while falling housing prices can make it harder for people to relocate if their home is underwater. Housing prices can also determine whether some households will choose to be renters or homeowners, and even among renters, expected house price changes can affect their savings decisions if, for example, they are trying to save for a down payment. Housing prices also matter for equilibrium rents, so beliefs about the evolution of housing prices can matter to renters who have no intention of ever buying a home, through their implications for rents. In this chapter, we discuss new causal evidence from recent research on how individuals form beliefs about housing prices and the ways in which these beliefs affect their decisions.

The Formation of Housing Price Expectations

"All real estate is local" goes the old saying. So, measuring beliefs about local housing prices is a natural starting point. This is the approach used by Armona, Fuster and Zafar (2019, AFZ henceforth). They added a special module of questions to the New York Fed's Survey of Consumer Expectations (SCE) focusing on housing price expectations of both homeowners and renters in

February 2015. The survey included questions about perceptions of recent home price changes in their area as well as their beliefs about future home price changes. In both cases, respondents were asked these questions at shorter horizons (12 months) and longer horizons (five years). Other questions targeted beliefs about financial conditions, past housing-related decisions (e.g. did you buy a home in the past?), and the future likelihood of purchasing a home. The authors also added a special follow-up module to the regular SCE survey in April 2015, which allowed them to track the persistence of housing price beliefs as well as the effects of their information treatments.

As there was only limited evidence on housing price expectations prior to AFZ, they experimented with the sensitivity of responses to question formulations by measuring perceptions and expectations of price changes as point forecasts expressed in levels or in percent changes. In addition, respondents were asked to assign probabilities to four possible ranges of home price changes (less than −5%, −5% to 0%, 0% to 5%, and more than 5%) at the one-year horizon, with an equivalent formulation asking for five-year-ahead price changes. These questions allowed AFZ to measure the perceived downside risk to home prices and the respondents' overall uncertainty about future home price changes.

On average, respondents believed that home prices had risen by nearly 4% over the previous year and at an annualized rate of 1.5% over the previous five years. Disagreement about past home price changes was large. Expectations of home price changes over the next year and the next five years were very similar, on average, to perceptions of recent home price changes over the corresponding horizons, with similar amounts of dispersion in forecasts as in perceptions. In general, perceptions and forecasts were correlated: those who thought local home prices had risen more rapidly tended to also predict faster growth in home prices, in both the short run and the long run. Because AFZ asked about the zip codes that respondents lived in, they could compare respondents' beliefs about recent home price changes with actual ones, as measured by Zillow (an American real-estate marketplace tech company). Perception gaps were relatively small on average. Again, the dispersion was quite high, indicating that some respondents were significantly overestimating recent home price changes while others were significantly underestimating them.

To assess how households respond to new information about housing prices, AFZ randomly assigned survey participants to either a control or one of two treatment groups. One treatment involved being told about the percentage change in home prices in the respondents' zip codes over the last year, as measured by Zillow. The second treatment was about the total change in housing prices in the zip codes over the previous five years. These treatments therefore provide individual-specific information as a function of zip codes, capturing the very local nature of housing prices.

The effects of each treatment on housing price expectations found in AFZ are shown in Figure 16.1. Each panel represents a binscatter in which respondents are ordered by either the size of their initial one-year perception gap (the actual one-year housing price change minus their perceived one-year housing price change) on the horizontal axis in row 1 or the five-year perception gap in row 2. The vertical axis shows the average revision in either the one-year home price expectations before and after the treatment (row 1) or the longer-term housing price expectations (row 2). The different columns show results for each group separately. Note that for the control group, the lines representing the average relationship between perception gaps and expectation revisions are essentially flat, indicating that respondents did not systematically alter their revisions during the survey in a way that varies with their perception gap, consistent with them not being provided with any information about local housing prices.

For respondents who were told about one-year housing price changes, however, we see pronounced revisions in beliefs. For those who initially underestimated local housing price growth (positive perception gaps), expectation revisions are positive, indicating that they were increasing by how much they expected housing prices to rise over the next year. In contrast, those who initially overestimated recent housing price growth tended to lower their expectations of subsequent housing price growth. This is consistent with a belief in *momentum* in housing prices, i.e., that higher-than-average price growth one year tends to lead to the prediction of higher-than-average price growth the following year. This is indeed a feature of housing prices, although AFZ found that there is actually more momentum at the one-year horizon in housing prices than what is implied by the revision in respondents' beliefs to information about recent prices. In other words, respondents should be changing their beliefs by even *more* if they realized just how much momentum there actually is in housing prices. Information about one-year price changes did not lead to any meaningful revisions in beliefs about price changes over the next five years, which is consistent with the fact that one-year housing price changes have little predictive content for actual changes in housing prices over the next five years.

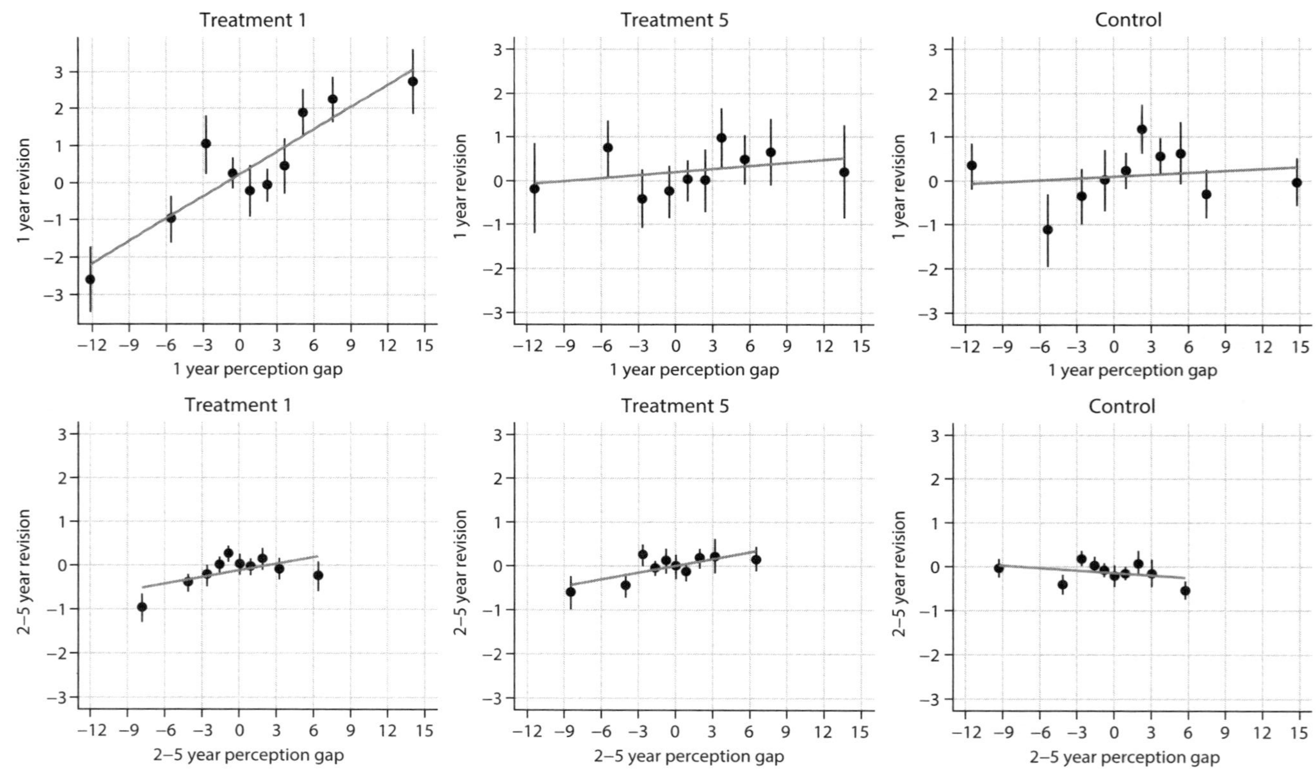

FIGURE 16.1. Effects of treatment on housing price expectations.
Source: Armona, Fuster and Zafar (2019).

In the case of the information treatment involving local housing price changes over the last five years, column 2 of Figure 16.1 indicates that households that initially underestimated by how much housing prices had risen in the previous years (positive perception gap) tended to raise their forecasts of both one-year and five-year housing price changes in their area. Looking at historical home price changes in the U.S., AFZ showed that the five-year change in housing prices in a zip code is not informative about housing price changes over the next year and is negatively correlated with subsequent five-year home price changes. In other words, housing prices over the medium run follow mean reversion: an above-average period of rising housing prices in a zip code is generally indicative that the next five years will display below-average housing prices. This means that the way in which households were revising their forecasts when told about recent five-year price changes was sharply at odds with the data. Someone realizing that local housing prices have risen by more than they thought should revise their beliefs about future home price growth downward, yet in practice they were raising them on average. Unlike with short-run price dynamics, households are therefore significantly *overestimating* how much momentum there is in local housing prices at longer horizons.

Home Price Expectations and Intended Home Purchases

To assess whether these beliefs about housing price changes are likely to affect individual behavior, AFZ considered several possible outcomes. One is how respondents answered a question about what fraction of $1,000 they would allocate to either a risk-free savings account earning 2% or a fund that invested in local housing and paid an annual return equal to the percentage change in local housing prices. They regressed this individual-level outcome on the revision in one-year-ahead home price expectations of respondents and, in the same spirit as that of the method described in Chapter 10, instrumented for these expectation revisions using the information treatments. They found that higher expectations about local housing price growth led individuals to allocate a higher share of this windfall to the housing fund, indicating that beliefs about housing prices are likely to affect financial portfolio decisions. Another outcome they considered is the probability that a respondent would buy an investment house in the next three years. They found that as respondents expected higher growth in housing prices, they also reported that they would be more likely to purchase a house as an investment. A third outcome AFZ examined was, conditional on moving, how likely respondents were to purchase a home. Those who expected higher home price growth tended to report that they would be more likely to purchase a home. Those same individuals also reported being more likely to make new investments in their home.

While all of these outcomes were based on hypothetical scenarios or planned decisions, we have seen in prior sections that responses to such questions are informative about how people actually behave. Hence, an important takeaway from AFZ is that housing price expectations are likely to have meaningful effects on the investment and home-purchasing decisions of households.

Home Price Expectations and Actual Home Sales

Because individuals only infrequently purchase and sell houses, it is quite difficult to assess how home price changes affect their decisions in practice. One approach is that used in AFZ, which is to ask survey respondents about the probability that they may purchase or sell a home in the future. But, ideally, one would like to observe whether they actually do or do not engage in these transactions. A second approach would be to run a follow-up survey of respondents but, unless the survey sample is very large, there will be very few home transactions visible in the data due to how infrequently these transactions take place.

A recent study by Bottan and Perez-Truglia (2025, BPT henceforth) came up with an ingenious field experiment that allowed them to get around this issue. They decided to focus their attention on people who had already listed their homes online, and sent them information about local housing prices. They then tracked whether and how this information affected the probability of a home being sold and its price using administrative records for home sales. Their approach relied on the random provision of information to home sellers, with large-scale external data on housing transactions. The result was crisp evidence on the effects of beliefs about housing prices on subsequent home sale outcomes.

Their starting point was to scrape online information from a major real-estate listing website, thereby collecting a wide range of information on listed properties, such as their listing price and the characteristics of the home (number of bedrooms, square footage, etc.). These real-estate listings also included a unique Assessor Parcel Number (APN). These APNs could then be linked to publicly available tax rolls from county assessors, which includes information on the names of the owners and their mailing addresses. They focused on 36 large U.S. counties in which this tax information was made easily accessible.

After dropping nonresidential properties, they randomly selected 60,000 properties from their total available pool of listed properties for which they had mailing addresses and names of homeowners along with characteristics of the listed property.

Armed with this large number of listed properties, BPT then considered how to affect owners' home price expectations. They allocated each of these properties to one of six treatment groups. Every single subject was sent an identical-looking letter, and all of the letters included information on the median price of a home comparable to theirs, based on the zip code and the number of bedrooms. For one group, no additional information was provided beyond this median home price. For each of the other five groups, some form of information was provided. As in AFZ, two of the groups were provided with the average price change for such properties (by zip code and number of bedrooms) either over the last year or over the last five years. The other three groups were each provided with a forecast of prices for these properties over the next year, but from different forecasting models. All three models were statistical representations of housing prices that the authors used to generate forecasts, but the models varied somewhat, so their predictions differed as well. Hence, depending on which group a specific property was randomly assigned to, the respondents could receive, above and beyond the information on the median selling price of a home like theirs, forecasts with different numerical values or recent home price changes. Each letter also included a link to a survey, which helped the authors track the receipt of letters over time. The experiment had two different sources of variation in information. One was that, within a given zip code, people with similar houses were provided with different information (e.g., different forecasts). The second source of variation was geographic: because the signals were stronger on average in some regions than others, the average effect of treatments was larger in some regions than others. Finally, the authors were able to track subsequent home sales through weekly scraping of the same online listing website as well as through tax records.

The main downside of this type of field experiment is that it is not possible to measure either the prior or the posterior beliefs of the property owners. To get around this, the authors ran a survey of other households in parallel that replicated the information treatments in a context where they could observe the effects on expectations of respondents. Of course, the two approaches should not be expected to yield identical results given the different sets of participants, their different exposures to the treatments (e.g., some letters went unread in the field experiment), and so on. Nonetheless, the joint implementation is an illustration of how one can still try to measure both beliefs and outcomes even when they cannot necessarily be observed jointly.

BPT focused on two main outcomes in the field experiment. The first is the probability that the home was sold by a specific time horizon after the start of the experiment. How these probabilities are related to the size of the information treatment is shown in the left panel of Figure 16.2. On the horizontal axis, properties are grouped by the size of the information effect, which is the value that was provided relative to the minimum possible signal the respondents could have received. The vertical axis shows the probability that the property was then sold within three months of the mailing. There is a clear negative relationship: the higher the information shock (i.e., the more the information induced people to expect higher subsequent price growth), the lower was the probability of selling the home. This is what we would expect, since, when predicting higher prices in the future, home sellers perceive a greater incentive to wait for future offers, thereby delaying the timing of the home sale on average. This is precisely what the data indicates. In Panel B, we present a similar plot from BPT, but now with the revision in expected home price growth, as measured in the survey. The positive relationship confirms that, at least within the survey, those who received more positive information about home prices raised their expectations of future home price growth. This is supportive of the expectations mechanism being the source of the delay in home sales, apparent in Panel A.

Of course, given that mail takes time to be delivered and property owners may open their mail only with a delay (if ever), we would expect the effects on their decisions to take time to materialize in terms of actual home sales. The authors were then able to determine how rapidly home sales responded to the mailing of the letters because they could track, each week, home sales in each market. They were therefore able to assess not only how the probability of the home being sold varied according to the information shock, but also how long it had been since the experiment began. The results can be seen in Figure 16.3, which plots the estimated effects week-by-week of information shocks on the probability of the property being sold after the start of the experiment, as well as the share of letters that were likely to have been read over time as indicated by the U.S. Post Office. Consistent with a gradual receipt and opening of the letters over time, as well as with delays before homes were actually sold, there was an increase in the size of the estimated effects over the first few weeks of the experiment, peaking around 12 weeks after its start.

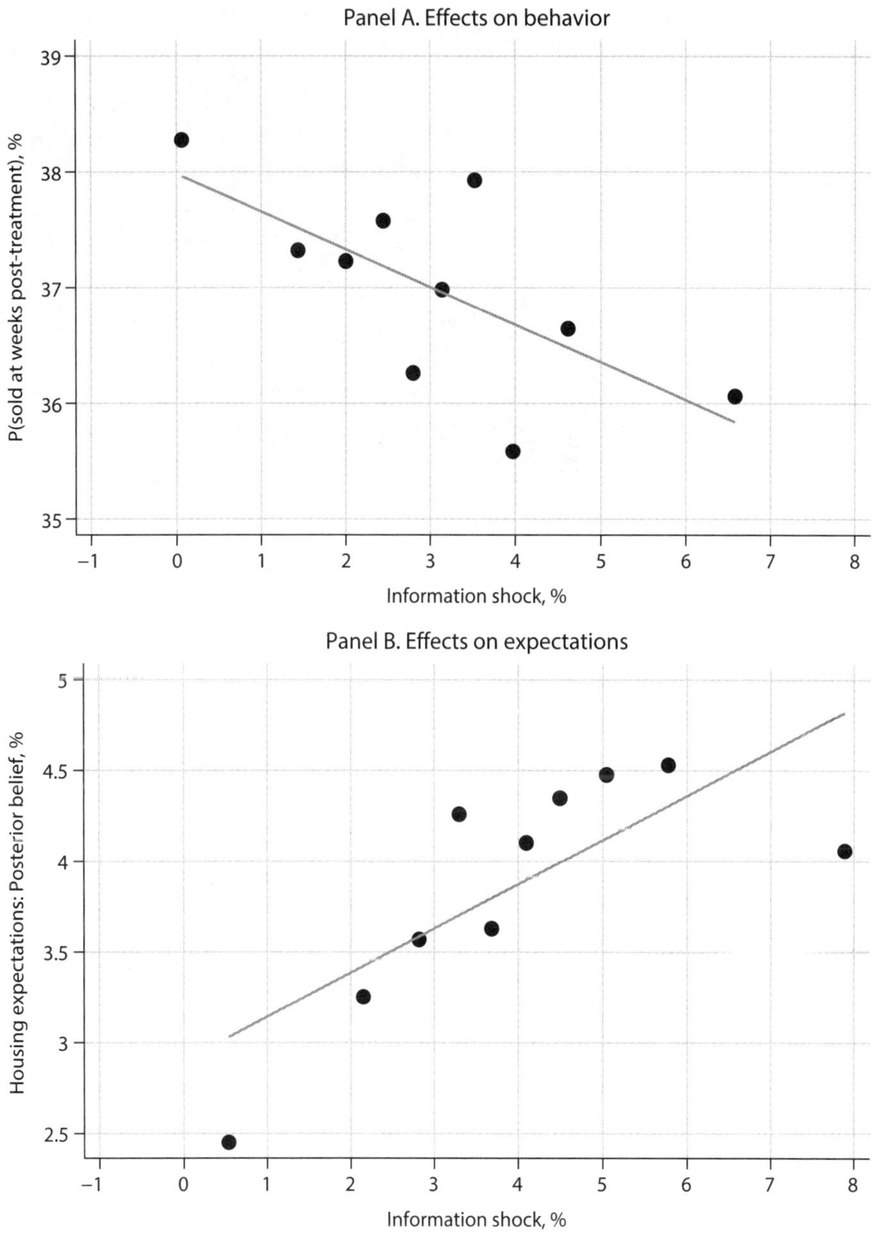

FIGURE 16.2. Effect of information shocks on expectations and probability of house sold in three months.
Source: Bottan and Perez-Truglia (2025).

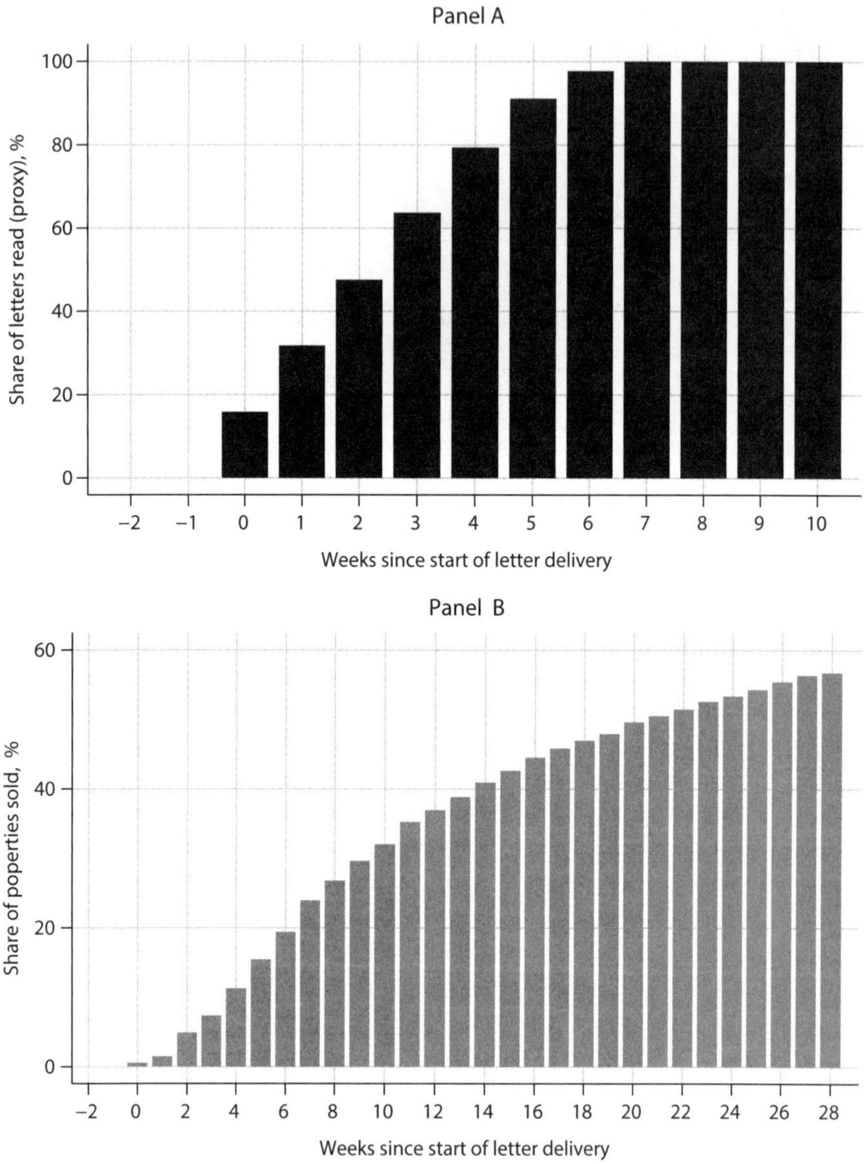

FIGURE 16.3. Timing of read-receipt.
Source: Bottan and Perez-Truglia (2025).

The second outcome is the effect on the prices of the properties when they were sold. One would expect that, if homeowners are more likely to hold out for a higher offer when they expect rising home prices, then we should see higher home price sales among those who received more positive information shocks. Again, the authors could assess these effects week-by-week by regressing home sale prices for properties sold each week after the experiment began on the information shock of those properties. The results are presented in Figure 16.4. Here, we see that the effect on prices conditional on the home being sold can be identified fairly quickly, but the estimates are noisy. This is because, within each week, there were not many properties being sold, so estimated home prices are imprecise. Nonetheless, we can see the expected effect: as property owners were provided increasingly positive information about local housing markets, they only sold their properties if it was at a premium relative to those who received less positive information about local housing prices.

BPT is quite different in its approach from many papers that we have discussed. Intuitively, the low frequency of home price transactions makes it very challenging to directly measure how housing price expectations affect home sales through a survey. BPT used a field experiment with a large number of

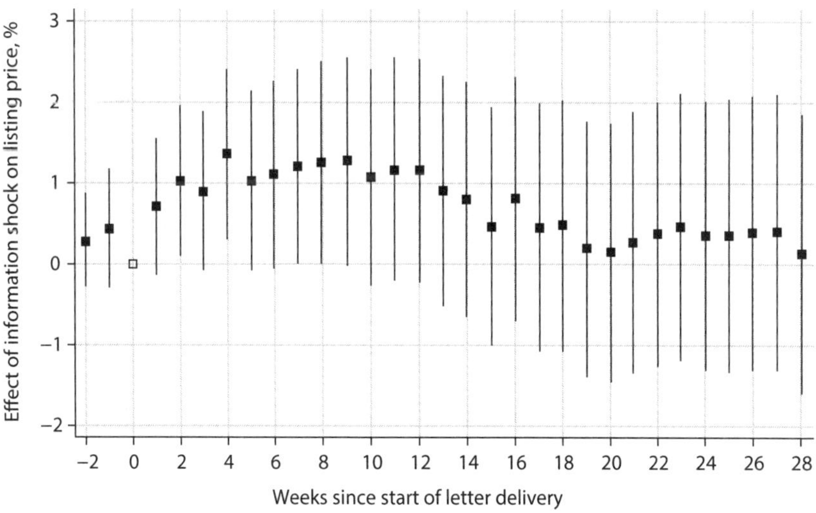

FIGURE 16.4. Effect of information shock on weekly home sale prices.
Notes: Squares show point estimates and whiskers show 90% confidence intervals. The square at time 0 is normalized to a value of 0. See Bottan and Perez-Truglia (2025) for more details.

actual home sales measured using administrative data and a well-executed information treatment, which provides clear causal evidence that the treatment had an effect on the home sellers' decisions; but the absence of information on the actual expectations of the home sellers means that the mechanism and its quantitative magnitude are harder to pin down. Nonetheless, BPT provides some of the best available evidence on the key role that home price expectations play in affecting the decisions of homeowners to sell their homes.

Home Price Expectations and Consumer Spending

Beyond the decision to purchase or sell a home, beliefs about future housing prices might be expected to affect individuals in other ways. For example, for homeowners, a rising value of their home means that they should perceive themselves as wealthier, which could make them spend more. Or, if they do not plan to sell their home anytime soon, they could view changing home values as "paper gains" that they do not want to touch. Even if they plan to sell their home, they might expect that the next house they buy will also be more expensive, thereby offsetting any gains from the higher value of their own home. Or, since homes can serve as collateral, rising home prices could make some homeowners believe that they will have more access to credit in the future, thereby relieving them of borrowing constraints. Among renters who would like to buy a home, rising future housing prices mean that they will need more money for a down payment, which may require more saving on their part. Even among renters who have no plans to buy a home, they could expect that if houses are going to become more expensive, then so will their future rent, which again could increase their incentive to save. There are therefore a variety of channels through which beliefs about future home prices could affect the saving and spending decisions of individuals, whether they own a home or not.

These effects of expected housing prices on spending decisions were carefully assessed in a paper by Chopra, Roth and Wohlfart (2025, CRW henceforth). They combined scanner-level spending data on Nielsen Homescan participants with surveys of these same respondents that included an information experiment. The information treatment generated exogenous variation in expected housing price growth that they could then link to the actual spending decisions of respondents, along with additional spending measures from a follow-up survey. Jointly, this allowed them to provide clear causal evidence on how home price expectations affect the spending decisions of households, of both homeowners and renters. They combined this with additional survey evidence (relying on open-ended questions) that helped them identify the motives underlying these spending decisions.

Their starting point was the group of households that participate in the Nielsen Homescan panel. As discussed earlier, these are households that track their spending on food and other retail items, allowing economists and others to observe in exceptional detail on what, where, when and how these households do their spending. Because Nielsen allows researchers to occasionally run surveys of these households, CRW was able to implement an information experiment to assess the role of expected housing prices on them.

The survey itself was administered to approximately 3,800 respondents in November 2019. A follow-up survey four weeks later was not completed by everyone, leading to a sample size of around 2,500 across the two surveys. Unlike AFZ, CRW focused on respondents' beliefs about home prices across the U.S. over the next ten years, which is different in both its focus on national home prices and its much longer time horizon. Following the information treatment, respondents were asked to answer another question on future home prices, in which they allocated probabilities to different bins for possible future national home price growth rates. In addition to these particular beliefs, the survey measured other economic expectations as well as characteristics of respondents, such as whether they owned a home or were renters.

The information treatment implemented in this case was an "active control," which, as described in earlier chapters, is when *all* groups receive information. In this case, respondents were randomly assigned to one of two groups. Both groups were provided with a professional forecast of housing price changes over the next ten years, but one forecast was low while the other was high. Specifically, the forecasts were formulated as follows:

> According to this expert forecast, the average annual growth rate of home prices in the US over the next ten years will be [1.5 or 6] percent. In the case where home prices increase by [1.5 or 6] percent in each of the next ten years, this would mean that a home worth $100,000 today will be worth about [$116,054 or $179,085] in ten years from now.

Whether they received the 1.5% or 6% number (and the corresponding values of the home after ten years) defines whether they were in the "low" or the "high" group, respectively. The advantages and disadvantages of "active control" designs were discussed in more detail in Chapter 5.

CRW focused on two main outcomes. One is total monthly expenditures of the household as measured by Nielsen. The second is whether a household purchased durable goods over the month following the information treatment, which was measured using a follow-up survey. This follow-up survey also remeasured home price expectations, which can be used to assess the persistence of treatment effects. With these two outcome measures, prior and posterior beliefs about home price growth, and a randomized information treatment, CRW was then in a position to quantify the causal effect of home price expectations on spending decisions. It did so using a two-step procedure similar to the one described in Chapter 10. In the first stage, it estimated the average effect on home price expectations of getting the "high" treatment relative to the "low" treatment:

$$F_{it}^{post} HP_{t+1} = \alpha + \beta \times \mathbb{I}(i \in Treatment \text{ ``}High\text{''}) + Controls_i + error, \qquad (1)$$

where i,t index households and time, $\mathbb{I}(i \in Treatment \text{ ``}High\text{''})$ is an indicator variable with value 1 if a household is in the "high" forecast treatment and 0 otherwise, and $F_{it}^{post} HP_{t+1}$ is the posterior expectation of home price growth. Controls include the prior home expectations of the household as well as a number of observable characteristics. They found that the "high" treatment raised home price expectations by approximately 1.5 percentage points across all participants, with the effect being larger for renters (2.2 percentage points) than homeowners (1.3 percentage points).

The second stage for spending on nondurables was given by:

$$\log(expenditure_{i,t+1}) = \gamma \times \mathbb{I}(i \in Treatment \text{ ``}High\text{''}) + \tau_i + \mu_t + error, \quad (2)$$

which was estimated using monthly expenditures in the three months prior to as well as after the treatment. The specification includes individual fixed effects and time fixed effects. Across all participants as well as for homeowners specifically, the estimates of γ are small and statistically insignificant, indicating that the treatment did not affect spending for these groups. However, for renters, the researchers found that γ is around -0.08 and significant, so that renters who were told about the high home price forecast reduced their spending by about 8% relative to renters who were told about the low home price forecast. The implied pass-through of home price expectations into nondurable goods spending is given by the ratio of the coefficients γ / β, which is approximately 3.9 for renters: every 1 percentage point increase in home price expectations of renters reduces their spending on nondurable goods by almost 4 percentage points, a large effect in economic terms. When they focused on durable goods purchases one month after the treatment as the outcome variable, CRW again found a negative effect of the treatment for renters but not for homeowners. Thus, the evidence of CRW points toward large negative effects of home price expectations on the spending decisions of renters but little effect on that of homeowners.

By itself, this is already a useful result that is cleanly identified and an important contribution to the literature. But CRW took another step in understanding the mechanisms at work through an additional survey. In this separate survey of 500 respondents (not in the Nielsen Homescan panel), they presented all participants with the following hypothetical scenario:

> Imagine that you expect home prices to grow by 1.5% per year over the next 10 years. Now imagine that you increase your expectations about future home prices. You now expect home prices to increase by 6% per year over the next 10 years.

This is precisely equivalent to the qualitative and quantitative exercise done in the RCT. After seeing this hypothetical, respondents were asked whether they would expect their economic situation to improve, worsen or stay the same, and then asked to explain why in their own words. Following this, they were presented with the same hypothetical, and asked whether they expected to increase, decrease or maintain their spending, and again asked to explain why in their own words. These open-ended questions helped avoid any priming of respondents, but were more time-intensive for them as well as for researchers to process. CRW had research assistants code whether the answers identified specific pre-defined mechanisms, yielding qualitative measures of the mechanisms that respondents had in mind.

As illustrated in Panel A of Figure 16.5, the respondents' answers to the hypothetical scenario were qualitatively consistent with the results of the RCT: renters were more likely to report that they would reduce their spending than homeowners when they expected higher home price growth in the future, and they viewed this scenario as making them worse off. This consistency between the results of the RCT and a hypothetical scenario is, as discussed in Chapter 11, in line with other evidence that hypothetical scenarios generally seem to be able to recover the same effects as RCTs. Panel B of Figure 16.5 shows the distribution of answers across different mechanisms for homeowners and renters separately. For homeowners, 41% mentioned the value of their home,

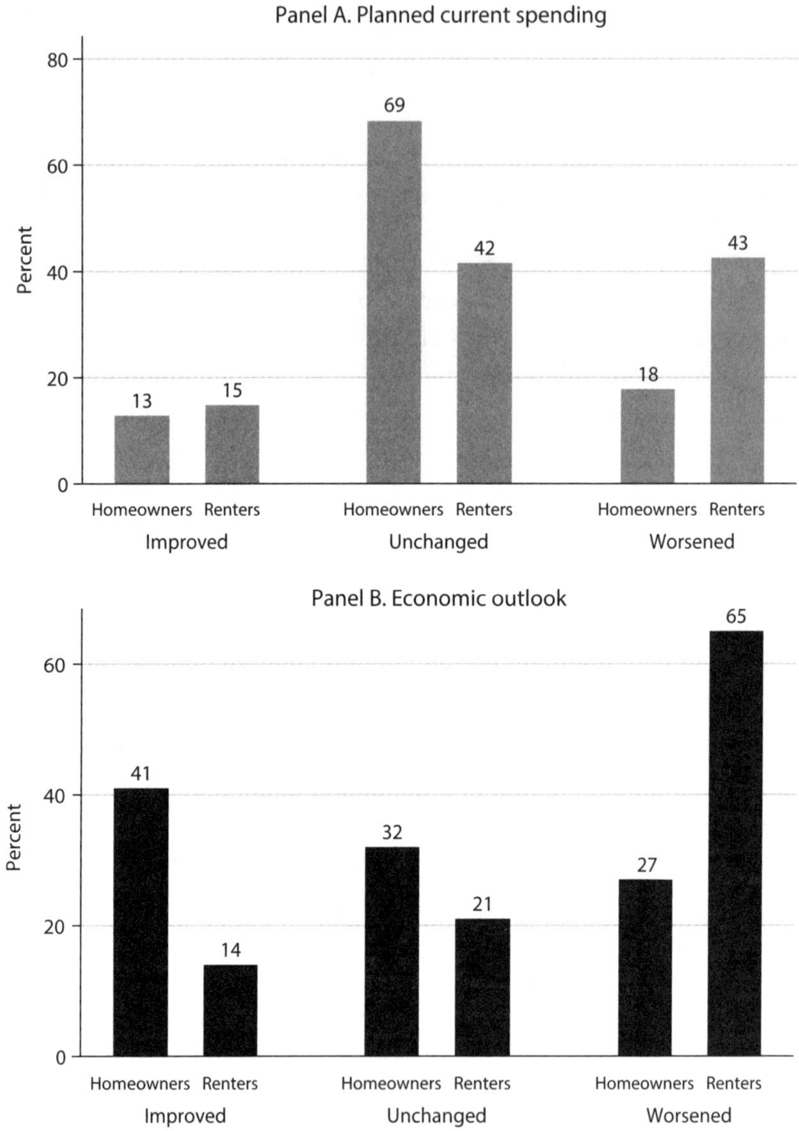

FIGURE 16.5. Effects of an increase in expected home price growth on respondents' economic outlook and planned current spending.
Source: Chopra, Roth and Wohlfart (2025).

which would generally be a positive effect for them, while 32% mentioned that home price growth was irrelevant for them (likely because they either perceived the gains as paper gains or did not plan to sell the home) and another 27% emphasized the negative effects of higher home prices (higher cost of buying a new house, inflation). In contrast, renters primarily identified the higher cost as the mechanism for their behavior, consistent with the increased saving that they displayed in the RCT. This illustrates how open-ended questions, in combination with more quantitative survey questions, can be helpful to researchers in identifying which mechanisms are driving specific behaviors.

Summary

Home prices can affect households in many ways, reflecting the fact that homes are partly consumption, partly investment, and partly collateral. Expected future prices matter directly for homeowners since homes are assets for them; but even for renters they should be expected to play an important role, as the evidence just discussed suggests they do. Understanding the mechanisms through which these effects operate, and quantifying them, can be cleanly done through a combination of surveys, information treatments and external data on decisions. These are not the only ways, and a large body of literature on the role of housing prices has utilized many different methods, but it is a promising way to break new ground in this area, as the early papers discussed have already demonstrated.

Conclusion

HOPEFULLY ONE MESSAGE has come across clearly in this book: randomized controlled trials (RCTs) can be applied to help address many questions that are of importance to macroeconomists. While some macroeconomists have been rather skeptical about measuring expectations or using microeconomic methods to establish causality for macro questions, we believe that RCTs can bring in decisive evidence for many key debates in macroeconomics. We have focused on how inflation expectations affect the decisions of firms and households in particular, but far more can be done.

Where Do We Go from Here?

Looking forward, we see several fronts along which progress seems particularly promising and should help make this methodological approach a more systematic and useful tool for all economists.

Matching survey and administrative data: The first and lowest-hanging fruit is to match surveys with administrative or other external data sources much more systematically. As we have discussed at length, one can measure outcomes through repeated survey waves in which respondents are asked about their recent decisions. But this can be less than ideal for at least two reasons. First, self-reporting through surveys tends to be much noisier than measures that come from administrative data. Matched survey-administrative data can help address this source of measurement error and increase the precision of empirical estimates. Second, by not having to ask respondents about their recent decisions, precious space in the survey is left open to ask about other areas of interest. This expands the scope of what can be asked in the survey and therefore the range of research questions that can be studied. This is particularly important for surveys of firms, in which the need to keep surveys short is paramount. More systematic linking of surveys with administrative data would therefore open the door to many additional research projects.

Expanding who gets surveyed: A second important avenue is the expansion of surveys to more targeted groups of economic participants. We have discussed extensively surveys of "firms" and "households," but these mask important differences across respondents that likely matter for economic dynamics. For example, retailers that produce only in one region have a different incentive to be informed about aggregate conditions than retailers that produce nationwide (Wu 2024). Within a firm, CFOs are rarely price-setters and HR representatives who typically set wages are not generally making investment decisions. Trying to assess how expectations affect a firm's decisions will be hampered if one cannot talk to the relevant decision-makers in each case. This extends beyond households and firms as well. There are many different groups of agents whose expectations are likely to be important. Real-estate agents' beliefs about inflation will matter for the listing prices of the houses they represent (Guglielminetti and Loberto 2024). Loan officers in banks are responsible for credit supply decisions that likely significantly impact macroeconomic outcomes (D'Acunto et al. 2024). Systematically being able to measure expectations for many different types of economic actors would allow researchers to estimate the pass-through of beliefs into decisions in a much more targeted and useful fashion than what is currently feasible.

Applications to new questions: In this book, we've discussed at length how RCTs have been used to assess how inflation expectations affect decisions. We also covered some additional applications such as the effects of macroeconomic uncertainty, beliefs about asset returns and housing prices, and peer effects. But given how pervasively expectations matter for decisions, this is only scratching the surface of questions that can be asked and answered with RCTs in surveys. New research has already begun to address a diverse set of topics with these methods, including automation (Golin and Rauh 2022), energy conservation (Castillo and Petrie 2023), maternal labor supply (Boneva et al. 2023) and exchange rates (Delgado et al. 2024). Future work can and should go much further. It's hard to predict which areas will be most fruitful at this stage. As Yogi Berra, a famous baseball player, said, "It is difficult to make predictions, especially about the future." And if we knew the future for sure, we would already be working on them ourselves! But what is clear is that there is tremendous scope for applying this approach to a wide range of questions.

Replicate, replicate, replicate: Another general direction that will be important for this approach addresses concerns about external validity through the more systematic implementation of replications of experiments. In fields like physics or genetics, new scientific experiments and measurements are immediately put to the test by other teams of scientists. With the growing access to surveys, it will become increasingly possible for economists to adopt a similar model. This will be useful along at least two dimensions. First, from a scientific point of view, more evidence is better than less, and the availability of multiple studies for a given question will provide a more precise understanding of economic relationships in the data. Second, there are many cases in which we expect estimates to differ based on the environment (for example, at the zero bound on nominal interest rates), so having multiple estimates of the same experiment but applied at different moments or in different settings will provide new ways to test and guide economic theories.

Partial vs. general equilibrium effects: While RCTs can address some shortcomings of typical macroeconomic empirical estimates, they can measure only partial equilibrium responses of individuals, not the aggregate outcomes that we typically care most about. Making the jump from partial equilibrium estimates to predictions about aggregate outcomes requires a model. Hence, RCT-based strategies like the ones we have described should be viewed as complements to models and dependent upon them to make claims about aggregate effects. Better understanding how to map estimated pass-throughs from RCTs into macroeconomic models should therefore be a priority for this line of research. We discussed some initial ways of doing so in Chapter 12. One could entertain others as well. For example, in a macroeconomic model with imperfect information, one could simulate how agents would respond to an information treatment like the one in an RCT and estimate the underlying parameters of the model through a Simulated Method of Moments approach that minimizes the distance between the moments of the data (the effects of the RCT on beliefs and/or decisions) and the moments of the model (the simulated effects of the same RCT applied to economic agents in the model). Yet another strategy to quantify how partial equilibrium effects could translate into general equilibrium effects is to apply RCTs in a laboratory setting in which participants interact in an economic task. Laboratory settings are not commonly used by macroeconomists, but like a macroeconomic model, they provide a closed and controlled environment in which we can study how shocks, policies and communication affect aggregate outcomes in general equilibrium (see Pfajfar and Zakelj 2018, Kryvtsov and Petersen 2021 for examples). In such a setting, one could compare the partial equilibrium responses of participants to RCTs and their subsequent general equilibrium behaviors, helping establish how one relates to the other, just as in a macroeconomic model.

Application to policy in real time: Finally, we believe it would be useful to start applying RCTs and hypothetical scenario questions much more systematically in real time to help address policy questions. Consider, for example, the design of a stimulus package, for which policymakers could be unsure about the strength of the spending response of households to transfers or tax rebates. A hypothetical question in a survey could provide immediate guidance about the likely effectiveness of the two prior to their implementation. Another example is with policy reforms such as the adoption of flexible average inflation targeting (AIT) by the Federal Reserve in 2020. We ran daily surveys of households with colleagues at the Federal Reserve Bank of Cleveland before and after Chairman Powell's announcement at the Jackson Hole conference to assess to what extent the announcement was heard by the general public and affected their beliefs (answers: not at all and not at all). In these surveys, we also presented hypothetical scenarios to respondents in which we tried to explain what AIT would mean, in an attempt to assess whether one should expect any effect on inflation expectations if people learned about the announcement (Coibion et al. 2023). We found that, even when we explained AIT in the simplest possible language, it still had no discernible effect on people's inflation expectations relative to traditional inflation targeting. Had the Federal Reserve run such a survey prior to its policy switch, it would have become clear ahead of time that some of the theoretical gains from AIT (those operating through households' inflation expectations) were unlikely to materialize in practice, diluting much of the potential benefits of the new policy regime. More generally, each new economic crisis tends to be unprecedented in some way, whereas the empirical evidence that macroeconomists have available to them is based entirely on the available history, meaning that it very often cannot speak to the relevant questions or policy options under consideration. With the use of real-time surveys, RCTs and hypothetical scenario questions, policymakers could assess *in real time* how different potential policy responses might affect the behavior of economic actors, providing useful guidance as to what policies would be best suited to the problem at hand.

Together, these steps would help expand the scope to which this methodology can be applied, would bring theory and empirics closer together, and would contribute in a practical and immediate way to better policymaking. There is a long way to go, and much more still to be learned. But we are very hopeful that RCTs can contribute in a meaningful way to macroeconomics and ultimately to policymaking.

RCTs and the Future of Macroeconomics

RCTs are not a panacea, and they cannot directly answer the big macroeconomic questions that we ultimately care about. But neither can any other modeling or econometric method. That should not be a death blow to a new instrument in our toolkit. Instead, we think that this approach can help macroeconomics along three main directions.

Scientific credibility: In 1991, Larry Summers published an article provocatively titled "The Scientific Illusion of Empirical Macroeconomics," in which he argued that most recent econometric estimates in macroeconomics had contributed essentially nothing to our knowledge and policies. As empirical macroeconomists ourselves, we are more sympathetic to empirical research in macroeconomics, and especially to the type of work that has been done since Summers's article. For example, work since then has successfully provided new and important facts about price-setting (e.g., Bils and Klenow 2004, Nakamura and Steinsson 2008), the size of fiscal multipliers (e.g., Auerbach and Gorodnichenko 2012, Ramey and Zubairy 2018), consumers' propensity to spend (e.g., Johnson, Parker and Souleles 2006, Shapiro and Slemrod 2003) and other key elements of macroeconomic analysis. But in each of these cases, controversy remains about how to interpret the resulting facts and estimates. There are few debates in macroeconomics that have been successfully resolved through empirical work, besides perhaps the non-neutrality of money. Summers's skepticism about what empirical macroeconomics has contributed is, we suspect, not uncommon.

There are many reasons for such skepticism. With aggregate time series data, assigning causality generally requires heroic assumptions. The historical experience covered by the available data is limited and confounded by the many shocks and policy changes taking place simultaneously. A lot of recent work has turned toward microeconomic data in the hope of resolving some of these issues, but even there, causality is often difficult to establish convincingly (see Nakamura and Steinsson 2018b for a review). And moving from micro estimates to macro implications can often be challenging.

The RCT approach adds three important dimensions that have not been successfully addressed by prior work. First, causality is much clearer with RCTs than with most other applications and can be applied to study relevant questions *by design*, rather than by relying on whatever narrow historical experiences permit a causal interpretation. Second, RCTs can be readily replicated while natural experiments such as the collapse of the Soviet Union (Gorodnichenko, Mendoza and Tesar 2012) or military buildups in the U.S. (Ramey and Shapiro 1998) cannot. Third, the RCT approach can answer questions where endogeneity and unobservable variables such as expectations interact in important ways. Indeed, how expectations shape decisions is a topic that has been largely absent from prior work due to the endogeneity of expectations and the limited availability of joint information on expectations and decisions. As a result, we think the RCT approach can break a lot of new ground in empirical macroeconomics and strengthen the scientific foundations of the field through well-designed experiments that can be repeated and tested by multiple research teams in different settings. Over time, this can help break through the scientific illusion emphasized by Summers.

Taming the wilderness of non-FIRE expectations: A major limitation facing macroeconomics is how to move beyond full-information rational expectations (FIRE). Even in the early days of the rational expectations revolution, Tom Sargent, a Nobel laureate and a leader of this revolution, was already looking ahead to possible deviations from FIRE, and described those departures as a "wilderness." Indeed, one can deviate from both full information and rationality along so many dimensions that it is difficult to even know where to start. Yet start we must. The evidence against the null hypothesis of FIRE is decisive, as strong as anything we ever observe in empirical macroeconomics. But the source of those deviations remains to be pinned down. Fortunately, through the growing availability of survey data on expectations combined with RCTs that are explicitly designed to study how expectations adjust to new information, we have already begun to make some progress in distinguishing between different models of expectations formation. There is a long way to go before there is a consensus on which deviation from FIRE is most appropriate to integrate into the "standard" macroeconomic model, but with these new tools, we can eventually map out Sargent's wilderness and determine the right path to follow.

Building Block: Economists are known to disagree on almost everything and one can hardly expect the profession to embrace RCTs right away for various reasons. For instance, some macroeconomists will be concerned that the approach is too "micro", too small to really help us answer the big macro questions. It's true, we won't be able to use these RCTs to identify the sources of business cycles, to explain why some countries are richer than others, or to determine optimal stabilization policy. But it's also clear that after decades of using other methods designed explicitly to do so, we have not made much progress in this respect (see, for example, Ramey (2016) for a review of how little we have learned about the sources of business cycles), and not for a lack of trying. Of course, we should continue to try to improve these methods, but we should also try new ones.

In the last 20 years, macroeconomics has become increasingly empirical, particularly in moving toward the use of microeconomic data and methods. Incorporating RCTs and survey experiments is clearly another step in that direction. But in its emphasis on the role of forward-looking expectations in shaping decisions, it has a uniquely macro flavor and it can tackle fundamental mechanisms and questions at the heart of macroeconomic models that we could not possibly address otherwise.

A well-established strategy of scientists when taking on big problems (and big, "macro" problems are in the name of our field) has long been to break them into smaller manageable ones and gradually work their way back up to the bigger questions. RCTs can, we think, help us go far in this way. There is a whole new set of questions that we can ask and hopefully answer using these methods that simply could not be done before. With each new study we learn more about the role of expectations in affecting economic decisions, and, for macroeconomics, being able to quantify this forward-looking behavior is central to better understanding aggregate dynamics and policy. With each new study we add a rock to our growing wall of macroeconomic knowledge. It may be slow going, and some of the rocks may fall from time to time, but eventually it will be tall enough and sturdy enough that answers to the big questions will be within reach.

REFERENCES

Abberger, Klaus, Anne Funk, Michael Lamla, Sarah Lein, and Stefanie Siegrista, 2024. "The Pass-through of Inflation Expectations into Prices and Wages: Evidence from an RCT Survey." CEPR Discussion Paper 19595.

Adam, Klaus and Mario Padula, 2011. "Inflation Dynamics and Subjective Expectations in the United States," *Economic Inquiry* 49(1): 13–25.

Afrouzi, Hassan, 2024. "Strategic Inattention, Inflation Dynamics, and the Nonneutrality of Money," *Journal of Political Economy* 132(10): 3378–3420.

Afrouzi, Hassan and Choongryul Yang, 2017. "Dynamic Inattention, the Phillips Curve, and Forward Guidance." Manuscript.

Afrouzi, Hassan, Joel Flynn, and Choongryul Yang, 2024. "What Can Measured Beliefs Tell Us about Monetary Non-Neutrality?" NBER Working Paper 32541.

Agarwal, Sumit, Vyacheslav Mikhed, and Barry Scholnick, 2020. "Does Keeping Up with the Joneses Cause Financial Distress? Evidence from Lottery Winners and Neighboring Bankruptcies," *Review of Financial Studies* 33(1): 433–472.

Ahn, Hie Joo, Shihan Xie, and Choongryul Yang, 2024. "Effects of Monetary Policy on Household Expectations: The Role of Homeownership," *Journal of Monetary Economics* 147: 103599.

Aidala, Felix, Olivier Armantier, Gizem Koşar, Jason Somerville, Giorgio Topa, and Wilbert van der Klaauw, 2024. "Gasoline Price Changes and Consumer Inflation Expectations: Experimental Evidence," *Journal of Economic Behavior & Organization* 220(C): 66–80.

Akarsu, Okan, Emrehan Aktug, and Huzeyfe Torun, 2024. "Inflation Expectations and Firms' Decisions in High Inflation: Evidence from A Randomized Control Trial." Manuscript.

Aktug, Emrehan and Orhan Erem Atesagaoglu, 2024. "Inflation Expectations and Household Spending in High Inflation: Evidence from a Randomized Control Trial." Manuscript.

Albrizio, Silvia, Allan Gloe Dizioli, and Pedro Vitale Simon, 2023. "Mining the Gap: Extracting Firms' Inflation Expectations from Earnings Calls," *International Monetary Fund Working Paper* 23/202.

Allcott, Hunt and Dmitry Taubinsky. 2015. "Evaluating Behaviorally Motivated Policy: Experimental Evidence from the Lightbulb Market," *American Economic Review* 105(8): 2501–2538.

Alexopoulos, Michelle, 2011. "Read All About It!! What Happens following a Technology Shock?" *American Economic Review* 101(4): 1144–1179.

Alexopoulos, Michelle, Xinfen Han, Oleksiy Kryvtsov, and Xu Zhang, 2024. "More than Words: Fed Chairs' Communication during Congressional Testimonies," *Journal of Monetary Economics* 142(C): 103515.

Alfaro, Iván, Nicholas Bloom, and Xiaoji Lin, 2024. "The Finance Uncertainty Multiplier," *Journal of Political Economy* 132(2): 577–615.

Altig, David, Jose Maria Barrero, Nicholas Bloom, Steven Davis, Brent Meyer, and Nicholas Parker, 2022. "Surveying Business Uncertainty," *Journal of Econometrics* 231(1): 282–303.

Andrade, Philippe, Gaetano Gaballo, Eric Mengus, and Benoit Mojon, 2019. "Forward Guidance and Heterogeneous Beliefs," *American Economic Journal: Macroeconomics* 11(3): 1–29.

Andrade, Philippe, Erwan Gautier, and Eric Mengus, 2023. "What Matters in Households' Expectations," *Journal of Monetary Economics* 138: 50–68.

Andrade, Philippe, Erwan Gautier, Eric Mengus, Emanuel Moench, and Tobias Schmidt, 2025. "Household Beliefs about Fiscal Dominance." Manuscript.

Andrade, Philippe, Olivier Coibion, Erwan Gautier, and Yuriy Gorodnichenko, 2022. "No Firm Is an Island? How Industry Conditions Shape Firms' Expectations," *Journal of Monetary Economics* 125(C): 40–56.

Andrade, Philippe, Richard Crump, Stefano Eusepi, and Emanuel Moench, 2016. "Fundamental Disagreement," *Journal of Monetary Economics* 83: 106–128.

Andre, Peter, Ingar Haaland, Christopher Roth, and Johannes Wohlfart, 2022b. "Narratives about the Economy." Manuscript.

Andre, Peter, Carlo Pizzinelli, Christopher Roth, and Johannes Wohlfart, 2022a. "Subjective Models of the Macroeconomy: Evidence from Experts and Representative Samples," *Review of Economic Studies* 89(6): 2958–2991.

Ang, Andrew, Geert Bekaert, and Min Wei, 2007. "Do Macro Variables, Asset Markets, or Surveys Forecast Inflation Better?" *Journal of Monetary Economics* 54(4): 1163–1212.

Angeletos, George-Marios, and Zhen Huo. 2021. "Myopia and Anchoring," *American Economic Review* 111(4): 1166–1200.

Angeletos, George-Marios, Zhen Huo, and Karthik A. Sastry, 2020. "Imperfect Macroeconomic Expectations: Evidence and Theory," *NBER Macroeconomics Annual* 35: 1–86.

Armantier, Olivier, Scott Nelson, Giorgio Topa, Wilbert van der Klaauw, and Basit Zafar, 2016. "The Price Is Right: Updating Inflation Expectations in a Randomized Price Information Experiment," *Review of Economics and Statistics* 98(3): 503–523.

Armantier, Olivier, Argia Sbordone, Giorgio Topa, Wilbert van der Klaauw, and John Williams, 2022. "A New Approach to Assess Inflation Expectations Anchoring Using Strategic Surveys," *Journal of Monetary Economics* 129(S): S82–S101.

Armona, Luis, Andreas Fuster, and Basit Zafar, 2019. "Home Price Expectations and Behaviour: Evidence from a Randomized Information Experiment," *Review of Economic Studies* 86(4): 1371–1410.

Aruoba, Boragan, Andrés Fernández, Daniel Guzman, Ernesto Pastén, and Felipe Saffie, 2024. "Pricing Under Distress," NBER Working Paper No. 32538.

Ash, Elliott, Heiner Mikosch, Alexis Perakis and Samad Sarferaz, 2024. "Seeing and Hearing is Believing: The Role of Audiovisual Communication in Shaping Inflation Expectations," KOF Working Paper No. 515, KOF Swiss Economic Institute, ETH Zurich.

Atkeson, Andrew and Lee Ohanian, 2001. "Are Phillips Curve Useful for Forecasting Inflation?" *Federal Reserve Bank of Minneapolis Quarterly Review* 25(1): 2–11.

Auerbach, Alan and Yuriy Gorodnichenko. 2012. "Measuring the Output Responses to Fiscal Policy," *American Economic Journal: Economic Policy* 4(2): 1–27.

Avalos, Edgar, Jose Maria Barrero, Elwyn Davies, Leonardo Iacovone, and Jesica Torres, 2024. "Business Uncertainty in Developing and Emerging Economies." CESifo Working Paper 11368.

Axelrod, Sandor, David Lebow, and Ekaterina Peneva, 2018. "Perceptions and Expectations of Inflation by U.S. Households," Finance and Economic Discussion Series 2018–073, Federal Reserve Board.

Bachmann, Rüdiger, Tim Berg, and Eric Sims. 2015. "Inflation Expectations and Readiness to Spend: Cross-Sectional Evidence," *American Economic Journal: Economic Policy* 7(1): 1–35.

Bachmann, Ruediger, Benjamin Born, Olga Goldfayn-Frank, Georgi Kocharkov, Ralph Luetticke, and Michael Weber, 2021. "A Temporary VAT Cut as Unconventional Fiscal Policy," NBER Working Paper 29442.

Bachmann, Ruediger, Kai Cartensen, Stefan Lautenbacher, and Martin Schneider, 2020. "Uncertainty Is More Than Risk—Survey Evidence on Knightian and Bayesian Firms." Manuscript.

Bachmann, Ruediger, Kai Cartensen, Stefan Lautenbacher, and Martin Schneider, 2021. "Uncertainty and Change: Survey Evidence of Firms' Subjective Beliefs," NBER Working Paper 29430.

Bachmann, Rüdiger, Steffen Elstner, and Eric Sims. 2013. "Uncertainty and Economic Activity: Evidence from Business Survey Data," *American Economic Journal: Macroeconomics* 5 (2): 217–49.

Baek, ChaeWon and Vitaliia Yaremko, 2022. "Spillovers in Macroeconomic Expectations and Labor Supply: Implications for Wage-Price Spirals." Manuscript.

Baker, Scott, Nicholas Bloom, and Steven Davis, 2016. "Measuring Economic Policy Uncertainty," *Quarterly Journal of Economics* 131(4): 1593–1636.

Baker, Scott, Nicholas Bloom, and Stephen Terry, 2024. "Using Disasters to Estimate the Impact of Uncertainty," *Review of Economic Studies* 91(2): 720–747.

Baker, Scott, Tucker McElroy, and Xuguang Sheng, 2020. "Expectation Formation Following Large, Unexpected Shocks" *Review of Economics and Statistics* 102(2): 287–303.

Barro, Robert, 1974. "Are Government Bonds Net Wealth?" *Journal of Political Economy* 82(6): 1095–1117

Barsky, Robert, Thomas Juster, Miles Kimball, and Matthew Shapiro, 1997. "Preference Parameters and Behavioral Heterogeneity: An Experimental Approach in the Health and Retirement Study," *Quarterly Journal of Economics* 112(2): 537–579.

Barsky, Robert and Eric Sims, 2011. "News Shocks and Business Cycles," *Journal of Monetary Economics* 58(3): 273-289.

Barsky, Robert and Eric Sims, 2012. "Information, Animal Spirits, and the Meaning of Innovations in Consumer Confidence," *American Economic Review* 102(4): 1343–1377.

Bauer, Michael, and Eric Swanson, 2023. "An Alternative Explanation for the 'Fed Information Effect.'" *American Economic Review* 113(3): 664–700.

Baumann, Ursel, Annalisa Ferrando, Dimitris Georgarakos, Yuriy Gorodnichenko, and Timo Reinelt, 2024. "SAFE to Update Inflation Expectations? New Survey Evidence on Euro Area Firms," CEPR Discussion Paper 19161.

Ben-David, Itzhak, Elyas Fermand, Camelia M. Kuhnen, and Geng Li, 2018. "Expectations Uncertainty and Household Behavior," NBER Working Paper 25336.

Bertrand, Mariane and Adair Morse, 2016. "Trickle Down Consumption," *Review of Economics and Statistics* 98(5): 863–879.

Beutel, Johannes and Michael Weber, 2023. "Beliefs and Portfolios: Causal Evidence," Chicago Booth Research Paper No. 22–08.

Bholat, David, Nida Broughton, Janna Ter Meer, and Eryk Walczak, 2019. "Enhancing Central Bank Communications Using Simple and Relatable Information," *Journal of Monetary Economics* 108(C): 1–15.

Bianchi, Francesco, Renato Faccini, and Leonardo Melosi, 2023. "A Fiscal Theory of Persistent Inflation," *Quarterly Journal of Economics* 138(4): 2127–2179.

Bils, Mark and Peter Klenow, 2004. "Some Evidence on the Importance of Sticky Prices," *Journal of Political Economy* 112(5): 947–985.

Binder, Carola C., 2017. "Measuring Uncertainty Based on Rounding: New Method and Application to Inflation Expectations," *Journal of Monetary Economics* 90: 1–12.

Binder, Carola, 2020. "Coronavirus Fears and Macroeconomic Expectations," *Review of Economics and Statistics* 102(4): 721–730.

Binder, Carola, Jeffrey Campbell, and Jane Ryngaert, 2024. "Consumer Inflation Expectations: Daily Dynamics," *Journal of Monetary Economics* 145(S): 103613.

Binder, Carola, Rupal Kamdar, and Jane Ryngaert, 2024. "Partisan Expectations and COVID-Era Inflation," *Journal of Monetary Economics* 148(S): 103649.

Binder, Carola, Pei Kuang, and Li Tang, 2023. "Central Bank Communication and House Price Expectations," NBER Working Paper 31232.

Binder, Carola and Alex Rodrigue. 2018. "Household Informedness and Long-Run Inflation Expectations: Experimental Evidence," *Southern Economic Journal* 85(2): 580–598.

Bloom, Nicholas, 2009. "Impacts of Uncertainty Shocks" *Econometrica* 77(3): 623–685.

Bloom, Nicholas, Philip Bunn, Scarlet Chen, Paul Mizen, Pawel Smietanka, and Greg Thwaites, 2019. "The Impact of Brexit on UK Firms," NBER Working Paper 26218.

Bloom, Nicholas, Philip Bunn, Paul Mizen, Pawel Smietanka, and Greg Thwaites, 2025. "The Impact of COVID-19 on Productivity," *Review of Economics and Statistics* 107(1): 28-41.

Bloom, Nicholas, Philip Bunn, Paul Mizen, Pawel Smietanka, Gregory Thwaites, and Garry Young, 2017. "Tracking the Views of British Business: Evidence from the Decision Maker Panel," Bank of England *Quarterly Bulletin* 2017 Q2.

Bloom, Nicholas, Max Floetotto, Nir Jaimovich, Itay Saporta-Eksten, and Stephen J. Terry, 2018. "Really Uncertain Business Cycles," *Econometrica* 86(3): 1031–1065.

Bloom, Nicholas, Takafumi Kawakubo, Charlotte Meng, Paul Mizen, Rebecca Riley, Tatsuro Senga, and John Van Reenen, 2021. "Do Well Managed Firms Make Better Forecasts?" NBER Working Paper 29591.

Boctor, Valerie, Olivier Coibion, Yuriy Gorodnichenko, and Michael Weber, 2024. "On Eliciting Subjective Probability Distributions of Expectations," NBER Working Paper 32406.

Boneva, Teodora, Marta Golin, Katja Kaufmann, and Christopher Rauh, 2023. "Beliefs about Maternal Labor Supply," CEPR Discussion Paper 17790.

Bordalo, Pedro, Katherine Coffman, Nicola Gennaioli, and Andrei Shleifer, 2016. "Stereotypes," *Quarterly Journal of Economics* 131(4): 1753–1794.

Bordalo, Pedro, Nicola Gennaioli, Yueran Ma, and Andrei Shleifer. 2020. "Overreaction in Macroeconomic Expectations," *American Economic Review* 110(9): 2748–82.

Bottan, Nicolas and Ricardo Perez-Truglia, 2025. "Betting on the House: Subjective Expectations and Market Choices," *American Economic Journal: Applied Economics* 17(1): 459–500.

Braggion, Fabio, Felix von Meyerinck, and Nic Schaub, 2023. "Inflation and Individual Investors' Behavior: Evidence from the German Hyperinflation," *Review of Financial Studies* 36(12): 5012-5045.

Brick, J. Michael and Douglas Williams, 2013. "Explaining Rising Nonresponse Rates in Cross-Sectional Surveys," *The ANNALS of the American Academy of Political and Social Science* 645(1): 26–59.

Broer, Tobias and Alexandre Kohlhas, 2024. "Forecaster (Mis-)Behavior," forthcoming in *Review of Economic and Statistics* 106(5): 1334–1351.

Bruine de Bruin, Wändi, Wilbert van der Klaauw, Giorgio Topa, Julie S. Downs, Baruch Fischhoff, and Olivier Armantier, 2012. "The Effect of Question Wording on Consumers' Reported Inflation Expectations," *Journal of Economic Psychology* 33(4): 749–757.

Bruine de Bruin, Wändi, Wilbert van der Klaauw, Maarten van Rooij, Federica Teppa, and Klaas de Vos, 2017. "Measuring Expectations of Inflation: Effects of Survey Mode, Wording, and Opportunities to Revise," *Journal of Economic Psychology* 59: 45–58.

Bursztyn, Leonardo, Georgy Egorov, Ingar K. Haaland, Aakaash Rao, and Christopher Roth. 2023. "Justifying Dissent," *Quarterly Journal of Economics* 138(3): 1403–1451.

Caldara, Dario, Cristina Fuentes-Albero, Simon Gilchrist, and Egon Zakrajšek, 2016. "The Macroeconomic Impact of Financial and Uncertainty Shocks," *European Economic Review* 88(C): 185–207.

Calvo, Guillermo, 1983. "Staggered Prices in a Utility-Maximizing Framework," *Journal of Monetary Economics* 12(3): 383–398.

Candia, Bernardo, 2024. "Inflation Expectations and Household Spending: Different Patterns in Low and High-Inflation Settings." Manuscript.

Candia, Bernardo, Olivier Coibion, and Yuriy Gorodnichenko, 2020. "Communication and the Beliefs of Economic Agents," in *Navigating the Decade Ahead: Implications for Monetary Policy*, Economic Policy Symposium (Jackson Hole, WY) Proceedings, Federal Reserve Bank of Kansas City, 2020.

Candia, Bernardo, Olivier Coibion, and Yuriy Gorodnichenko. 2022. "The Macroeconomic Expectations of Firms," in *Handbook of Economic Expectations*, Ruediger Bachmann, Giorgio Topa, and Wilbert van der Klaauw, eds. Elsevier.

Candia, Bernardo, Olivier Coibion, and Yuriy Gorodnichenko, 2024. "The Inflation Expectations of U.S. Firms: Evidence from a New Survey," *Journal of Monetary Economics* 145(S): 103569.

Caplin, Andrew, Victoria Gregory, Eungik Lee, Søren Leth-Petersen, and Johan Sæverud, 2023. "Subjective Earnings Risk," NBER Working Paper 31019.

Card, David, Alexandre Mas, Enrico Moretti, and Emmanuel Saez, 2012. "Inequality at Work: The Effect of Peer Salaries on Job Satisfaction," *American Economic Review* 102(6): 2981–3003.

Carroll, Christopher, 2003. "Macroeconomic Expectations of Households and Professional Forecasters," *Quarterly Journal of Economics* 118(1): 269–298.

Carson, Richard, Nicholas Flores, Kerry Martin, and Jennifer Wright, 1996. "Contingent Valuation and Revealed Preference Methodologies: Comparing the Estimates for Quasi-Public Goods," *Land Economics* 72(1): 80–99.

Carvalho, Carlos, Stefano Eusepi, Emanuel Moench, and Bruce Preston. 2023. "Anchored Inflation Expectations," *American Economic Journal: Macroeconomics* 15(1): 1–47.

Castillo, Marco and Petrie, Ragan, 2023. "Incentivized Learning and Attention-Driven Treatment Effects: A Field Experiment on Energy Conservation." Manuscript.

Cavallo, Alberto, Guillermo Cruces, and Ricardo Perez-Truglia, 2016. "Learning from Potentially Biased Statistics," *Brookings Papers on Economic Activity* 47(1 (Spring)): 59–108.

Cavallo, Alberto, Guillermo Cruces, and Ricardo Perez-Truglia. 2017. "Inflation Expectations, Learning, and Supermarket Prices: Evidence from Survey Experiments," *American Economic Journal: Macroeconomics* 9(3): 1–35.

Chopra, Felix, Christopher Roth, and Johannes Wohlfart, 2025. "Home Price Expectations and Spending: Evidence from a Field Experiment," *American Economics Review* 115(7): 2267–2305.

Christelis, Dimitris, Dimitris Georgarakos, Tullio Jappelli, and Maarten van Rooij, 2020. "Consumption Uncertainty and Precautionary Saving," *Review of Economic and Statistics* 102(1): 148–161.

Christiano, Lawrence, Martin Eichenbaum, and Charles Evans, 2005. "Nominal Rigidities and the Dynamic Effects of a Shock to Monetary Policy," *Journal of Political Economy* 113(1): 1–45.

Clarida, Richard, Jordi Galí, and Mark Gertler, 2000. "Monetary Policy Rules and Macroeconomics Stability: Evidence and Some Theory," *Quarterly Journal of Economics* 115(1): 147–180.

Coibion, Olivier, 2010. "Testing the Sticky Information Phillips Curve," *Review of Economics and Statistics* 92(1): 87–101.

Coibion, Olivier, Dimitris Georgarakos, Yuriy Gorodnichenko, Geoff Kenny, and Michael Weber, 2024. "The Effect of Macroeconomic Uncertainty on Household Spending," *American Economic Review* 114(3): 645–677.

Coibion, Olivier, Dimitris Georgarakos, Yuriy Gorodnichenko, and Maarten van Rooij. 2023. "How Does Consumption Respond to News about Inflation? Field Evidence from a Randomized Control Trial," *American Economic Journal: Macroeconomics* 15(3): 109–52.

Coibion, Olivier, Dimitris Georgarakos, Yuriy Gorodnichenko, and Michael Weber, 2023. "Forward Guidance and Household Expectations," *Journal of the European Economic Association* 21(5): 2131–2171.

Coibion, Olivier and Yuriy Gorodnichenko, 2011a. "Strategic Interaction among Heterogeneous Price-Setters in an Estimated DSGE Model," *Review of Economics and Statistics* 93(3): 920–940.

Coibion, Olivier and Yuriy Gorodnichenko, 2011b. "Monetary Policy, Trend Inflation, and the Great Moderation: An Alternative Interpretation," *American Economic Review* 101(1): 341–370.

Coibion, Olivier and Yuriy Gorodnichenko, 2012. "What Can Survey Forecasts Tell Us about Information Rigidities?" *Journal of Political Economy* 120(1): 116–159.

Coibion, Olivier and Yuriy Gorodnichenko, 2015a. "Information Rigidity and the Expectations Formation Process: A Simple Framework and New Facts" *American Economic Review* 105(8): 2644–2678.

Coibion, Olivier and Yuriy Gorodnichenko, 2015b. "Is the Phillips Curve Alive and Well after All? Inflation Expectations and the Missing Disinflation," *American Economic Journal: Macroeconomics* 7(1): 197–232.

Coibion, Olivier and Yuriy Gorodnichenko, 2015c. "Inflation Expectations in Ukraine: A Long Path to Anchoring?" *Visnyk of the National Bank of Ukraine* 233: 6–23.

Coibion, Olivier, Yuriy Gorodnichenko, and Rupal Kamdar, 2018. "The Formation of Expectations, Inflation, and the Phillips Curve," *Journal of Economic Literature* 56(4): 1447–1491.

Coibion, Olivier, Yuriy Gorodnichenko, Edward S. Knotek II, and Raphael Schoenle, 2023. "Average Inflation Targeting and Household Expectations," *Journal of Political Economy—Macroeconomics* 1(2): 403–446.

Coibion, Olivier, Yuriy Gorodnichenko, and Saten Kumar. 2018. "How Do Firms Form Their Expectations? New Survey Evidence," *American Economic Review* 108(9): 2671–2713.

Coibion, Olivier, Yuriy Gorodnichenko, Saten Kumar, and Matheiu Pedemonte, 2020. "Inflation Expectations as a Policy Tool?" *Journal of International Economics* 124: 103297.

Coibion, Olivier, Yuriy Gorodnichenko, Saten Kumar, and Jane Ryngaert, 2021. "Do You Know that I Know that You Know . . . ? Higher-Order Beliefs in Survey Data," *Quarterly Journal of Economics* 136(3): 1387–1446.

Coibion, Olivier, Yuriy Gorodnichenko, and Tiziano Ropele, 2020. "Inflation Expectations and Firm Decisions: New Causal Evidence," *Quarterly Journal of Economics* 135(1): 165–219.

Coibion, Olivier, Yuriy Gorodnichenko, and Mauricio Ulate, 2019. "Is Inflation Just Around the Corner? The Phillips Curve and Global Inflationary Pressures," *AEA Papers and Proceedings* 109: 465–69.

Coibion, Olivier, Yuriy Gorodnichenko, and Michael Weber, 2020a. "Political Polarization and Economic Expectation Outcomes," NBER Working Paper 28044.

Coibion, Olivier, Yuriy Gorodnichenko, and Michael Weber, 2020b. "How Did U.S. Consumers Use Their Stimulus Payments?" NBER Working Paper 27693.

Coibion, Olivier, Yuriy Gorodnichenko, and Michael Weber, 2021. "Fiscal Policy and Households' Inflation Expectations: Evidence from a Randomized Control Trial," NBER Working Paper 28485.

Coibion, Olivier, Yuriy Gorodnichenko, and Michael Weber, 2022a. "Monetary Policy Communications and their Effects on Household Inflation Expectations," *Journal of Political Economy* 130(6): 1537–1584.

Coibion, Olivier, Yuriy Gorodnichenko, and Michael Weber, 2022b. "Does Policy Communication during COVID Work?" *International Journal of Central Banking* 18(1): 3–39.

Coibion, Olivier, Yuriy Gorodnichenko, and Michael Weber, 2025. "The Cost of the COVID-19 Crisis: Lockdowns, Macroeconomic Expectations, and Consumer Spending," *Journal of Economic Behavior & Organization* 229: 106846.

Colarieti, Roberto, Pierfrancesco Mei, and Stefanie Stantcheva, 2024. "The How and Why of Household Reactions to Income Shocks," NBER Working Paper 32191.

Conlon, John J., Laura Pilossoph, Matthew Wiswall, and Basit Zafar, 2018. "Labor Market Search with Imperfect Information and Learning," NBER Working Paper 24988.

Croushore, Dean. 2011. "Frontiers of Real-Time Data Analysis," *Journal of Economic Literature* 49(1): 72–100.

Cruces, Guillermo, Ricardo Perez-Truglia, and Martin Tetaz, 2013. "Biased Perceptions of Income Distribution and Preferences for Redistribution: Evidence from a Survey Experiment," *Journal of Public Economics* 98: 100–112.

Crump, Richard, Stefano Eusepi, Andrea Tambalotti, and Giorgio Topa, 2022. "Subjective Intertemporal Substitution," *Journal of Monetary Economics* 126: 118–133.

Curti, Filippo and Sophia Kazinnik, 2023. "Let's Face It: Quantifying the Impact of Nonverbal Communication in FOMC Press Conferences," *Journal of Monetary Economics* 139(C): 110–126.

Curtin, Richard, 2019. *Consumer Expectations: Micro Foundations and Macro Impact.* Cambridge University Press.

D'Acunto, Francesco, Andreas Fuster, and Michael Weber, 2021. "Diverse Policy Committees Can Reach Underrepresented Groups," NBER Working Paper 29275.

D'Acunto, Francesco, Janet Gao, Lu Liu, Kai Lu, Zhengwei Wang, and Jun Yang, 2024. "Subjective Expectations and Financial Intermediation." Manuscript.

D'Acunto, Francesco, Daniel Hoang, Maritta Paloviita, and Michael Weber, 2020. "Effective Policy Communication: Targets versus Instruments," University of Chicago, Becker Friedman Institute for Economics Working Paper No. 2020–148.

D'Acunto, Francesco, Daniel Hoang, Maritta Paloviita, and Michael Weber, 2022. "IQ, Expectations, and Choice," *Review of Economics Studies* 90(5): 2292–2325.

D'Acunto, Francesco, Ulrike Malmendier, Juan Ospina, and Michael Weber, 2021. "Exposure to Grocery Prices and Inflation Expectations," *Journal of Political Economy* 129(5): 1319–1666.

D'Acunto, Francesco, Ulrike Malmendier, Juan Ospina, and Michael Weber, 2023. "What Do the Data Tell Us about Inflation Expectations," in *Handbook of Economic Expectations,* Ruediger Bachmann, Giorgio Topa, and Wilbert van der Klaauw, eds., ch. 5. Elsevier.

Davis, Steven and Pawel Krolikowski, 2025. "Sticky Wages on the Layoff Margin," *American Economic Review* 115(2): 491–524.

De Quidt, Jonathan, Johannes Haushofer, and Christopher Roth, 2018. "Measuring and Bounding Experimenter Demand," *American Economic Review* 108(11): 3266–3302.

Deaton, Angus, 2008. "Income, Health and Well-Being around the World: Evidence from a Gallup World Poll," *Journal of Economic Perspectives* 22(2): 53–72.

Delgado, Martha Elena, Juan Herreno, Marc Hofstetter, and Mathieu Pedemonte, 2024. "The Causal Effects of Expected Depreciations." Manuscript.

Demmelhuber, Katrin, Stefan Sauer, and Klaus Wohlrabe, 2023. "Beyond the Business Climate: Supplementary Questions in the ifo Business Survey," *Jahrbücher für Nationalökonomie und Statistik.* 243(2): 169–182.

Dräger, Lena, 2015. "Inflation Perceptions and Expectations in Sweden—Are Media Reports the Missing Link?" *Oxford Bulletin of Economics and Statistics* 77(5): 681–700.

Dräger, Lena and Michael J. Lamla, 2024. "Consumers' Macroeconomic Expectations," *Journal of Economic Surveys* 38(2): 427–451.

Dräger, Lena, Michael Lamla, and Damjan Pfajfar, 2023. "How to Limit the Spillover from an Inflation Surge to Inflation Expectations," *Journal of Monetary Economics* 144: 103546.

Dräger, Lena and Giang Nghiem, 2021. "Are Consumers' Spending Decisions in Line with A Euler Equation?" *Review of Economics and Statistics* 103(3): 580–596.

Dräger, Lena and Giang Nghiem, 2023. "Inflation Literacy, Inflation Expectations, and Trust in the Central Bank: A Survey Experiment," forthcoming in *Review of Economics and Statistics*.

Drenik, Andres and Diego Perez, 2020. "Price Setting under Uncertainty about Inflation," *Journal of Monetary Economics* 116: 23–38.

Easterlin, Richard A., 1974. "Does Economic Growth Improve the Human Lot? Some Empirical Evidence," in *Nations and Households in Economic Growth: Essays in Honor of M. Abramovitz*, Academic Press.

Ehrbeck, Tilman and Robert Waldmann, 1996. "Why Are Professional Forecasters Biased? Agency versus Behavioral Explanations," *Quarterly Journal of Economics* 111(1): 21–40.

Ehrmann, Michael, Dimitris Georgarakos, and Geoff Kenny, 2023. "Credibility Gains from Communicating with the Public: Evidence from the ECB's new Monetary Policy Strategy," CEPR Discussion Paper No. 17784.

Ehrmann, Michael, Damjan Pfajfar, and Emiliano Santoro, 2017. "Consumers' Attitudes and their Inflation Expectations," *International Journal of Central Banking* 13(1): 225–259.

Enders, Zeno, Franziska Hünnekes, and Gernot J. Müller, 2019. "Monetary Policy Announcements and Expectations: Evidence from German Firms," *Journal of Monetary Economics* 108: 45–63.

Enders, Zeno, Michael Kleemann, and Gernot Muller, 2021. "Growth Expectations, Undue Optimism, and Short-Run Fluctuations," *Review of Economics and Statistics* 103(5): 905–921.

European Central Bank, 2021. "ECB Consumer Expectations Survey: An Overview and First Evaluation," Occasional Paper Series, No 287, December.

Evans, George and Seppo Honkapohja, 2001. *Learning and Expectations in Macroeconomics*. Princeton University Press.

Faberman, Jason, Andreas Mueller, Aysegul Sahin, and Giorgio Topa, 2022. "Job Search Behavior among the Employed and Non-employed," *Econometrica*, 90(4): 1743–1779.

Facchini, Giovanni, Yotam Margalit, and Hiroyuki Nakata, 2022. "Countering Public Opposition to Immigration: The Impact of Information Campaigns," *European Economic Review* 141, 103959.

Fehr, Dietmar, Johanna Mollerstrom, and Ricardo Perez-Truglia, 2022. "Your Place in the World: Relative Income and Global Inequality," *American Economic Journal: Economic Policy* 14(4): 232–268.

Ferrer-i-Carbonell, Ada, 2005. "Income and Well-Being: An Empirical Analysis of the Comparison Effect," *Journal of Public Economics* 89(5–6): 997–1019.

De Fiore, Fiorella, Marco Lombardi, and Johannes Schuffels, 2019. "Are Households Indifferent to Monetary Policy Announcements?" CEPR Discussion Paper 17041.

Fischer, Johannes, Christoph Herler, and Philip Schnattinger. 2024. "The Effect of Inflation Uncertainty on Household Spending." NBER Working Paper 32939.

Fisher, Jonas D. M., 2006. "The Dynamic Effects of Neutral and Investment-Specific Technology Shocks," *Journal of Political Economy* 114(3): 413–451.

Frache, Serafin and Rodrigo Lluberas, 2019. "New Information and Inflation Expectations among Firms," BIS Working Paper No. 781.

Friedman, Milton, 1968. "The Role of Monetary Policy" *American Economics Review* 58(1): 1–17.

Fuhrer, Jeff, 2017. "Expectations as a Source of Macroeconomic Persistence: Evidence from Survey Expectations in Dynamic Macro Models," *Journal of Monetary Economics* 86: 22–35.

Fuster, Andreas, Greg Kaplan, and Basit Zafar, 2021. "What Would You Do with $500? Spending Responses to Gains, Losses, News, and Loans," *Review of Economic Studies* 88(4): 1760–1795.

Gabaix, Xavier, 2020. "A Behavioral New Keynesian Model," *American Economic Review* 110(8): 2271–2327.

Galashin, Misha, Martin Kanz, and Ricardo Perez-Truglia, 2020. "Macroeconomic Expectations and Credit Card Spending," NBER Working Paper 28281.

Galí, Jordi. 2015. *Monetary Policy, Inflation, and the Business Cycle: An Introduction to the New Keynesian Framework and Its Applications*. Princeton University Press.

Galí, Jordi and Mark Gertler, 1999. "Inflation Dynamics: A Structural Econometric Analysis," *Journal of Monetary Economics* 44(2): 195–222.

Gambetti, Luca, Dimitris Korobilis, John Tsoukalas, and Francesco Zanetti, 2023. "Agreed and Disagreed Uncertainty," CESifo Working Paper 10463.

Garciga, Christian, Edward S. Knotek II, Mathieu Pedemonte, and Taylor Shiroff, 2023. "The Survey of Firms' Inflation Expectations," Federal Reserve Bank of Cleveland *Economic Commentary* No. 2023–10.

Gautier, Erwan and Jeremi Montornes, 2025. "Measuring Households' Inflation Expectations in the Euro Area: The Effect of Panel Conditioning." Manuscript.

Gennaioli, Nicola, Yueran Ma, and Andrei Shleifer, 2016. "Expectations and Investment," *NBER Macroeconomics Annual* 30: 379–431.

Gennaioli, Nicola and Andrei Shleifer, 2010. "What Comes to Mind" *Quarterly Journal of Economics* 125(4): 1399–1433.

Georgarakos, Dimitris, Yuriy Gorodnichenko, Olivier Coibion, and Geoff Kenny, 2024. "The Causal Effects of Inflation Uncertainty on Households' Beliefs and Actions," NBER Working Paper 33014.

Georgarakos, Dimitris and Geoff Kenny, 2022. "Household Spending and Fiscal Support during the COVID-19 Pandemic: Insights from a New Consumer Survey", *Journal of Monetary Economics* 129: S1-S14.

Georgarakos, Dimitris, Kwang Hwan Kim, Olivier Coibion, Myungkyu Shim, Myunghwan Andrew Lee, Yuriy Gorodnichenko, Geoff Kenny, Seowoo Han, and Michael Weber, 2025. "How Costly Are Business Cycle Volatility and Inflation? A Vox Populi Approach," NBER Working Paper 33476.

Gertler, Mark and Simon Gilchrist, 1994. "Monetary Policy, Business Cycles, and the Behavior of Small Manufacturing Firms," *Quarterly Journal of Economics* 109(2): 309–340.

Gertler, Mark, and John Leahy. 2008. "A Phillips Curve with an Ss Foundation," *Journal of Political Economy* 116 (3): 533–572.

Giglio, Stefano, Matteo Maggiori, Johannes Stroebel, and Stephen Utkus, 2021. "Five Facts about Beliefs and Portfolios," *American Economic Review* 111(5): 1481–1522.

Glennerster, Rachel and Kudzai Takavarasha, 2013. *Running Randomized Evaluations: A Practical Guide.* Princeton University Press

Goldstein, Nathan, 2023. "Tracking Inattention," *Journal of the European Economic Association* 21(6): 2682–2725.

Golin, Marta and Christopher Rauh, 2022. "The Impact of Fear of Automation," Janeway Institute Working Paper 2229, Faculty of Economics, University of Cambridge.

Gorodonichenko, Yuriy, 2008. "Endogenous Information, Menu Cost and Inflation Persistence," NBER Working Paper 14184.

Gorodnichenko, Yuriy, Enrique Mendoza, and Linda Tesar. 2012. "The Finnish Great Depression: From Russia with Love," *American Economic Review* 102(4): 1619–44.

Gorodnichenko, Yuriy, Tho Pham, and Oleksandr Talavera. 2023. "The Voice of Monetary Policy," *American Economic Review* 113(2): 548–84.

Gorodnichenko, Yuriy, Debora Revoltella, Jan Svejnar, and Christoph Weiss, 2018. "Resource Misallocation in European Firms: The Role of Constraints, Firm Characteristics and Managerial Decisions," NBER Working Paper 24444.

Gorodnichenko, Yuriy and Xiao Yin, 2024. "Higher-Order Beliefs and Risky Asset Holdings," NBER Working Paper 32680.

Graefe, Andreas, 2014. "Accuracy of Vote Expectation Surveys in Forecasting Elections," *Public Opinion Quarterly* 78(S1): 204–232.

Gründler, Klaus, Lena Dräger, and Niklas Potrafke, 2025. "Political Shocks and Inflation Expectations: Evidence from the 2022 Russian Invasion of Ukraine," *Journal of International Economics* 153: 104029.

Guglielminetti, Elisa and Michele Loberto, 2024. "Inflation Expectations and the Housing Market: Insights from Real Estate Agents." Manuscript.

Haaland, Ingar, Christopher Roth, Stefanie Stantcheva, and Johannes Wohlfart, 2024. "Understanding Economic Behavior Using Open Ended Survey Data," NBER Working Paper 32421.

Haaland, Ingar, Christopher Roth, and Johannes Wohlfart, 2023. "Designing Information Provision Experiments," *Journal of Economic Literature* 61(1): 3–40.

Hajdini, Ina, Edward S. Knotek II, John Leer, Mathieu Pedemonte, Robert W. Rich, and Raphael S. Schoenle, 2023. "Low Passthrough from Inflation Expectations to Income Growth Expectations: Why People Dislike Inflation," Federal Reserve Bank of Cleveland Working Paper No. 22–21.

Hajdini, Ina, Edward S. Knotek II, John Leer, Mathieu Pedemonte, Robert W. Rich, and Raphael S. Schoenle, 2024. "Indirect Consumer Inflation Expectations: Theory and Evidence," *Journal of Monetary Economics* 145(S): 103568.

Hajdini, Ina and Andre Kurmann, 2023. "Predictable Forecast Errors in Full-Information Rational Expectations Models with Regime Shifts." FRB Cleveland Working Paper No. 24-08.

Haldane, Andrew, Alistair Macaulay, and Michael McMahon, 2021. "The 3 E's of Central Bank Communication with the Public," in *Independence, Credibility, and Communication of Central Banking,* Ernesto Pastén and Ricardo Reis, eds., pp. 279–342. Banco Central de Chile, Santiago, Chile, 2021.

Haldane, Andrew and Michael McMahon, 2018. "Central Bank Communications and the General Public," *AEA Papers and Proceedings* 108: 578–83.

Hamilton, James D., 1994. *Time Series Analysis*, Princeton University Press, Princeton, NJ.

Hassan, Tarek, Stephan Hollander, Laurence van Lent, and Ahmed Tahoun, 2019. "Firm-Level Political Risk: Measurement and Effects," *Quarterly Journal of Economics* 134(4): 2135–2202.

Havranek, Tomas, Marek Rusnak, and Anna Sokolova, 2017. "Habit Formation in Consumption: A Meta-Analysis," *European Economic Review* 95: 142–167.

Hazell, Jonathon, Juan Herreño, Emi Nakamura, and Jón Steinsson, 2022. "The Slope of the Phillips Curve: Evidence from U.S. States," *Quarterly Journal of Economics* 137(3): 1299–1344.

Hoffman, Mathias, Emanuel Moench, Lora Pavlova, and Guido Schultefrankenfeld, 2022. "Would Households Understand Average Inflation Targeting?" *Journal of Monetary Economics* 129: S52-S66.

Hoy, Christopher and Franziska Mager, 2021. "Why Are Relatively Poor People Not More Supportive of Redistribution? Evidence from a Randomized Survey Experiment across Ten Countries," *American Economic Journal: Economic Policy* 13(4): 299–328.

Hsieh, Chang-Tai and Peter Klenow, 2009. "Misallocation and Manufacturing TFP in China and India," *Quarterly Journal of Economics* 124(4), 1403–1448.

Huber, Peter, 1964. "Robust Estimation of a Location Parameter," *Annals of Mathematical Statistics* 35: 492–518.

Huber, Stefanie, Daria Minima, and Tobias Schmidt, 2023. "The Pass-through from Inflation Perceptions to Inflation Expectations," Deutsche Bundesbank Working Paper No. 17/2023.

Huo, Zhen, Marcelo Pedroni, and Guangyu Pei. 2024. "Bias and Sensitivity under Ambiguity," *American Economic Review* 114(12): 4091–4133.

Hvidberg, Kristoffer, Claus Kreiner, and Stefanie Stantcheva, 2023. "Social Positions and Fairness Views on Inequality," *Review of Economic Studies* 90(6): 3083–3118.

Indarte, Sasha, Ray Kluender, Ulrike Malmendier, and Michael Stepner, 2024. "What Explains the Consumption Decisions of Low-Income Households?" Manuscript.

Jaeger, Simon, Christopher Roth, Nina Roussille, and Benjamin Schoefer, 2024. "Worker Beliefs about Outside Options," *Quarterly Journal of Economics* 139(3): 1505–1556.

Jain, Monica, Olena Kostyshyna, and Xu Zhang, 2024. "How Do People View Wage and Price Inflation?" *Journal of Monetary Economics* 145: 103552.

Jens, Candace E., 2017. "Political Uncertainty and Investment: Causal Evidence from U.S. Gubernatorial Elections," *Journal of Financial Economics* 124(3): 563–579.

Jiang, Janet Hua, Rupal Kamdar, Kelin Lu, and Daniela Puzzello, 2024. "How Do Households Respond to Expected Inflation? An Investigation of Transmission Mechanisms," CAEPR Working Paper 2024-004, Indiana University, Bloomington.

Johnson, David, Jonathan Parker, and Nicholas Souleles. 2006. "Household Expenditure and the Income Tax Rebates of 2001," *American Economic Review* 96(5): 1589–1610.

Jonung, Lars. 1981 "Perceived and Expected Rates of Inflation in Sweden," *American Economic Review* 71(5): 961–968.

Jordà, Òscar. 2005. "Estimation and Inference of Impulse Responses by Local Projections," *American Economic Review* 95(1): 161–182.

Juodis, Artūras and Simas Kučinskas, 2023. "Quantifying Noise in Survey Expectations," *Quantitative Economics* 14(2): 609–650.

Jurado, Kyle, Sydney Ludvigson, and Serena Ng, 2015. "Measuring Uncertainty," *American Economic Review* 105(3): 1177–1216.

Kamdar, Rupal, 2019. "The Inattentive Consumer: Sentiment and Expectations." Manuscript.

Kamdar, Rupal and Walker Ray, 2024. "Attention-Driven Sentiment and the Business Cycle." Manuscript.

Kaplan, Greg and Sam Schulhofer-Wohl, 2017. "Inflation at the Household Level," *Journal of Monetary Economics* 91: 19–38.

Kieren, Pascal, Christian König-Kersting, Robert Schmidt, Stefan Trautmann, and Franziska Heinicke, 2025. "First-Order and Higher-Order Inflation Expectations: Evidence about Households and Firms," *Journal of Economic Behavior & Organization* 233: 106988.

Kim, Gwangmin and Carola Binder, 2023. "Learning-through-Survey in Inflation Expectations," *American Economic Journal: Macroeconomics* 15(2): 254–278.

Knotek II, Edward, James Mitchell, Mathieu Pedemonte, and Taylor Shiroff, 2024. "The Effects of Interest Rate Increases on Consumers' Inflation Expectations: The Roles of Informedness and Compliance," Federal Reserve Bank of Cleveland Working Paper No. 24–01.

Kohlhas, Alexandre and Ansgar Walther, 2021. "Asymmetric Attention," *American Economic Review* 111(9): 2879–2925.

Korenok, Oleg, Stanislav Radchenko, and Norman Swanson, 2010. "International Evidence on the Efficacy of New-Keynesian Models of Inflation Persistence," *Journal of Applied Econometrics* 25(1): 31–54.

Kostyshyna, Olena and Luba Petersen. 2024. "The Effect of Inflation Uncertainty on Household Expectations and Spending," NBER Working Paper 32939.

Kreiner, Claus Thustrup, David Dreyer Lassen, and Søren Leth-Petersen, 2015. "Measuring the Accuracy of Survey Responses Using Administrative Register Data: Evidence from Denmark," in *Improving the Measurement of Consumer Expenditures,* Christopher Carroll, Thomas Crossley, and John Sabelhaus, eds. The University of Chicago Press: Chicago, IL; Chicago Scholarship Online (21 Jan. 2016), online edition.

Kryvtsov, Oleksiy and Luba Petersen, 2021. "Central Bank Communication That Works: Lessons from Lab Experiments," *Journal of Monetary Economics* 117(C): 760–780.

Kuchler, Theresa, Monika Piazzesi, and Johannes Stroebel, 2022. "Housing Market Expectations," NBER Working Paper 29909.

Kuchler, Theresa and Basit Zafar, 2019. "Personal Experiences and Expectations about Aggregate Outcomes," *Journal of Finance* 74(5): 2491–2542.

Kumar, Saten, Hassan Afrouzi, Olivier Coibion, and Yuriy Gorodnichenko, 2015. "Inflation Targeting Does Not Anchor Inflation Expectations: Evidence from Firms in New Zealand," *Brookings Papers on Economic Activity* 46(2 (Fall)): 151–225.

Kumar, Saten, Yuriy Gorodnichenko, and Olivier Coibion, 2023. "The Effect of Macroeconomic Uncertainty on Firm Decisions," *Econometrica* 91: 1297–1332.

Kumar, Saten, Oleksandr Talavera, Olivier Coibion, and Yuriy Gorodnichenko, 2025. "Using Online Prices to Measure High-Frequency Price Responses to Information Treatments." Manuscript.

Kuziemko, Ilyana, Michael Norton, Emmanuel Saez, and Stefanie Stantcheva, 2015. "How Elastic Are Preferences for Redistribution? Evidence from Randomized Survey Experiments," *American Economic Review* 105(4): 1478–1508.

Kydland, Finn and Edward Prescott, 1982. "Time to Build Aggregate Fluctuations," *Econometrica* 50(6): 1345–1370.

Lamla, Michael and Dmitri V. Vinogradov, 2019. "Central Bank Announcements: Big News for Little People?" *Journal of Monetary Economics* 108: 21–38.

Lamont, Owen, 2002. "Macroeconomic Forecasts and Microeconomic Forecasters," *Journal of Economic Behavior & Organization* 48(3): 265–280.

Leeper, Eric, 2010. "Monetary Science, Fiscal Alchemy," Proceedings—Economic Policy Symposium—Jackson Hole, Federal Reserve Bank of Kansas City, pp. 361–434.

Lewis, Daniel, Christos Makridis, and Karel Mertens, 2020. "Do Monetary Policy Announcements Shift Household Expectations?" FRB of Dallas Working Paper 1906.

Loungani, Prakash, Herman Stekler, and Natalia Tamirisa, 2013. "Information Rigidity in Growth Forecasts: Some Cross-Country Evidence," *International Journal of Forecasting* 29(4): 605–621.

Lucas, Robert, 1972. "Expectations and the Neutrality of Money," *Journal of Economic Theory* 4(2): 103–124.

Lucas, Robert, 1994. "Review of Milton Friedman and Anna J. Schwartz's 'A Monetary History of the United States, 1867–1960,'" *Journal of Monetary Economics* 34(1): 5–16.

Lucas, Robert, 2003. "Macroeconomic Priorities," *American Economic Review* 93(1): 1–14.

Ludvigson, Sydney, Sai Ma, and Serena Ng, 2021. "Uncertainty and Business Cycles: Exogenous Impulse or Endogenous Response?" *American Economic Journal: Macroeconomics* 13(4): 369–410.

Lusardi, Annamaria and Olivia S. Mitchell, 2014. "The Economic Importance of Financial Literacy: Theory and Evidence," *Journal of Economic Literature* 52(1): 5–44.

Luttmer, Erzo, 2005. "Neighbors as Negatives: Relative Earnings and Well-Being," *Quarterly Journal of Economics* 120(3): 963–1002.

Maćkowiak, Bartosz, Filip Matějka, and Mirko Wiederholt, 2023. "Rational Inattention: A Review," *Journal of Economic Literature* 61(1): 226–73.

Mackowiak, Bartosz and Mirko Wiederholt, 2009. "Optimal Sticky Prices under Rational Inattention," *American Economic Review* 99(3): 769–803.

Maćkowiak, Bartosz and Mirko Wiederholt, 2024. "Rational Inattention during an RCT." CEPR Discussion Paper 18875.

Malmendier, Ulrike and Stefan Nagel, 2011. "Depression Babies: Do Macroeconomic Experiences Affect Risk Taking?" *Quarterly Journal of Economics* 126(1): 373–416.

Malmendier, Ulrike and Stefan Nagel, 2016. "Learning from Inflation Experiences," *Quarterly Journal of Economics* 131(1): 53–87.

Mankiw, Gregory, 1997. "Comment" in *Reducing Inflation: Motivation and Strategy*, Christina D. Romer and David H. Romer, eds., pp. 13–65, University of Chicago Press.

Mankiw, Gregory and Ricardo Reis, 2002. "Sticky Information versus Sticky Prices: A Proposal to Replace the New Keynesian Phillips Curve" *Quarterly Journal of Economics* 117(4): 1295–1328.

Mankiw, Gregory, Ricardo Reis, and Justin Wolfers, 2004. "Disagreement about Inflation Expectations," *NBER Macroeconomics Annual* 18: 209–248.

Manski, Charles, 2004. "Measuring Expectations," *Econometrica* 72(5): 1329–1376.

Maronna, Ricardo, Douglas Martin, Victor Yohai, and Matías Salibián-Barrera, 2019. *Robust Statistics: Theory and Methods (with R)*. 2nd Edition. Wiley Series in Probability and Statistics.

Mavroeidis, Sophocles, Mikkel Plagborg-Møller, and James Stock, 2014. "Empirical Evidence on Inflation Expectations in the New Keynesian Phillips Curve," *Journal of Economic Literature* 52(1): 124–188.

McClure, Ethan, Vitaliia Yaremko, Olivier Coibion, and Yuriy Gorodnichenko, 2025. "The Macroeconomic Expectations of U.S. Managers," *Journal of Money Credit and Banking* 57: 683–716.

Melosi, Leonardo, 2017. "Signaling Effects of Monetary Policy," *Review of Economic Studies* 84(2): 853–884.

Meyer, Brent and Xuguang Simon Sheng, 2024. "Unit Cost Expectations and Uncertainty: Firms' Perspectives on Inflation," Federal Reserve Bank of Atlanta Working Paper 2021–12b.

Mikosch, Heiner, Christopher Roth, Samad Sarferaz, and Johannes Wohlfart, 2024. "Uncertainty and Information Acquisition: Evidence from Firms and Households," *American Economic Journal*: *Macroeconomics* 16(2): 375-405.

Milani, Fabio, 2005. "Adaptive Learning and Inflation Persistence." Working Paper.

Mitra, Anushka, 2023. "Macroeconomic Sentiments and Job Search Behavior." Manuscript.

Murphy, James, Geoffrey Allen, Thomas Stevens, and Darryl Weatherhead, 2005. "A Meta-analysis of Hypothetical Bias in Stated Preference Valuation," *Environmental and Resource Economics* 30(3): 313–325.

Nakamura, Emi and Jón Steinsson, 2008. "Five Facts about Prices: A Reevaluation of Menu Cost Models," *Quarterly Journal of Economics* 123(4): 1415–1464

Nakamura, Emi and Jón Steinsson, 2018a. "High-Frequency Identification of Monetary Non-Neutrality: The Information Effect," *Quarterly Journal of Economics* 133(3): 1283–1330.

Nakamura, Emi and Jón Steinsson. 2018b. "Identification in Macroeconomics," *Journal of Economic Perspectives* 32(3): 59–86.

Natali, Luise, Sudhanshu Handa, Amber Peterman, David Seidenfeld, and Gelson Tembo, 2018. "Does Money Buy Happiness: Evidence from an Unconditional Cash Transfer in Zambia," *SSM Population Health* 4: 225–235.

Nghiem, Giang, Ami Dalloul, and Lena Dräger, 2024. "Anchoring Households' Inflation Expectations when Inflation Is High." Manuscript.

Nordhaus, William D., 1987. "Forecasting Efficiency: Concepts and Applications," *Review of Economics and Statistics* 69(4): 667–674.

Orphanides, Athanasios, 2003. "Monetary Policy Evaluation with Noisy Information," *Journal of Monetary Economics* 50(3): 605–631.

Ottaviani, Marco and Peter Norman Sorensen, 2006. "The Strategy of Professional Forecasting," *Journal of Financial Economics* 81(2): 441–466.

Patterson, Christina. 2023. "The Matching Multiplier and the Amplification of Recessions," *American Economic Review* 113(4): 982–1012.

Patton, Andrew and Allan Timmermann, 2010. "Why Do Forecasters Disagree? Lessons from the Term Structure of the Cross-Sectional Dispersion," *Journal of Monetary Economics* 57(7): 803–820.

Pfajfar, Damjan and Blaz Zakelj, 2018. "Inflation Expectations and Monetary Policy Design: Evidence from the Laboratory," *Macroeconomic Dynamics* 22(4): 1035–1075.

Phelps, Edmund, 1967. "Phillips Curves, Expectations of Inflation and Optimal Unemployment over Time," *Economica* 34(135): 254–281.

Phillips, A. W., 1958. "The Relation Between Unemployment and the Rate of Change of Money Wage Rates in the United Kingdom, 1861–1957," *Economica* 25(100): 283–299.

Pilossoph, Laura and Jane Ryngaert, 2024. "Job Search, Wages, and Inflation," NBER Working Paper 33042.

Pischke, Jorn-Steffen, 2011. "Money and Happiness: Evidence from the Industry Wage Structure," NBER Working Paper 17056.

Ramey, Valerie, 2016. "Macroeconomic Shocks and Their Propagation," in *Handbook of Macroeconomics*, J. B. Taylor and Harald Uhlig, eds., edition 1, volume 2, pp. 71–162. Elsevier.

Ramey, Valerie and Matthew Shapiro, 1998. "Costly Capital Reallocation and the Effects of Government Spending," Carnegie-Rochester Conference Series on Public Policy 48(1): 145–194.

Ramey, Valerie and Sarah Zubairy, 2018. "Government Spending Multipliers in Good Times and in Bad: Evidence from US Historical Data," *Journal of Political Economy* 126(2): 850–901.

Reis, Ricardo, 2006a. "Inattentive Consumers," *Journal of Monetary Economics* 53(8): 1761–1800.

Reis, Ricardo, 2006b. "Inattentive Producers," *Review of Economics Studies* 73(3): 793–821.

Roberts, John, 1995. "New Keynesian Economics and the Phillips Curve," *Journal of Money, Credit, and Banking* 27(4): 975–984.

Romano, Joseph and Michael Wolf, 2016. "Efficient Computation of Adjusted P-Values for Resampling-Based Stepdown Multiple Testing," *Statistics and Probability Letters* 113(C): 38–40.

Romer, Christina and David Romer, 1989. "Does Monetary Policy Matter? A New Test in the Spirit of Friedman and Schwartz," *NBER Macroeconomics Annual* 4: 121–170.

Ropele, Tiziano, Yuriy Gorodnichenko, and Olivier Coibion, 2022. "Inflation Expectations and Corporate Borrowing Decisions: New Causal Evidence," NBER Working Paper 30537.

Ropele, Tiziano, Yuriy Gorodnichenko, and Olivier Coibion, 2024. "Inflation Expectations and Misallocation of Resources: Evidence from Italy," *American Economic Review: Insights* 6(2): 246–61.

Roth, Christopher, Sonja Settele, and Johannes Wohlfart, 2022. "Risk Exposure and Acquisition of Macroeconomic Information," *American Economic Review: Insights* 4(1): 34–53.

Roth, Christopher and Johannes Wohlfart, 2020. "How Do Expectations about the Macroeconomy Affect Personal Expectations and Behavior?" *Review of Economics and Statistics* 102(4): 731–748.

Rothschild, David and Justin Wolfers, 2012. "Forecasting Elections: Voter Intentions versus Expectations." Manuscript.

Rudd, Jeremy and Karl Whelan, 2005. "New Tests of the New-Keynesian Phillips Curve," *Journal of Monetary Economics* 52(6): 1167–1181.

Ryngaert, Jane, 2022. "What Do (and Don't) Forecasters Know About U.S. Inflation?" forthcoming in *Journal of Money, Credit and Banking*.

Salle, Isabelle, Yuriy Gorodnichenko, and Olivier Coibion, 2023. "Lifetime Memories of Inflation: Evidence from Surveys and the Lab," NBER Working Paper 31996.

Sandri, Damiano, Francesco Grigoli, Yuriy Gorodnichenko, and Olivier Coibion, 2023. "Keep Calm and Bank On: Panic-Driven Bank Runs and the Role of Public Communication," CEPR Discussion Paper 18448.

Savignac, Frédérique, Erwan Gautier, Yuriy Gorodnichenko, and Olivier Coibion, 2024. "Firms' Inflation Expectations: New Evidence from France," *Journal of European Economic Association* 22(6): 2748–2781.

Schmidt, Jonas and Tammo Bijmolt, 2020. "Accurately Measuring Willingness to Pay for Consumer Goods: A Meta-Analysis of the Hypothetical Bias," *Journal of the Academy of Marketing Science* 48(3): 499–518.

Sergeyev, Dmitriy and Yuriy Gorodnichenko, 2021. "Zero Lower Bound on Inflation Expectations," CEPR Discussion Paper 16729.

Shapiro, Matthew and Joel Slemrod, 2003. "Consumer Response to Tax Rebates," *American Economic Review* 93(1): 381–396.

Shiller, Robert J., (1997). "Why Do People Dislike Inflation?" in *Reducing Inflation: Motivation and Strategy*, Christina D. Romer and David H. Romer, eds., p. 13–65. University of Chicago Press.

Sims, Christopher A., 2003. "Implications of Rational Inattention," *Journal Monetary Economics* 50(3): 665–690.

Smets, Frank, Anders Warne, and Raf Wouters, 2013. "Professional Forecasters and the Real-time Forecasting Performance of an Estimated New Keynesian Model for the Euro Area," *ECB Working Paper* 1571.

Smets, Frank and Raf Wouters, 2003. "An Estimated Dynamic Stochastic General Equilibrium Model of the Euro Area," *Journal of the European Economic Association* 1(5): 1123–1175.

Stantcheva, Stefanie, 2024. "Why Do We Dislike Inflation?" *Brookings Papers on Economic Activity* 55(1 (Spring)): 1–46.

Stevenson, Betsey and Justin Wolfers, 2008. "Economic Growth and Subjective Well-Being: Reassessing the Easterlin Paradox," *Brookings Papers on Economic Activity* 39(1): 1–102.

Summers, Lawrence, 1991. "The Scientific Illusion in Empirical Macroeconomics," *Scandinavian Journal of Economics* 93(2): 129–148.

Sung, Yeji, 2022. "Macroeconomic Expectations and Cognitive Noise." Manuscript.

Swanson, Eric, 2021. "Measuring the Effects of Federal Reserve Forward Guidance and Asset Purchases on Financial Markets," *Journal of Monetary Economics* 118(C): 32–53.

Tanaka, Mari, Nicholas Bloom, Joel M. David, and Maiko Koga, 2021. "Firm Performance and Macro Forecast Accuracy," *Journal of Monetary Economics* 114: 26–41.

Tversky, Amos and Daniel Kahneman, 1974. "Judgement under Uncertainty: Heuristics and Biases," *Science* 185(4157): 1124–1131.

Ungar, Meyer and Ben-Zion Zilberfarb, 1993. "Inflation and Its Unpredictability—Theory and Empirical Evidence," *Journal of Money, Credit and Banking* 25(4): 709-720.

Van Rooij, Maarten, Olivier Coibion, Dimitris Georgarakos, Bernardo Candia, and Yuriy Gorodnichenko, 2024. "Keeping Up with the Jansens: Causal Peer Effects on Household Spending, Beliefs and Happiness," CEPR Discussion Paper 19133.

Vellekoop, Nathanael and Mirko Wiederholt, 2019. "Inflation Expectations and Choices of Households." Manuscript.

Weber, Michael, Bernardo Candia, Olivier Coibion, and Yuriy Gorodnichenko, 2023. "Do You Even Crypto, Bro? Cryptocurrencies in Household Finance," NBER Working Paper 31284.

Weber, Michael, Francesco D'Acunto, and Andreas Fuster, 2021. "Diverse Policy Committees Can Reach Underrepresented Groups," CEPR Discussion Paper 16563.

Weber, Michael, Francesco D'Acunto, Yuriy Gorodnichenko, and Olivier Coibion, 2022. "The Subjective Inflation Expectations of Households and Firms: Measurement, Determinants and Implications," *Journal of Economic Perspectives* 36(3): 157–184.

Weber, Michael, Bernardo Candia, Hassan Afrouzi, Tiziano Ropele, Rodrigo Lluberas, Serafin Frache, Brent H. Meyer, Saten Kumar, Yuriy Gorodnichenko, Dimitris Georgarakos, Olivier Coibion, Geoff Kenny, and Jorge Ponce, 2025. "Tell Me Something I Don't Already Know: Learning in Low and High-Inflation Settings," *Econometrica* 93(1): 229–264.

Wehrhofer, Nils, 2023. "Energy Prices and Inflation Expectations: Evidence from Households and Firms," Deutsche Bundesbank Discussion Paper No. 28/2023.

Werning, Iván, 2022. "Expectations and the Rate of Inflation," NBER Working Paper 30260.

Woodford, Michael, 2001. "Imperfect Common Knowledge and the Effects of Monetary Policy," in *Knowledge, Information and Expectations in Modern Macroeconomics*, Aghion, P., R. Frydman, J. Stiglitz, and M. Woodford, eds. Princeton: Princeton University Press.

Woodford, Michael, 2003. *Interest and Prices*, Princeton University Press, Princeton, NJ.

Wu, Edson, 2024. "Rationally Inattentive Seller: The Geographic Dispersion of U.S. Retail Chains and its Aggregate Implications." Manuscript.

Yang, Choongryul, 2022. "Rational Inattention, Menu Costs, and Multi-product Firms: Micro Evidence and Aggregate Implications," *Journal of Monetary Economics* 128(C): 105–123.

Yotzov, Ivan, Nicholas Bloom, Philip Bunn, Paul Mizen, and Gregory Thwaites, 2024. "The Speed of Firm Response to Inflation," NBER Working Paper 32731.

Zhang, Chengsi, Denise Osborn, and Dong Heon Kim, 2008. "The New Keynesian Phillips Curve: From Sticky Inflation to Sticky Prices," *Journal of Money, Credit and Banking* 40(4): 667–699.

INDEX